HELEN
MIRREN

IVAN WATERMAN

HELEN MIRREN

The Biography of Britain's
Greatest Actress

metro

Published by John Blake Publishing Ltd,
3 Bramber Court, 2 Bramber Road,
London W14 9PB, England

www.blake.co.uk

First published in paperback in 2007

ISBN: 978-1-84454-397-7

British Library Cataloguing-in-Publication Data:

A catalogue record for this book is available from the British Library.

Design by www.envydesign.co.uk

Printed in the UK by CPI Bookmarque, Croydon, CR0 4TD

1 3 5 7 9 10 8 6 4 2

This book is dedicated to Alice Lara,
who loves a good drama.

ACKNOWLEDGEMENTS

This book would not have been possible without the assistance, knowledge and in some cases the contribution of a number of people, just occasionally unwittingly. To those I know personally, many thanks. To those I have never met in the flesh, I am doubly indebted.

I should like to thank: Dame Eileen Atkins, Colin Baker, Sophie Bowell at Channel 4, the British Newspaper Library, Mike Bygrave, Sue Clancy from St Bernard's High School, Michael Coveney, Dick and Cathy Durham, Hunter Davies, *Empire* magazine, Friends Re-United, ex-Essex CID officer Fred Feather, Quentin Falk, Nigel Farndale, Alan Franks, Ed Guilliamy, Andy Harries, Nicky Henson, David Hall in France, Linda Hall in Los Angeles, Roddy Llewelyn, John Heilpern, Brian Heggarty, Jasper Humphreys, International Movie Data Base, Peter Kane, Barrie Keeffe, Charles McDonald, The Helen Mirren Appreciation Society, News International Researchers, *OK!* magazine, Barry Norman, Elsa O'Toole, Penny Oswald of the Essex Yacht Club, Phil Penfold, the late Maggie Parker, Amy Rennert, John Rendell, Byron Rogers, Peter Rushton of

Carlton Television, Sara Keene at Premier Public Relations, Terry Wynn, Douglas Webb, Charlie West at The Neeld Arms, Grittleton, Edward Wilson, Director of the National Youth Theatre. A special thanks to Holly Palin at Granada Television for her endless co-operation and kindness. Amy Rennert edited an earlier book on Helen Mirren and *Prime Suspect* which was enormously informative as was John Heilpern's *Conference of the Birds*.

Contents

PROLOGUE

The echo of the bullet leaving the chamber and the dull thud as it struck Jane Tennison in the chest would, without question, be one of the TV highlights of the year. That moment as the camera panned down, her green eyes closing, blood pumping out from her chest.

As she lay on the cold ground, at least she knew in those darkening seconds that another killer had been brought to justice. Not only had she 'taken' a bullet to save the life of her chief witness, she'd also had time to fire off one round from her standard police automatic pistol. And that had been enough. The prime suspect lay motionless just feet away from her tortured body.

Vivid pictures of the horror she had witnessed in her years as a detective would soon be flashing past her. And then it would be over. Or at least that's how writer Paul Billing and director John Madden saw Det. Supt. Jane Tennison's final moments in *Prime Suspect*. Revelling in glory, numbed by pain but ready to bid adieu. They hadn't worked out the grim details but they had planned to 'kill off' TV's favourite lady cop as a Christmas ratings buster.

The industrious Billing had just penned *Prime Suspect 4: The Lost Child* in which actor Robert Glenister played a wicked child abuser and Lesley Sharp was the mother of two young daughters who were under threat. Madden was the director of the two-part series and the film maker who three years later was to step up on a podium in Hollywood to collect an Oscar for masterminding the modern classic *Shakespeare In Love*. He could count among his friends both Gwyneth Paltrow and Dame Judi Dench who also won Oscars that warm night in California.

Billing felt the time was right for Tennison to go after four helter-skelter years and four compelling adventures. They were getting ready to present their ideas to senior executives at Granada Television, the backers of the series, and its creator Lynda La Plante. But suddenly they got word of 'changes at the top' at the TV station which was then based in both Manchester and London. And the new management were not keen on killing off their golden goose. La Plante, so it was understood, wasn't ready to see her go either. She was from the school of 'leaving things open'. So, Billing and Madden trailed off into the night unable to convince the 'suits' that they could have 20 million viewers pinned to their sofas.

Executive producer Sally Head and her 'team' who had been with the series since its 'birth' were leaving. Gub Neal was taking control of the drama department. New faces, new ideas.

Billing said, 'It just seemed to be the obvious thing to do. We thought Tennison had a good run for her money and there weren't too many places left to go to. I haven't changed my mind really. I won't be at all surprised though if they try to keep her going for a while longer.'

He couldn't have been more accurate. There have been three more *Prime Suspect* adventures since his prophetic words and the much loved detective who – Inspector Morse apart – dominated television in the UK for 15 years has been, so to speak, 'laid to rest'.

Today, Dame Helen Mirren, no less, is as ever holding court in the West End of London, with the recent transmission of *Prime*

Suspect 7 and the huge success of the controversial film *The Queen* in which she played the British monarch in the days following the tragic death of Princess Diana in a car crash in Paris.

Mirren has had much to do with the reshaping and formulisation of Jane Tennison since La Plante created the character. And, as the climax to the series draws closer, she again has ensured that her parting scenes bear the hallmark of distinction.

Dame Helen ... sorry, Helen ... is now 61, though she looks a full 40 years younger, and must count a carpenter among her best friends, as she has won so many awards that her shelves are groaning with trophies. A critic once wrote of the late Dame Edith Evans that she glided on to a stage like 'a battleship in full sail'. Mirren arrives rather like a trim little frigate, jaunty in the afternoon sun.

For the record, she is five feet four tall, slight of figure, grey in hair, is nicknamed 'Popper' by her close friends, and wears a beautifully cut dark slate-blue two-piece suit, with a white top underneath it, some rather spectacular gold chains, and a huge diamond on her wedding finger. There's a very large watch to match and – rather incongruously – some faux-leopardskin sling-backs on her feet.

When she curls up on the rather large armchair, she kicks off the shoes and takes a sip of Perrier water. Almost immediately, she is protective of the no-nonsense sleuth who made her a household name. As she put it, 'I feel she is a good friend of mine. When I start to play her again after a period away, it's like coming back to someone I know well. It's then that I discover different sides to her. But she doesn't fit me like a glove. There are elements I do identify with like the intense ambition for getting on, which is something that I have only lately come to realise I have myself.'

Mirren's commercial career was in fact languishing in the doldrums until Lynda La Plante dreamed up the idea of the tough female detective who, like so many men in a similar position, found it almost impossible communicating with the opposite sex at a romantic level. And she was a brilliant woman detective who could command respect from both sexes.

It was the actress in La Plante who gave Mirren the key to playing Tennison in the opening *Prime Suspect* adventure. Pundits and critics believed she had pulled off something of a two-faced trick by allowing herself to appear sour-faced, miserable and without make-up. In fact, she had her hair cut by top crimper Trevor Sorbie and was trying to look glamorous. So, what was the clincher? What made Tennison a triumph? She says, 'Lynda had given me a brilliant piece of advice on how to play the role. It was two words: Don't smile. She said, "You are smiling too much, don't smile." It's a very female thing to do, to smile, to charm people, and Lynda said, "That's not Jane Tennison. She doesn't work that way." And she was right. It was a wonderful piece of advice. For Tennison, to try to beguile and charm people was wrong. She is strict and intimidating. She uses her smiles very, very carefully. As a woman, you smile and nod and look interested as a way of getting around people. Women grow up imagining their job is to make men feel good about themselves. But Tennison was not there to make you feel good. She wasn't there to stroke egos. She was her own woman.'

The other piece of sound advice came from *Prime Suspect* adviser and real-life cop Jackie Malton. 'She told me never to cry and never to fold my arms. If you are a woman in the force, you don't cry, and, if you are going to cry, you go and lock yourself in the loo where nobody can see or hear you. If you watch *Prime Suspect* from start to finish, you will never see me fold my arms. It is a defensive act and, while you might imagine it makes you look strong, you're actually putting up a barrier to defend yourself. The police are so into body language they understand it perfectly. A good detective can read you so easily.'

Suddenly, Mirren was public property. She had leaped over the barrier of being an 'art-house' film star and 'serious' stage actress for 20 years and was basking in the glory of being in the public arena. She does, however, get edgy when she suspects that the body of her work over four decades is being ignored and that she owes her current status to a television series.

'Certainly not,' she responds sharply. 'I was known for a lot of things before that, a whole variety of work on stage and screen and TV, and I have continued to do work during it, and after it. I didn't do *Prime Suspect* for seven years, and then returned to it. It's not as if it was a continuing cop drama, and as if I was in someone's home on the box every night of the week! I haven't been there, on the screen, in your face, for the best part of the last two decades. I cannot stand it when modern drama becomes unrealistic, and if I was ever offered anything that I couldn't believe personally in, then I would not for a second get on board.' There is a pause. 'No matter how tempting the offer was, financially.'

Everybody rated Mirren from the moment she set foot on stage back in the Sixties. Inside the business, she was a 'sexual powerhouse', the former 'sex queen of the Royal Shakespeare Company'. As actor Nicky Henson put it, having worked with her on a TV version of *A Midsummer Night's Dream*, 'What do you think of when you think of Helen? Sex.'

Perhaps the mischievous Henson was simply being glib, but what was true was that the uninhibited, unchained Mirren was always ready to strip for the cause of her art. Though she had gained over the years a certain reputation for disrobing, nobody questioned the excellence of her work, especially when she took to the stage. Three times she had played the Queen of the Nile in stage adaptations of *Antony and Cleopatra* and the critics lapped up her interpretations, at least on the first two assaults on the impossible role. There was very little she couldn't do as an actress. And yet, and yet …

Was it that she intimidated the wrong people? When she made her bid for Hollywood success, she put some of her ideals into cold storage in the cause of progress. She boxed clever. She played it their way. But her patience finally ran out under the tropical rain clouds of Belize in Central America on the film *Mosquito Coast* when a certain Harrison Ford kept calling her 'Mother'.

Dark clouds still occasionally settle over moody Mirren. They were there from her formative days in Leigh-on-Sea, Essex. She would often peer out across the Thames Estuary and wonder about her Russian heritage. She'd fantasise about being a heroine struggling through the snowy wastes as Larissa does in Boris Pasternak's *Doctor Zhivago*. Or she'd be the mysterious girl hovering around the casino while Gregory Peck gambled his last rouble in the film of the Dostoevsky classic *The Gambler*. She'd be confused as to the details of her background and exactly what was expected of her. Who were the Mironoffs? Was it fate which had led them to Britain? What was left of her family on Russian soil? So many questions but so few answers. She never felt as though she entirely fitted in the equation unless she was on a stage. Only there did she enjoy complete freedom. And that also scared her. She'd argue, in conversations with herself, that she would never find true 'happiness'. Either she would dedicate herself to her craft or she would spend a life wasted.

Ironically, Mirren recently returned to her Eastern European roots in the BBC Radio 4 play *The Mironoff Legacy* in which she was asked to portray her own real-life great-aunt. She explains, 'My grandfather was in Britain in the First World War, a rather high-ranking official at the Russian Embassy, their Military Charge d'Affaires.

'And the revolution happened, the Tsar was assassinated, and the government changed. So, from being a somebody, he became a nobody. From a diplomat to a displaced immigrant. I realised with a shock that I knew hardly anything about him. I knew that my great-great-grandfather was Field Marshal Kamensky, one of the amazing heroes of the Napoleonic Wars, but my own grandfather, who I used to talk to as a little girl, was a mystery to me!

'He wrote so many letters home, and his sister then wrote back to him … my father changed the family name to Mirren from Mironoff, and, instead of being known as "Elena" at school, Dad asked that I be called "Helen" so that I could fit in better, and Grandfather was (there's no other word for it) disgusted as this betrayal of his Imperial Russian heritage. He was a proud man, and he found other work – he became a taxi driver. Imagine. Taxi driving is fine – we all need taxis. But considering what he had done before! When he died, I found this vast archive of letters that he and his sisters had written until about 1930 when they stopped replying for some reason, and I was intrigued to know what they said – because my father had always made us speak English, and they were all penned in Russian! And, despite my ancestry, I am *not* fluent in the language.

'I was doing one drama, and there was a Russian actor in the cast, and I told him about this treasure trove, and he said, "Helen, let me look at them," and, dear darling man that he is, he translated *all* of them for me. And then I mentioned this to a dramatist friend, and she thought that it might make a short play, and out of that came *The Mironoff Legacy*.

'It was *so* strange, to be playing one's great-aunt, and to watch and listen to another actress playing me as a little girl … not spooky, just very moving, very emotional. I'm now seriously thinking of returning to the piece, and maybe turning it into something for television. I think that it would work. Or maybe a stage play?

'I'd only discovered my great-aunt very recently through getting the letters written to my grandfather translated, so she was a revelation to me. I'd known nothing about her at all as a personality. That was incredibly moving, to find this part of my personal family history.'

The Mironoff Legacy came about as a direct result of her being able to research her family's roots while promoting *Calendar Girls* at the British Council's New British Cinema Festival in Moscow in April 2004. She employed a translator to work through her grandfather's memoirs and letters spanning nearly half a century from the collapse of Tsarist Russia to the mid-1950s when he died. She and her sister stumbled on the unfinished memoirs and a typewriter with Russian keys in their grandfather Pyotr Vasielivch Mironoff's old chest. And within lay an abundance of clues to the family.

Mirren, who was brought up on her grandfather's stories of pre-

Revolutionary Russian nobility, explained, 'My grandfather was in the Tsarist army and had been sent to London to do an arms deal with the British government during the Russo-Japanese war, so it was impossible for him to come back during or after the Revolution. He left behind six sisters who lived on the family estate at Gzhatsk near Smolensk. The letters show they had to leave to live in small rooms in Moscow.'

While in Moscow for the premiere of *Calendar Girls*, she wandered the vast Vagankovskoye Cemetery in search of her great-grandmother's grave. Though she failed to locate the grave, she did find the church close to the Pushkin Museum which held a requiem service for her. It was now a warehouse. She said, 'I was seven or eight when he [her grandfather] died. He used to draw me little maps of what the house at Gzhatsk was like, where the stables were and what the grounds were like. Reading his memoirs, I found out stuff I had never known before. He found the whole business of being part of a family and respect for your ancestors hugely important. To be ripped away from all of that must have been incredibly painful. Not just the wealth side of it but the sense of the past.'

Though fluent in Russian, her father, who was to take the first name Basil, 'rejected all of that and wanted to move away from it'. She said, 'It was he who anglicised the family name, not because he wanted to forget his roots, but to blend in better, to feel less of a stranger in a foreign land. What I had were memories of sitting on my grandfather's knee while he told me stories about Russia. He made it sound so much like something out of Chekhov.'

Mirren soon realised as a youngster in Essex that she was not cut out to be a housewife, mother or drudge behind a desk at the local council offices. The time was the austere Fifties in Britain. Well-spoken, well-educated young ladies were expected to marry and be content with their husband and 2.5 children. But she felt a new mood approaching. And she wanted to be part of that 'movement'. A classmate described her frame of mind thus: 'It was as though she was having premonitions. She said a new age was beginning and she would be part of that age. But then she'd go into a shell and you'd never guess what she was thinking. What was plainly obvious was that she was convinced there was a "special" place waiting for her, somewhere.'

She confided after joining the National Youth Theatre that she had even considered saving to have plastic surgery. She hated the ridge across her nose and cried in a moment of insecurity, 'I'm not pretty enough and I'm too fat. I did think of going to one of those doctors who could put it all right, who could make me look beautiful but that kind of thinking is destructive and I can't afford it in any case.'

People misunderstand her still. They think of her as intimidating, that she possesses an outer ring of platinum and an inner of cast iron. But she protests, 'I am not tough at all. I am quite soft hearted actually. I couldn't even drown a moth if it flew into the shower. I'm independent but not when it comes to carrying my own luggage. I don't want to get out of cars at two in the morning to change tyres. I think men do that kind of thing far better. But I can and would do it if I had to.

'I tend to cry in confrontations which is really pathetic and very irritating. I dissolve into this horrible snivelling creature. It drives me crazy. But they are tears of rage. It's to do with being inarticulate and not being able to confront people as I should be able to.'

But she managed to turn the tap marked 'angry' off when she once appeared on Michael Parkinson's chat show. She claimed that he couldn't take his eyes off her breasts. 'He annoyed me,' she said. 'I tried not to show it but he tried to suggest there was a relationship between my career and the size of my bosom. The only thing was that he refused to say the word "breast". I said, "My what ? ... Go on, Michael, spit it out." He just gestured. They [her breasts] keep coming up ... they always will.'

Mirren has been brave enough to let the camera come in close to reveal lines and wrinkles on numerous occasions, displaying the kind of confidence rarely seen in an actress of her years. She says,

'Listen, I've had my sixtieth birthday. What you see is what you get. All you have to do on a film is to look really crap, and everyone thinks, How brave, what a brilliant actress, whereas all you've actually done is look crap.'

She loves working with young actors 'because, although we are often culturally very far apart, I really enjoy seeing the next generation coming up. People my age start thinking, Oh, it's all moved on, we are no use any more, and yet I've learned *so* much from these youngsters. Their energy, their vivacity, their eagerness to try new things. I am truly excited by the way things have moved on in this business. In the classical theatre, maybe not so much, because you are appearing in plays where the female roles are not that thick on the ground, or not so substantial for the female actor, especially when she is over 30! But, in today's contemporary theatre, there are *so* many more parts for women and they reflect the society that we live in today.

'I am especially pleased that there are so many more parts for black and Asian actors today. When I was starting out, 40 years ago, that was *not* the case. It hardly ever happened. Rampant racism was rife, and galloping sexism too – you were patronised all the time as a woman. I sometimes wondered if a lot of casting directors, producers and directors thought that we women checked our brains in at the door! But we have seen so many changes in the last quarter of a century. Women are far more high profile in politics, in medicine, in acting, in the law and in life generally, and, slowly, that is being seen in drama as well. In another 20 years, the change will be there, for all to observe.'

Helen Mirren has luxurious homes in Los Angeles and in Wapping in Central London, close to the River Thames, following her lengthy occupation of a mansion apartment overlooking Battersea Park.

Her range extends from playing Shakespearean heroines for the Royal National Theatre and the RSC to a trio of real-life British Queens – Charlotte in *The Madness of King George*, *Elizabeth I* and

Elizabeth II – the monarch who asked her to become a Dame of the British Empire. In fact, she is the only actress ever to have played both Elizabeth I and Elizabeth II on screen. Not to mention 15 years, on and off, during which she enjoyed seven adventures in *Prime Suspect*.

She adores antique jewellery and street markets. If she's back in town taking lunch, you'll usually find her at her favourite restaurant Corelli's not far from her former London pad in Battersea Park Road. Or, if her husband, award-winning film director Taylor Hackford, is around, they might drop into an Indian tandoori restaurant near the Oval in Kennington. If she's feeling 'up for it', she'll take a table at The Ivy. She used to swear by Ossie Clark and Elizabeth Emmanuel frocks and now wears Max Mara but she doesn't follow fashion. She loves France and likes to 'lose' herself in Provence. Her literary icon is Joseph Conrad. Somewhat surprisingly, she enjoys watching television.

The circle has now truly turned for Helen Mirren. At the start of her career, she removed her clothes for the film *Age of Consent*, with James Mason playing the artist who wanted to 'capture' her voluptuous body on canvas somewhere off the Great Barrier Reef. She has never been allowed to forget her state of undress. Either then or in subsequent films such as Ken Russell's *Savage Messiah*, the painfully inept *Caligula* and director Peter Greenaway's explicit, full-frontal, gastronomique black comedy *The Cook, The Thief, His Wife and Her Lover*.

Today, largely through being able to rightly access quality roles, she has somehow managed to reach yet another career peak. First, she found new film success in the British comedy drama *Calendar Girls*, playing the leader of a pack of middle-aged women from a Women's Institute in Yorkshire who stripped for charity, and then made her successful return as Tennison in *Prime Suspect 6*. And she has rapidly moved on to find even greater international acclaim through *Elizabeth I* on television and the intriguing real-life movie drama *The Queen*.

Ah, Mirren the Misunderstood. Becoming a sex symbol, she insists, was never actually high on her agenda. 'I didn't invent Helen Mirren,' she says. 'You are what you are. I was never interested in films at first probably because we got such lousy ones at home in Southend. I wanted to do the classics because they had the best stories and the richest characters. But it took me ten years of struggle and torture before I felt comfortable on stage. Then I realised I knew nothing about films and had to start learning all over again.

'But when I am filming I go into retreat, I don't go out or party. I feel as though I'm one of those nuns in a monastery. I put everything aside. I am terribly disciplined. I think perhaps that does come from my family background. My father was an organiser and he liked things in their place. That's me. I like to know where things are, where things go. I feel like that professionally and at home.

'I think as an actress if you let these things pass you by you are destined for mediocrity. You must know what is happening around you and who is doing what. You have to protect yourself against the inept and the amateurish. The thing that is always waiting to gobble you up like a demon.'

Mirren has not been forgotten in America where she recently worked on *The Clearing* with Robert Redford and Willem Dafoe, playing a wealthy businessman's wife who has to negotiate her husband's freedom in a hostage situation, and the New York high-flyers comedy *Raising Helen* with Kate Hudson and John Corbett. In the pipeline to be made in 2007 is the Great War drama *Angel Makers* directed by Jon Amiel and due to co-star Anne-Marie Duff, John Hurt and Anna Friel. The writer is her old *Prime Suspect* chum Paul Billing. Also due for release shortly is the period piece *America*, written by Frederic Raphael and filmed in Paris and Venice. She co-stars with Isabelle Huppart and Jennifer Jason Leigh in Polish director Jerzy Skolimowski's take on Susan Sontag's best-seller about an actress who sets out to found and open a commune in San Francisco.

She has also become an active campaigner internationally in

support of Oxfam's crusade against the small arms trade. She said, 'It started from being in America. It's a great country for all its faults. It is bold and brilliant but there is this cancer, the accessibility of guns which kill thousands of potentially great Americans. Then Oxfam approached me and told me about the situation internationally. It just struck me that the underlying cause of so much of the misery is the unstoppable availability to any group of a flow of guns from Britain, Russia, France, China or wherever. The people are hungry but the food doesn't get through because of the people with guns. How many times have we heard of this?'

At Universal Studios, there is still much talk about Michelle Pfeiffer or Glenn Close filling the shoes of Det. Supt. Jane Tennison in a £40 million movie version of *Prime Suspect* set against the backdrop of Bel Air and Downtown Los Angeles or possibly San Francisco. Mirren was naturally as miffed as the character's creator La Plante that the Americans should want to hijack her dream role. But Mirren prefers to play the pragmatist. At least it eases the pain of missing out on a possible £2 million pay day. 'Films are expensive things and they can't afford to put someone like me in them,' she said. 'They want to try the Hollywood approach which is basically to recoup the cost of the movie within the first two weekends of showing it. If they can do that, it doesn't really matter if it's no good because, by the time the word is out that it isn't up to much, they might have already got their money back. Maybe I am underestimating my profile a little but all I am saying is that I understand the realities of the world and it doesn't bug me any more.'

So, who exactly was, or is, Helen Mirren, the misfit who could never quite shake off her middle-class roots, the 'beatnik' from a convent school in Leigh-on-Sea, Essex who shook the Royal Shakespeare Company down to its administrative foundations? She wanted to become a great actress and that she has achieved. She was never interested in 'stardom' just for the sake of it. What set her apart from the other youngsters who filed through the ranks of the National Youth Theatre?

She says, 'There must be a million people on earth who would be brilliant actors. It's a very common talent but the thing that's comparatively rare is the thing that takes people there and that seems to be irrespective of talent. I often think this when I'm on stage. I suddenly wonder why we're here, why we are the people who are standing there and they are the people who are out there.

'I have always considered myself serious about what I do and it is very important to me. But I hate the phrase "serious actress". It sounds like the civil service, humourless, pathetic and boring. It is important not to take yourself too seriously, to be able to laugh at yourself.'

If she'd have you believe it, she's an enigma, a mysterious, vulnerable creature staring over the edge of an emotional abyss. That may have been the Helen Mirren of old. Today, I suspect, she's very much at home sipping her cup of tea in her converted super modern duplex in London's East End or quietly plotting her next move in the Hollywood hills guzzling a chilled glass of Krug champagne.

When she was at convent school, the most senior nun summoned her and warned her about her constant 'resident' enemy – fear. 'She told me that fear was one of the most destructive things in life,' she recalled. 'What you must learn is not to be afraid. But I still haven't learned that lesson.'

Mirren claims that, due to press attention and some of the more lurid roles she has played, her image has been widely misinterpreted.

'I am not gregarious or an exhibitionist,' she says. 'On a first day's rehearsal, when you walk in and meet 20 people you have never met before or going to the bar after the show can be torture. As an actor, you confront fear on such a scale that you think it would be easy to cope with fear in your own life … but it doesn't.'

Many who have worked with her say her career has been characterised by a mild non-self-destructive bohemianism. Actor Mark Rylance who runs The Globe at Southwark recalled her at a party he threw in Stratford-upon-Avon in 1982 shortly before she left for America. He said, 'We hired a bus and picked up 30 or 40 actors at the end of the night's performances, all in costume, and asked them to stay in character and improvise. The late Bob Peck was there as Caliban with Sinead Cusack and Helen Mirren as Cleopatra. The invitation said that God had decided to end the world in a couple of hours and needed to find a new Adam and Eve from the characters in Shakespeare. I was the Angel Gabriel in drag as the host and everyone got very crazy with drink and drugs and stuff.' But most of all he remembered Mirren controlling all around her by using a very quiet voice, an aspect of a technique which served her well during her Shakespearean days.

Mirren has seen her 60-plus years as a series of challenges and hurdles. And she has 'cleared' most of them. But she always liked to shock, to surprise. That was part of her psyche. When she slips into her self-deprecation mode, Mirren amusingly likes to describe herself as 'an old bird'. So, what, apart from the sales of small arms, concerns her just before she closes her eyes at night? 'Time,' she confides. 'There is not a lot of time in the world and my problem is that basically I am quite lazy. I think of myself as a bit of a wimp deep down. I've decided that people need energy more than talent. That's the greatest gift anyone can give you. My worry is that I need to try and put more energy into my life and work. Do I still have that kind of time?'

Let's not start at the very beginning. Instead, we shall return to a day when the unpredictable actress astounded her family and friends – in fact, just about everybody who knew her. It was New Year's Eve 1997 and the venue was a tiny Scottish church. She was very definitely the centre of attention. And a man with a well-groomed white beard sporting a kilt was placing a gold band on her finger, her mother's wedding ring.

1

THE ACTRESS, THE DIRECTOR, THE GHOST AND HER WEDDING

Nobody, least of all Helen Mirren, ever expected to see her trooping up the aisle with her lover, American film director Taylor Hackford, to become man and wife.

For 12 years, the couple had been an item sharing homes in various locations – the hills high above Los Angeles, a bijou apartment in New Orleans and Mirren's own opulent base close to London's Battersea Park.

Mirren herself was in her fifties and had firm views about marriage – almost all of them anti – which went all the way back to her twenties and the non-conformist Sixties, when she sipped her frothy coffee in a King's Road pavement cafés in Chelsea.

'Marriage, who needs it?' she'd later smile to curious backstagers at the Royal Court Theatre. 'I can't see too much point. I'm not sure that I could promise to obey. I'm not terribly good at obeying. "Obey" does not figure so well in my vocabulary.'

Only two months before the wedding, she was waxing lyrically on the subject comparing marriage to lobster. She definitely was *not* about to become a bride. 'It's not to my taste,' she said. 'Lobster is supposed to be this wonderful, fantastic thing, but it's not for me. I don't see why people get so excited about it. I feel the same about marriage.

'My parents had a wonderful marriage and I have some great role models around me. But none of my friends who got married are together any more. It's only in retrospect that I have realised I knew something subconcsiously that they didn't. But you don't need to be married to be with somebody in an intense, loving and supportive relationship. I don't want to be with anybody else. I just hope he feels the same way.' He did and he does.

Yet, here she was on New Year's Eve 1997 looking resplendent in an off-the-peg gold brocade, Cossack-style jacket with a flowing, full-length, peach silk skirt. The theme of her outfit was something old, new, borrowed and blue.

She also wore a new string of pearls, a present from Hackford, while her elder sister Kate loaned her two diamond rings for the occasion. Her shoes were well worn. Significantly, the 'blue' item had something to do with a sewing machine left to her by her mother who had died 18 months earlier. Mirren brought the machine back into service to shorten her skirt for the wedding and discovered it was still threaded with blue cotton – the last thread her mother Kit had used before she died. 'That was so strange,' Mirren later confided to Kate. 'It was as though Mother knew, had some vision of the future. She had never quite given up on me getting married. It was so sad that she went before I'd made up my mind to marry Taylor. But that was the way it was obviously meant to be.'

The groom was immaculate, as you'd expect if you knew anything about Taylor Hackford's pedigree. Though Hackford was raised in sunny Santa Barbara nestling against the Pacific Ocean, he was decked out in tartan, sporting a kilt and family crest proudly denoting his north-of-the-border ancestry. Only a small group of 18 took the night train to Inverness to what turned out to be a triple celebration – the wedding, Hogmanay and Hackford's birthday.

In the background were his two sons – Rio, 32, and Alex, 23 – from his previous marriages, along with Kate Mirren and her son

Simon who acted as Best Man. His cute daughter Natasha was the only bridesmaid. Helen's mother Kathleen – or Kitty to friends – had died the previous year, while her father Vasily – better known as Boris – had died many years earlier.

From the showbusiness fraternity was Mel Smith, one half of the comedy duo Smith and Jones and now an established film director responsible for features such as *Mr Bean*. He stood out as an instantly recognisable, flamboyant figure in a small sea of anonymous faces in the small ancient chapel.

The setting for the wedding, Hackford's third, was the Presbyterian church in the Highland village of Ardersier (population 1,200), perched on a hill overlooking the Moray Firth. The venue had also been kept a closely guarded secret until the day itself. Only a handful of reporters had time to make the arduous trip to the quiet backwater, an hour's drive from Inverness.

Local Mary Douglas, who had run her flower shop, Mary's Flowers, for ten years, had been sworn to secrecy. For six weeks, she had been wanting to gossip about the celebrity wedding on their doorstep. But she felt bound to honour Ms Mirren's wishes.

And low-key it was, even on the day. 'She decided on sprays of terracotta-coloured roses,' recalled Mrs Douglas. 'Though she was very demure, you could also see she was over the moon, really excited. The first thing that struck me about her was how cool, calm and collected she was. Not in the least bit bossy or showy.'

Few of those attending the 30-minute-long ceremony could have known that Mirren had been on the verge of calling the whole thing off only two weeks earlier. Hackford had proposed on several occasions, always for her to declare, 'Why change things? Aren't we happy as we are?'

As she approached her fiftieth birthday, a string of friends were signalling the end to their marriages. Her sister Kate's marriage had ended in divorce, leaving her to bring up Simon alone, leaving Helen with serious doubts as to whether a change in their status would make them any happier. Far from it, she semi-convinced

3

herself that any move towards Mr and Mrs would prove disasterous. 'It could prove the undoing of us,' she confided to close friends. 'I have already told Taylor that it won't change me or my attitude or feelings. He was just so happy to be getting married again. He had no doubts.

'For a while, I felt like calling the whole thing off and saying to him, "Let's just jump on a plane ... anywhere." I don't normally get pessimistic, especially when it comes to us. I'd trust Taylor with my life.

'But I find marriage so important that I don't see how anybody ever gets the courage to do it. I believe in love of all ilks. By saying that, I put myself in a vulnerable position because it isn't cool. Not that I mind. It's not important to be cool. People who call themselves cool are usually the least cool of all.'

A confused Mirren revealed that she spent a troubled 48 hours 'walking on glass', hardly able to eat or drink. Amusingly, she caught a late-night screening of the Oscar-winning movie *As Good As It Gets* which starred Helen Hunt and Jack Nicholson as a waitress and pulp-fiction writer drawn to each other by loneliness and fear of commitment.

'Not only did she think it was a great movie, she sobbed her heart out watching Hunt,' recalls a confidante. 'She felt this was the moment in her life, the time, to make that commitment. To be past 50 and unmarried is quite something. She didn't want to have waited this long to be making any mistake. Then she realised you have to gamble sometimes. You have to take a risk. There are no guarantees.

'Helen had spent much of her career and life developing this image of being tough, of having this inner and outer steel. The truth is that she was the one frightened of getting hurt.'

Arriving ten minutes late at the Presbyterian church, Mirren, her fair hair neatly cut to shoulder length, thrilled the waiting crowd of villagers by inviting them all inside to share her happiness.

The sun had already set at 5.00pm when the Rev Alex Whiteford, a relative 'new boy' to the village, ushered the remaining guests into the Victorian church. Among them was the dark, dapper and urbane Prince George Galitzine, one of Mirren's oldest pals and ex-flames, and the fiery socialite Lady Sarah Ponsonby. They were the posh rebels from the past who, during the Seventies, lived in an up-market rural commune in Gloucestershire preaching love and peace while occasionally swilling down a bottle of Bollinger. Here they were, now pillars of society, singing 'Amazing Grace' and 'To Be a Pilgrim'.

What was unusual about the day was that it also happened to be Hackford's fifty-third birthday. As they exchanged rings and the groom kissed the bride, Rev Whiteford led the laughing ensemble into a rousing chorus of 'Happy Birthday'. Mirren and Hackford then gathered their guests around them for a four-day wining and dining treat at nearby Castle Stuart.

Rev Whitehead, who hails from Ayrshire and has three children, recalls, 'They wanted to be married in church rather than a hotel. They thought it was more meaningful. But I had no idea what was happening until only a few days before. I didn't realise we were getting a celebrity.'

But the wedding didn't go off completely without a hitch. Documents which needed to be signed by the bride and groom were temporarily 'lost' and had to be forwarded to elegant Castle Stuart at Petty Parish where the reception was soon in full swing.

The wedding party trooped into the ancient seventeenth-century home of the Earls of Moray, singing as they went. They had taken over the entire castle at a cost approaching £10,000.

Waiting for them with his staff was Renfrewshire-born businessman Charles Edward Stuart and his wife Elizabeth. He had spent the best part of 20 years restoring the Jacobean structure to its former glory. Hackford joked to his bride that it was like being in a movie as they gazed down from their honeymoon suite, the Murray Room in the West Tower, across the Moray Firth to the mountains beyond.

In keeping with the period, the bedrooms had been named after the clans who battled at nearby Culloden in 1746 and was carpeted in that family's tartan. Guests slept in 400-year-old four-poster beds. The temperature outside may have been dipping below zero, but some chose to use the copper warming pans hanging in their rooms. The not-so-medieval central heating dealt well enough with the chill night air.

Inside the beamed and oak-pannelled Great Hall, the wedding party tucked into a traditional Hogmanay meal, a spread of haddock mousse, venison, salmon and haggis, the famed Scottish dish made of well-seasoned offal and oatmeal. The cake, decorated by Kate and Natasha, sported both the British and American flags. The entire Hackford clan were wearing kilts while Rio Hackford, in his speech, appropriately dubbed his father and stepmother 'free spirits who shall remain free spirits'.

At midnight, they joined hands to sing 'Auld Lang Syne' before taking a peek at The Three Turret Haunted Room at the top of the East Tower. The Earl of Moray, so the story goes, once searched for a brave soul to spend the night at Castle Stuart to prove to everyone that it was not haunted, so he asked the minister at the nearby Petty Church to offer a £20 reward. A local poacher, known as Big Angus, and said to be afraid of neither man nor beast, apparently took up the challenge. But the next morning, his body was found in the courtyard, quite dead, with a look of frozen horror on his face.

As Charles Stuart joked to Mirren shortly before she entered the room, 'Aye ... but did he jump, or was he pushed?'

As midnight tolled, the entire wedding party rattled pots and pans in the courtyard and around the ramparts, a traditional ceremony to ward away evil spirits. Multi-millionaire comedy star Mel Smith did his own spectacular impression of a banshee, complete with white sheet, taking up a prominent position on the battlements.

It was all, as one might put it, very un-Mirren like. One of the guests observed, 'Even those who had known her for decades were taken aback by how relaxed she was. It was as though we had all gone back in time to the Seventies and were kids again. She has always looked happy and relaxed with Taylor but now there was something more. The wedding and the romance had broug. the child in her again. She was a serious woman, for the most part who had needed to be taken seriously. She always felt it was the only way. But here she was dancing away, letting her hair down in every sense. It was a revelation.'

Charles Stuart, who had never met Mirren or Hackford previously, had picked them up in his Rolls-Royce from the church and brought them to his home. He commented, 'She became very emotional as the evening wore on. There were often tears in her eyes and she was crying when she left with Mr Hackford. She said it had all been very moving, and indeed it had.

'I think you could safely say we cater for people with taste and style looking for something a little different and they found it. They were a delightful group.'

Mirren, who was 52 when she slipped Hackford's gold band on to her finger, remembered the day as 'clear but cold'. At the time, the usually forthright Mirren had left it to her thrilled elder sister Kate, a teacher, to do the talking for her.

'It was a very low-key affair,' she said. 'But it's not a tradition in our family to have big weddings, so it was just how Helen wanted it. They both wanted to be with a small group of special people to them. Neither of them are up for showy events.'

They had talked the logistics of the wedding through over the previous two months, with Kate doing most of the fretting for both of them. They wanted the atmosphere to be 'intimate and comfortable' and more like a 'classic country weekend'.

She said, 'We played silly games, went for walks and chatted around the fireside doing pretty much what we wanted when we felt like doing it.'

Mirren later recalled having what amounted to an out-of-body experience. She said, 'As I arrived at the church, many of the villagers whom I had met while shopping for flowers and food were braving the chill standing outside, so I invited them in. When we reached the castle, we walked across the bridge singing and dancing.

The sky was clear and star-filled. It felt as though we were living out a romantic sonnet.'

Hackford was equally ecstatic about his wife's extraordinary change of attitude. For 15 years, she had proclaimed that she was content being single and childless. The concept of making 'the final commitment' left her cold and gave her instant panic attacks. Hackford was later his usual supercool self about his third marriage and the sudden turn in events. 'I would always have been happy to marry her,' he said. 'I had asked her several times before and she had always smiled, given me a peck on the cheek, and said, "Why ... we're happy, aren't we?" I was never able to beat that. It wasn't as if we weren't committed to each other before. I know she had been moved emotionally by something she had seen and heard. I know there was an influence of some kind which got us to having a wedding. Why analyse it though?

'But I have to say there is a certain ring to the expression "my wife" as opposed to "my girlfriend", "lover" or "partner". Our relationship is based on each other, not on our careers, even though that's how we got together. She is a great artist but there is more to us than that.'

Hackford also stressed that they had agreed to make each other the priority in their lives rather than put their hectic work schedules before all else. He said, 'Both of us have lived our lives and made errors of judgement on a private front. So when you do find somebody special and you know they are right for you, you just seize that moment. I try to spend all my time with her. We're both growing as people, as a couple. We can be apart for days, weeks, even months. But we never feel separated. To me, she's the greatest actress in the world. Her talent has always turned me on.'

Back in the Eighties, the lady who was now the centre of Hackford's universe was a dedicated member of the anti-marriage brigade, though she considered the concept romantic enough. Soon after making *Pascali's Island* with Charles Dance, she told writer Quentin Falk, 'Marriage? I just don't feel the need for it. I never have done and I still don't. There is, I agree, something very romantic about the idea. I love the pull men and women have towards being married. That's wonderful, but not for me. I guess it has a lot to do with ownership, the idea of owning somebody else. Someone else "owning" me is too crazy. I do love children but, as for having my own, that's never really been for me either.'

Hackford was taken aback and delighted when she decided to take him up on his proposal. In a very business-like way, he joked that he'd left the 'offer' on the table for years before she took him up on it.

Today, friends of Mirren still express their surprise and delight that she underwent such a change of heart on the subject of marriage. She certainly had them fooled as to her intentions right up to the wedding itself. One commented, 'Just before she took off to Scotland, she said something "traumatic" was about to happen but she wouldn't say anything more. We feared the worst and it turned out to be the best.'

But Mirren now denies being a feminist icon who kept the flame against marriage alight for most of her adult life. She merely says that she felt it wasn't right for her. 'It felt different for about three weeks, fantastic, so romantic,' she said. 'It was a feeling of not being owned but possessed, which I'd never had before. That euphoria passed but I still get the odd pang. It's like you wake up at two in the morning, look over and think, Hold on, that's my husband! I never expected that. I thought most things would remain the same. I was surprised by how this new "thing", this new feeling, influenced me.

'I don't think I ever felt insecure about us but I suppose I must have done to a degree. I must have been looking over my shoulder without even realising it because here I was, almost smugly, feeling settled and totally comfortable.

'That doesn't mean the edge of excitement or danger had gone. I couldn't live without that kind of danger. But it gave me this sense of wonderful belonging. We'd been together for 15 years and he had given me respect and loyalty but I was still terrified that getting married might change us. But it hasn't and it has, because everything did change.

'I got this tremendous sense of pleasure out of calling him "my husband" and buzzed when I heard him address me to other people as "my wife". This shiver went down my spine it sounded so good.

'To wake up every day and know you are with the right person and nothing is going to change – that may sound arrogant but that is the way it is. I like to think that is the way it is for both of us and the rest of my family. Oddly, I was also convinced, quite suddenly, that they wanted this to happen for me. That they knew it was right.

'Certain people had this weird idea about me because of my career and perhaps parts in which I took my clothes off. Perhaps they thought of me as wild, off the wall, always the unpredictable. Now I'm this older married bird and they find it terribly unexciting. Well, I hope not. I hope I have not lost my sexual allure. Indeed, I think not because work is still there and there are taxi drivers still going "Cor ..." which is certainly a very good thing from where I am sitting.'

Taking her vows as Mrs Taylor Hackford made her confront her fears about divorce and fractured relationships. In the Eighties, she was almost a 'sounding board' for actress chums who'd been betrayed by their husbands and others who were playing away from home themselves. She told her closest friends in London that she was 'horrified' by the sex games being played out by the LA movie set, especially the 'suits' running the major studios.

Another friend who was going through a messy divorce to a studio executive in Beverly Hills recalled, 'Helen was brilliant even if you didn't see her for six months. She was like this walking, talking Samaritan person. I was really being squeezed by my husband who seemed to have mistresses coming out of the woodwork everywhere. We had two lovely kids and I didn't want them destroyed through all the bitterness. I knew Helen was in town so I called her up and we had coffee. I explained things to her and she thought for a second and said, "Who is more important, you and the children or his flights of fancy?"

'I said it had to be us and she dwelled on this for a second or two before saying, very calmly, "Then it's simple. Screw him into the ground. Tell him you're taking an extra million for every new affair you get to hear about unless he wants to stop now and make a settlement."

'That worked a treat. I think the fact she wasn't married and had no interest played a huge part in her clear thinking. I was forever grateful. She made me a stack of money.'

Romance, it has to be said, was the last thing on Mirren's mind when she arrived in Hollywood to make the science fiction film *2010* in 1983. She was already nudging 40 and was not about to be subjected to the pressures of the casting couch syndrome which were rife in the movie game for attractive girls fresh to the Los Angeles movie scene. Though seen as a stunning sex symbol by many, especially in Europe, bronzed, well-manicured Californian men largely found her intimidating and threatening.

Not that this concerned Mirren. She found them mostly superficial, to a large part juvenile and totally wrapped up in themselves and their next facelift. A confidante revealed, 'She said she was too old for most of them. They were too old and weird or too young and stupid for her. And she spoke, in LA terms, proper English, which put her in the position of them not being able to understand her and she rarely understanding them.' She'd joke at their expense and they wouldn't get it. The guys were gay or they wanted 'meaningful' relationships. She didn't. She joked to a friend, 'No, they have virtually no interest in me that way ... thank goodness.'

And though she treated the men who did try to penetrate her ultra-cool shield with a blend of charm and levity, she largely found their superficiality, in the context of relationships, nothing less than appalling. Until, that is, Hackford came along.

She explained to a member of her circle, 'The weirdest thing is that men in very important positions in Hollywood can be charming and sophisticated. They can also say the most lewd, vulgar things without a thought for what they are actually saying. They generally have little respect for women and treat them as meat. Divorce means next to nothing which is why their lawyers are among their closest friends.'

But, with Taylor Hackford, she discovered a very different species of American male. It took her 15 years, however, to convince herself that she was ready for marriage and one day to wear a wedding ring, even if it was her mother's.

She wore it for the ceremony in Scotland and was going to slip it into her top drawer the day after. Instead, she couldn't bring herself to take it off. She said, 'It seems that my fears about what marriage can do to a happy, contented couple were completely unfounded. Though we have spent a lot of time apart, we are close and committed. Before I met Taylor, I'd had four lengthy relationships, so I guess I think of myself as serially monogamous. When it comes to the crunch, though, fidelity isn't everything. I could forgive a lover who has a one-night stand but I couldn't forgive a lover who showed me no respect in front of other people. Trust is much more important. Trust can be ... everything.

'If I add up the days and the months, I have spent much of my life celibate. I think perhaps the problem for me there was that I didn't think at one time in my life that I needed to be in love to have sex. But I also learned because of my job to be without cuddles, to be alone, to be independent. I hate not being able to give my partner time when I am working, so it is better if he is not there.'

Typically Mirren, she could also use moments like these to become her most enigmatic. 'There have been a lot of great loves in my life,' she said, almost in a whisper, 'But he is the love of this part of my life. That part is by far and away the happiest.'

2

THE
END-OF-THE-PIER
SHOW

The smiling sister – a whimsical Irish lady, so it is said, at Queen Charlotte's Hospital in Chiswick, west London – hit it right on the button when she turned to a midwife with the words, 'Oh, she's a star, that's for sure ... a real star.'

When Ilynea Vasilieuna Mironoff – as Mirren was christened – came into the world on the night of 26 July 1945, she was already setting records. Her birth took a mere 20 minutes, which turned out to be a 'speed' record for natural deliveries at the world-famous maternity hospital.

Her mother was thrilled, as was her father, Vasily-Petrov Mironoff, a strikingly handsome Russian gentleman who arrived in England shortly before the Kaiser called a halt to the Great War.

Both mother and father were understandably delighted. They already had another daughter, Katrina – plain Katie to other toddler chums – who was three, and what better way to celebrate the end of hostilities with the Germans than their sparkling addition to the Mironoff clan. But behind Vasily-Petrov's smile was cause for concern.

His father, and Helen's grandfather, was a Tsarist colonel

stranded in London while hoping to clinch an arms deal with the British Government when the Bolsheviks grabbed power in late 1917. Lenin and his cohorts snatched their land and money before the Mironoffs could react. Her maternal grandfather was a butcher and horse dealer in London's East End. Her grandmother had a total of 13 children.

Mironoff was basically a proud, serious man interested in world affairs and, in particular, any Eastern European developments. Like many patriots of the old school from the Ukraine to Latvia, he dreamed of the fall of Communism and one day being able to return safely to his homeland. He rarely found humour in his heritage but, when pressed, would joke that the Communists had at least improved their techniques on the soccer field and the 'art of destruction'. His granddaughter Helen later dryly remarked, 'The deal took so long ... the Revolution happened and my grandfather stayed. He lived for 20 years but still referred to the Bolshevik uprising as just a peasant revolt.'

Mirren grew up without learning a word of Russian though the family observed Russian religious holidays, such as Orthodox Easter. 'It was funny, in a nice way.' she says. 'When my sister and I argued and she was being very passionate or emotional or depressed about something, we always say "Don't be so Russian".'

She remained sure that somewhere in Russia, following her 2004 Moscow initiative, there existed the remnants of the Mironoff dynasty, those left from Stalinist purges who had not been sent to Siberia. There were six great-aunts and on her grandmother's side there was the legendary Marshal Kamensky who fought against Napoleon. In fact, it was left to the UK *Mail on Sunday* some two years later to trace the whereabouts of the remaining Mironoffs in the form of modern-day relatives - Ilyena Bogacheva, 34, and Lydia Gvozdeva, 62 - who expressed their surprise at the connection to the British actress. Mirren was beside herself with glee, suggesting that both she and sister Kate would be flying out to meet the last of the long-lost Mironoffs as soon as possible.

What the exasperated Mironoff did find in Britain – despite being eternally grateful for being allowed to remain in the country – was a 'grey nation, largely ruled by grey people'. He remained unimpressed to the end.

What also pained and angered him, because of his fine education, was being unable to find a position to suit a man of his stature. He was a superb musician who played the violin with the London Philharmonic. But above all, he wanted and needed respect. Friends said he offered his linguistic services on several occasions to the British Government, only to be flatly rejected on 'security' grounds. And he felt a general distrust of the British ruling class because of his Russian background.

An old family friend observed that Mironoff, who was just two years old when his father's ship docked at Tilbury, was used to being subjected to racial taunts and jingoism. He said, 'During and after the war, all foreigners were treated with suspicion. Naturally enough, there was sympathy for the Russians because of what the Germans were doing to them but ... they were still Communists and deemed to be a very dodgy lot. He resented the attitude of the Brits but kept it to himself. But he was concerned about his family facing prejudice.'

Vasily-Petrov married London girl Kathleen Rogers from Pimilco during the Blitz and they moved to the East London suburb of Ilford in Essex, working in a fabric shop before settling after the war in nondescript Leigh-on-Sea in Essex, overlooking the Thames Estuary. He was a former viola player who once slugged it out with Oswald Mosley's right-wing Blackshirts in the East End and she was from a family of butchers. And he was anxious that he and his young family should make a fresh start. He was also a Socialist on the verge of becoming a Communist, according to his youngest daughter. But he was never a card-carrying member and harboured a deep-rooted contempt for Stalin and red Russia.

They purchased a modest, red-brick, three-bedroom terraced house in the cul-de-sac, Queen's Road, an anonymous road of terraced houses sandwiched between the busy shopping centre and the Grand Parade with its landscaped gardens meandering down to the water's edge and the fabulous vista across the estuary with Southend Pier on the horizon. Somewhat grandly, the previous owners of the run-down Victorian property had named it Ilfracombe, which meant absolutely nothing to Mr and Mrs Mironoff. Other homes in the street were similarly grandly titled, considering their state of repair and worth, with names such as 'Mossbank' and 'Heathbank'. They duly painted over the stone sign with whitewash and made as many adjustments as they could, within their meagre budget.

Vasily-Petrov was nudging 30 and looking towards an uncertain future while millions celebrated victory over Adolf Hitler's Germany. He shared the joy of his neighbours, but he had his reservations. The Communists and Joe Stalin were in power in Moscow and he wouldn't be welcome back in what was now the mighty USSR.

Instead, he turned his attention towards his family and career, making money as a taxi driver in those foggy, austere days of post-war Britain while his wife Kitty, a bright outgoing woman of Scottish parentage, raised the children. Life was never going to be easy for an aristocratic Russian gentleman with no friends in the right places hoping to advance himself. Though he had no association with the Communist regime, his patience, naturally enough, wore thin when he was treated with suspicion. He confided to one neighbour that he had been interested in securing a position in the Foreign Office but felt he had the wrong 'pedigree'. There were already too many Eastern European exiles seeking opportunities in the South-East in secure, white-collar occupations.

He was also prone to melodrama, which always amused those close to him. He had become, as he once described it, 'this peculiar, often excitable piece of flotsam in a sea of lost souls'. His amiable, thoroughly supportive wife spent many a long hour convincing him, in true Micawber style, that something would turn up. She was eventually proved to be right.

Their eldest daughter Katrina was a studious, quiet and introverted little girl, quite unlike her sister, while the Mironoffs' youngest child, Peter, was so distant at times that he might be in a room for an hour before anybody noticed. In later years, his behaviour would be described as 'eccentric' or 'odd'. He became an engineer, developed a *wanderlust* and took off in his twenties to build roads in the Kalahari Desert, Somalia and New Guinea. He left school at 15, which upset his parents, and he never truly returned to the fold, despite being the only son.

When the Mirren family home was eventually sold in the late 1990s to a couple who were in their thirties, Peter played little or no part in the negotiations or the tedious paperwork which his sister Katie oversaw. Tragically, he died at the age of 53, by which time he was teaching, while Helen was working on *Calendar Girls*. Though profoundly shocked and disturbed by his death, she continued to work to a tight schedule. When commiserations were offered and gracefully accepted, she could only say, as she had said in the past, 'I'm afraid this goes with the territory. It's a cliché but there it is. I can't expect everyone to pack up and go home and come back again in six months when I feel better about things.'

The intensely private Mirren never discussed her brother or sister or her nephew Simon with outsiders and she expected and received the same courtesy from them. Theirs was a family who kept their deepest problems and traumas within the family, rarely giving much more than a general surface picture of life with the Mironoffs. For Helen, in later years, it was part of her seemingly indestructible defence mechanism.

In contrast to her elder sister, Ilynea Vasiliena Mironoff was an absolute firebrand from the moment she made her triumphant début as a baby. She would scream and shout to get attention. And she was prone to beaker-chucking temper tantrums which led her mother to nickname her 'Popper'.

The Mironoffs had little spare cash for luxuries in those dim, dark days when the ration book ruled in the high street and few families could afford the luxury of a television. Her father, like so many from 'royal' Russia, had gone from riches to poverty in a very short time. But he accepted his lot as he showed his brood photographs of the Mironoff estates they were forced to leave behind. Mirren rarely spoke of her father, respecting his wishes for privacy with comments like, 'He was very Chekhovian in class and attitude.'

The family was ahead of its time, she later joked. They ate yoghurt long before other families knew what it was. There was no television and, over dinner, they usually discussed local or even world events.

Life was thoroughly unexciting in Leigh-on-Sea for little Popper. But the hamlet warranted a mention in the Domesday Book as a 'port of considerable importance' between Harwich and Gravesend. Plantagenet and Lancastrian monarchs embarked from the shoreline on their foreign travels and its sheltered position on the estuary gave it some naval significance before the area fell into decline in the eighteenth century.

In 1940, the Southend Corporation began ripping dilapidated dwellings down around the wharfs. Rows of crumbling old cottages, once part of Anne Boleyn's wedding dowry to Henry VIII in 1225, were also demolished on the grounds of public safety.

Helen, as a teenager, discovered romantic links to the past. Princess Beatrice, the daughter of Henry III, eloped on a vessel with the dashing but not sufficiently wealthy soldier-of-fortune Ralph de Binley, while her father discussed her wedding to the Lord of Castille. In Victorian times, mistress Sarah Moore – the Sea Witch as she was known – was almost lynched by a mob for putting curses on locals sickened by the sight of the unfortunate creature with the hare lip and hooked nose.

Truth be told, there were few incidents in Leigh's history to warrant record. The odd whale was washed up, the sea froze over in 1927 and high tides threatened to overwhelm the town. They never did. And, until the arrival of the Mironoff clan, there were few celebrities raised in the Essex backwater.

Helen was dispatched to Hamlet Court Road Junior Mixed School which once stood on the main A13 London Road, but today has been levelled to make way for a car park. Like her sister, she was a bright child and made good progress academically, breezing past the 11-plus examination. Even then, she dreamed of acting but she had to be the best. She was an angel in a nativity play and a 'blackbird in a pie'. The first real challenge came when she was ten and was asked to play Gretel in a production of *Hansel and Gretel*. She says, 'My first reaction was to say no because I wanted so much to do it that I thought I would not live up to my expectations. I didn't want to test myself and find myself wanting. I have the same fear today, but now I overcome it. If, when I read a script, my first feeling is one of fear, then it means I have to do it.'

There were several highly regarded girls' schools in the area at the time, but her parents were drawn to the high academic standards and discipline at St Bernard's High School. Their judgement was confirmed by Katrina's experiences at the school which sits at the junction of Milton Road and Canewdon Road in Westcliff-on-Sea, just a couple of minutes' stroll from the railway station.

Mirren, as a child, liked the idea of being close to her sister but was uncertain and wary about spending the next six years of her life being dominated by nuns, especially after endless teasing by her sister about the severity of their Order. But her mother talked her round and her father, Russian Orthodox by birth but atheist by belief, confidently put his faith in the nuns of the Roman Catholic St Bernardine Order, which was French in origin.

It was the grey mid-Fifties in England as Helen Mirren made the switch to secondary education. The move coincided with her father deciding to change his family's name to the Anglicised and more simple 'Mirren'. The 'foreigners' from the corner house in Queen's Road suddenly found that their faces fitted like never before. The taunting, slightly ridiculous cries of 'Russky spies' from other children in the neighbourhood gradually faded away and the continuous, tired prank of having 'coded messages' shoved through their letterbox abruptly ended.

As one neighbour put it, 'Nobody likes to think of themselves as particularly xenophobic but there was this thing about Russians at the time. They were depicted by the Government and the media as "the enemy". A lot of families did change their names when they re-settled in Britain after the war. It certainly didn't do Basil and Kit any harm. Their house was quite a lively place, often full of people enjoying themselves. They were a very popular couple.'

It wasn't long before Vasily-Petrov – who soon adopted the more pronounceable English name 'Basil' – with job security in mind, made a decisive career move to became a Driving Test Examiner spending most of his weekdays based in Ipswich. He finished his career as a civil servant, the much-respected Chief Driving Examiner at the Southend Test Centre under the auspices of the Ministry of Transport.

The biggest row her parents ever had, recalled Mirren, was over his job and their education. She explained, 'My mother may have East End roots but she had learned to talk properly. She was very strict about the way we talked when we were growing up. She was obsessed with us not having bad accents or poor grammar. When my dad got a job in the North as a driving examiner when I was about ten, I remember her saying she didn't want us growing up with northern accents. She felt it was beneath her. She scraped enough money for me and my sister to have elocution lessons.'

Her father also became a member of the local sailing community, joining the nearby Essex Yacht Club which today is based on the yacht *Bembridge*, moored a short walk away from the Mirren family home. Basil became an enthusiast, winning the prestigious Sydney Bromiley Memorial Cup in 1960 and 1961 in his modest but lively yacht *Curlew*. Peter came out of his shell when he accompanied his father to the well-supported club. And the whole family proudly watched as the teenager was first past the finishing line in his dinghy *Glass Slipper* in 1961. He also won a junior sailing cup in 1963 and a racing cup in 1964.

The Union Jack still flutters high over St Bernard's where Mirren's reputation as a budding actress of the future rapidly gathered pace. She excelled in all things Shakespearian and her performances during the annual nativity play are legend to this day. Her parents encouraged Mirren and her elder sister Katrina to look to the future and a teaching career, but she set her heart on the theatre after seeing a local amateur production of *Hamlet* when she was 13.

'It was probably terrible,' she recalls. 'I remember the guys couldn't keep their tights up and they were all wrinkly around the ankles. But what an incredible story!'

The tough regime enforced by the nuns throughout the rock 'n' roll years of the late Fifties into the early Sixties was often treated with humour. Former pupil Linda Hall, née Louis, recalls the girls in their blue pleated skirts and white shirts and ties and Panama hats undergoing inspection by the likes of the 'ghastly' nun, Mother Mary Vincent. She said, 'We'd have to kneel on the floor in assembly at the beginning of each term so the nuns could check the length of our skirts. No jewellery was permitted. Prefects would be on guard duty by the gates to ensure the girls were wearing their hats properly. If not, it meant detention.

'After school, the nuns would also be at the gates in a very menacing manner dispersing any boys who'd dared to show up. They would quite literally chase them off. There was most definitely no sex education and I don't recall a male teacher.'

At St Bernard's, she was elected to play Caliban and won a cup for playing Ophelia. Norma McCleverty, née Thorp, remembers Mirren well in *Hamlet*. She has vivid memories of her with her best chum Jennifer May trooping off in the direction of the famous Kursaal Amusement Park in Southend after school. She says, 'They were both very attractive and walked so proudly, some people thought they were a bit stuck up. I personally didn't. I always found Helen very enthusiastic. She was even good at sport, in particular tennis.'

Another pupil, Bernice Welland, has a hazy recollection of Mirren running a market stall in her spare time, occasionally sneaking off to smoke behind the school bike sheds with other girls. 'But she [Mirren] was mesmerising in school plays,' she says. 'Especially a nativity production in which she played King Herod. But what stood out about her was apparent much later on, when her mother was dying in Southend General Hospital. She was very pleasant, natural and friendly to all the staff, something which surprised many of them. My sister Lesley works at the hospital and she said they expected such a big star to have airs and graces, but she was just ... ordinary.'

Jill Smith, then a teenager by the name of Jill Dent, was in the same house – Fountain – as Helen. The nuns once upset Helen by objecting to her playing the Virgin Mary in the nativity play as they 'doubted her authenticity'.

When the nativity play was being performed, parents from other schools in the borough would crowd the school hall to suffocation. She says, 'Helen would invariably play Eve in *Adam and Eve*. Even then her performance would be intriguing and I would watch in envy at her obvious talent. I can remember standing in the wings with her at some school play and asking her if she wanted to be a professional actress. She replied that she thought she might be a teacher. I was aghast as, at the time, I wanted to be a drama teacher and longed for her natural aptitude. She was also a good artist. I found her one day sitting on the stairs of the art block in tears. A jealous malicious rival had slashed one of her huge oil paintings.'

During the summer holidays, Helen worked at the Kursaal Amusement Park on the breathtaking Rotor Wheel as a 'screamer', tempting boys to drag their girlfriends through the turnstile on to the fast-moving steel cylinder which pinned their bodies to the walls. Her knee-length skirt would be blown sky high by the spinning motion, causing an even greater rush of young lads to one of the park's main attractions. Working at the Kursaal in her spare time was most definintely fun for the young Helen. She recalls,

'That was a marvellous place to work in, extremely noisy and violent and dirty, slightly decayed and very exciting.'

Other girls from St Bernard's once spotted her displaying her natural talents in the game Knock the Lady out of Bed. She wore a skimpy nightie borrowed from her mother's bottom drawer. Lines of boys armed with three wooden balls apiece queued up to hit the bullseye and catch a glimpse of Helen in old-fashioned underwear being thrown on to a mattress below.

South African-born drama teacher Clare Angel, who finally left the school to return to her homeland, was Helen's inspiration, according to her friends, along with Mrs Alyce Welding, a spirited, supportive English teacher.

Diana van Bunnens acted as stage manager for some nativity productions and saw the relationship grow between Angel and aspiring actress Helen. There was almost a rebellion one year, she recalls, when the girls wanted to run the school play themselves but the nuns would not be moved.

Helen Greco, now Helen Pawsey, recalls Helen's 'quite brilliant' Caliban in *The Tempest* in which she had a character part as a drunk. She said, 'Helen always knew she could act and wanted to go into the theatre. She had a ruthless streak even then. She was going for it and nothing deterred her. The fact we had to perform Shakespeare in school uniforms which could be quite tricky didn't put her off either.

'My mother adored her because she "sparkled". She could look like a million dollars one moment and then just be terribly ordinary. Just by throwing one look, one expression, she could change herself completely.

'She didn't have to be glamorous. Seeing her recently as a dowdy housekeeper in *Gosford Park* brought it all back. She was glamorous, exciting and ordinary. Helen was fond of Mother Aildred, who taught Latin. She could be very amusing. But the younger nuns were scary. They were only a couple of years older than us and wanting to appear as authority figures.'

The Mirren family would often drop by the Essex Yacht Club where Basil soon became a regular, popular member of the local boating set. One of his dreams was to own an ocean-going vessel and take holidays criss-crossing the channel. His wife was not so keen on the idea. They were both also keen bridge players and members of the local club.

Mirren was able to raise extra cash for herself 'blagging' (pitching the ride to the customers) at the Kursaal, while every other Sunday afternoon was spent 'stomping' at Arlington Hall in the Chalkwell district where the Ken Collier or Chris Barber jazz bands would perform.

She recalls mobs of girls including Helen and her buddies Mary Greco and Helen Skordis sipping frothy coffee on Saturday afternoons at The Shrubbery just off the Grand Parade and the underground basement hang-out, The Capri. In those days, Mirren ran a gang of six screaming aggressors called 'The Beatniks' who did their utmost to infuriate the nuns.

'We were all Bohemian and beatniks ... well, that's what we wanted people to think,' recalled another ex-pupil Julia Gee, who now lives in Sunbury-on-Thames, Middlesex. 'But where Helen truly excelled was at drama and Shakespeare. There was nobody to touch her in school and she won the Shakespeare Cup for her Ophelia. She was just 13 and nobody had ever seen Ophelia played like that. It was as though she was possessed. Helen was different. She was very confident, her own person but still well liked.'

What does any convent school girl do about sex? Pleasures of the flesh remained a tabboo subject and in summer, by way of reminding them of 'temptation', the girls were sternly directed to keep their shirts buttoned and never lie stretched out on the grass on the recreation ground opposite the school. When she was 13, she read three volumes of the erotic tale *A Thousand and One Nights*, having found the books at the bottom of her parents' wardrobe while they were out shopping. But she confessed to being a prude as a youngster, even to the degree of being embarrassed by the sight of couples kissing on television.

When she was fourteen, she briefly went out with a French boy who was staying in Leigh-on-Sea with a penfriend. But she soon showed him the door, saying that she found him too young to be truly entertaining.

Local lads soon learned on the grapevine that she was not 'good for a snog' and she confesses, 'I had this terror of going to the toilet if I was with a boy. I just couldn't bring myself to say, "Excuse me, I need to go to the loo," because I had visions of them trying to visualise what I was doing. I would insist on being taken home. I'd be so desperate that I couldn't speak. Then I'd just race in and say goodbye. There was no kissing. I was totally and ridiculously inhibited.

'My parents didn't want me to get married. They were happily married themselves but they didn't see it as something everyone should do. When I was about 22 and it became evident I was going to bed with men, I had a tricky time with them. They disapproved. They thought I was being taken advantage of. I wasn't. They were especially upset when my first boyfriend was Jewish. This was a bit hypocritical considering they had been on anti-Mosley marches. They liked to think of themselves as Bohemian.

'I suppose people have this image of me fucking everyone, but actually I've only had a handful of serious long-term relationships. Guys taught me stuff, brought me on. I am like I am because of those men.'

What Mirren refused to disclose until much later was that she became the victim of date-rape on several occasions. She revealed that the 'terribly upsetting and disturbing' attacks happened between the ages of 16 and 25, leaving her distrustful of men for many years. She said, 'I was being pursued by them purely for sex and absolutely nothing else.' She became so hostile before she embarked on her first serious relationship that she regarded men as 'so vile and so cruel and alien and nasty. I felt most men despised me as a person. It was like I was a piece of meat.' She says now that she was never as confident of herself as she appeared. She was shy and, despite herself, always later looked to men for support. 'I was very uncertain,' she confessed. 'I had panic attacks. In my job, you have to meet people constantly and deal with people you don't know. It was very difficult on the first day's rehearsal of a play having to walk in and assume control of a situation. What anyone might call sexuality often had to do with the fact of me having blonde hair and big tits and absolutely nothing else. Sometimes I deeply hate men. They're so gullible sometimes and so stupid a lot of the time, young men especially.'

Life at St Bernard's had an emphatic effect on her beliefs. By the age of 21, she had discarded her family's long association with the Russian Orthodox Church. She later said, 'I'm utterly confused about faith in general because I don't have any. I can't get my head around it, so I can't get my head around people needing to have it. Yet I know all the cultures in the world have faith, different faiths.'

The nuns, meanwhile, had been reading about certain goings-on at rock 'n' roll rave-ups. One of the Sisters felt it only wise, according to an ex-pupil, to implore the girls to beware of 'certain chocolate and cookies' which might tempt them at parties and which would almost certainly make them do 'awful things'. The girls took the Sister to mean 'hash brownies'.

Mirren later said with a smile, 'It was as though these so-called "chocolates" were going to make us strip all our clothes off and run around, jump on people and have sex orgies.'

The nuns cast a wary eye over the young Mirren, one of the school's known rebels and anti-authority figures. If she bent the rules, she expected to pay the price. One morning, she arrived at school with her red hair up and her skirt far from the standard length, and incurred the wrath of the starchy music teacher Maureen Sparey. Voices were raised and a crowd gathered. Mrs Gee said, 'There was quite a stir. Then the teacher turned on Mirren and told her she looked like a "Russian tart" and was "in need of a bath". The distraught teenager burst into tears and went home.

'The girls were generally afraid of the the nuns,' added Mrs Gee.

'Nobody challenged them. Helen was a fighter but even she knew her limitations. I loved drama and was terribly envious of Helen because she had what it took to go all the way.'

Senior staff at the school were convinced that Helen had 'special gifts' of almost religious proportions when she took to the stage. Sister Mary Stephens, who later became head teacher, saw her development under Clare Angel during the 'reign' of the formidable Sister Mary Mildred in the early Sixties at St Bernard's and was hugely impressed.

Sister Stephens said, 'I was a very green young Sister and the sixth form then was very arty, very *au fait* and quite dramatic in their reactions, sophisticated. I remember studying Genesis with them and they got quite excited. Helen became quite dramatic about the creation process. I think she was amusing herself and winding me up. She was so expressive. Whatever she was doing, it worked. I was totally unnerved. She wasn't prefect or head girl material, though, she was too free and artistic and didn't want to be tied down to authority.'

It was 1963 and, outside the school gates, the times they were a-changin'. Girls once gripped by the TV series *77 Sunset Strip* and the comb-thrusting antics of 'Cookie', alias Edward Byrne Jr, were now deeply in love with hopelessly handsome Richard Chamberlain who was making them swoon in the Accident and Emergency Department as the smooth talking Dr Kildare.

At the local picture house, those thoroughbreds Albert Finney, Alan Bates and Tom Courtney had 'arrived' from Up North as fresh-faced, working-class lads to join the stylish, charismatic but more traditional Peter O'Toole as magazine pin-ups. Ironically, one of the biggest matinée idols of the day was James Mason, who would also be taking Helen's hand in his during her début film drama *The Age of Consent* just six years later. He had just caused a minor morality sensation himself as the middle-aged lecher Humbert Humbert chasing a pert Sue Lyons in *Lolita*. But it was still, in many artistic ways, most definitely the age of innocence.

Julie Andrews waited in the wings to take her place in the hall of fame with the Beatles. Elvis dominated the charts from America with crooners such as Perry Como, Gene Pitney and Bobby Vinton on the flanks. Our teens were, meanwhile, lapping up Cliff Richard and Tommy Steele before the surf sound of the Beach Boys caused a new worldwide musical deluge. Nothing, of course, shook civilisation quite like those four long-haired lads from Liverpool.

But Helen Mirren, armed with seven O-levels and three A-levels in English, Art and Spanish, had other things on her mind as she gazed dreamily across the shoreline from her favourite bench overlooking the Thames Estuary on the Grand Parade. She fantasised over the idea of being a movie star, of having a cigar-munching Hollywood producer arrive in a Rolls-Royce to whisk her away to Sunset Strip. There would be glamour, applause and laughter.

At home, Mr and Mrs Mirren wanted their daughter to find a 'fall-back' profession if they were not going to be able to talk her out of her true ambition. The local authority, according to Helen, took a dim view of youngsters seeking grants to become actors and her parents could not afford the fees required by the Royal Academy of Dramatic Art. So she packed herself off – 'forced by economic circumstances' – to the New College of Speech and Drama in Hampstead, North London, to complete a teacher's training course, specialising in speech and drama. During the course, she did a spot of 'field training' at a tough East End secondary school in Bethnal Green. 'It could be quite frightening, intimidating,' she said. 'I was really seeing the other side of the tracks for the first time.'

But she found her time spent at the college, once the home of the Russian prima ballerina Anna Pavlova, to be largely unspectacular and unproductive. She made few friends and could hardly wait to leave. She said, 'I would have left earlier but I had no courage. I was told that I would have to pay back my grant and I couldn't afford that. Sadly, my grant was a complete waste of money for Southend Council. They might well have supported my application to attend drama school.'

Her fellow students, it must be said, were not largely impressed by her. Mother-of-two Stella Campion recalled, 'She cut us all dead as if we were just nobody. She wouldn't even speak to us and, if you spoke to her, she wouldn't even acknowledge the fact that she came from Southend with that kind of background like the rest of us. She had an ambition the rest of us didn't have.' Former lecturer Pauline Stuart said, 'Gratitude wasn't a strong streak in Helen. It's as though she thinks she has done it all herself, out of her own brilliance. Well, she was undoubtedly talented, though her singing was so bad it was on the threshold of pain.' But Mirren certainly made an impression, even through her dress sense. Ex-student Felicity Crow laughed, 'She let it all hang out. She'd often arrive barefoot and she was very well endowed. You couldn't miss her.'

During a summer break, she auditioned 'in a moment of madness' for a prize place at the National Youth Theatre under its founder, the late Michael Croft. She portrayed Queen Margaret from *Henry VI* in her piece and was snapped up as the establishment's new star pupil. She was given a bit-part in *Julius Caesar*, was a member of the court in *Hamlet* and played Helena in *A Midsummer Night's Dream*. She then became a NYT legend, selected by the revered Croft as a raw 20-year-old to play the lusty middle-aged Queen of Egypt in *Antony and Cleopatra* to sell-out houses at the Old Vic in September 1965.

Even today, Mirren fondly recalls her formative dramatic period at the NYT with a beaming smile. She made many friends, who remain so to this day. Edward Wilson, the current director of the group, said, 'She created such a stir here as one of the first young girls to be involved. She set a standard and that in itself was tremendous. She was very popular and very talented.'

Mirren saw her term at the NYT as a period of complete rejuvenation and said soon after leaving, 'Coming as I did from a smallish provincial town and convent school, it opened a far wider social life than I could otherwise have expected ... perhaps, at first, too wide.

'Being plunged into the middle of so many new faces made me very shy and inhibited at first. It was in the NYT, however, that I made many of my greatest friends ... there are a mass of people centred around the NYT headquarters, some new, some old, that I have an immediate interest in and communication with.'

Playwright Barrie Keeffe, who was to work with Mirren a decade later in his film *The Long Good Friday*, recalls, 'The place used to be almost all boys from the public school system when we were there, and yet she showed no fear. She was one of the first women there and, bearing in mind she came from a convent school, she really handled herself with great dignity and style. She was absolutely stunning and very sexy and she spoke her verse quite beautifully. I didn't realise Shakespeare was so sexy until I heard Helen reading. When she appeared in *Cleopatra*, the first thing I saw her in, she was a star waiting to happen. She stood out ... in every sense!'

Ex-schoolmaster Croft founded the organisation in 1956 to give school-age actors the chance to appear in professionally directed Shakespearian productions during their summer breaks. They were then based in Dulwich and had at least one prospective star of the future in a certain Derek Jacobi. Croft, who died in 1986, was equally convinced that his new student would also scale the dizzy heights.

'Helen's performance as Cleopatra was remarkable by any standards,' he said in an ecstatic tribute. 'It wasn't simply a question of a young girl making a big stab at a difficult part. She gave the part something which English actresses for generations have failed to do and that is really to get inside the sheer sexuality, the built-in sexuality of the woman.

'She had a remarkable capacity to use herself on stage with a kind of zest and a joy ... and she gave this without ever losing the Shakespearian side or the poetic side of the part.'

The NYT and Cleo were recalled with the fondest memories. 'I wore low-cut dresses which emphasised my breasts and with a combination of sex and Shakespeare we made the most of the national papers,' she said. 'The Youth Theatre is a marvellous way of breaking out of your background and seeing what the theatre is really like.' What she couldn't comprehend was why so few women made it in comparison with the numbers of men, such as Simon Ward, Michael York and Kenneth Cranham. She added wryly, 'I suppose it's because the women's parts are so crummy there as everywhere else.'

Though Helen may have had her doubts, what she did at the NYT was enough to win her a winter's season away in repertory with the Manchester Century Theatre and get her on the books of the top theatrical agent Al Parker, who'd 'discovered' both Rudolf Valentino and Richard Attenborough. She, in turn, was totally bemused by the adulation. 'I was a round girl with a large bottom ... and on the fat side,' she recalled.

But it wasn't long before she was snapped up by then plain Peter Hall, the founder of the Royal Shakespeare Company, to appear alongside his contracted players at Stratford-upon-Avon and the Aldwych Theatre off The Strand in London. She played the beleaguered Castiza in Trevor Nunn's production of *The Revenger's Tragedy* and Diana, the easy-going Italian tart in *All's Well That Ends Well*. She played the shepherdess Phoebe in *As You Like It* and Hero, the slandered heroine of *Much Ado About Nothing*. Then came *Troilus and Cressida* in which she gave a magical performance as the Trojan wanton who gives herself to her Greek captors. One scribe later wrote, 'Her mind might be that of a child ... but her body, independent and mature, knew just where it was, took fire and acted for her.' Another commented, 'On the surface she looks like the *ingénue* next door, pretty, innocent, young for her age ... but the moment she moves, something about her stride and carriage proclaims the temptress lurking inside.'

They were largely happy days for Helen earning £50 a week – 'it seems an enormous amount of money' – and roaming the banks of the Avon when she wasn't on stage. She had a 'happy' relationship with fellow company member Bruce Myers and said, 'We had a lot of fun. It was quiet, a calm sort of sun in the countryside.'

Another actress who was at the RSC recalls, 'Though she won't know it, she broke his heart. He was totally infatuated with her but she had places to go and he wasn't quite up to the same speed. She was like a child in the toy shop at the time and he was one of the toys, but not in a nasty kind of way. He had a great time with her. He couldn't actually tell why she bothered with him. She was just this Ursula Andress thing with a mind. When she finished with him, he was totally distraught and way over the top in a Shakespearian sense, saying it was "the end". But a few drinks later, he was bubbling away like there was no tomorrow. We figured Helen would break quite a few more hearts before she was through, though. Not because she was callous or insensitive, but because she was this tremendous free spirit, like a bird never wanting to be caged.'

Television and film offers were pouring in. She was given her first taste of filming by supremo Peter Hall who directed her as Hermia in a glittering new filmed version of *A Midsummer Night's Dream*. The cast oozed the cream of British acting talent with the likes of David Warner, Michael Jayston, Ian Richardson, Judi Dench and Diana Rigg on parade.

At the age of 23, she took six months' leave from the Royal Shakespeare Company to go to Australia to co-star with James Mason in the film *Age of Consent*. Both Ken Russell and Sam Peckinpah were already breaking new censorship ground in movies such as *Women in Love* and *Straw Dogs*. 'Art' was now taking preference to gratuitous sex.

But movers and shakers in the film industry had their doubts about the integrity of legendary director Michael Powell. Here was Helen Mirren facing her first taste of on-screen nudity ... and hating every second of it. 'I saw there was nudity in the script but I didn't think I would have to do it,' she recalled. 'I thought I would be able to get around it. But I couldn't. At worst, I thought I would be wearing a body stocking. But I was wrong. I took a deep breath and decided it was just a job of work. I tried to be cool but actually I felt rather strange, as if I'd walked into a nudist colony.'

And so the Mirren myth was born. The actress who has stood condemned for taking every opportunity to show her heavenly form was dismayed about the issue of nudity before she'd even stepped on to a film set. She said, 'What I have discovered is that nudity takes away all ideas of acting. I think most of today's sex films are very unsexy. In the Fifties, directors showed a bloke unbuttoning a woman's blouse, then they cut to his face and everyone's imagination was raging like mad. That's far sexier than bare flesh. Sex is in the mind.'

The opportunity to film with Mason and the veteran Powell on scorching locations off the Great Barrier Reef was irresistible. She had never worked abroad before. Apart from school trips, she had never ventured far from our shores.

So it was an absolute thrill to be travelling to the other side of the world, all expenses paid, to be working on a movie with none other than the imposing James Mason who had her and a band of her classmates giggling furiously when she'd seen him leching away in *Lolita*. What wasn't quite so thrilling was unpredictable Powell's attitude towards her. The master director, who made the classic *Peeping Tom*, shouted a lot in her direction and, according to members of the crew, treated her like a 'juve' (juvenile). 'I didn't like that,' she said. 'When I'm bullied, I tend to stick out my chin and fight back.'

Mason played an elderly artist past his sell-by date in the story, based on Norman Lindsay's novel. Jubilant Helen beat scores of other British starlets, including Judy Geeson and Jenny Agutter, to the role of his innocent muse Cora Bryan. She didn't have much useful dialogue but she made a certain impact. Another veteran, the wonderful Irish character actor Jack McGowran, actually walked away with the film as Mason's scrounging mate Nat Kelly. The critics chided Mason, who was nudging 60 and in the twilight of his career, for bothering with the film. They suggested he was slipping back into Humbert Humbert mode. Writer, producer and director Powell was also nearing the end of his illustrious career which started in the silent-movie era in the early Thirties.

Mirren travelled first class to Australia, stopping off in Honolulu on the Hawaiian island of Oahu. It was a trip she was never to forget. 'The first-class section of the plane was empty,' she recalled. 'I remember having two stewardesses dance attendance on me and serving me as much champagne and caviar as I could want. It was all quite unbelievable. Until then, I was a walk-on nobody and suddenly I was being given this star treatment.' But she came down to earth with a bump at Honolulu at two in the morning where there was a mix-up over her accommodation. She had left England with just a pound in her purse having spent the last £30 in her bank account on a smart new leather outfit. She was told James Mason would greet her on arrival and that there would be an envelope with cash and her hotel details waiting for her. The airline desk was, however, deserted.

She grinned, 'I got a bit teary, my bottom lip started to tremble and I didn't know what the hell to do. Finally, I pulled myself together and marched into the Lost and Found Department which, for some reason, was run by a burly American cop, straight out of a TV series. After I poured my heart out to him, he found me accommodation at the Hilton and personally escorted me there in his police car.

'The next morning when I woke up, I flung back the curtains and, seeing a blue sky, palm trees and everything else that went with Honolulu, I threw my arms back and let out a yell of joy, which was returned by a yell from the next room. When I stepped out on to the balcony to see who it was, there was James Mason himself. He invited me to have breakfast with him and, from then on, nothing went wrong.'

They travelled onwards together and she spent six weeks Down Under on an island paradise living in a little hut with a creaking roof before returning to the sanctuary of the RSC and her beloved MG sports car.

She was more terrified of what her mother might say when the film opened to almost deafening silence in London in November 1969 due to a limited release, and took a modest amount at the box-office. Her parents, much to her relief, approved of her portrayal of the alluring Cora. She said, 'They didn't mind, surprisingly enough. There was nothing offensive about it and they accepted it as I did. Even if I say so myself, I was pretty good in the film.'

The distinguished Powell, according to aides, was not in the best of health during the production and was concerned about Helen's lack of experience. A senior source said, 'He started behaving like a headmaster with his pupil and Mirren didn't take kindly to that. She was a feisty type and made it clear that she was also the sort who stood up for herself. Powell was very much of the old school and there was an instant bond between him and Mason. She was right out of it in that way and she wanted to be so much part of it. They all parted with smiles on their faces. Nothing could dampen her excitement and enthusiasm.

'But she learned a good couple of lessons about dealing with directors and experienced film actors. She also learned a word called "compromise".'

The erudite Mason was thoroughly taken by Ms Mirren. 'Don't bother looking at me on screen' he later dryly remarked. 'Just look at Helen Mirren's bottom.' Most, especially those of the male variety, keenly took his advice.

The nuns at St Bernard's and the Mirren clan were transfixed by their television sets on the night of 23 June 1970 when ITV broadcast *Doing Her Own Thing*, a documentary account of her ascent as an actress and obvious superstar of the future. The programme, a genuine piece of 'star spotting', had been made by producer/director John Goldschmidt for Lord Lew Grade's old company ATV, later to become Central Television on the ITV network. It was a time to revisit old haunts such as her primary school, Southend Pier and the Rotor Wheel experience at the Kursaal Amusement Park. She chatted away sipping coffee at The Shrubbery Coffee Bar on the Royal Terrace and got into the 'mood' for tackling the Bard by wandering through the Warwickshire countryside and the atmospheric churchyard of Shakespeare's Church in Stratford-upon-Avon.

Times do not seemed to have changed much. 'I wouldn't be recognised walking down the street or asked for my autograph. I think I prefer it that way. I mean, I enjoy my anonymity,' she said. 'The people in your local street would say, "Er ... you're not doing so well, are you all right? We haven't seen you on television." However much you have been working in the theatre, they don't think you have made it until you are on telly. If you are on telly, you are famous.'

Wearing a blue duffle coat, her red hair in a pony tail, she told how she used to dream about being 'discovered' while dancing on the nearby beaches as a 15-year-old. Her family would have disapproved of her spending so much of her time in the local coffee bars and she explained how she kept her ambitions to herself as her parents would not have been impressed.

She never told her family or friends that she was auditioning for the National Youth Theatre through the simple fear of failure. 'My parents were not very keen on me becoming an actress. They would, originally, have preferred me to be a teacher or something like that. It was a very feminine occupation for me, acting. I was very nervous and embarrassed in front of men anyway at the best of times, just sitting in the coffee bar. But to actually have to stand in front of them was a very humiliating experience.'

Ironically, Helen was then acutely insecure when it came to her 'body work'. Thinking men, from judges to MPs, might have lusted over her when she was at the RSC, but she confided, 'I honestly and truly don't find myself attractive and I'm very embarrassed in a way about what I look like. I find other people much more attractive than I am and I don't think I am going to succeed because of what I look like. I don't look interesting enough. I'm just not enough of whatever it takes. I'm not as sexy as Raquel Welch and I'm not as beautiful as Brigit Bardot or Anouk Aimee. I have a basically very ordinary face and it's not going to make my fortune.'

It wasn't long before Helen was briefly back at St Bernard's High School presenting the Shakespeare Cup she once proudly clutched herself as a pupil. But the nuns brought back the painful memories of her more difficult days under Mother Mary Mildred and her staff. They would often monitor her movements, 'spy' on her during breaks and ask other girls to 'report' if she said anything remotely blasphemous or against the school's ruling body. As one former pupil said, 'They had her under the cosh from quite early on. If it hadn't been for the fact she had talent, she would have had a nightmare time. There was a lack of respect and it was a two-way thing.'

And some 35 years were to pass before the rift between Mirren and her old school was genuinely healed, when Leigh-on-Sea's favourite daughter returned triumphant to her old 'stomping' ground.

Local journalist Terry Wynn from South Benfleet in Essex was instrumental in offering her an olive branch from the school and luring her back, work permitting, to present the Helen Mirren Drama Award. She was so thrilled she telephoned him personally from Hollywood to finalise the details.

He said, 'There was a certain degree of emnity which took a long time to put aside. The school had her marked down as a "bad girl" and so she had kept her distance. It was a sad thing but, at last, that is over. Helen actually placed the nuns as being an important influence on her career. She didn't have much courage as a child to get on the stage or as an adult. But the one thing the nuns taught her was to have "courage" above all else. Now she had come back into the fold which had a marvellous effect on the girls. The fifth and sixth forms were always excellent at acting. Now, they really have somebody to look up to.'

To this day, he said, Mirren has kept in contact with the first pupil, a 17-year-old black girl, to win the prize named after her.

Past feuds and bitter rows were put aside as Mirren returned to deafening applause in the school hall in the summer of 1997. Nearly 100 girls queued for an hour for autographs and every second of her visit was recorded by the BBC and local TV cameras from Anglia Television. Mirren herself made a speech joking about how 'frightening' she looked as the gang leader of the Beatniks in the summer of 1963, and how her reputation was now ruined because she was considered to be a 'good girl'.

No sooner had she restored a link with the past than another was sadly broken. Mirren's house was sold not long after her mother Kit died at a nursing home in Southend following a short illness at the end of the summer in 1996. Her sister Katrina, who still teaches, assisted her with the paperwork. Their strangely absent, apparently disinterested brother Peter had nothing to do with the transaction.

The infamous nuns of St Bernard's – they were to be replaced in the Eighties by a lay teaching staff – had a custom of listing Helen's latest achievements in morning assembly, no matter what her status or sins from the past. They had one other quietly successful 'star', the actress Anne Stallybrass, better known as the wife of Captain James Onedin in the long-running nautical BBC series *The Onedin Line*. Another household name to follow Mirren in the late Sixties was the singing, dancing livewire Gemma Craven, who went on to find fame in the Seventies through the musical film adaptation of *Cinderella, The Slipper and the Rose* and Dennis Potter's *Pennies from Heaven* in which she played Bob Hoskins's shy, prissy wife.

Helen said nervously, soon after leaving the NYT, 'It's quite impossible to say what's going to happen to me. I can't judge myself as an actress. I don't know what I'll be doing in three years' time.'

But the winds of change were starting to blow fiercely in the direction of the Thames Estuary. As one teacher at the school observed, 'There had been all manner of sociological changes in the previous decade from acid tripping with the Beatles to Flower Power at Haight-Ashbury. It was only going to be a matter of time, in any case, before the nuns had to make way for lay teachers.

'The twentieth century had suddenly caught up with dear old Westcliff. But, in the meantime, there were still morals, standards to maintain. To the nuns, Helen represented the new order of chaos and free love and danger. A number of them, a mix of the old and new order, saw her as an anarchist, albeit a talented anarchist.'

To this day, however, she believes the nuns were not in the least offended by her nudity in her erotic early work. Early in her career while at Stratford-upon-Avon with the Royal Shakespeare Company, she felt for the most part that she was in 'goody-two-shoe roles'.

But Mirren, so everyone was predicting, was destined for greater stage and screen glory. She was in a league of her own. She wasn't so sure. She dubbed herself 'The End-of the-Pier Show' in self-deprecation, recalling her many days spent roaming the Grand Parade promenade and beaches close to her home.

Shedding the more dark memories of her youth, there were to be triumphant returns to St Bernard's, culminating in her unveiling a plaque to mark the opening of a new arts building in the summer of 2005. But for many years she carried mixed images of her schooldays. She wasn't over-enamoured with the nuns of St Bernard's but, as time wore on, she saw the logic in their protectionist policies. She said, 'The convent would approve of anything done well. I don't believe the school's morality is so simplified and crude to appreciate only what is overtly good. The convent gave me much of my appreciation of the theatre. Drama there was highly developed and an interest in it was encouraged.'

Looking back, she'd often think her mini-rebellions were harmless and yet spectacular in their own way. 'We'd walk down Southend High Street wearing one red stocking and one blue,' she said. 'Women would stop us in the street and shout rude things at us.'

One day, she was summoned into the presence of Mother Mary Mildred who advised her, 'Helen, one of the most destructive things in life is fear. What you must learn is not to be afraid.'

'But I still haven't learned that lesson,' Helen says. 'I have spent most of my life being afraid and hating my own fear. If I hadn't been an actress, I would have been a teacher. My sister was a teacher and I have an immense respect for the profession. We owe our teachers a great deal.'

And though there is no question that she was deadly ambitious, she also possessed a mystical quality in keeping with her Sixties-child status.

If pressed about her destination, she insisted she wanted to direct the traffic in The Mall. 'It is one of the most beautiful streets in London,' she'd grin, childlike. 'The only one with a plinth in the middle of the road from which I could indicate stop or go. I have seen police directing traffic there, waving their arms about. They look so ... ecstatically happy.'

3

MIRREN FEVER –
THE SEX QUEEN OF
STRATFORD

The roused league of mainly irritable gentlemen known as theatre critics were beside themselves with a heady mix of excitement and anticipation over Helen Mirren. They hurled a string of superlatives such as 'sensual', 'graceful' and 'buxom' around as though the Venus de Milo had risen from the River Thames. And it wasn't long before the green-eyed beauty from Leigh-on-Sea was a tabloid pin-up.

Then, much to the amusement of the upmarket theatrical Establishment, the 'above it all' broadsheets muscled in on the act by dubbing her 'the sex queen of Stratford-upon-Avon'. Mirren fever was running high.

It was just before Christmas 1971 and the more mature nuns at her old school averted their eyes when mischievous sixth formers left a copy of the *News of the World* pinned to a wall in the dining room and took cover in the shadows, waiting for a reaction. There was much giggling in the corridors. '*The Screws*', as it was affectionately known in Fleet Street newspaper circles, was hardly required reading at St Bernard's.

They were not amused by the contents. There was a photograph of Helen naked from the waist up, nipples hard and erect, her red curls tumbling across her bare shoulders. The grimace of pleasure on her face signified a sudden sexual encounter of some sort. Behind her was an elderly military figure, lines of medals covering his chest. Actor Philip Locke wore the expression of an ageing gentleman in the throes of a heart-attack having satisfied his lust.

The scene was not from a tatty strip revue or from a Brian Rix farce with the cast taking turns at getting 'em off. This was the Royal Shakespeare Company performing a sequence set in a brothel from the play *The Balcony* written by the French literary icon Jean Genet and showing at the Aldwych Theatre in London. The complex plot revolved around a trial taking place during a revolution. And it wasn't only the critics who warmed to her portrayal of a mischievous prostitute, even if the nuns who once presided over her choice of play were far from impressed. Pupils had been warned only a month earlier about bringing 'certain publications' into the school.

Sir Larry Lamb, the brains behind Rupert Murdoch's new *Sun*, was so excited by the new girl on the block that he decided to devote an entire spread to the sex siren from the RSC.

Was the super, soaraway *Sun* gliding upmarket? Was it heck. There was Ms Mirren in a low-cut, black, gold-striped Moroccan dress by John Bates, her red hair covered by an Arab-style scarf. Her pouting full lips were well glossed, her ample breasts protruded in typical *Sun* style. And she wore the look of a woman welcoming a very close friend into the kasbah.

Her verdict? 'This is a dress you have to act your way into.' Another photograph portrayed her in Little Bo Peep mode, her hair tied up, all frills in a white jersey dress by the same designer. 'I feel like a sex object in this. Women's lib wouldn't approve,' she commented with a grin.

Helen Mirren had arrived.

The *Sun*, showing true wizardry in picking tomorrow's superstars, was convinced that Mirren had got the required 'armoury' to appeal to Shakespearian devotees no matter what their background. She was appearing in a varied selection of roles displaying her extraordinary range.

In *Enemies*, she had to play it grand but calm as a 30-year-old actress. In *Man of Mode*, she was a fresh, lively 18-year-old, while in Strindberg's *Miss Julie*, she took the intense, over-sexed title role.

'I am incredibly ambitious,' she said. 'But it is an ambition for travel, love and adventure ... I just want to live life to the full, for today. I want to squeeze everything I can out of every minute. Others may disapprove, but there it is. That's me.'

If only she'd adopted that philosophy the night a certain Warren Beatty drifted into town and saw her in action at the Aldwych Theatre in *Troilus and Cressida*. It was spring 1970 and Mr Beatty was esconced at the Savoy Hotel under one of his many aliases and searching for 'action', which only meant one thing in his Californian vocabulary.

Mr Beatty was in his early thirties and certainly in his prime. He had already left a trail of broken hearts in his wake – Natalie Wood, Leslie Caron and Joan Collins (who had a wedding dress hanging in her wardrobe for almost a year) had come and gone in an ocean of tears and recriminations. He had been invited over by a British producer and director who wanted to sound him out about the possibility of playing an 'egocentric' Count Dracula who was semi-alive and well in a château in the Loire Valley. Beatty was amused by the concept, though consciously aware he was in familiar territory. His Polish director and actor buddie Roman Polanski had been down 'Transylvania Avenue' with the offbeat 1967 yarn *The Fearless Vampire Killers* which had already achieved cult status. Polanski's wife Sharon Tate, who was to die tragically later at the hands of Charles Manson's gang, also starred in the movie.

The insatiable Beatty had been declaring his love for his new 'sweetheart', British beauty Julie Christie. They had met starring together in Robert Altman's quirky warts 'n' all western *McCabe and Mrs Miller*, in which he played a self-centred entrepreneur launching a brothel in the frozen Great North with Christie as his enthusiastic madame. The blonde actress who enticed male civilisation from Huddersfield in *Billy Liar* to Hollywood in *Dr Zhivago* had put lothario Beatty under her spell. Or so she thought. In fact, Beatty and his buddie Jack Nicholson had been on a two-week-long spree, 'knocking over' Hollywood's latest but unknown starlets like pins in a bowling alley.

But here he was in London, ready to declare his love for dazzling Christie who had yet to star with him again in *Shampoo*. The only problem was that she had, at very short notice, to fly to New York for a series of meetings.

Beatty had become used to having his 'pleasure' laid on for him on his travels but his film company friend was also tied up on business. It was a mild night in The Strand as he drifted across to the Aldwych Theatre and embarked on what he later described as a 'cultural exercise', taking his seat in the stalls for *Troilus and Cressida*. He was instantly captivated by the sight of Helen in white lace, dominating the stage as the tragic daughter of a Trojan priest. So much so that he later joined a pack of autograph hunters at the stage door, leaving a note suggesting she make contact while he was in England. Helen played on his mind the following day and, when he heard nothing, he telephoned the stage door at the Aldwych.

He explained who he was to a somewhat cynical stage doorman who called her on the in-house tannoy. According to his highly amused British friend, standing only a few feet away in his hotel suite, the conversation went along the following lines:

> Helen: Who is this?
>
> Beatty: Oh, hello, hi there, Ms Mirren, we haven't
> spoken before but my name is Warren Beatty ...
> I was just ...
>
> Helen: Not the absurdly handsome, sophisticated
> American movie star?

Beatty: Well ... that's very kind of you ... but I was saying ... I was just wondering whether ...

Helen: OK, OK, that must be you, Johnny ... very funny ... now, get on with it will you, I'm on stage soon ...

Beatty: Er, I think you are under the misapprehension ...

Helen: I'm under nothing, but you will be in a minute. Get on with it!

Beatty: Anyway, I was hoping we could meet up to discuss a few projects I am interested in ... and ...

Helen: That's it, I'm off. If that's not you, Johnny, or Bruce or whoever, stop being silly whoever you are. Just grow up, will you?

And with that, Mirren had put Mr Beatty firmly in his place.

Dumbfounded, Beatty made one last attempt to reach Mirren before returning to Los Angeles but was not even able to draw her to the telephone point at the theatre. The stage doorman gave him some parting advice, telling him, 'If I were you, I wouldn't bother with that Warren Beatty lark any more. It's daft.'

His pal was brimming with admiration at her refusal to tolerate 'hoax' calls. 'To this day, she doesn't know she turned down the chance to date Warren,' he said. 'She had no reason to believe it really was Warren Beatty, she just assumed it was a friend clowning around. He was absolutely desperate to get into her knickers.

'But something tells me they would not have bonded very well, in any case. She wanted to get out there and have fun. But much as she loved a glass of bubbly, she was also happy with a glass of cheap plonk. He was "Hollywood" and was not her style then. Mind you, it would have appealed to her sense of humour to have gone out with him to have their picture taken together. She would have liked a laugh with him ... he blew it.'

The rejected Beatty for once took it on the jaw and put his vanity aside. To this day, he remains a fan, having avidly watched *Prime Suspect* on PBS. He also saw the amusement and irony on hearing she had made a new TV version of *The Roman Spring of Mrs Stone*, a frothy romantic comedy which helped launch him on his career in 1961 with Vivien Leigh and Oscar-winning Lotte Lenya.

Mirren was definitely moving up a gear career-wise. Unattached, though coolly romantic, she was not desperately seeking a serious relationship. She, instead, turned her attentions towards her first major dramatic TV role in a new version of Honoré Balzac's classic *Cousin Bette* which starred Margaret Tyzack, Ursula Howels and the dashing Colin Baker who, 13 years later, became TV's sixth Dr Who. Children's favourite Sally James and roly-poly Bella Emberg, one of Russ Abbott's favourite stooges, represented a racy supporting cast in Ray Lawler's adaptation for BBC2 in collaboration with the PBS network in America. The series was broadcast in August 1971 and Mirren did not go unnoticed in the part of the delicious courtesan Valerie who is in league with Bette, played by the dynamic Tyzack.

Most agree that the relatively low-budget production – now on the video racks – was a cut above the glossy 1997 American-backed movie version starring Jessica Lange and Elisabeth Shue.

LAMDA-trained Baker, now approaching his sixtieth birthday, was already something of a TV idol when he landed the lead role of the weak-willed artist Steinbock in the five-part drama. But he was ill-prepared for what was to greet him at Television Centre in London's White City when he arrived to record the period piece. The red-blooded chap that he was, bachelor Baker was totally enamoured and in awe of Mirren whose powerhouse reputation was sweeping through the ranks of Equity.

And, for once, Baker, who was absolutely no slouch with the ladies, feared the worst biological threat of all – an obvious state of arousal – when he was about to clamber into bed with Mirren. The actor was desperate at all costs to keep his embarrassment somehow 'under wraps'.

But a wardrobe girl saved his blushes. He says his lasting memory of the production was being asked on the day of his love scene with Mirren whether he required flesh-coloured knickers to cover his private parts.

'Being a bloke and things being as they are, I thought it best in case I needed to hide my embarrassment, so to speak,' he said. 'Bless my heart, on the day, she turned up, dropped her gown and was completely starkers. She looked absolutely knockout. She had an incredible figure. But she wasn't at all self-conscious which really helped me a good deal. We didn't actually have to be seen on camera doing anything, it was like the morning after.

'But I kept looking straight into her eyes to avert glancing down, thereby avoiding any biological accident. Boys will be boys. If you think Helen is beautiful today, you should have seen her then. I had to keep a grip on myself in every sense!'

Word of the love scene whispered its way through the circular corridors of the building and it wasn't long before technicians totally unconnected with the production drifted into the studio. Baker said, 'It was amazing how many scene painters and engineers were required on the day on a closed studio set when we were filming, fiddling around, taking a long time.

'She wasn't intimidated in the least by me, either. Not in the least. Everyone fancied her. She was very confident as an actress and as a woman, like a female Kenneth Branagh. She had that gift of being sexy and yet being able to be taken seriously. She may have been naked but she was in control.

'Even then she had this quality as though she could eat you alive for breakfast but couldn't be bothered for the moment. It was an animal thing. It was her whole personna. Sex is great but sex can get in the way. It can obscure how talented somebody like her is. But men still lust after her. The sex thing has done her no harm.'

Indeed. Fresh from his roaring success with Twiggy in the art-deco musical *The Boyfriend* came the fiery, eccentric film director Ken Russell and his new drama *Savage Messiah* which was stacked with his usual wild, visceral imagery. Mirren was instantly drawn to the film's Catholic themes, though mainly in an irreligious or sacriligious way, and his daring sexual insights. From incest to homosexuality, he knew no taboos and was, from her schooldays, a champion of artistic liberalism. Russell certainly had a thing about kitsch, nuns, snakes, phallic symbols and marching Nazis. He expected his leading ladies to strip and often strip again. He recognised few boundaries and his early movies drew large audiences and much publicity. The former BBC man who worked on the *Monitor* programme, stunned the movie business with his controversial adaptation of DH Lawrence's *Women in Love* which featured the landmark naked wrestling bout between Alan Bates and Oliver Reed. He then went hopelessly over the top with his musical biopic *The Music Lovers*, again featuring Glenda Jackson, but with the miscast American idol Richard Chamberlain portraying the sexually lost Russian composer Piotr Ilyich Tchaikovsky. As his protégé Glenda Jackson later commented, 'I just wish he would find a really good scriptwriter he could respect because he needs to be dragged by someone with a talent as large as his own. Then he could get out of this fearful rut. He'll spend hours getting the set right or screaming abuse at people because a costume isn't actually correct in every fine detail and then he'll leave you to play a scene entirely on your own. He can't do anything to help a bad actor.'

But the combustible Russell thought he was on relatively safe ground with *Savage Messiah*, a bizarre study of the life and times of artist and sculptor Henri Gaudier-Brzeska. Born in 1891, the Frenchman was regarded as one of the outstanding sculptors of his generation, having studied art in Bristol, Nuremberg and Munich. He became a member of the English Vorticist movement which sought to reflect the energy of the industrial age through a semi-abstract style. His work was influenced by Jacob Epstein and primitive art. He was tragically killed in action during the Great War, though romantics believe he fled the battlefield and started a new life on the other side of the world under an assumed name.

Russell's film focused on Gaudier's relationship with the much older, somewhat dowdy Sophie Brzeska, a friendship which led to them sharing names though they never married. The young, unknown American actor Scott B Anthony played Gaudier, with the late stage star Dorothy Tutin playing Sophie. Mirren's role is probably best remembered for her ascending a staircase slowly, imperiously, in the nude while wandering around her father's mansion. She played a French artist's model, a bubbly suffragette-type, aptly named Gosh Smith-Boyle. Peter Vaughan, Michael Gough (latterly Batman's indispensible butler, Alfred) and one of the director's firm favourites, dancer/choreographer Lindsay Kemp, battled away gamely in support.

Russell associated strongly with the artist. He read HS Ede's biography on which the film was based when he was a young man and said, 'I was impressed by Gaudier's conviction that, somehow or other, there was a spark in the core of him that was personal to him, which was worth turning into something that could be appreciated by others.'

Posters emblazened with the slogan 'ALL ART IS SEX' and 'EVERY MAN HAS A DREAM THAT MUST BE REALISED' did little to sell the feature to the movie-going public. As the film was largely self-financed by Russell, its commercial failure was a particular blow. Problems piled up throughout the shoot. His son Alex, who made a brief appearance in the film, recalls, 'We were on the coast and some oil or tar got on the lens but this was not discovered until the end of the day, so a whole day's shooting was lost. It didn't stop there. We had some fake Gaudier charcoals made up which were stolen and then sold as originals through Bond Street and Sotheby's.'

The deeply thoughtful Mirren was among those impressed by Russell's painfully observed study of Gaudier and his brief but turbulent life. She mentally put the cult masterpiece down as a 'fascinating experience, soul-enriching'.

Russell, no matter how much criticism was being hurled in his direction, believed that, in Mirren, he had found a new 20-carat diamond among the fake starlets. He was unfamiliar with her work and, on the recommendation of a friend, went to see her on stage in Strindberg's *Miss Julie*. That was enough. 'I was totally knocked out by her presence. I simply had to have her for the film,' he recalls today. 'Helen was extremely co-operative during the filming. She is a markedly intelligent woman, able to mesmerise, but too emotionally articulate to let the character coast on that alone. She came up with many suggestions for the interpretation of her role as a spoiled brat who goes slumming, who satisfies her vigour and appetite under the aegis of the emergent feminist banner. Audiences found her unforgettable. People still ask me about her. What is she like? She impressed me as a very confident and sensitive young woman, alert to nuance and with a first-rate mind. She can't have been unaware of her enormous allure. She has a quality of self-possession that is irresistible. She's no one's fool. I dare anyone who sees the film to forget her slapping those marble columns to punctuate her promenade around the room. I go to her films expecting that marvellous blend she's developed of instinct and cunning and compassion and vulnerability she reveals in her characters. She's juicy. She invests her characters with a hint of steel that reads as pride of strength. I don't know how she does it, really. There'll be that element of grandeur, of *hauteur*, and an undertone of sheer dogged bravery, or survival instincts, then a melting vulnerability or pathos, any number of layers.

'If Helen has ever expressed doubts about the nude scene in *Savage Messiah*, I don't know about them. Much to my delight, she had no problems about the scene of the "nude descending a staircase", which she carried off with great aplomb. And with a figure like hers, who could blame her? One of these days, I hope we get the chance to work together again.'

Mirren, in fact, was not so agreeable. She suggested wearing something in her nude scene, at which Russell's wife Shirley appeared with white stockings. But they were later discarded.

Savage Messiah inspired Mirren with a novel idea about actresses having to deal with nudity based on the theory that everyone on the set should be wearing their birthday suits. She said, tongue piercing cheek, that she was going to Equity with her scheme. 'Actresses won't have hang-ups about stripping then,' she said. 'Why should the producer, director and the whole crew get away with it? No wonder a girl can feel self-conscious, like an outcast. People are sensitive about their naked bodies. They think of their ugly features first. Nudity should be done only in the focus of the loving eye.'

Mirren was then sleeping on floors and sofas around London staying with friends, while hoping to buy herself a small property in Parsons Green, West London. The role in the film, she quipped, would at least cover the cost of a bathroom.

On the nudity issue she confessed, 'It's just rubbish, all that stuff. It's put into films to cater for an audience who want to see chicks with their clothes off. I would have thought that it would be extremely boring, because I suppose when people see the film they'll say, "Here comes that dear old nude scene again." But it doesn't worry me any more. We're in a society where it doesn't matter whether I appear naked or not. Taking your clothes off is easy for a girl. The only thing you can do wrong when you're stripped is to look awful.' When pressed over her motivation, she claimed she was only doing the movie to pay for central heating in her new home. 'I stripped off to keep warm, if you see what I mean.'

Was she beautiful minus her clothes? She said, 'In the right circumstances, I can be. But I wouldn't say a film set qualifies.' Future director Derek Jarman mingled with the cast of *Savage Messiah*, keeping a close eye on his ingenious sets. He was to hail Russell as an 'important but disturbing' influence on his career.

She was later angry with the film company distributing the Russell movie for releasing unauthorised nude photos of her to publicise the film. 'I certainly don't want my body appearing in some nudie magazine. I wouldn't have minded if it hadn't been such a disgustingly horrible picture. I was so cross about it. It was against my contract which said that no pictures could be issued or published without my consent and approval. I wasn't ever going to sue because that is an expensive, laborious and silly business. I was, though, going to track down the culprit and put a custard pie right in his face. But everyone denied responsibility,' she complained. 'I was basically unhappy with the nude scene because I thought, like so much else in the film, it was rather vulgar. Ken Russell said he was very concerned it should be tasteful and that I shouldn't feel in any way exploited. But when I think back on it, he always chose to be vulgar. I didn't want to do it. I got myself into a terrible state over it. Everybody else makes money, but girls are constantly the losers. I don't mind stripping, though. Compared to the way some people earn their money, stripping is an extremely gentle pastime.' The convent school girl confessed with a tiny degree of embarrassment that she only did the film for the money, because she was broke and had debts. She was running a car and a girl has to eat!

Another part of Mirren's audacious game plan for longevity was not to get caught up in some of the more tacky British movies going into production at Pinewood and Elstree Studios. Offers flooded through, tempting her to capitalise on her figure. But the siren from the RSC wasn't about to make *Confessions of a Classical Actress* with Robin Askwith or join the late Barry Evans for a romp in *The Adventures of a Drama Queen*. *Confessions* producer Greg Smith and Stanley Long who made the *Adventures* series saw Mirren as the icing on the soft-porn cake, a certain draw in an overcrowded movie marketplace. They were already luring some high-quality, glamorous names to their cast lists through the sheer power of a fat pay cheque, while others waited for the phone to ring.

A film industry source said, 'The producers of the *Confessions* series and the *Adventures* series were both in the same marketplace and she would have been a huge prize. They offered her five times the going rate in a bidding war to join them, just for one film, but she didn't want to know. She could have made an absolute fortune. If she'd made three or four of them, she could have taken a year off. They wanted her as a gimmick. But she wasn't interested.'

Colin Baker today believes her long-term strategy paid off. 'I think it's fair to say that those actresses who did get involved in that kind of material largely disappeared from the scene. They lost their value. But Helen stood her ground. She believed in herself and her ability to come through, no matter what.'

Mirren also knew that the nuns of St Bernard's, apart from her dear mother and father, would be mortified if she'd suddenly changed direction into the British sex comedy zone. Stockings and suspender belts could be treated as 'art', when displayed on the right stage. On screen, however, pursued while scantily clad by the likes of rotund Bill Maynard, now that was an altogether nightmarish image.

And it wasn't going to happen, not even if the character offering the wad of greenbacks was the legendary James Bond producer Cubby Broccoli. The gregarious American movie mogul Broccoli was also on Mirren's trail anxious to secure her services. The huge financial success of *Diamonds Are Forever* in 1971 had assured his company Eon Productions of another box-office jackpot, whether it was going to be with or without Sean Connery as 007. His right-hand executives started another talent search for a new James Bond for their next project, *Live and Let Die*.

Hollywood macho man Burt Reynolds was considered as well as our own up-and-coming TV stars Anthony Valentine and Patrick Mower.

But Roger Moore, with his good looks and sophisticated edge, was soon edging out the front-runners in the field. The uncompromising Broccoli insisted that he had to have a 'true Brit' in the golden role and his mind was made up. Roger the Dodger was perfect. His attention was also drawn to Mirren as ideal to play the mysterious, frightened and vulnerable Tarot card-playing Solitaire.

But Mirren's advisers, principally her agent Maggie Parker, were shrewd enough to want to know more about the role of Solitaire before committing their girl to the major part. Graduating to the dizzy, glamorous heights of being a 'Bond beauty' had never been high on her agenda, not that she was about to knock the likes of

Honor Blackman or Diana Rigg. But Mirren never saw herself, even from the early days, as a man's plaything. The thought of posing for photographs crouched by Sean Connery's knees was just about repellent. One of her associates said, 'Helen wasn't being a snob. There were quite a few fine actresses who'd been in the Bond movies but it simply wasn't for her. She didn't see any particular credibility factor in having that on her CV or even in getting that kind of universal recognition. At the time, Bond girls tended to be flash in the pans.'

Maggie Parker met again with Broccoli. She had thumbed through the latest draft of the screenplay by Tom Mankiewicz. Ian Fleming's original story had been thrown out because it was felt that the novel's treatment of black people was patronising. Guy Hamilton was again to direct the tale about a high-class crime syndicate operating out of the Caribbean and led by the dreadful Dr Kananga. Parker was privately unimpressed. She felt Solitaire was left little to work with and ultimately came across as a naïve little girl. On the plus side, her client could have picked up a super-cool £250,000 and got a taste of the way they treat celebrities in Hollywood. Broccoli was perplexed, while Mrs Parker attempted to explain their reasoning in Verrey's restaurant in London's Regent Street. Finally, an exasperated and somewhat confused Broccoli rose to his feet and muttered, while trying to retain control, 'If this young lady thinks she is above our little film and just wants to hang out with these people from RAC, then let that be her problem.'

Parker found herself roaring with laughter. She later said, 'I felt terrible and totally unprofessional. But I think Helen would have laughed if she'd been there. I didn't go into any of the details with her. There was no point. I knew she wasn't interested. The money would have been lovely and the promotional tour great fun, but she'd never done it for the size of the cheque before and wasn't about to go that way.'

It was the summer of 1972, and Mirren was the leading figure in another RSC success story in August Strindberg's *Miss Julie*, and later starred in the filmed version with new Irish star Donal McCann and Heather Canning in full support at Pinewood Studios in Buckinghamshire.

But her mind was now turning to matters much further afield, geographically and intellectually. She had at last finished work on *Savage Messiah* before being fêted for her body of work with the RSC at a two-day tribute to Shakespeare during the Positano Arts Festival.

In late 1972, the in-demand Mirren upped and left Britain for over three months, surprising both friends and family, to join the revered and now much-lamented stage and film director Peter Brook on what she described as a 'voyage into the unknown'.

Brook, a mentor figure from her days at the RSC, had spent time in Paris forming the independent theatrical company Le Centre International de Créations Théâtrales. He wanted Mirren to join his small troupe on a tour of West Africa and through the Sahara Desert. They'd 'entertain' the indigenous people who'd never laid eyes on white Europeans with a new brand of improvised theatre. The extraordinary African trip and a briefer additional visit to a Native American reservation were to change her life for ever.

Mirren later recalled, 'Peter is difficult to work with because he always demands the best of you. I could have stayed in Britain and done TV and plays and made a lot of money but I had total faith in what Peter was doing.' She could hardly wait to get out into the bush and sleep under the stars. The journey lived up to expectations.

Exhausted and exhilarated, she bounced back to Britain full of new enthusiasm for her craft and emotionally 'enlightened' by her dangerously close encounter with Third World poverty. She had learned much from her theatrical 'safari' with Brook, and the subsequent tour to the Native American reservation in Minnesota. She said, 'I was aware of Peter Brook's work and I'd been a great admirer. That was the time he was doing *Marat/Sade*, work that was so revolutionary and extraordinary and entertaining. Pure theatre.

There was no one else out there like him. So I very much wanted to work with him and learn from him.

'In that era, American theatre was pretty extraordinary. There were some amazing theatre groups that were exploding out, all around. It was an extraordinary learning time of my life. What I learned was that, as you travel through life, you think Oh, that's what that was about ... now I understand. It wasn't something that you walk away from with a few quick, easy tricks that you've learned. It was much more to do with understanding yourself as a person and, it seemed at the time, constantly confronting your failures as an actor and as a person. It wasn't a particularly comfortable experience. But it was wonderful and, in retrospect, it was very righteous.'

Mirren was also getting to be something of a rabid political animal with heavy leanings towards Vanessa Redgrave's Workers' Revolutionary Party as a radical alternative to Labour's cloth-cap image, standing for the WRP in Equity elections. She was a firm believer in women's rights and had been commissioned to write on the subject by *Cosmo* magazine. And she didn't hold back if she felt she had a genuine grievance and the cause was worth knocking a nose or two out of joint for. She went public in print for the first time to tell her peers how disenchanted she was by the way things were being run at the cash-starved RSC. Her intense feelings led to her firing off a volley of criticism in the *Guardian*, largely aimed at the administration of the prestigious organisation which was then in a state of perpetual 'crisis'. The *Guardian* pubished her views, which included a thinly veiled broadside at 'lazy' actors.

Mirren, slightly uneasy about her début as a seen-and-heard protester, said audiences had been conditioned to expect lavish standards, such as real leather on Roman uniforms, so actors have become confused and made lazy by them. She said, 'I just feel that, if all that money was yanked away, it would force actors to find a new and more truthful form.'

The permanent set for that season's four Roman plays was said to have cost £250,000 and had not been used thereafter. Des Wilson, then Head of Public Affairs, was quick to go on the counter-attack insisting they had done everything to keep costs down. The RSC was quietly, privately, furious with its 'princess' and she knew it. She said they were 'intensely polite' about her barbed comments and 'kept saying things like, "Of course, you are free to say what you like about us but we do wish you had talked to us first." In other words, they wanted the right to censor what I had to say, which I suppose was natural enough in the circumstances. I'm not sure I'll be asked back there for a while, nor whether I want to go.' She was right. It was five years before the RSC called a truce and invited her back through its hallowed doors.

The acid-spitting scribe Bernard Levin even joined in the verbal punch-up, outraging her to the extent that she promised to chuck a cup of tea over him, or worse, if she ever stumbled across him at the BBC. She claimed he was being at his most sexist, writing a piece suggesting that it was 'extraordinary that this girl with big breasts can think, and how strange that an actress should have an actual idea about the theatre.'

Mirren was certainly making her mark. Her contemporaries noted that though she showed little ambition in the context of local or national political office, she would stand up to be counted on certain issues.

Politically, she leaned heavily towards the Left, though she professed, attempting to discard her dull middle-class upbringing, to be 'spiritually' an anarchist.

And with perfect timing, the mercurial Lindsay Anderson entered her life. Educated at Oxford University, he created the Marxist film magazine *Sequence*, and was originally a documentary film-maker. He was also a founder member of the anti-censorship Free Cinema Group with Karel Reisz and Tony Richardson.

The maverick doyen of the stage from the Royal Court Theatre had broken out to direct classics on screen such as *This Sporting Life* in 1963. But he had been strangely quiet on the movie front until he launched the career of Malcolm McDowell through his anti-Establishment epic *If* in 1968. Mirren was thrilled when Anderson asked her to join him and the cream of Equity in the marathon second part of his social trilogy *O Lucky Man!*

McDowell made his name as the scowling Travis spraying his automatic weapon from a public-school roof. *O Lucky Man!* was a surreal black comedy, accompanied by music from Alan Price, charting the rise and fall of coffee salesman Mick Travis as he criss-crossed Britain following a trail of corruption and intrigue. At every turning loitered a bent politician or police officer, while the Government was active on a daily basis at bending the minds of the population using drugs or scientific experimentation. The late, lamented *Dad's Army* veteran star Arthur Lowe played against type magnificently as a local councillor with a penchant for porno movies, while the likes of the sublime Ralph Richardson and Rachel Roberts played multiple eccentrics. The underrated Graham Crowden portrayed an unbalanced boffin, while Mirren was the mysterious, comforting but unattainable Patricia. The film was viewed as 'art house' by the critics and was a box-office failure, but it still remains as a rich tapestry of Anderson's artistic legacy.

Mirren was ecstatic at the company she was now keeping and the quality of work being ushered in her direction, even if the dialogue was no more than a few sentences. She was being noticed by the right people for the right reasons. Headstrong Malcolm McDowell, like a grinning vulture, sidled up to her at every opportunity. He was particularly impressed and the feeling was mutual. They were to star together on several occasions over the next decade and there was no mistaking the heart-shaped mushroom cloud on the horizon whenever they met.

McDowell had a profound effect on Mirren, who kept her feelings to herself. But she did confide in a close friend, 'I was brought up to keep myself pure and to believe that most men are brutes on the quiet. The result is that men are a mystery to me, though I wouldn't say I was an innocent any more.

'I am a victim of that type of upbringing as much as any girl of my age. I fight against it but I can't change it. Who are the most important men in your life? The ones who break my heart. I am in love, but it isn't reciprocated. I don't think he knows I love him.'

The mid-Seventies, however, were not productive times in terms of Helen Mirren's movie output. The industry was in a pitiful malaise due to a lack of investment and interest. But for Lew Grade and his ITC operation and Sir Nat Cohen and EMI, business in Wardour Street where many of the big film deals were hammered out was desperately quiet. The unions had priced too many films out of the country and it wasn't long before the only feature being made on our shores was the James Bond series which was based at Pinewood Studios. The two other main studios at Shepperton and Elstree were on the verge of closure.

Some British beauties, like Reading doctor's daughter Jacqueline Bissett and Susan George, were preparing to pack their bags and quit Britain to take their chances in Hollywood where *The Godfather* had just been voted Best Picture at the Oscars. Twelve-year-old Linda Blair was turning heads in *The Exorcist* and *Deep Throat* had been judged to be obscene by a New York court.

Former Boots shopgirl Glenda Jackson was well on the way to becoming Britain's top female draw through films such as *A Touch of Class* with George Segal. Although Mirren had taken a giant step towards international recognition via Ken Russell's wild and wayward *Savage Messiah*, she was staying put.

Instead, she turned her attention towards television and the stage. In January 1974, she partnered Stanley Baker in the BBC *Play of the Month*, *The Changeling*, which was based on the five-act seventeenth-century work of Thomas Middleton and William Rowley. The Jacobean tragedy was full of blood and sexual passion and also starred Susan Penhaligon, prior to her emergence in the TV series *Bouquet of Barbed Wire*.

Mirren played the rich, beautiful and spoiled Beatrice-Joanna who developed an overwhelming desire for a heroic sea captain. But before she could have her romantic way, she had to rid herself of her fiancé. She employed her despicable manservant De Flores (Baker) to do the job. But he also desired her and she found herself being sucked into a pit of evil.

It was also good timing for Mirren to make her move into contemporary thriller land via commercial television in ITV's *Coffin for the Bride*, which was shown in June 1974. She co-starred with Michael Jayston, a TV pin-up through his role in *The Power Game*. And though she enjoyed the foray into modern dialogue and settings, she still felt more at home in the classics. It was no surprise when she signed to play the king's mistress Orinthia in a new BBC production of George Bernard Shaw's *The Apple Cart* with Peter Barkworth, Nigel Davenport and Beryl Reid, before starring in a BBC adaptation of JM Barrie's *The Little Minister*.

And there was more success to follow for her in the commercial theatre in the summer of 1975 as sexually ravenous, booze-drenched pop icon Maggie Frisby in David Hare's switched-on Sixties rock show *Teeth 'n' Smiles* which was set at a May Ball in Cambridge circa 1969. Once again, she was able to turn on that quality – once defined as 'sluttish eroticism' – which heralded her first stage appearance at 18 as Cleopatra.

Hare's acclaimed new work, which also starred Jack Shepherd, was first performed at the Royal Court to rave reviews before transferring the following year to Wyndham's Theatre in the West End. Comedian and song 'n' dance man Dave King, who in the 1950s had been the only British entertainer to have his own American network prime-time TV show alongside Perry Como and Andy Williams, played Saraffian. Shepherd played Arthur the songwriter and, for the first time, London audiences were able to see Antony Sher, Karl Howman, Cherie Lunghi, Hugh Fraser and Mick Ford.

Teeth 'n' Smiles was a massive landmark in Mirren's career and Maggie Frisby 'haunted' her in her private life. No wonder her close friends around this time nicknamed her 'Hell'. The role also required her to belt out two rock songs and she said, 'Every character I play takes me over off-stage for a while. In a limited way, I had to do some soul-searching to find Maggie. She is a bitchy person and I could not find the same quality of bitchiness in myself.'

Playwright David Hare, who recently revived *Teeth 'n' Smiles* at the Crucible Theatre in Sheffield, admits that the musical was his only 'nakedly' autobiographical work. But he says he was thrilled by the musically untested, unprimed Mirren, whom he didn't rate as a *chanteuse*. Today, however, he insists it was only a 'small risk' to hand her the role of Maggie, commenting, 'Helen herself would probably admit that the capacity to soar in song is one of the very few gifts that she does not possess. But the power of her performance swept all before it, in the most extraordinary way. She was so brilliant that she had every member of the audience believing she could sing, even when some of the notes she was hitting seemed to have travelled quite a long way from home. It is something of a tribute to those who surrounded her that the impression of the evening remained half with Helen and half with the ensemble.'

In the autumn of 1975, the magical call came for her to join Laurence Olivier, Alan Bates and her friend Malcolm McDowell in a prestige ITV version of Harold Pinter's *The Collection* at Granada's Studios in Manchester, in which she was to play Bates's sexually ambiguous screen wife Stella. The forever-joking McDowell still had a crush on her and rushed to greet her while Olivier, then a sprightly 68-year-old, charmed her into an immediate glass of champagne. She was totally overawed, though later said to a member of the production team, 'I just had to keep my cool but I didn't know whether to call him "Larry" or "Mr Olivier". He just said, "Whatever takes your mood, my dear." He was such a wonderful man. The whole thing just took my breath away. I was so, so lucky to be in that kind of company. The most amazing thing was that there was this acceptance of you, as though you also belonged. That blew my mind. That's the kind of boost to the old self-esteem everyone needs.'

Amusingly, Granada and the ruling Bernstein clan, who lived under the shadow of their founder Sidney Bernstein, were so thrilled by their illustrious 'catch' that they assembled luxury dressing rooms and toilets for Sir Laurence and Co. But the stars of other ongoing productions, including *Coronation Street* – then viewed by less than nine million homes and way down in the ratings – were forbidden from using the facilities.

So impressed was Olivier by Granada's 'professional attitude' that he returned in 1983 to make the epic *Brideshead Revisited* for them with Jeremy Irons and Anthony Andrews. The ruling TV classes in Manchester viewed and tolerated the *Street* as a 'downmarket' but necessary product.

The cast of the *Street*, however, were infuriated by what became known as the 'Bog Wars'. The legendary Pat Phoenix and Peter Adamson, who played Elsie Tanner and Len Fairclough, formed a deputation, backed by Bryan Mosley, who played Councillor Alf Roberts, to protest to drama executives. The usually affable Mosley was particularaly infuriated by Granada's 'divide and rule' tactics and was heard shouting, 'If we can't wipe our arses on the best soft loo paper paid for by you, I, for one, will bring my own in.' True to his promise, he arrived the following day carrying a bumper packet of 12 rolls which he distributed in the Green Room where the cast spent their relaxation periods.

Other members of the cast got in on the joke for the best part of the following three months much to the chagrin of Granada and the producers of the series. Actress Lynne Perrie, who played 'Poison Ivy' Tilsley, made a special visit to an ironmonger's store to buy a plunger and kept it with her at all times for the next month.

Mirren, Olivier and Co were unaware of the fuss in the background and senior staff and security were almost always on hand to guide them away from 'that soap mob' when they weren't in the studios.

The late Michael Elphick sought to redress the balance of lavatorial power when he returned to Manchester two years later to make the drama series *Holding On*. The stroppy Chichester-born actor, who had a personal loathing of all things pompous, had briefly played landlord's son Douglas Wormold in the *Street* in 1974. When he heard about Bog Wars and how 'the suits' had created a two-tier loo system, he sneaked into the security office and announced to all and sundry through the tannoy system that 'with immediate effect, through a change in policy, the special bathroom facilities are now open and available to everyone'.

There was much giggling and cheering before the likes of *Street* regulars Bernard Youens (Stan Ogden) and Adamson led a line of chums through the hallowed doors. Mischievous Elphick, who was to become better known on TV through the sitcom *Three Up, Two Down* and as the character Boon, laughed as he told me, 'It was The Day of the Great Unwashed. Of course, all hell broke out when the suits got word of what was happening. But the point was made. Granada was not a place fit for snobbery. In fact, there was no place for that kind of stuff in British television ... apart from at the BBC!'

Mirren had just turned 30 and starred with Laurence Olivier. And she'd rubbed shoulders with the mob from the *Street*. What tales her mum Kit would have to tell the bridge club in Leigh-on-Sea.

Yet, Helen lapsed into one of her deep, dark moods. 'Between 18 and 30 were the worst years of my life,' she confided. 'I tried never to show it by just getting on with things, but during those decades I cried myself to sleep most nights simply because I felt afraid of what was ahead, of the unknown. I have talked about this to other women and found that it was similar for them. Odd, isn't it, when you consider that, at the time, you're at your physical best? In reality, there is all the misery and fear of wondering what is to become of you.'

Mirren proudly returned to London armed with a string of anecdotes about her conversations with Olivier to make a virtually unseen but innovative new screen production of *Hamlet* in which she played both Ophelia and Gertrude. The casting of the play was bizarre, with brothers Anthony Meyer and David Meyer portraying Hamlet and Laertes, with the pre-eminent homosexual of that period, Quentin Crisp, playing Polonius. The Royal College of Art backed the production, which was directed by the unknown Celestino Coronada.

Mirren confided that the Bard would probably not have approved of Mr Coronada's peculiar vision of his work but then the film was not about to cause a sensation.

Her sanity was duly restored by a starring role in Ben Travers's last play *The Bed Before Yesterday* at the Lyric Theatre, playing a prude who's put off sex on her bridal night but rediscovers her passion with an impoverished widower.

And there was an early Christmas present in December 1975. Her reunion with director Lindsay Anderson and his fledgling repertory company, starring Joan Plowright and Peter McEnery, paid off. The London theatre critics voted her joint winner with Diana Rigg of the Plays and Players Best Actress Award. She shared the award, for making her West End début with her portrayal of Nina in Anton Chekhov's *The Seagull* at the Lyric, and for *Teeth 'n' Smiles* which had earlier burst into life at the Royal Court. The awards flowed. She was also voted TV Actress of the Year by the Variety Club of Great Britain. Her portrayal of Fascist dictator Benito Mussolini's mistress Clara Petacci in the BBC's *Caesar and Claretta* from their *Private Affairs* series swung the vote her way.

Mirren had no intention of standing still, even though her career, in an international sense, had almost ground to a halt. Dull, mediocre movie offers, almost all requiring her to strip off, came and went. There was talk of her co-starring with Lynda Bellingham in *Stand Up Virgin Soldiers*, the sequel to Leslie Thomas's pulp paperback hit about warfare in the Malaysian jungle. She wasn't at all keen and felt relieved when a little-known Australian actress, Pamela Stephenson, signed on the dotted line.

And she found her clout waning when they started dealing out roles worthy of an Oscar. She badly wanted the lead part opposite Alan Bates in Paul Mazursky's *An Unmarried Woman*, but Jill Clayburgh's star was soaring faster in the eyes of studio chiefs. She would have killed to take Jane Fonda's place as Lillian Hellman alongside Vanessa Redgrave in *Julia*. It was not to be. And much as she admired David Bowie, she did not want to be seen urinating on screen playing his human lover in *The Man Who Fell to Earth*.

Instead, the following year she headed North to Glamis near Dundee in Scotland on what was to be another mind-expanding trip to play Rosalind in a new atmospheric, rustic adaptation of *As You Like It*, being co-produced by the BBC and Time Life. Directed by Basil Coleman, the cast of the comedy included James Bolam as Touchstone and Angharad Rees as Celia. A relaxed Mirren had never truly surveyed the landscape of the Highlands before and was instantly bewitched. A member of the crew recalled, 'She was deeply contented and felt totally at home. But she said that most of all she needed to be totally and absolutely in love.'

She made a romantic pledge to herself that her association with the Highlands would run deep. By the turn of the Eighties, she was miraculously able to buy a chunk of land which would forever remain unblemished. A friend said, 'That was one promise she truly believed she would never be able to keep. It wasn't about her owning land, she's no rank-and-file capitalist. It was about conservation, owning a spot in Stirlingshire that nobody would be able to touch, a place she could go and belonged. She made a film and the salary paid for it. That's what she wanted to use the money for. It wasn't money she felt happy about using just for herself on frivolous things.'

Twenty years later, she also selected a haven a two-hour drive away where she would wed the American director Taylor Hackford. And, as though to prove the RSC was not able to survive without her, she was finally forgiven for her condemnation in the media of the powers that be, and was invited back to return in Henry VI

Parts 1, 2 and 3. Terry Hands, then the the Joint Artistic Director of the RSC, described her as 'the most exceptionally gifted actress of her generation'.

All's well that ends well, they might have said. But not quite. After a magnificent summer to remember in 1976, Mirren was to embark on what would be a despairing journey into the depths of blood, gore and pornography. Never a dull moment when you're a convent schoolgirl from Leigh-on-Sea.

4

Roman
Scandals

In the movie world, they still talk about Gore Vidal's *Caligula* – or 'Caligola', as the Italians prefer to call him. Infamous, expensive, extremely graphic, sexually explicit and pretty awful. Correction – downright appalling.

If you happened to be one of the main players in the cast, you could also add the words 'degrading' and 'demoralising'. In fact, there's hardly anyone around with virtually a good word to say about the movie which was premièred in America to howls of derision in late 1979.

The movie, a two-and-a-half-hour-long biopic of Rome's most demented leader, was the brainwave – or brainstorm – of Robert Charles Joseph Edward Sabatini 'Bob' Guccione. The former chef and truck driver had become the Chief Executive of a multi-millionaire soft porn empire, dominated by *Penthouse* magazine, when he decided it was time to get into the movie business.

He'd already invested in the classic Jack Nicholson gangster yarn *Chinatown* and the Burt Reynolds prison caper *The Longest Yard*. But now he fancied his chances as a major international player.

Guccione naïvely thought he could shoot anything, anywhere, however he wanted and get away with it. As he put it, 'Instead of just shooting for two hours in a motel room, shoot a serious film with serious actors and actresses and an important writer and director. Have all the trappings of a major film but let it go all the way for a change.' Indeed he did. By the time he was through as producer and then 'substitute' director, his little offering to history depicted scenes of decapitation, necrophilia, rape, bestiality and sado-masochism. And, as some people have suggested, that was even before the crew arrived on set.

Guccione targeted Caligula as the 'perfect' subject matter for an epic. Had he got it right? Tabloid historians had unearthed some amazing revelations about the emperor. He was, apparantly, a bisexual, cross-dressing psychopath, who had slept with all three of his sisters. He declared war on the ocean. He stocked brothels with noblemen's wives. And he made it a capital offence to mention goats in any context.

But when Guccione realised the finished product was going to cost him upwards of £12.5 million, he wanted writer Vidal to make 'certain adjustments' to the script by adding explicit material. Vidal left the project. But Guccione wasn't going to let go of his dream of recreating the story of the mad Roman emperor in every last sensational, gory detail.

At the beginning of the project, the signs of an epic in the making couldn't have been better. The Vidal screenplay was based on his own book reinterpreting Caligula's bloodthirsty reign as the most powerful man on earth from AD12 to AD41. Also on the payroll and allegedly in control was 'generalissimo' director Tinto Brass, a radical film-maker formerly involved in Italian underground film-making who possessed strong anti-censorship leanings. Guccione liked his *Salon Kitty*, a World War II thriller set in a Nazi brothel.

Anything the outrageous director Pier Paolo Pasolini could do, Brass could do better. Fellini? So what! That was kid's stuff. Italy's film-makers were shocking the world in the Seventies and Eighties with their daring imagery and anti-Establishment sentiments, often with lashings of grisly violence and explicit sex. They knew no boundaries and the British censor was loath to use his power against continental 'artistes'. Unfortunately, even in these more liberal and accepting times, Pasolini overstepped the mark with wild scenes of torture and cruelty in *Saló or 120 Days of Sodom*, ensuring his film was banned before it even arrived in Britain.

Brass came to *Caligula* with a reputation for gratuitous sex. But given a decent opportunity, so Guccione believed, he might just make a half-decent movie with some commercial appeal outside Europe.

The story, depending which historian you believe, was still fascinating. Gaius Caesar Augustus Germanicus, as he was fully titled, was the youngest son of the revered Germanicus Caesar. Educated in the camp, he was nicknamed Caligula from his soldier's boots, 'caligae'. Following his father's death, he appointed himself co-heir along with the emperor's grandson Gemellus, with the Senate later granting Caligula complete control. But he soon squandered his wealth and murdered most of his relatives, apart from his sister Drusilla and uncle Claudius. Rome flowed red until he was assassinated in a quick but decisive coup with his family, leaving the supposedly dim-witted Claudius to wear the laurel crown.

If *Penthouse* organisation chief Guccione had done his homework, he might have chosen a more romantic period in Roman history ... or American history ... or not bothered at all. But associates of the no-nonsense businessman said he was constantly irritated by being dubbed by the media as a kind of poor man's Hugh Hefner, a reference to the womanising, presidential style of the *Playboy* magazine boss. Hefner may have his store of in-house Playboy movies, but he'd never been able to pull off any kind of success on the silver screen. This was going to be Guccione's bid, albeit an expensive one, for real street cred. He would create the first ever historic adult epic as a hands-on co-producer. In one cinematic swoop, he'd make that pipe-smoking pseudo-intellectual choke on his tobacco in a hot tub at the Playboy Mansion.

The critics were waiting, chainsaws at the ready, long before his Italian director Tinto Brass started to organise the 'troops' in Rome.

Malcolm McDowell was everyone's choice to play Caligula. When it came to 'mad, bloodthirsty and without scruples', there was no debate. McDowell – from spraying the lead indiscriminately in *If* to raping and beating in Stanley Kubrick's *A Clockwork Orange* – was undoubtedly their man. Brass met McDowell in London where he was told he would meet his Caesonia. He took him to see Mirren in Ben Travers's *The Bed Before Yesterday* at the Lyric Theatre. Brass was enthralled. They chatted backstaged, by which time Brass was in a trance.

Meanwhile, at his Penthouse base in New York, the inexperienced movie-maker Guccione was heading for disaster and nobody was about to bail him out. He'd reckoned on producing a 'masterpiece ' a 'classic for adults'.

But the horse was, in fact, already long past the post. From London to Los Angeles, everyone was still busy applauding the BBC's serialisation of Robert Graves's *I, Claudius* and *Claudius the God* by that deft wordsmith Jack Pulman. The absolutely riveting piece was condensed into 13 pulsating, enthralling episodes and not a single scene came in for criticism. Even hardcore members of Mary Whitehouse's right-wing Viewers' and Listeners' Association were silent. This was 'art'. When Sheila White, as Claudius's man-eating wife, had the entire male population of Rome in a couple of sittings, it was 'art'. Hooray for the BBC.

A veritable *Who's Who* of Equity filed into the BBC rehearsal rooms to 'break bread' with director Herbert Wise and producer Martin Lisemore, led by Derek Jacobi who was playing Claudius, Sian Phillips as the deadly Livia, Patrick Stewart as the devious Sejanus and John Hurt as the often restrained, effete Caligula. He was simply awesome, well on his way to becoming one of Britain's leading chameleon-like character actors.

The irony for Mirren was that she would have been in the cast but for her own galloping success story. Producer Lisemore was dismayed. It was late 1975 and she was already tied up on several projects and unable to fill the role of Caligula's manic sister Drusilla. She had business in Manchester with Sir Laurence Olivier and her pal Mr McDowell. Then Beth Morris stepped in and nobody complained. The serial won three BAFTA Awards with Best Actor for Jacobi and Best Actress for Phillips. When the serial was shown in America, it also won an Emmy for set designer Tim Harvey. *I, Claudius*, complete with Hurt as Caligula, was one of the greatest, if not *the* greatest, dramatic achievement of the Seventies, certainly on television..

Back in Rome ... much of this seemed to escape Guccione and Brass as they plotted, Caligula-like, in a bar somewhere near the Spanish Steps. The cast was splendid. They, after all, had one of the most promising actors of his generation in McDowell – or 'Mr Orange' as Brass would often jokingly refer to him. This seriously irritated the usually affable McDowell.

Peter O'Toole, still highly regarded from his Sixties epics with David Lean, had put his signature on the contract to play the disintegrating, vindictive Tiberius. O'Toole was delirious – he actually grinned at McDowell, 'Look, don't call me Tiberius, call me "Delirious", because I'm getting out of here long before you lot.'

John Gielgud was also in the line-up as Tiberius's cunning eyes and ears, the loyal Nerva. He, too, was destined to make an early exit. But his parting was in the script.

The neurotic French actress Maria Schneider, late of *Last Tango in Paris* with Marlon Brando, had been cast to play the incestuous Drusilla, but she bolted in tears after only one day on the set, ranting, 'This I cannot do ... I cannot do ... enough ... enough ...' She later labelled the film a 'grotesque pornographic parody'. And she was barely seen again in the movies for a decade.

The wild card to take her place – and 'they didn't come much wilder', according to McDowell – was a little-known actress called

Teresa Ann Savoy. One of Brass's favourite ladies, Savoy was a mysterious creature from the backstreets of Fulham in London. He had spotted Savoy – not her real name – while she was a teenage model on a photographic shoot in Rome. He then used her talents, or rather her ample curves, to star in his wartime anti-Fascist stocking-top-filler *Salon Kitty*, in which she portrayed the most popular hooker in a Berlin brothel.

'Johnny', as Gielgud preferred to be addressed by other thespians, was beside himself with glee as naked young men rehearsed for orgy sequences. The Knight of the Realm was soon at his most outrageous when he noticed a band of Roman musicians in the centre of the mêlée. They were also naked under their see-through, flimsy white togas. McDowell, who's still capable of an almost perfect Gielgud impression, complete with a rather haughty walk, grinned, 'He was out of this world. He touched me on the arm when he saw the band and couldn't believe his eyes. It wasn't that he was a promiscuous man, it was just that he'd never seen anything like it and he'd been around since time began.

'He said [adopting his Gielgud accent], "Just look, dear boy, just look. That boy with the harp ... his balls are down to his knees! Oh dear boy, what are we to do ... what are we to do?" I think it was just as well Gielgud wasn't with us for too long. He might have exploded.'

The late Knight of the Realm later recalled how the director was a 'very peculiar man'. He said, 'Nobody seemed to speak the same language and one actress walked out because she said her dress was indecent.' He was an onlooker in a swimming pool scene in which Peter O'Toole rose from the water surrounded by young boys and girls. Gielgud continued, 'There were about 20 more boys and girls splashing about, very good-looking all of them, the girls shaved to make them look younger and all stark naked. Then, the moment the bell rang for lunch, they all put their hands in front of their genitals and rushed out to have a pizza with their families, who were waiting in the corridors with lunch baskets.'

Though Vidal's screenplay may have been dull and lifeless,

bordering on the juvenile, money and manpower had been thrown at the sets. Countless numbers of extras filed into a specially built Roman stadium on the outskirts of Rome which spanned the length of three soccer fields. Mile-long Roman streets were pieced together along the route to the stadium. One of their most sickly 'inventions' was a gigantic wooden, 50ft-high, blood-splattered 'head-clipper'which stuttered slowly along severing heads. Often, the spectacular instrument of death would break down and more extras were sent in to push it from behind. Off the coast, an hour's journey from the city, they constructed a full-scale 175ft-long Roman galley, complete with 120 carved oars. It was the largest prop ever built at that time and was supposed to depict a floating brothel. But it leaked the moment it hit the water.

Under the supervision of Danilo Donati, 3,592 costumes were designed, 5,000 handcrafted boots and sandals were worn and the 2,000 wigs were stitched from over 1,000 pounds of human hair. McDowell was impressed, though nervous, when Brass informed him that they had hired a Yugoslav stallion named 'Davide' to portray Caligula's fiery steed Incitatus. 'Fine, so long as they keep the bloody thing away from me,' muttered McDowell to a visiting chum. 'They're lunatics. Lunatics. I'm not breaking my neck for Mr Guccione, believe me.'

The budget soared through continuous hold-ups. And as each day wore on under the burning sun, Guccione's patience was running out. Mirren and Co stood well back, avoiding confrontation. Her opening sequence involved her 'dancing' semi-naked for Caligula, an event which filled her with total dread. She barely got any sleep the night before and refused to eat in case the biological elements worked against her. 'If I was sick in the middle of a scene, even a dance scene, they'd probably use it,' she sighed in exasperation to McDowell. 'What have we let ourselves in for?'

Indeed. But at least she was surrounded by friends. It was a 'war zone' and, somehow or other, they would see it through together. One day, they would see the humour in it.

Mirren still holds dear a silver medallion made out of an ancient Roman coin, a gift from McDowell during the shoot. The Leeds-born publican's son was raised on the Mersey where his ex-RAF father bought The Royal Rock Hotel at Rock Ferry and then the Station Hotel at Ellesmere Port. With one sister who was six years older and another eight years younger, he always felt like an only child. He was a rebel at Cannock House School in Eltham, London, though the dicipline did him some good. At the age of 11, he was cast in *Aladdin* in the school pantomime and he loved it. He took LAMDA exams in speech and drama when he was 20 and passed. Eventually, he squeezed into the RSC but didn't feel as though he fitted, saying, 'I'm just not a company person ... it's the politics ... it can't be done.'

Small parts on television followed in *Dixon of Dock Green* and *Emergency Ward Ten*, before Lindsay Anderson saw his curled lip and streak of arrogance and handed him the role of Mick in *If*. The lad did well, showing a more sympathetic side in the tragic drama *The Raging Moon*, but it was Stanley Kubrick's *A Clockwork Orange* which brought him international acclaim. His portrayal of a vicious, futuristic thug lingers on some 30 years later for obvious sociological reasons, in the context of Britain's spiralling violent crimewave.

The *enfants terribles* sniffed around each other like curious big cats during the making of *O Lucky Man!*. Helen was both infatuated and intimidated by the charismatic extrovert by the time they bopped together at the wrap party. By the time they were back in each other's arms, on screen at least, alongside Sir Laurence Olivier at Granada's studios in the mid-Seventies, McDowell's marriage to American actress Margot Bennett Dullea, the ex-wife of *2001* star Keir Dullea, was decidedly rocky. He was ripe for a fling with Mirren, and friends said they barely left one another's side while working together on the ITV drama.

One friend said, 'It wasn't just that he was exciting and talented. There was such an amazing physical attraction between them, bordering on lust. We're sure they did the deed, so to speak, while they were doing the Olivier thing in Manchester. She wasn't in a solid relationship and neither was he. His marriage was a mess. But Helen was concerned because he was just going through a divorce.

'By the time they'd finished work on that, they had decided to "cool it", at her suggestion. He had other fish to fry in Hollywood. Helen would have been too much for him. She had too much fire. It would have been exciting though!'

Mirren always insisted that they were 'friends' rather than lovers to those in her inner circle. She didn't want to get 'seriously involved', even though McDowell had raved on in private about them 'conquering the world in harness'. She felt he was moving too fast and she wasn't going to be able to keep up. 'I think if I were together with Malcolm for any long period as a couple, I would become possessive, jealous and aggressive,' she confided. 'That could destroy me and both of us. I think our careers and our lives are more important. We are so much better as friends, anyway.'

Secretly, she always kept a special place in her heart for the dynamic McDowell, conjuring up images of them as a comedic double-act when they were together. Now here they were in Rome. He was her confidant and the man she should have married if she had married at all, back in the early Seventies.

But firm friends they remained. For a spell, she lived like a star with McDowell and Margot during one of their reconciliations, in a huge, marble-floored villa outside Rome, complete with swimming pool and live-in staff.

But she also needed to discover the city during her four-month-long stay and found a commune in a rough district of the Italian capital which was 'educational and instructive', until she woke up one morning to discover she was sharing her bed with two other strangers. Then, as Mirren was prone to do, she ran out of money. By a series of accidents. she met a roving street dancer called Valentino who performed in the dark squares of the Trastevere in order to pay for her to stay in a small hotel. She lived under his protection for a while in another less desirable district of the city.

Until it was time to go home, she'd face adversity with McDowell, her head held high with dignity. She joked that she was given the best possible warning of what was to come by Brass himself over dinner with Guccione, just before filming got under way. He leaned over to her while Guccione was out of earshot and whispered, 'I've got Malcolm McDowell, the best film actor there is; I've got Peter Toole, the best movie star; I've got Sir John Gielgud, the very best stage actor; and I've got Gore Vidal, the best screenplay writer, all to make ... the worst movie.' Never had a prediction been more accurate.

McDowell thought the whole affair was a hoot when there wasn't total chaos around him. He later told me, with a wide, cheeky grin, how impressed he'd been by Teresa Ann Savoy's body. 'I had to make love to her time after time after time,' he gushed, feigning exhaustion. 'I kept saying, "Sorry about this, Terry, here we go again!" I got to know her extremely well. At one stage, I had to have her and Helen at the same time. Then they made love to each other. I remember saying to Helen, "Don't talk to me any more about sex after this week!"

'There we were, going at it like alley cats and howling with laughter, saying, "What are they going to make us do next week, for God's sake?" But I survived. I rewrote some of my own lines to make the part speakable. I didn't want to look a complete idiot.

'Fortunately, I wasn't asked to do the full-frontal stuff, though in one scene I actually suggested it because I thought it was necessary and in context. But, believe me, the stuff I was doing was tame by comparison with the rest.'

Off set, Mirren meditated and kept her mind and body in trim with a series of exercises recommended by a Canadian Air Force manual. She was not terribly impressed by Brass. She said, 'He appeared to be deliberately pushing the film to the limits of what is permissible, just daring anyone to censor him. Every scene I was in appeared to include two or three naked couples doing odd things in corners. I always seemed to be filmed standing in front of giant phallic objects. There was little acting to be done. It was mostly just a clash of gigantic visual images.'

Meanwhile, back in 'Uncle Bob's Empire', as the set became known, there was a clear groundswell of animosity at almost every level. Writer Vidal, angry at changes made to his script by Brass and Guccione, was the first to walk, departing the scene with an emotional verbal volley and the use of the well-worn phrase, 'You'll be hearing from my lawyers.' He sued to have his name removed from the credits.

Then, the noisily volatile Brass found Guccione 'redirecting' the movie during the rushes, the nightly examination of what has been filmed that day prior to the editing stage. The explosion which followed led to Brass threatening to quit the film, though he also later claimed he'd been fired.

Brutal Guccione took firm control, much to the dismay of Mirren and McDowell. And there appeared to be prolonged activity between the American businessman and his entourage. He was dissatisfied with his historic epic, which, in his humble opinion, was no more 'dangerous' than a midnight stroll through Central Park. He arranged for extra scenes to be shot which would take Caligula to a 'higher erotic plain'. In effect, he was secretly hiring porno stars to shoot graphic sexual inserts in small studios usually reserved for TV commercials, understood to be in Frankfurt, Germany.

Mirren later made no excuses for deciding to be part of the mad romp. 'Malcolm [McDowell] wanted me to be in it,' she said. 'I think because he wanted a friend in it. He knew it was going to be tough and he wanted to have a good mate for moral support. Few people had ever asked me to do films, and it seemed like a sort of bad, mad adventure which was exactly what it was.' And then she smiled. 'Actually, making *Caligula* was rather like being paid well to visit a nudist colony.'

What also failed to impress Mirren was the constant attention of swarthy young Italian gentlemen who pestered her all the way from the sparkling Via Veneto, to the steps to her digs. On several occasions, she was forced to resort to physical counter-attacks and McDowell came to her rescue during one particularly unpleasant incident when she was in danger of being dragged into a car and kidnapped.

A handgun was brandished by one of the would-be kidnappers, but the lightning-fast and courageous McDowell screamed for Mirren to 'run for it'. He then pulled a whistle from his pocket and blasted away until the thugs drove off at speed. A girlfriend who visited Mirren in Rome soon after said that the actress was 'absolutely terrified' of stepping out alone in the evenings following the incident.

She said, 'Helen was molested everywhere she went. Well-known Italian actresses like Claudia Cardinale, who lived just outside Rome, and Sophia Loren would always have protection if they were in the city after dark. Ursula Andress, who lived in the centre, just put up with all the clowning and laughed it off. But Helen couldn't take it. She didn't like being touched by perfect strangers and many of them went a whole lot further than just touching. It was impossible for her in the end. She was glad to get out of there alive and in one piece.'

The erotic inserts were only ever to be seen in a German version of the movie which was rapidly pirated and sold across the world. By the time the movie wrapped, both Mirren and McDowell were mentally and physically exhausted.

The cast were unaware of how the finished product had been tampered with but had heard rumours. That would be for a battery of lawyers to sort out. McDowell warned that he had agreed with Mirren and Gielgud not to 'dub' the film (a process which involves the main actors adding their voices in a studio) if pornographic sequences had been edited into the drama.

In Italy, the furious and bitter Tinto Brass had gone to a judge in Rome and tried to block the film's worldwide release. The judge sided with him but the ruling meant next to nothing outside his courtroom. Guccione was in the clear. He countered that Brass was fired from the film while he was editing it for, among other things, his 'alteration and distortion without consultation with the producers of the basic idea of the film'. He accused Brass in his magazine of trying to sabotage the production and referred to him as 'a very sick guy'. Veteran director and producer Brass, who still lives in Rome, feels much the same way about Guccione who, in autumn 2002, was fighting a battle against throat cancer.

Brass today says from his Rome residence, 'Mirren was perfect for the role. She brought grace, sensuality and bravura. I think most of all, style and talent. She was also willing to do what we asked her to do without argument. She wanted to work hard for the film to give depth and artistic credibility to the part. She had the capacity which only great actors have to believe in the character they are playing in the film, and she could detach herself from it.'

Brass claims he directed the entire movie apart from the inserts which Guccione shot himself. The nudity was 'fine', until there was 'outside interference'. He says, 'Girls who worked for *Penthouse* were suddenly included. It was sad and very wrong.' He added, 'I have no regrets. I saw the film originally as anarchistic. The power of the orgy against the power of the Establishment.'

Brass later saw the more mature power of Mirren at work in Peter Greenaway's *The Cook, The Thief, His Wife and Her Lover* and said, 'I knew she was good. I just didn't know how good.'

Caligula – minus the obscene inserts – finally opened in the UK in autumn 1980 after Guccione had banned the UK critics from seeing it. Not one British star was 'available' to promote it, all being 'out of town' or 'involved in other projects'.

Those critics who did sneak in to catch a glimpse of *Caligula* were largely appalled by the scenes of a bride being raped on her wedding night and a man casually castrated after having had his penis tied into a knot. What staggered them most, however, was the total ineptitude of the camera work and emphasis on inconsequential explicit sexual activity on the fringe of almost every frame. Apart from the screen presence of Savoy and Mirren, the film's makers stood accused of runaway tastelessness and ineptitude. But Guccione didn't give a damn about the universal critisism and condemned livid McDowell for his 'poor attitude' through the columns of his own *Penthouse* magazine. They didn't get on from the start, with Guccione attacking the British actor for being 'shallow' when the going got tough.

Before becoming too ill to speak, Guccione said recently, 'McDowell just sucked up to the director as most actors do, and O'Toole was never sober. He was very very difficult to work with. At the end of the film, he ran off to Ireland, even though he knew he was scheduled to revoice his part. I had to send someone to get him.'

He claimed O'Toole then flew on to South Africa and Canada, giving them the slip until the producer threatened to use a stand-up impressionist to mimic him. As for Tinto Brass, 'He went out of his way to find ugly women and put them in the foreground. All the beautiful girls [actually Penthouse Pets] I sent over from America sat around all day doing nothing. He did it deliberately to subvert and undermine the film.'

O'Toole rejected every accusation thrown at him by Guccione and warned that his lawyers were watching the situation closely. McDowell, in turn, refused to be drawn into yet another bust-up. But he was unrepentant over his involvement. 'I hated *Caligula*, but I have no regrets about making it. It's probably the most expensive amateur film ever made. It was supposed to take 12 weeks but it went on for me for seven months. During one scene, a Penthouse Pet ran on to the set and began whipping me, which had nothing to do with the scene at all. Somebody had told her I was the star and if she wanted to get on she should make an impression with me! The soundtrack was hopeless because of the screaming and shouting going on.'

The highlight of the movie for him, he laughed, was when they cantered in his trusty steed Davide, who had the honour of being made a senator by Caligula. The emperor was quickly fading away from a bout of fever, and his horse was brought to his deathbed. 'He was a very beautiful beast,' McDowell recalled. 'He was the star of the picture. He was very famous, he'd been in *Ben Hur* and other Roman epics. I'd heard 18 families survived through his earnings. It's not easy for a horse to get into bed with anybody, you know.

'The first time we tried, the bed collapsed. This huge 20ft-wide bed fell apart. They then drugged the poor horse and lifted him on to the bed. I was supposed to whisper to him but, when I did, he started to get up, lashing out with his hooves. I was trapped by a microphone cable and then the handler was sent sailing through the air when the horse kicked him. He was in hospital for months. In future, I shall work with monsters who are at least being professional.'

But, humour apart, McDowell also disowned the film on Russell Harty's TV chat show, advising movie-goers to stay away. Producer Tom Gutteridge later commented dryly, 'The stars usually come on to plug their movies, not trash them. This was a first.' McDowell then remarkably changed his tune and said he thought the film was 'actually rather good'.

Mirren listened carefully to all the arguments and commented, 'I loved Tinto Brass and he became a friend. I thought he was an absolutely wonderful guy and I have to say that it is a film I have never bad-mouthed, partly because I never got around to seeing it. I don't really like excessive violence. Actually, Bob Guccione was very straightforward about who he was and what he is and what his intentions were. I thought people were hypocrites.'

She laid low for some months, staying well away from publicity machines and the controversy surrounding *Caligula*. At least she'd hit the jackpot for her bank manager.

Instead, Mirren bought herself a massive plot of land, a conservation area in Scotland, filled with forests of beech and oak trees, the little bit of heaven she had promised herself while making *As You Like It* for the BBC in the Highlands.

'My parents take it all in good spirit, all the publicity,' she said after the rumpus over *Caligula* had petered out. 'It can't have been much fun for them when *Caligula* came out.' She paused and grinned. 'You can only imagine what it must have been like at the bridge club.

'There was no reason to fear the outcome at first. The film was as it should be, and it had some anarchic elements to it. Malcolm, who is an old friend, wanted me to be in it with him ... and it was Rome. In the end, you do things for such funny reasons. It's like having kippers one day instead of hamburgers. I do remember thinking during the film that all this could be quite good for me. I'm quite prudish and I feel I shouldn't be uptight. I thought I wouldn't be, not after all those naked extras.'

She was also angered by critics who refused to condemn gratuitous violence and nudity in other so-called 'tasteful' Hollywood movies. She said, 'If *Caligula* has done anything, it is to reveal hypocrisy in its most naked form ...'

Why did she get involved? Was it purely the money? She said, 'If you're asked to be in a movie, a big movie, you don't usually say no, not unless something is terribly wrong. In this instance, there didn't seem to be.

'I was freeing myself of my inhibitions. It also gave me the down-payment for my flat and that is something I don't regret. It was very important for me to have a home and I was instilled with this working-class ethic about not getting into debt.'

She was paid £40,000 for four months' work, the biggest cheque she'd ever seen. And the money gave her economic stability for the first time in her life. She now owns a wood. Her accountant advised her to make a tax-effective investment – 2,000 beech trees and 2,000 oak trees set in 100 acres of virtually untouched Highland near Stirling. She said, 'I can go there and think, This is my wall, this is my waterfall. But most of all, I feel protective about the land. Nobody can spoil it.'

And now? 'Now? I can sit back and do nothing for a while.' That, however, has never been Mirren's way.

She may have joked to friends that she was 'recovering' or

'convalescing' after her Roman experience, but typical of the beast that is an actor, she was already looking forward to her next job. And there was plenty of work on offer. She had already reached the point in her career where independent British film-makers were continuously knocking on her door. They didn't have much money but they usually came armed with the more interesting scripts. She usually had her pick of the best that Soho's watering holes had to offer and would find herself quietly competing behind closed doors with the likes of Diana Rigg for the top-notch commercial stage and screen roles. They were few and far between in any case.

Mirren had a more attractive string to her bow because, paradoxically, she was willing to strip off for a role without having to have a crescendo of insane arguments, so long as the material wasn't gratuitously obnoxious. Others, like Rigg and Jane Fonda – she used a body double in the Vietnam War drama *Coming Home* – refused to peel away the layers under any circumstances. Hollywood still wanted girls who said 'Yes'.

But the Mirren of old didn't want to be Marilyn Monroe. 'I've never been attracted to the idea of being a movie star,' she said. 'It's very much manipulation and hype and I like the idea of being an actor – the touring, the backstage jokes, despair, tears, cheap hotels and drunken evenings in the bar. You feel insecure and frightened and there are times when it is impossible to read the Sunday newspapers because it seems everyone is working apart from you.'

Dennis Potter was already being hailed as the new TV messiah. The writer's unorthodox tableau of the suburban middle classes in *Pennies from Heaven* was the talk of the BBC and had many a senior ITV drama executive wondering where their next 'biggie' was coming from. Potter's offbeat adventures of song sheet pedlar Arthur Parker and the beautiful young teacher played by Cheryl Campbell mesmerised the nation as they mimed to a superb compilation of pre-war hits. Bob Hoskins was the star and the emerging Gemma Craven, another St Bernard's High School old girl, stole tabloid headlines as his prim and proper wife when she rouged her nipples to excite the frustrated Arthur. It was billed as 'a play with music in six parts'. And it caused a sensation.

And the magical, untouchable Potter struck gold again with another completely offbeat piece called *Blue Remembered Hills*, which the BBC had drawn up on their *Play for Today* list.

The charming tale was, on the face of it, a simple study of seven West Country children idling the summer away in 1943. But what made the production unique was that the 'kids' would all be played by mature actors regressing to precocious childhood and being able to bring an intelligence and quirkiness to Potter's lively, witty script. Potter was fascinated by the theme that, while adults can be horrible, children can also be pretty unpleasant. Author and TV writer Fay Weldon was later to call the ex-TV critic 'the best television playwright in the world'. Nobody argued, not even those who had been quick to slam his dance with the devil in the earlier *Brimstone and Treacle*.

Mirren leapted at the opportunity to spend the summer of 1978 in the West Country with Michael Elphick, Janine Duvitski, Colin Welland, Robin Ellis, John Bird and Colin Jeavons for six weeks under the direction of Brian Gibson. They rehearsed in Soho, at the BBC's uninspirational 'Acton Hilton', and Barnes Common in south-west London, before setting off like a mob on a beano to the coast.

Duvitski, who had already booked her place in TV history via her irritating nurse in Mike Leigh's *Abigail's Party*, sensed the mood was 'pure fun and games' as they approached their hotel in the village of Mere on the road to Yeovil in Wiltshire.

'I didn't twig at first ... I spent ages looking through the script for my part before I realised what was going on, that we were the children. We all went a bit mad, I think, because we were playing kids,' she recalled. 'We actually had a day on Barnes Common together playing as children before we left. God knows what people passing by must have thought, with us running around building dens, kicking balls, shoving and pushing each other.

Doing the stuff children do. We reverted back at speed and didn't get a grip on ourselves.'

Once they'd unpacked and got their instructions and call sheets for the first day's work, they set about the hard business of rehearsing a professional, high-profile production ... by enjoying themselves. Led by the late Michael Elphick, a lovable, drunken, clown-like figure and something of a womaniser, the adults had no problems regressing in the saloon bar or the countryside surrounding Mere for six generally hilarious weeks.

'I think it's fair to say we drank copious amounts of alcohol,' laughed Duvitski. 'Michael Elphick got straight down to it. He was such fun, even when he was drunk.

'Once, while Helen and I were waiting to do a scene, we found this wonderful wine store and bought a couple of bottles. When they had gone, we bought a crate and dragged it around the hills close to the town with us. We were in this kind of open truck the BBC had hired and made a right old mess.'

One production underling was far from impressed when he saw the debris and witnessed the girls' behaviour. He accused them of 'abusing' BBC property, demanding that they immediately return their clothes to wardrobe and leave the vehicle in the condition in which they found it. Mirren, now almost in character as the precious, pretty but far from angelic Angela, stood her ground. The public-school type who fancied himself as a producer of the future gave her another tongue-lashing. Slowly, provocatively, she started to undress. And as he implored her to 'desist', she let the last garment fall to the floor of the open truck. She was stark naked. 'Now what? Here are the clothes ... take them!' she said. In the background, the lads in the crew whistled and applauded. Her chum Duvitski, who played sad, plain Audrey, howled with mirth. 'We were very naughty,' she said. 'This chap just didn't know what to do with himself. His face was a picture.'

Mirren, then in a relationship with photographer James Wedge, had something of a crush on the director Gibson and the feeling was most definitely mutual. The lecherous Elphick was also offering to give Mirren nightly massages, an offer which she politely declined.

Duvitski said, 'Brian was very keen on Helen. Very keen. We devised this plan in the end. We'd wait until he was fast asleep and put Helen into his bed so when he woke up he thought she had spent the night with him. He was so pissed most of the time in the evenings that he didn't have a clue as to whether he'd actually "performed", so to speak. But he looked so pleased with himself on set those mornings, he had that gleam in his eye. We never ever let on ... well, at least I didn't.'

Some of the mob, including Duvitski, Mirren and Gibson, stayed on for a couple of days after filming was over. 'We had a riot,' said Duvitski. 'I think it was something to do with the mood of the piece, plus the fact only a few of us had any responsibility waiting – no children or husbands then to deal with. After six weeks or so, it wasn't surprising we knew each other pretty well! Everyone just lost their inhibitions. I think Dennis Potter got the result he wanted because of that.'

She didn't work again with Mirren for another 16 years, playing a small part in *The Madness of King George*. She said, 'Helen was already very well known but she was not at all grand. She just wanted to do good work. But she was quite a catch and she felt she had this responsibility because of her image. She thought people expected her to be this awful sex symbol which she didn't want to be. She was a very intelligent woman with this fantastic body. It was daunting for her being our kind of Marilyn Monroe. She didn't want that kind of pressure. It just wasn't her, in any case. She was never full of herself or showed any vanity.'

Towards the end of 1978, she starred as a busty barmaid pulling a lot more than pints in the TV play *The Quiz Kid* which was produced by ATV in February 1979. The family comedy about how a bright young lecturer revives the fortunes of a hopeless quiz team brought her back in partnership with Michael Elphick, who was still offering her the opportunity to sample the 'life-giving power of touch' from his nimble fingers. RSC veteran John Woodvine was in support, with Peter Jeffrey and Sheila Steafel.

In another rapid return to the BBC, she played the legendary prophetess Kassandra in the star-studded trilogy *The Serpent's Son*, which had been adapted from Aeschylus's Greek drama *The Oresteia*. Her long pre-Raphelite locks had been snipped away to combine with dark eye shadow, which left her looking like a very modern temptress, a Grecian Bond girl no less.

There was no way she was going to escape her voluptuous image, especially with the *Caligula* affair still on many people's lips. 'People see what they want to see in you and, thereafter, that's all they seem to expect,' she admitted. 'I have been acting in Shakespeare and other classical plays since I was 19, but people only seem to remember the sleazy or sensational roles.' *The Serpent's Son* was hardly going to change anyone's mind about her. 'It's marvellous, really over the top,' she said. 'I come on and rant and rave for 20 minutes and then I am stabbed to death.'

Mirren's sexuality was still a vibrant element in her personal repertoire. It formed a large part of her appeal as she glanced back at the rapidly fading Seventies. And nothing was about to change.

It was late spring 1979 when she arrived on stage at the Riverside Theatre in Hammersmith, London, to star as Isabella, the nun whose virtue is tested in a new production of *Measure for Measure* directed by Peter Gill, following his earlier successes there with *The Cherry Orchard* and *The Changeling*. Her pay was £50 a week, but she was close to home around the corner off the Fulham Broadway and getting a real buzz out of playing a nun, even though she would not be dressed in a wimple and habit in Gill's interpretation. Little did she realise, but two extremely important but anonymous figures drifted in to see her in action. They were to have a major impact on her fledgling movie career.

Neither did she have to leave home for Lord Delfont's EMI Group, in order to make a new version of the disaster movie, *SOS Titanic*. She played a real-life survivor, sympathetic but cool stewardess Mary Sloan, among a cast which included American stars David Janssen as John Jacob Astor and Cloris Leachman, with a fine British line-up represented by David Warner, Ian Holm and Harry Andrews. The drama, which focused firmly on three couples in the three different classes on board, was made largely at Shepperton Studios in Surrey on a sound stage. Sadly, nobody took director William Hale's pedestrian remake of the naval tragedy seriously. Originally, there had been high hopes of a major theatrical release. Janssen was a hugely popular TV celebrity from the long-running *The Fugitive* series, and the subject matter was gigantic enough. But the budget wasn't and Hale needed more than 'serious personal interacting' between the shipmates to make the feature work. They also developed a sinking feeling when the ship struck the iceberg in James Costigan's script. Hale and Co were so hard up that they were forced to use footage from the earlier Titanic drama *A Night to Remember* which starred Kenneth Moore. *SOS Titanic* was released in America in September 1979. It sank without trace.

'My own film career has been peculiarly disastrous,' Mirren observes, drawing a veil over the Seventies. 'Even *O Lucky Man!* was a box-office failure, though I think it's the kind of film people will come back to in 20 years from now.' And she has been proved right.

Things were going to get better. Much better.

5

HIPPIE DAYS ARE
HERE AGAIN

The weird, indecipherable tattoo on Helen Mirren's left hand
close to the base of her thumb has long been a cause of debate
and fascination. She has spent most of her career covering it up,
hiding it away from the cameras. Policewomen were banned back in
the Nineties from having tattoos so she was forced to keep the
designs out of sight for *Prime Suspect*.

In fact, the tattoo, which left many a producer confused and
exasperated, is there as a result of a little-known but bizarre chapter
in her life and career.

She'd joke about the two interlocking V shapes to strangers,
telling them she'd got drunk as a teenager in Southend and meant
to have 'Mum & Dad' etched there instead. Occasionally, she'd spin
a yarn about being in the navy – before having a sex-change
operation. The truth? She once explained with a grin, 'I'm a
member of a secret society and I'm not allowed to say any more.'

The answer to the strange drawings lay in a trip she made to the
African continent and then on to the Badlands of America where a
Pueblo Native American artist left his mark on her body. She later

claimed she was drunk with other actors. Others said she had a brief romance with the artist. The message, according to a close friend, was a 'spiritual' birthmark and a sign of good fortune. The symbolic momento, which she will carry to her grave, in fact, comes down to two words – 'equal' and 'opposite'.

What was true about the Sixties child was that she'd never quite left her treasured visions of the Hippieland of San Francisco's Haight Ashbury behind. But the sound of the Beatles's 'All You Need Is Love' was still ringing in her ears as the Seventies gathered pace. She woke up most days with metaphoric 'flowers' in her hair. Perhaps it was her genteel middle-class upbringing or her disciplined education under the close scrutiny of nuns which made her want to break away from the norm, free herself of the restrictive chains of her youth. Either way, she'd never really cut loose. She'd never quite had the courage to take one extra puff on a joint or 'blow her mind' until she wasn't in control any longer. She could even count on one hand the number of times she'd drunk more than she should.

Mirren was a divided soul – part Bohemian, part Establishment. Her off-kilter temperament could lead to quiet but massive depressions. She'd say it was her Russian heritage, the neurotic Eastern European in her. The moodiness was part of her driving force. One friend who knew her from her days at the RSC said, 'Though she was hugely successful and well liked, she'd just roll up into an emotional ball for days on end, barely saying a word. You'd never know what would trigger it off. It could be an innocently made remark. She was very very sensitive, especially to critisism of any kind.

'You worried for her. She took the work extremely seriously and gave that 100 per cent. But she also had this thing about the way we all were, from governments to the City, from the administration at the RSC to Third World poverty. She wanted to do her bit and felt rather useless. She wanted to take up issues but didn't feel capable. She lacked confidence when she wasn't on that stage or behind that camera. She wanted to be taken "seriously" and then she just wanted to have "fun". She created her own series of crises that didn't exist. The depressions, if that's what they were, would just disappear overnight. She'd just snap out of it. She'd just turn up with a smile on her face and say, "Now, what are we all doing?" and that would be it.

'She was certainly a bit of a handful for any fella, though, who cared ... she looked absolutely fantastic. Anyway, a lot of blokes found that kind of electricity and "mystery" very exciting.

'But she'd made up her mind she wanted to "expand", to just face a new challenge but have a completely different experience. She also wanted to see the world as it truly was. We didn't know what she meant until she made her announcement.

'There was a clear division between those who thought, fantastic and were terribly envious and others who thought she'd gone crackers. But, generally speaking, most were envious of what she was about to do and do it with.'

It was the autumn of 1972 and, bag by bag, she was preparing to race across to Paris to join an international troupe of actors who were being drawn together by her mentor Peter Brook, who had taken her under his wing at the RSC. After a spell living close to Stratford-upon-Avon, he rented an apartment on the Left Bank where he lived but also owned a house in the fashionable district of Kensington in London. Outside Paris, he kept a small country cottage.

The innovative director, the son of Russian scientists, was a genius. He was born in 1925, and when he was seven he directed a four-hour version of *Hamlet* for his parents. At 16, he left school to write scripts for commercials. He went to Magdalen College, Oxford University, and at 21 directed his first production at Stratford. At 22, he was the first Director of Productions at the Royal Opera House, Covent Garden and was already the 'Golden Boy' of the theatre. He had worked with the RSC from 1962 and his work included the 1970 production of *A Midsummer Night's*

Dream which was set in a white gymnasium combining elements of circus and *commedia dell'arte*.

Having directed some 60 productions, as he neared 50, he packed up and left England needing a 'greater theatrical challenge'. He was, without question, one of the world's leading stage directors and was called a 'guru' and an 'ogre' in the same breath.

In 1971, he had founded the independent initiative Le Centre International de Créations Théâtrales in the French capital. His later productions aimed to combine elements from different cultures. The revered stage and film director had also made the excellent film version of William Golding's *Lord of the Flies* which today ranks as part of the staple diet for many teenagers taking their GSCE in English.

Strangers misunderstood Brook, whose brooding could be associated with his Russian blood. He could be seen as austere or withdrawn but, in fact, he loved New York's vibrant nightlife and could be daringly spontaneous.

But what he now had in mind was, indeed, ground-breaking territory in every sense. He intended going where no stage or screen director had ever gone before, on an experimental and potentially extremely dangerous three-month-long, 8,500-mile expedition of the African continent. To take mime, music and theatre where it had never gone before. After their fleet of Land Rovers had snaked its way through the Sahara Desert from Algeria, they would be 'entertaining' the locals in remote villages in Nigeria, Togo, Dahomey and Mali. The eccentric English poet Ted Hughes would be joining them en route, perhaps to record their finest hours in verse.

The plan was to perform four improvisational plays which dealt with traditional themes such as love and death. The highlight of the production was Brook's mankind-meets-nature piece called *The Conference of the Birds*, in which a variety of species meet to discuss how best to find God, the journey involving the crossing of seven valleys from the Valley of the Quest to The Valley of Poverty.

What they'd also be doing was dodging fist-sized flying bugs and a variety of deadly snakes as they camped out in sleeping bags. And that wasn't allowing for the odd angry elephant or wild dog. The risks of suffering ill-health or being hurt were enormous.

The ten-strong company included Mirren, her eccentric RSC chum Bruce Myers and Brook's actress wife Natasha Parry, who courageously and perhaps foolishly allowed their two young children – 11-year-old Irina and Simon, aged six – to join the party when they reached Nigeria. Parry's mother was Russian and her father half-Greek.

The naturally stunning actress, who'd appeared in movies with the likes of Rex Harrison, Orson Welles and John Mills, had married Brook in 1951 but her career had been seriously disrupted through hellish attacks of tuberculosis.

The Russian background links between her and her husband had always been strong and there was an instant bonding with Mirren partly due to her parentage.

Myers, then an adventurous 30-year-old, had made history by being expelled from the Royal Academy of Dramatic Art for being drunk on stage while playing Napoleon in *Man of Destiny*. He was in Brook's production of *A Midsummer Night's Dream* after another actor fell ill and gave the performance of his life. But he suffered from severe recurring stage fright and left the RSC after three years because of the perpetual terror. He went off to the Lake District to teach sailing. He was clearly infatuated with Mirren and the word was that they had the briefest of flings before she decided to cool the situation. The outrageous lawyer's son from the North of England had more or less given up the theatre when Mirren urged him to join Brook's 'mission impossible'.

There were other notables in the party. From France there was charming television actor François Marthouret and Sylvain Corthay, and from Germany the black actress Miriam Goldschmidt with her wild, surreal imagination. The incomparable Yoshi Oida flew in from from Japan, while athletic Malick Bagayogo from Mali would be travelling through his own homeland where he was a legend, having recovered from a crippling illness as a child to become the nation's leading actor. There was also a French Government 'observer', the shy, awkward Daniel Charlot.

Members of the group said Mirren's late arrival, two months before departure as the last recruit, left her as an outsider, making her feel 'depressed and threatened' during her introductory spell.

Writer John Heilpern who kept a diary of events was to note, 'When she's vulnerable she can be curt and stand-offish, mannered almost. There's a melancholy side to her which surprises people. When she's on form, when she's confident and happy, she's unbeatable.'

Nobody had ever attempted anything like it before or since and, in December, they left their base in Paris to take their raw, fringe-style company off to bring a new art form to the indigenous population in their mud-hut village environment. Famine, disease and danger awaited. Their plan was to reach the town of Kano in Nigeria by Christmas. Mirren's pay? Next to nothing. Did she care? Not a jot. Was she frightened? She was terrified.

But she was equally fanatical about exploring the artistic soul of civilisation with Brook. She said, 'Peter is difficult to work with because he always demands the best of you. I could have stayed in Britain and done TV and plays and made a lot of money but I had total faith in what Peter was doing.'

Mirren's friends and family were concerned and bemused by her rejection of lucrative work on offer in Britain and her exit into darkest Africa, in the pre-tourist days of the early Seventies. But they also knew how determined she could be. As one friend put it, 'Her mind was made up and it was a mind she was determined to expand. She was in a hurry to learn and a hurry to establish herself. She was trying to find that balance. Her mother was frantic and spent months talking about inoculations and eating the right food. Helen thought it was hilarious when the word "pyjamas" came up. That would have certainly scared the natives off, apart from giving Bruce Myers the biggest laugh of his life!'

She could hardly wait to get out into the Bush and sleep under the stars. And so off she jolly well went. The tour was backed by $60,000 worth of American money (worth about £250,000 today) with photographer Mary-Ellen Mark recording events for *Life* magazine. The tour company Minitrek, used to dealing with big-game hunters, suddenly found themselves dealing with eccentric, egotistical actors. The omens were not good.

On arrival in Algiers, they were briefed by their Camp Master, Royston Bennett, a 31-year-old former schoolteacher. He was responsible for their survival and explained that, during the desert crossing, they would be restricted to one wash a day. They didn't bother bringing a portable lavatory because of the large number of travellers, so people would have to make use of the abundant sand. They would sleep in the nude to keep warm. Mirren was nonplussed, enquiring, 'Can't I even wear my socks?'

There was, however, not a Land Rover in sight and her first night was spent in a small hotel in the city centre. Once they did get going, they drove only 130 miles on their first day, ending up freezing to death in their overcoats on sand hills with the half-crazed Myers getting his vehicle stuck in the mud. Mirren had made up her mind that she was going to be one of the 'workers' and volunteered for the roughest job, daily digging a hole to bury rubbish. But she became tense and unhappy during her first spell with the company, using sign language to talk to an African in the party and taking refuge in a Land Rover at night where she read Graham Greene's *Brighton Rock* or made entries in her diary. Some suggested that she was 'jealous and contemptuous' of others in the group. She was certainly feeling homesick as she wrote, 'We are supposed to live this journey as a disciplined, thoughtful, organised, organic, inspired, fun in fun time, which is not too often time, alert, helpful, hard working, oh so together and admirable group. I dream homely banal dreams.'

And she must have wished she was back in Blighty when they performed halfway across the Sahara in the town of In Salah. A stick suddenly flew out of somebody's hand and struck her above the eye, causing a flow of blood and tears. It wasn't long before she was sobbing again.

In the eerie darkness of the desert, her unpredictable buddie Myers, who'd wash in freezing cold water to 'test and amuse' himself, had disappeared. Search parties were sent out as the scorching sun began to rise. Myers caused widespread panic for close to eight hours before being brought down from one of the highest mountains in the area by one of the search parties. He was apologetic, while the normally unruffled Brook was apoplectic. Mirren was in tears and hugged the ex-RSC man before admonishing him for his behaviour.

Though Brook may have been something of a theatrical 'messiah', Mirren wasn't alone in questioning exactly why he had chosen Africa as a New World for their art. But his explanation was enough to get their adrenalin pumping. 'Why Africa?' he said. 'You will never have a greater opportunity to answer the question. Why are we here? You will never have a greater chance to learn and understand. We must use our eyes every second of the day.'

True to her reputation, one of the first opportunities Mirren had to shine as an actress with Brook's troupe was portraying, totally against type, the 'Old Hag' in his improvised piece, *The Shoe Show*. The story revolved around a shoe collector who abandons a pair of shoes which are found by an old hag who is given back her youth.

A monarch falls in love with her but the romance ends in tragedy due to her duplicity and his greed. Mirren danced and sang, bent double creeping and cursing her way around a carpet, and had the crowd in the poor Tuareg village of Tamanrasset under her spell. And, perhaps more importantly, she felt as though she had at last bonded with her own nomadic community.

Onwards they went, deep into Niger where Brook's performing warriors were struck down by bouts of diarrhoea and nausea. The gravest danger was malaria and they had to take pills every morning and sleep under nets. Christmas was spent just outside Zinder, close to the border with Nigeria, where Mirren made Christmas decorations out of baking foil. She became so emotional she burst into a flood of tears.

Mirren finally succumbed to a light strain of malaria as they rested outside the Nigerian city of Kano in the grounds of the university campus. Her only consolation was that most of the crew and almost every other actor had also contracted the disease. The better news was that they were able to make themselves English-style breakfasts and take cold showers in the student quarters which were more like army barracks.

And all was well until, in what closely resembled a biblical farce, Mirren refused to have anything to do with the slaughtering of a ram as a 'a form of theatre' in the village of Dungung. The animal had been offered to Brook by way of payment for bringing *The Conference of Birds* to them. The natives had not got enough food to feed the entire cast and crew. Voices were raised against any kind of sacrifice, especially by a vegetarian in their line-up. A vote was taken before the dissenters lost the day and the ram had its throat slit by the French actor Sylvain Corthay, a disciple of the famous stage icon Jean-Louis Barrault. Many of the blood-spattered actors turned various shades of white and green with shock, as they watched the blood pour out. It was then skinned, boiled and eaten. Unsmiling, Mirren's only comment to one of Brook's closest allies was, 'If you feel hungry and want to eat, then kill and eat it honestly. Do not kill to bring anyone closer to their work.'

Brook and Mirren were then fearful for the safety of the group when the crew walked out on the expedition, claiming to be exhausted and demoralised by events. They headed for the city of Ife where they camped in a forest clearing by a swamp. Bullfrogs croaked all night and they were under threat from mosquitoes, snakes and hideously large bugs. When they woke up, they were covered in flesh-eating ants. To make matters worse, Myers and several of the other actors were knocked sideways by malaria again. Water filters were blamed for the outbreak and the medical dosages of salt and vitamin pills were doubled. A depressed and disillusioned Mirren went into one of her most sullen moods and, according to those closest to her at the time, felt threatened and unhappy, only relaxing when she sat African children on her knee in the villages they passed through. 'It's difficult to laugh any more,' she said, lapsing into another long silence.

But laugh she did when she realised her sexual allure had not vanished in the night, along with her sense of humour. Brook's company had reached the town of Oshogbo on the road to Lagos when their handsome African tribesman and accompanying musician Ayansola revealed his true feelings for her. For over two months, they had assumed that he had been talking to her in some strange African dialect. And she had been politely attempting to unravel his peculiar Swahili accent, often using sign language. But all of that changed when he suddenly announced through a translator that not only was he a poet, but also of royal stock. 'Who are you ... who do you think you are?' he told Mirren. 'The moon and stars are all very well ... but screw me! Screw me!' She thought it was hysterical that she thought she'd been having deep, meaningful conversations with the African night after night. Instead, he'd been trying to get her clothes off! She giggled again and whispered to Parry, 'It's interesting to note that men are basically the same the world over, whether you're in the West End or in the middle of Africa. Does it get any more flattering than this?'

Mirren and her new bunch of friends were soon to perform *The Conference of Birds* for the last time in Africa at a nearby open-air theatre to an audience of over 500.

Then they jumped into their Land Rovers and headed across the border to Dahomey where they slept and swam before the long drive north through the Sahara back to Algiers. Their 100 days of Africa was over and they had survived!

They returned to Paris and then went on to America where their tour started in the Californian mission town of San Juan Bautista and ended at the Brooklyn Academy of Music with three different versions of *The Conference of Birds* in one night.

To this day, the introverted side of Mirren takes over when anyone mentions her African experiences, regarding her voyage of discovery with Brook as mystical and sacred. Years later, she was still haunted by the sound of Brook lecturing her about how she should have delivered a line. 'I dream that he is telling me I am not good enough, which he did to all of us frequently. He was the person I was most afraid of in life. I think he was a genius, but I don't know whether I could have ever worked with him again.'

Brook is still with her, and is likely to be for ever. The tattoo on her hand is a constant reminder of the civilisations she left behind. Gone but not forgotten. Reflecting on her time with Brook, Mirren remembers particularly their work with 'a theatre group in San Juan and also with the American Theater of the Deaf. In that era, American theatre was pretty extraordinary; there were some amazing theatre groups that were exploding out. It was an extraordinary learning time of my life.'

Mirren bounced back to Britain and the RSC in Stratford-upon-Avon from Brook's tour full of new enthusiasm for her craft and emotionally 'enlightened' by her often dangerous close encounter with Third World poverty. She had learned much from her theatrical safari with Brook and the later 'teepee' tour to the Native American reservation in Minnesota, where she had briefly gone on to 'another plane' while she was being tattooed.

Mirren was still clearly light in head and hippie in spirit after her arduous travels, when she came to bed down with upper-crust pals Princess Margaret and Roddy Llewellyn.

It was the spring of 1973, and you could hear the sounds of Nepalese drums beating out across the Warwickshire countryside from Ditchford Farm near Shipston-on-Stour. In the background, girls sculpted horses in clay while others carved toy figures and a landscape which would later be seen at an exhibition in London. There were no rules or regulations about washing-up or cooking among the young crowd who retreated from the pressures of urban life to produce wood and fabric arts and crafts. The large, red-bricked farmhouse had been empty for over 20 years until, in November 1969, it was seen by a group of friends who wanted to get away from what had been 'Swinging London' and create a new constructive order. In America and France, they called it a 'commune'. Lady Sarah Ponsonby (though she claimed not to be a 'Lady'), the niece of the Earl of Bessborough and unofficial leader of the pack, preferred not to use the word.

They just wanted to get out of London, explained Sarah, who was then 25. 'I didn't like the hustle. People can't think properly in London. What I was doing was soul-destroying. I painted horses in a certain style and made a good living by it, but there wasn't any way I could expand on it.

'I thought if some of my friends could get together, all with talents of various sorts, something might emerge. None of us had too much talent in any direction so we thought we might put it all together. It was freezing cold and damp when we first saw the house but it looked friendly. We were full of optimism and energy. You get a feeling in your life that there is nothing you can't do.'

Her band of Establishment misfits included George Galitzine who was a freelance writer and soon to become Mirren's 'semi-serious' boyfriend. There was an Indian drummer, Sam Gopal, with his group of musicians and art student Sandy Campbell. And there was Australian wildlife expert-turned-society columnist John Rendell, who'd occasionally have a lion or tiger cub by his side. Rendell, who was later to marry society wheeler-dealer Liz Brewer, quipped, 'My parents are absolutely stunned that I have lived in one place for four months.'

They moved in on 1 January 1970, and over three years there was a hardcore of 20 'residents' at Ditchford. Ponsonby used savings to help renovate part of the house, plant fruit trees and lay turf. They put a new bathroom in and they plastered, and the apples from their orchard yielded 120 gallons of cider. A daily help came in three times a week to clean up. There was one clock in the house and nobody wore a watch. Everyone had to contribute £1 each towards dinner. They tried not to quarrel over money and anyone who found themselves with extra cash paid the bills.

Mirren said, 'I'd heard about it from a friend and I was scared about meeting a lot of nobby people, so I was a bit uptight. But they are not like that and I grew towards them so quickly I moved in.'

Outsiders and passing sceptics pointed at the line of smart parked cars, colour television and other expensive gadgetry on view. As one local puts it today, 'They were just messin' about at being these "of the land" mob, pretending to be anti-materialist. They liked money as much as the rest of us. They came from those sort of backgrounds. They didn't know what it was like to have to rough it.'

They did, however, have some businesslike intentions, with Ponsonby and Galitzine setting up their company Parsenn Sally & Co, named after a prized cow on the commune. The idea was to open a restaurant and grow as much of the food as possible to go on the menu at the farm.

Quiet in manner, introverted Ponsonby, who, to this day, remains one of Mirren's closest friends, was perplexed by the general reaction to them, while always sensing a politically hostile press. She said, 'I think we have gone back to childhood here. We play a lot of games, make short films and fill our cupboards full of jam.'

There was also a menagerie of pets including an Irish Wolfhound called Murphy, three horses and a gaggle of cats. For the most part, there was calm, interspersed with chaos, and they kept themselves to themselves. Ponsonby was convinced they were seeing the shape of things to come. 'We'll be here, all of us, very old, whizzing around in our wheelchairs, still getting things done,' she said. The owner of the property, which they rented, thought otherwise.

The fun was, in fact, about to start. By the sizzling summer of 1976, the middle-class rebels had moved on to Wiltshire and the equally remote Surrendell Farm, at the end of a dirt track through a field set against the backdrop of 47 acres of countryside.

The craze for commune living had more or less died out and the drive appeared to be away from alternative lifestyles back to what John Major later laughingly referred to as 'basics'.

But there was much excitement in the area when interior designer and architect Michael Tickner and several friends, including Rendell and Ponsonby, paid £50,000 for the nine-bedroom Jacobean farmhouse, which came complete with the alleged ghost of a Cromwellian soldier. The restaurant, Parsenn Sally, had now become a reality 15 miles away in Bath. Vegetables from Surrendell were supplemented by those grown by their neighbour. She was the actress Diane Cilento, Sean Connery's ex-wife, who lived on a nearby farm in Pinkney, near Sherston.

Happy Ponsonby and her weary bunch of Mother Earth devotees took little time settling in at dilapidated Surrendell, having raised the funds to guarantee their security of tenure. They sought freedom, peace, creativity and perhaps a small profit from Parsenn Sally. What they actually got were hordes of the dreaded media, photographs of Ponsonby gardening in the semi-nude and many column inches. And they must have left their business brains somewhere in Pall Mall because Parsenn Sally didn't last longer than the average frozen turkey as a gastronomic enterprise.

The new inhabitants were a heady mix of landed gentry and aristocracy. There was ex-debutante Susie Allfrey, who actually grew up at Balmoral where her stepfather, the nineteenth Earl of Caithness, was a leading administrative figure. Richard Courtauld, of the famous fibre and chemicals family, was often resident, along with another deb, Katie Windsor-Lewis, the daughter of a Welsh Guards colonel. And then Mirren would surface with Galitzine or her friend, American actor Ben Carruthers.

Mirren at that time was appearing in Ben Travers's farce *The Bed Before Yesterday* at the Lyric Theatre in the West End, which she had nicknamed 'the Cat House'. She was in a strange mood and had put the name 'Sweet Sugar Dumpling' on her dressing-room door.

Mirren and her band of farming artistes had been together for only a few months when it was discovered that their head gardener, Roddy Llewellyn, was holidaying with Princess Margaret on Mustique. The younger son of Lietenant-Colonel Harry Llewellyn, who won Olympic gold on Foxhunter, was Shrewsbury-educated and had been working at the Herald's Office while DJ'ing for the London social set. He now wore a silver earring and dreamed of becoming a market gardener and serious horticultural expert. He'd been introduced to Princess Margaret at a house party in Scotland and she had taken an instant shine to him.

Mirren had been given one of the better rooms by Tickner, whose sister slept in the attic while Ponsonby occupied an area of the barn. Mirren couldn't believe the scenes at what was supposed to have been 'secluded, scenic, soulful Surrendell', as the press went after Llewellyn in his blue Ford Transit van. The late Tickner became Pythonesque at the time, saying, 'The Princess has endeared herself to all of us. She is a nice lady and we don't want all of this distasteful gossip.'

HRH was given the most comfortable room in the house, with Indian blankets on the walls and ceiling and a comfortable mattress on the floor. In the evening, she joined sing-songs around a camp fire with 'Chattanooga Choo-Choo' apparently being her favourite number. And she was not adverse to 'roughing it' as the commune had no running water or electricity in its infancy. There was, however, a TV sited in the Victorian wing of the house.

Llewellyn, who is perenially youthful, despite being in his mid-fifties, maintains today that he slept at night in his van which was parked in the barn. He was recovering from a nervous breakdown caused by press attention. Remembering his time at the farm, he said, 'It was in a bit of a state. If the average visitor didn't have his wits about him, he'd walk through the front door and find the carpet swallowing him up before he landed in the cellar. It was drop-out time for all of us and it seemed a good place to go to.'

When the press first got wind that he was there, he fled. He said, 'The long lane down the farm was jammed with cars. Suddenly, something snapped in me and I made my escape across the fields to Diane Cilento's place. I made many dramatic escapes from the photographers. People would tell me I was "public property", but that's absolute nonsense. I didn't ask for it and it was a terrible shock. It is a very, very difficult thing to cope with.'

But cope he did. He returned to the fold and was introduced to Mirren. 'I was in awe of Helen,' he confessed. 'She was very striking. Irresistibly delicious. There are very few women I have ever met who exude sex from every pore but she was and is one. She would come and stay two or three days at a time with her nephew Simon, who was a kind of "escort". You could tell it was an adventure for her.

'Helen was more of a stage actress at this time. I think very few people had seen her in films. She had this amazing reputation from the RSC and we knew she was a fantastic star. She was this leading light with the Workers' Revolutionary Party. I can't even imagine what she thought of me and my associations.

'For my fiftieth birthday at Kensington Palace, I sat between her and Princess Margaret. Who knows what she thought of me, this gardening expert, this "friend of the royals" ... well, one royal. I think Helen represented a republican corner.'

And what did he think was the object of the 'commune' exercise? 'It was a bit like preach love, not war. We were all rejecting society for one reason or another. There was a backlash of disillusionment, a hangover from the Sixties, this wonderful period when we all felt free and not terribly responsible.

'People were still enjoying themselves, wearing outrageous fashions and following new spiritual beliefs, like gurus and going on spiritual trails. I'm not sure at the end of the day that any of us were truly being political. We just wanted to get away. We were terribly lucky to involve ourselves in totally irresponsible behaviour. It was cheap to live and we didn't need much money to survive.'

The 'deal', as he put it, was that he looked after the vegetable garden and provided enough food for the kitchen. 'There was no code or rules. Nothing like that. There was a lot of coming and going ... you'd come down to breakfast and see so many different people. I would spend most of my time in the garden. I couldn't spend time sitting around because I found that infuriating. It was also the best possible therapy.'

He stayed for almost a year before taking off to study horticulture at college. 'But I never saw any drugs being taken,' he said. 'The police started arriving regularly after I had gone.

'The locals had their eyebrows permanently raised in an expression of disapproval. They had goldfish mouths wide open in amazement when they saw us in our flowery shirts.'

Another local, retired farmer Vic Rawlins, had lived in the Wiltshire backwater for most of his life before Ponsonby and her set of upper-middle-class drifters arrived on the scene. All was well for some months until Mr Rawlins, not the most orthodox of characters, had his telephone moved from the farmhouse into a shed in the middle of a nearby field. Unknown to Ponsonby, guests at Surrendell began to creep out and make calls and the bill grew and grew until Mr Rawlins's patience ran out. They originally paid for their calls in a mutually acceptable and most novel way, by delivering bales of hay to Mr Rawlins's farm. But when a cheque for the amount due failed to appear, he threatened to sue. 'The whole business was daft. Some of them were calling friends in Australia. But they didn't like parting with cheques or money,' he said. 'But they were good fun.

'They had a vegetable patch outside the farmhouse but it was all weeds when I looked by. Whoever he was, I don't think they had an expert gardener, or maybe the land wasn't good, but it looked a mess. I am sure he has learned a lot since from his experiences. No wonder the restaurant didn't do well, though, if it was relying on food from there. There were some funny goings on all right ... they used my electric fan for the pigs to keep them cool because it was so warm that summer. The animals just roamed around. They were more like pets than for food. But Ms Mirren would always give you the time of day if you saw her in the field. She'd always be very smart, nicely dressed.'

By autumn, the farm commune had collapsed with Parsenn Sally also going bust, owing £28,000. Almost everyone dispersed, with only Ponsonby staying on. Michael Tickner said, 'Everyone has gone their separate ways. The main reason, I suppose, is that people have got to earn money. The days when you could just live in the country for nothing have passed by.'

The police, however, remained as regular visitors. They simply wanted to see exactly what Sarah Ponsonby was 'tending' in her garden. In May 1980, they raced through the fields of Wiltshire and found 292 cannabis plants growing at Surrendell. She was fined a total of £110. And they returned in July 1983 to seize 40 more plants which were sent away for analysis, though, on this occasion, no action was taken.

There were soon new impartial observers at Surrendell. The attached Snow White-style cottage, situated at the other end of the dirt track on the listed road, was purchased by businessman John and Patricia King, who had returned to England after ten years in Australia. They were amazed by some of the goings-on.

Mrs King bumped into Mirren on one visit to the farmhouse. She said, 'She seemed a very nice person. Very striking. I couldn't exactly say what the purpose of the place was, but they seemed to be getting away from their upper-class roots. As many didn't have money worries and probably had private incomes, they could let life pass them by. At least for a while. The place was in a terrible state, really falling to pieces. But that didn't seem to bother them. It had always been like that. Sarah slept in the barn and, apart from guests like Princess Margaret, everyone slept fairly rough.

'They did try to grow food for this restaurant they owned in Bath but it didn't come off. Princess Margaret apparently always enjoyed herself sitting by the large inglenook fireplace in the hall. They thought she was something of a pain in the neck. We never found them disruptive but enjoyed having them as neighbours. They made the place alive and were fun to know.

'It was hilarious when these plain-clothes drugs officers would arrive looking for evidence. Sarah would always say that whatever she had there by way of what they grew, it was for their own consumption, their own pleasure and they weren't doing any harm. She said it was like going to a drinks cupboard and helping yourself.

'By the time they left, the whole house smelled of pot. It was in an almost tumble-down state when Sarah finally left with the roof leaking, peeling walls and the bathrooms were disgusting. The best part was the gardens. They were in a terrible state.

'But Sarah was incredibly artistic and left me the model casting of a horse as a gift. I think she'd always been the black sheep of the family, something of a rebel. Somebody who wouldn't let go of the Sixties or Seventies.'

At least Roddy Llewellyn's dream came true. He went on to become a student at Merrist Wood Agricultural College and now lives in Oxfordshire with his wife Tania, the daughter of a Russian film producer, and their three daughters. He has written six books, lectures and writes a gardening column for the *Mail on Sunday*.

Rendell has remarried and had a spell charting society's hottest nights for *Hello!* magazine. Richard Courtauld went off to live in a farm in Chepstow before getting out of farming altogether in the late Seventies.

Sarah Ponsonby, it is understood, was the sole owner of the farm when it was sold in 1989 for a reported 'giveaway' price of £250,000 to a corporation for development. It is now owned by a wealthy industrialist and his family. They have spent an estimated £100,000 restoring the property and grounds which are now in magnificent condition. The wooden-beamed farmhouse itself is a luxurious mansion with a huge, modern, open-plan kitchen. The barns have been rebuilt with brand-new arched wooden doors, while the stone outhouses where Llewellyn tended to his vegetables have also been given a decorative makeover. Its current value with spectacular room for development on the adjoining lands is put in the region of £2 million.

Ponsonby now lives in the South of France and had a vet from nearby Chippenham assist her in transporting her 'ark' load of animals across the Channel to Normandy.

Pat King watched them being rounded up and prepared for their journey. She recalls, 'It was quite a sight. There were two horses, three dogs, twelve chickens and four cats. The pets of a smaller variety were taken in the back of a black London cab which was out of commission. The whole thing was just so weird.'

Ponsonby remained an artist and 'creative spirit'. She even later invented a board game called *The Garden Game*, a kind of horticultural Monopoly, which was one of the top ten toys of 1985.

And Mirren? She was never really into drugs in any case, remarking, 'Work was my drug, much more interesting than getting stoned. I desperately wanted to be cool, so I kept trying. But I'd get so frightened and feel miserable and stupid. Eventually, I had the courage to give it up.'

And she has long since dispensed with her sheepskin waistcoat. No longer does she wear bell-bottom trousers or long for a joint. She remained an occasional visitor to the farm until it was sold by Ponsonby. A friend says of Mirren, 'One of her character traits is loyalty. No matter what, she will stick by you ... unless you betray her. She cannot tolerate betrayal. Then she will cut you off. She expects the same kind of loyalty she gives. Meeting Sarah changed her life in the Seventies. The whole money thing didn't bother her. She liked the stuff, she hated the idea of being poor. But it was a different story in the Eighties. She bought a house and came in contact with people who earned small fortunes every week. If there had been any last particles of hippie life, they were soon expelled from her body and soul.'

Today in the hamlets of Grittleton and Hullavington, they chuckle over the antics of 'that hippie mob down on the farm'. Ah yes, and that 'famous actress person'.

Peacocks sweep across well-tended gardens in the model village of Grittleton which has often enjoyed the title of Best Kept Village with its rows of Cotswold stone designer cottages and luxurious converted terraced houses. The farming community may have dwindled, but the business fraternity is thriving with residents commuting west just 18 miles to Bristol or grabbing fast trains from Chippenham – a short drive away – into London.

And, oddly enough, there's still very much a royal link in existence. The Surrendell set, with Princess Margaret in tow, would frequently adjourn a short distance north to the village of Norton and The Vine Tree pub where they would quaff large amounts of her favourite bubbly.

Now the pub, which is within easy distance of Highgrove, has become one of the favourite haunts of Charlie's sons Prince Harry and Prince William. Landlord Charles Walker and his partner Tiggy Wood regularly have their work cut out when the Princes are around, preventing the 'groupies' from consuming too many alcopops on the premises.

A regular at The Neeld Arms in Grittleton said they missed the sight of John Rendell wandering through the countryside with a tiger cub at the end of a lead. On warm summer days, they'd get the village postman to strip down to his Y-fronts and join them for a dig in the Surrendell cabbage patch.

'Bring back the hippies, that's what we say,' the regular laughed. 'Let's have another revolution. Most of us would much sooner make love than war, especially with that actress lady!'

6

A VERY LONG
GOOD FRIDAY

It was 1980. At the box office, George Lucas was striking a blow for Darth Vadar with *The Empire Strikes Back*; Dustin Hoffman and Meryl Streep were making us weep in *Kramer v Kramer*; Monty Python's *Life of Brian* begged the question: 'What did the Romans ever do for us?', while *Airplane!* blazed a new trail through the skies as Hollywood at last learned to laugh at itself.

And in jolly old Blighty? We had another two years to wait for Colin Welland's perhaps premature clarion call, 'The British are coming', following the fabulous success of *Chariots of Fire*. Otherwise, there was a deafening silence from the British film industry. The word was not good. Margaret Thatcher had just climbed back into power and she viewed the cinema industry with utmost suspicion. It was either full of Lefties such as Ken Loach, champagne Lefties such as Richard Attenborough or Lefties with the right haircut – David Puttnam. Either way, nobody was expecting her to do the industry any favours in terms of tax breaks or handouts. Far from it. The cry was 'emigrate' or 'get thyself to television'. Many quality names were about to follow that dictum and go off into soapbox land in series such as *Dynasty* and *Dallas*.

But the fuse to a little firecracker that had been lit four years earlier was about to explode on the unsuspecting public. Nobody could have predicted that they were about to witness the best home-grown gangster yarn since 1971 when a scary Michael Caine took a cowering Ian Hendry to pieces with the wrong end of a shotgun in the marvellous *Get Carter*.

The backstagers didn't have that much of a pedigree. Producer Barry Hanson was a relative newcomer to the movie business, having made the low-budget *My Girl* with a then unknown Alison Steadman in 1975. The writer of the original stage play was Barrie Keeffe, an East End lad who began his career as an actor and journalist working on the *Stratford Express* newspaper where he penned his first novel *Gadabout*. His controversial plays were often premièred at the Theatre Royal, Stratford East. He painted an unromanticised portrait of modern England with a Big Brother-like Establishment at work in plays such as *A Mad World, My Masters* and *Sus*. On television, he'd had moderate success with *Gotcha* being the best of a politically conscious bunch of teleplays. He'd yet to write a film, but Hanson, who was allied to Thames Television in 1976, had a commission to create new product and approached Keeffe with a view to writing a pilot episode called *The Last Thriller*. Keeffe took six months to produce an 80-minute, highly charged piece called *The Paddy Factory* which Hanson optioned for Lew Grade's ITC empire.

Keeffe's work was soon to ignite a bitter four-year-long battle between film company executives George Harrison and rising star Bob Hoskins. Hoskins was already in the frame to play the lead role of Cockney gang boss Harold Shand with Helen Mirren at the top of the cast shopping list as his beautiful but tough lover Victoria.

The tale was simple enough. Hoskins, as East End hood Shand, planned to turn Docklands into a new Las Vegas with some help from the Mafia. But his violent methods inadvertently upset the IRA who infiltrated his 'patch', destroying everything and everyone in their path. The explosive, confused Shand believed the carnage must have been the work of a rival and started slaughtering his own mob to find the villains behind the plot. Victoria stood firmly by his side.

Hanson had worked with Hoskins previously on the TV version of Harold Pinter's comedic classic *The Homecoming* and knew that he was going to get full value for his money, of which he had very little at his disposal. But he also wanted to 'globalise' the story, bringing cultures into conflict, and decided he needed an American character actor to play a leading member of the Mob from the other side of the pond called Charlie.

Producer Hanson was involved in internecine warfare with Grade's leading executives Bernard Kingham and Jack Gill over the script. 'They hated it so much, they wanted to cut it and put it on television, which would have been disastrous,' he said. 'I knew we were going to have a lot of trouble by the time we were through.'

What he hadn't bargained for was what he described as 'Hollywood-style' behaviour from Italian-American actor Tony Franciosa who'd arrived in England to play his Mafia man. The then middle-aged Franciosa, who had been married to actress Shelley Winters, was in demonstrative form, bursting into a fit of rage when he heard that there had been script changes without his permission. He also complained about the lack of facilities and resources during the filming schedule. And then, before a final shot had been filmed, he packed his bags and flew home to New York.

Cool Hanson immediately signed up another craggy American acting stalwart Eddie Constantine to replace him. Veteran Constantine, who died in 1993, was going through one of his worst bouts of insecurity. He'd just finished making a low-budget movie called *Beware of the Holy Whore*. But Hanson was still convinced he could produce the goods. 'Eddie was more off-the-wall than Franciosa,' he said. 'You weren't sure what you were going to get, but at least you were going to get something. Franciosa was a real pain. He had all kinds of problems, not least his temperament.'

The part of Victoria had also changed radically from its original form. Hanson said, 'When we first saw her, she was a caricature, an emblematic character who said nothing during the film and then revealed a mouth of rotting teeth which wasn't what we really wanted. It certainly wasn't what Helen wanted either. We wanted somebody strong who wasn't going to be blown off the screen by Shand or Bob. She would "round" the character herself and take the director's lead.'

The director of *The Long Good Friday* was to be British television director John MacKenzie who went on to make the Michael Caine features *The Honorary Consul* and the thriller *The Fourth Protocol*. He was also to work with Hoskins again on *Mona Lisa*. With Keeffe for company, he went to see Mirren in action on stage in Peter Gill's production of *Measure for Measure* at the Riverside Theatre in Hammersmith. They were thrilled with what they saw. Keeffe, who trained as an actor with Mirren at the National Youth Theatre, commented, 'We were both blown away by her. I thought she was just the same as she had been ten years earlier – friendly, witty, funny and sharp. And wise. She was precocious but unspoiled as a teenager.'

With a budget of £811,000 – Hanson had agreed a 'partnership sharing deal' with the main players – MacKenzie had to watch every penny on locations in Greenwich and in Docklands.

Only three of the stars – Hoskins, Mirren and Constantine – had their own caravans to relax in, while the rest of the cast made do with their cars and made good use of local hostelries for the basic bodily functions.

A galaxy of stars were in the process of being born. Pierce Brosnan had a small part as an IRA assassin. Ulster-born Derek Thompson, still better known as nurse Charlie Fairhead from the long-runnning *Casualty* series, played Hoskins's right-hand henchman Jeff. The modest, softly spoken Thompson came out of his shell as a bad guy, especially when Shand's live-in love Victoria was in the vicinity. In one scene, they shared a lift and Thompson, slowly looking her up and down, says as though he really meant it,

'I want to lick you all over.' Members of the crew gave him a standing ovation and Mirren blushed.

Paul Barber, later to bare all in *The Full Monty*, was a small-time villain who had his buttocks slashed by Hoskins, while the late ex-stand-up comic Dave King loathed hanging on a butcher's hook in an abattoir, so much so that director MacKenzie dubbed him, 'A complete pain in the arse ... but great in the part'. King's protégé was another chirpy Cockney soul Karl Howman, later to star in the sitcoms *Brush Strokes* and *Babes in the Wood*.

The late Brian Hall, once Basil Fawlty's chef in *Fawlty Towers*, was also in the line-up, with hunky housewives' favourite Paul Freeman, rugged Kevin McNally and kids' idol Dexter Fletcher.

MacKenzie was nicknamed Frenzy MacKenzie for often moving things along at a frenetic pace. He said, 'We knew we had something very special. When you had such talent as Bob and Helen, something was bound to happen. But Pierce, along with so many others, also had this special spark.'

What he hadn't bargained on was the veteran Constantine's instant sexual obsession with Mirren as he set about stalking her for seven weeks. The crew lapsed into quiet hysterics as he'd use any pretext to enter her caravan. And though he may have been in his sprightly sixties, he'd get up to all kinds of mischief once he'd convinced himself she was bound to fall inside the first week of filming. To borrow one of Muhammed Ali's favoured expressions, he giggled, 'She will go in seven!' He'd sneak into her caravan and scrawl love notes in verse using lipstick on a mirror. Make-up girls would then dash in and wipe-off the provocative 'poetry' before she could see his handiwork. Once, Mirren expressed her concerns over what she thought was an on-set 'Peeping Tom', unaware that it was Constantine again on the prowl.

MacKenzie said, 'Eddie followed Helen around like a lapdog but she never understood what he wanted. He was hilarious. He did most of his movies in France and Germany and they always dubbed him. When I told him he had some speeches, he went white as a sheet and said, "But nobody ever asks me to say anything!" '

A member of the crew recalled, 'This old guy from the States had really got it into his mind that Helen would be his. He kept on asking us whether she'd like to live in New York and how she felt about older men. He said he would pay for information leading to him finding his way to her bed. He was hilarious. None of us actually knew whether to take him seriously, but he didn't have his evil way with her in any case. I think you could safely say he was not her type.'

What Mirren did to distinguish this role from earlier ones was to exude strength and maturity. As Victoria, she was sexy and beautiful, dangerous but attainable, loyal but demanding. And, perhaps more important, she is allowed to show her intelligence at every level. MacKenzie, Hanson and Keeffe didn't want her delivering just another gangster's moll and she wasn't about to go 'passive' on them.

Instead, and possibly for the first time in her movie career, they got the 'tiger' in Mirren. Her earlier escapades in *Savage Messiah* and *Caligula* had taught her an important lesson. Now was the time to stand up and be counted.

But as *The Long Good Friday* also happened to be 'a lads' movie', at least in the making, she knew she would have to roar loudly.

Hanson was on set the day Mirren noted a change in the script where she was expected to iron one of Harold Shand's shirts. Uneasily, she approached director MacKenzie. After some small talk, there was a meaningful pause before she said, trying to force a smile, 'Mmm, you see, the thing is that I don't iron shirts ... I am no handmaiden.' There was a hush on set as they went into a huddle.

MacKenzie, the wind taken out of his sails, suddenly wasn't living up to his nickname. Hanson said, 'It was basically a boys' film and there was a feeling abroad that Helen wouldn't mind getting in on the act going around with a sub-machine gun and cutting loose. Looking at the picture today, she was tremendously powerful in it. She's an actor's actor and she is very much aware of her status.

'In those days, she was defensive because women were fighting for their corners in the acting world and here she was in this all-male piece. She felt she probably had to fight harder than necessary.'

MacKenzie believed the film unleashed Mirren's feminist streak, especially when he openly described Victoria as an 'acolyte' in terms of her relationship with Shand. 'That set her off,' he said, instantly sensing Mirren's irritation. 'I said, "OK, then, you are his 'partner'." I took the word back. I decided, in the circumstances, that it was the wisest thing to do. When I explained that Victoria had to support Harold in the domestic sense, she said, "John, you are going too far … I have never made a cup of tea for a man in my life." But she did it, after some prompting. She was touchy but in control.'

The episode was to result in Mirren seeing the funny side 20 years later when one of the senior technicians from the film came to Los Angeles to see her director husband Taylor Hackford about work. He'd taken his place on a sofa in their home when Mirren asked the question, 'Would you like a cup of tea?' He didn't know whether or not she meant it, which she did, but it brought back all of these memories from the movie.

MacKenzie said, 'She is wonderful. She can certainly stand up for herself, which is admirable. My perception of her was always of this fantastic actress with lots of guts and balls.'

Writer Keeffe also happened to be in earshot while Mirren was airing her views on 'a woman's place'. He said, 'Helen could get uptight. There was a serious discussion between her and John and Barry over whether it was a woman's job to do a man's cufflinks on his shirt. You see, she wasn't just a moll. She was the one who kept the whole deal moving. Yup, I think she would have liked to have picked up an automatic weapon.

'But it must have been difficult for her being the only woman on the production. There were a lot of hard, tough people around but she kept her cool. A lot of actresses in those circumstances would have been timid and hidden away but she was phenomenal.'

Keeffe's wife, the writer Verity Bargate, was suffering from terminal cancer while the film was being made and he says he'll never forget Mirren's compassion. 'I was finding life very hard and I remember her incredible kindness. What was evident to me about Helen was that she had this attitude which cut through all classes. She wasn't up or down. She could play to anyone and she is always herself. Having said that, I was never sure whether I was meeting *her*. Does anyone really know who she is? But she had such strength and integrity.'

Mirren's cool, chic magic combined well with Hoskins's bruising, frightening portrayal of Shand. Hoskins, who was to work with Mirren on several more occasions, most recently on the ensemble romantic drama *Last Orders*, was basking in the glory of his breakthrough role in Dennis Potter's television epic *Pennies from Heaven*. Born in Suffolk but raised in North London, he was from the self-taught school of acting, coming into the business late.

Like his buddy Michael Elphick, another fully paid-up Equity *enfant terrible*, he'd be found drinking the nights away discussing the merits of Beckett and Shaw in smoke-filled dens next to various West End underground stations. The affable Hoskins could 'turn' on a sixpence. He once got nasty and thumped BBC executives who were out of line by gate-crashing a nude scene, and was the perennial champion of the underdog, mainly because he felt he'd been one himself for so long. Mostly, after a series of jobs ranging from plumber to painter, he was just thrilled to be an actor in good roles and getting paid well for it. Today, he's a huge star.

The violence in the film occasionally left members of the crew having to leave the set 'for air'. In one particularly infamous scene, which was shot in a real-life abattoir over three days, members of Shand's gang were suspended on meat hooks upside down and left to die. MacKenzie recalls, 'I'm afraid certain members of the cast didn't take too kindly to that scene. We had a great summer together for those seven weeks, but the most difficult days were spent in that abattoir. You could smell the blood in the air and it was sickening. The crew would rush out between takes so they could breathe properly. But David [King], in particular, took exception to this and got quite upset. I think he genuinely felt somebody was taking the mickey.'

Hoskins was then seen killing Derek Thompson's character off by plunging a broken bottle into his neck. Pierce Brosnan played a super-cool IRA assassin as though he were born to the task. As MacKenzie put it, 'We had more of the red stuff everywhere.' And, of course, Harold Shand gets his comeuppance, though nobody gets to see that.

The graphic violence was soon causing problems for Lew Grade's film company where his underlings wanted to take the film and slash it to ribbons, making it suitable for later TV use. They were also saying in private that it was 'unacceptable ' for the IRA to be seen coming out on top 'in any circumstances'.

Neither MacKenzie nor Hanson were having it, particularly when they also decided to re-dub Hoskins using an unknown actor from Wolverhampton in the Midlands. 'Bob was furious and threatening. He saw a rough cut of the film and thought what they had done had made the film plain boring.' Hoskins, stressed out from his marital problems – he was splitting up with his first wife, Jane, at the time – sought comfort with actress Patti Love, who had a small role as a gangster's girlfriend. He joked, 'Well, at least one good thing came out of the movie for me!'

For 18 months, rows and legal threats battered Hanson and Co from both directions until Hoskins met Monty Python comedy star Eric Idle at a party and told him about the 'brilliant' gangster movie which might never get a release. Idle's friend ex-Beatle George Harrison and his production arm Handmade Films, were soon negotiating with Grade's lawyers to remove the film and distribute it themselves.

Harrison and his partner Denis O'Brien paid £700,000 to 'rescue' the movie from the clutches of Grade and Co, though, in private, the TV and film company mogul told friends he thought the film was 'a gold nugget'. The irony was that his brother was also being accused of over-zealous censorship. Bernard Delfont, then head of EMI, was suffocating *The Life of Brian*, preventing its general release on the grounds that the Monty Python saga was 'blasphemous and offensive'.

Producer Hanson said, 'We were having major problems with funding and it appeared that some companies were operating a get out by way of delivering products to TV for tax reasons. We avoided any legal action in the end, either with Bob or Grade, but our hands were tied for a long time. We fought and fought and stopped the film being dumbed down. It was a weird experience which never seemed to end. I remember being in a bar in South London with Barrie Keeffe and somebody offered us a cheap pirated version of the movie. We just had to laugh. But in all honesty, we got what we were aiming for. It wasn't just another gangster movie. There were broader themes there about England and that period in history. But it stood the test of time. When we re-released many years later, there was a lot of interest.'

Finally, in May 1980, *The Long Good Friday* was seen by the critics and the verdict was almost unanimous. In America, though the cast was unknown to the cinema-going public, the movie rapidly took on a cult status.

Many now remember Mirren as being truly vulnerable in her portrayal of Victoria, especially the last scene in which Hoskins rapidly disappears in the back of a car to face his execution at the hands of the IRA. Mirren is seen in another car, her lips opening to form a silent scream. The terror in their eyes spoke volumes.

American author Kim Chernin, reviewing the film, remarked, 'Helen Mirren can play anything. She can play a repressed woman, a glamorous woman, a mobster wife. She fully enters the character. She's a psycho-analyst in acting form.'

A readers' poll later held by the movie bible, *Empire* magazine, voted *Friday* Best British Movie Ever Made. Critics raved that Hoskins was the natural successor to the legendary screen mobster Jimmy Cagney.

Mirren was at her unassuming best once the film had finally been released. She said, 'I am pleased the film has got through uncut, I am pleased for Bob. The film is more important for him than for me. I am just glad we can have a film made in England about England and reflecting our own culture.'

The bouquets rained down. But she wasn't smelling of roses for long. Before the year was out, she'd starred in the low-budget *Hussy*, most of which was shot in a dingy London nightspot, The Churchill Club. In it, she played a hostess-cum-hooker who gets caught up with Mob drugs deals. The rising American star John Shea added little to the budget or the appeal of the movie, which was directed by Matthew Chapman. But according to producer Don Boyd, he enjoyed his love scenes with Mirren. The lady herself rated Boyd's film so highly she usually left it off her CV and it doesn't even warrant a mention in Halliwell's *Film Guide*. Nigerian singer Patti Boulaye, who had just made her TV breakthrough, was offered the role of a cabaret artiste who also has a torrid nude sex scene. She said, 'They had this stereotypical view of the black girl. I was told nobody employs black actresses unless they take their clothes off. I was convent educated and there was no way I was doing this. I don't leap in and out of bed with strangers. I told them, so they said I could sing the song in the movie and they'd get somebody else to do the sex, even if it was simulated sex. When I went to a preview, I cringed. I sneaked out before the end. I was just glad my family never got to see it. The experience put me right off being in the movies.'

Boulaye saw little of merit in *Hussy*, apart from Mirren's work, and she was full of admiration for the manner in which the girl from the RSC dealt with her sex scenes. 'Mirren was amazing,' she said. 'I don't know how she was able to do some of the things she did, but that was, I suppose, what actors do. I didn't have her courage or her confidence to cope.'

Mirren sadly didn't fare much better playing it for laughs in what was to be Peter Sellers's last movie, *The Fiendish Plot of Dr Fu Manchu*, in which she had a small role as a London copper called

Alice Rage. The so-called spoof bordered on farce and total chaos as Sellers, taking control in Dr Strangelove mode, also played the dual role of the standard stiff-upper-lipped Scotland Yard detective Dennis Nayland Smith. There were two sub-plots: Fu running out of his age-regressing elixir, and the Yellow Peril returning from the Far East to Europe to mastermind a string of diamond thefts. The comedy was shot at Pinewood with a supporting cast of David Tomlinson, John Le Mesurier, Simon Williams and American comic Sid Caesar. They deserved better. And it was a rotten epitaph for the crazed genius that was Sellers. Mirren adored the job and the company, though the end product left much to be desired.

The film opened in London a month after his death from a heart-attack and Mirren said, 'I was very happy on that film and it was mainly due to Peter. We used to make each other laugh. By the end of the film, I counted him as one of my greatest friends.'

She had risen considerably in stature with *The Long Good Friday* and had come back down with two movie stinkers in a matter of months. On the helter-skelter barometer of being the flavour of the month, she was back to square one in a celluloid sense. Her artistic friends told her to forget it and take a world trip. Or go native and get herself back to countryside hippiedom in Wiltshire on Surrendell Farm.

On the plus side, Mirren had sold her bijou pine-and-lace-decorated flat in Parsons Green, West London, to buy a smart but modest terraced house a short distance away in Doria Road, Fulham, where her china pheasants could mature on the wall beside her piano. And she could at last buy a decent library case for her treasured volumes of leather-bound Shakespearian plays. She was also keenly proud of her sparkling new Honda Accord which caused much merriment among her more trendy chums.

What's more, *Daily Telegraph* theatre critic John Barber had just seen her give the 'performance of her career' in John Webster's charnel-house tragedy *The Duchess of Malfi* at the Royal Exchange in Manchester before its transfer to the Round House in Chalk

Farm, London. There was every good reason to be 'jolly', as she would have put it. Very soon, there would even be a new love in her life, the charismatic, studious Irish actor Liam Neeson.

But associates in the business arena were more solemn about what the future held. They told her it was time to take stock, time for a change in direction. Time for another challenge. Her career choices were thinning out. She should look west towards California and Hollywood. And, warily, she began to see it their way. Life was getting serious for Helen Mirren.

7

MIRREN'S
PASSIONS

The tall, softly spoken Irishman's eyes lit up when he was introduced to Helen Mirren by film director John Boorman. And the feeling was very much mutual as she glanced up and down at the frame of 6ft 4in actor Liam Neeson.

He was the novice, the newcomer, the ex-forklift operator for Guinness who'd also tried his hand and fists at truck driving and amateur boxing. The boxing left its mark, sure enough, with young Liam sporting a broken nose but holding on to his pride as an Ulster Youth champion at the age of 15. He also fancied himself as something of an architect, but that wasn't going to happen once he'd flunked his course at the University of Belfast.

But that was part of the appeal of the gangling Catholic who was born William John Neeson in the predominantly Protestant town of Ballymena in Ian Paisley's County Antrim. He'd never quite managed to finish what he'd started, in almost every aspect. He thought about being a teacher but that also went wrong, so he dropped out of St Mary's College in Belfast before ever setting foot in a staff room. His mother – her name, coincidentally, was also

Kitty – a school cook, and his father Barney, a caretaker, were often beside themselves with despair. They knew the lad was bright and likeable. He was 'special', but he just wouldn't apply himself. Hence the string of unsuitable jobs. 'What a waste,' they'd tell him. He'd nod and tell them it was going to be fine. His mother would say to friends, 'He's a funny boy, nothing seems to worry him.'

Neeson had, in fact, been educating himself. He'd go armed with books and was especially fond of Joyce and Beckett. Entertainment for him was the theatre and girls. In that order.

And so, after much messing about and far too many pints of Guinness, he got into amateur dramatics through his old English teacher, later joining the Belfast Lyric Players' Theatre to make his professional début in the play *The Risen People*. After two years, he moved to Dublin's famed Abbey Theatre where he performed in the classics and was spotted by Boorman in John Steinbeck's *Of Mice and Men*.

He was 28 and Mirren was 34. The siren was also a 'veteran' who'd starred with James Mason, Larry Olivier and Peter Sellers. She'd starred in Strindberg and Travers. She'd done *Macbeth*. She was, for goodness sake, 'the Sex Queen of the RSC'. He had some catching up to do, he figured. But, for the moment, he was in awe of the little filly with the green eyes and curly, tinted red hair. She was a picture all right.

She flashed him a smile, he was to recall to a close friend, and it was like a 'thunderbolt from above'. Boorman, hailed for his innovative brilliance, creating the first ever Green action thriller *Deliverance* with Jon Voight and Burt Reynolds, had himself something of a 'bonus' before he'd shot a frame of *Excalibur*, his pretty faithful adaptation of the classic *Le Morte d'Arthur*.

Neeson was playing the noble warrior Gawain with the late Nicholas Clay cast as Sir Lancelot to Cherie Lunghi's Guenevere. Nicol Williamson was in the pot as the wizard Merlin, along with Robert Addie, the wicked bastard son sired by Arthur with his evil sorceress half-sister Morgana, played by Mirren. For her, it was a role to die for – sex and death ... lust piled on lust.

Boorman had all the dark chemistry he needed before Mirren and Williamson acted out a single scene. They positively loathed one another. She grinned: 'I think Boorman cast the film that way because he knew that Mr Williamson and I could not STAND each other, and he [Boorman] thought that it would be great to see that hostility on screen. I think he was right. Now that, that was inspired. Although it took quite a bit for me to agree to do it - and I am sure that was in equal measures on Nicol's part as well!'

The story follows the path of the magical sword Excalibur through the Arthurian myth, from the violent, powerful hands of Uther Pendragon, played by Gabriel Byrne, to its year-long rest in a stone before being redrawn by Arthur.

He uses the sword to repel invaders and establish the great court at Camelot with his Knights of the Round Table. The emerging, highly respected newcomer Nigel Terry played Arthur. For him, at least, superstardom was to prove elusive.

Tax breaks led Orion and Warner Bros over to Ireland with Boorman where he shot *Excalibur* close to his own retreat in County Wicklow and on several picturesque castle locations in Tipperary and Kerry.

Alas, *Excalibur* fell on its own sword at the box office, barely causing a ripple of interest. The film was damned for falling between too many genres and never targeting itself at the appropriate market. Boorman took it all seriously, which was his intention. But the kids who queued at the local Odeon were still enthralled by *Monty Python's Life of Brian* and their version of the Holy Grail. It was hard to take anything in chainmail seriously.

Mirren may have had her infatuation with Malcolm McDowell, but this was her only real on-set romance to date. Once she got to know the gentle giant Neeson, they were rarely apart, leaving Boorman to grin with a certain amount of satisfaction, 'Looks like Morgana has bewitched Gawain.'

Neeson, from Mirren's viewpoint, was very unlike most of the actors she had known at close quarters. He was charming, intelligent but had the enthusiasm of an 11-year-old to learn more at every level. He had no fixed ideas. He wanted to see the world and he wanted to explore her world. He was ambitious but he didn't want a big house on a hill in Hollywood. He adored poetry and literature and was fascinated by the stories she had to tell of her adventures, especially her 'mission' to West Africa with Peter Brook's company. She didn't open up to many, certainly not the male of the species. She always expected trivia, silly jokes or arrogance.

But there was virtually no small talk with Neeson. To him, life was about issues and beauty. About love and loss. He wasn't just a charmer. He was genuine. He lived mainly out of a suitcase and had very few possessions. If she was looking for a character to keep her in a manner to which she had been accustomed, she was looking at the wrong chap, as he would constantly remind her with a beaming Irish grin. Ah yes, and he was also a gentleman. She was quick to tell her sister Katie of Mr Neeson's effect. 'He is absolutely gorgeous,' she revealed in a telephone conversation, 'but I must not get carried away!'

Mirren's love life had always been something of a grey, insignificant blur before Neeson entered the reckoning. But those closest to her believe it was the first time she 'clicked' with a man in every sense.

The Swinging Sixties had passed her rapidly by, largely eaten up by the constrictions of St Bernard's, where boys were a taboo subject, and her absolute determination to make a success of herself as an actress.

The nuns did make an effort, however, to bring sex into her life. When she was in the fifth form, she was bussed along with scores of other girls from the area to watch a documentary film about the birth of a baby, which was probably intended for midwives. It did not, however, show intercourse, or 'the creation', which she thought was particularly silly.

A good deal later, she blamed the film for her negative feelings towards motherhood. She said, 'Babies are lovely, but I was completely traumatised by the idea of having children. They did the most stupid thing to me at school. They discovered sex education when we had absolutely none. I had no idea at 15 how conception occurred. Then bureaucracy decided that we should find out, with a vengeance.

'We were taken with boys from a neighbouring school on to a bus, into a hall, to see this teaching film about what happens when a girl has a baby. There were enormous instant close-ups of the moment of birth. Halfway through, they had to stop it because all the boys were fainting.

'Finally, the lights went up on these frozen, terrified children. It was the most hideous thing that has ever happened to me and I am sure it put me off having children. The thought of giving birth was repellent.

'When the lights came up, I felt so embarrassed about my body that I didn't dare lift my eyes from the floor, imagining that all the boys were looking at me and thinking, We know what you've got under that gym-slip ... there's no point in hiding it. I couldn't look at a fella for a long time afterwards. I was just fantastically repulsed by it all and I decided I would never have sex myself!'

Her parents had done their best to support her when she took the route away from teaching. She vowed when Michael Croft gave her a place at the National Youth Theatre that she would prove any doubters wrong, be they the nuns of St Bernard's or her parents. She owed it to them and to herself not to blow the opportunity Croft had given her.

But there was time for some 'play' while she studied her lines. According to a long-standing chum, she lost her virginity to an 'older man' during her spell at the NYT and 'made up for lost time' in that department during her early days at the Royal Shakespeare Company. She had remained friends with her 'ex', Bruce Myers, and they were still just about in contact when she met George

Galitzine through his step-sister Sarah Ponsonby at Ditchford Farm in Warwickshire.

The tall, simian-like, wafer-slim and slightly wild Galitzine with his mop of unkempt hair closely resembled a Flower Power leftover or a lad about to grab an acoustic guitar and strum Bob Dylan songs.

He was a distant cousin of the Duke of Kent and was used to mixing in upmarket circles. He had no definite long-term career plans, but called himself a 'freelance writer' who simply enjoyed being an anti-Establishment rebel. Like Mirren, he was of good, sound Eastern European aristocratic stock with a Russian family tree which went back to Catherine the Great. He could, if he wanted, rightly claim the title 'Prince'. Members of his family sat on most of the thrones of Europe at one time or another.

The Galitzines were one of the foremost Russian émigré families in Britain. The new head of the line was the elder Prince George Galitzine – Queen Elizabeth was his sixth cousin once removed – who was born in 1916 and escaped with his family from the Bolsheviks at the age of three. His parents ran an antiques shop in Berkeley Square which was visited regularly by Queen Mary. He became an adviser to some very large companies who valued his contacts behind the Iron Curtain. He had a passion for Russian history and Anglo–Russian relations. He married former Dior model and fashion writer Jean Dawnay. Their daughter Katya went to Paris to learn Russian and, after the Berlin Wall came down, she went to live there. Her father died in 1992, having watched the Soviet flag lowered over their home town of St Petersburg and the old Russian flag unfurled. He also had dinner with Boris Yeltsin and the President asked him to autograph his napkin.

But the George Galitzine of Ditchford Farm didn't quite feel the same close alliance to 'the old country' back in the psychadelic Seventies. He carved, wrote and painted. And, according to those visiting the farm, he was totally devoted to Mirren and would do anything to please her. They were an odd couple, observers remarked.

'There was something about George that didn't look at all right next to Helen,' said one. 'Maybe it was just that he lacked confidence or always felt intimidated by her. But he gave off this aura that he was just incredibly lucky to hold her attention for more than five minutes. She appeared to humour him quite a bit, though we suspected she was very, very fond him. The Russian background bonded them quite a bit and he did, in his very straight moments, of which he had many, come over like a fatherly figure. She admired her own dad tremendously.'

Galitzine held out little hope of marriage to Mirren. She was too much of a free spirit and, perhaps because of his thoroughly conventional old-fashioned background, he could hardly bear to be with a woman who controlled the purse strings. She infuriated him more than once by talking about her bright financial state of affairs next to his acute money problems. No spite was intended. Her comments were meant to be amusing in the context of New Age Man and Woman. And she confessed that she was hell to live with, in any case, while she appeared in David Hare's *Teeth 'n' Smiles* at the Royal Court Theatre and later in the West End.

'I sort of support my boyfriend George, doesn't work very much, but that's all right ...' she said. 'He isn't extravagant either. It's the least I can do. After all, it's not that easy living with an actress. He gets terribly bored when I talk shop or mix with some of my colleagues and, during rehearsals of *Teeth 'n' Smiles*, I was rather awful to him. The character isn't very pleasant and, at home, I became this woman, which must have been a terrible strain on him.'

In truth, Mirren set too hot a pace for Galitzine and both recognised that, by Christmas 1975, their romance, if it could be described as such by then, was heading down a cul-de-sac. They had their happy days at Ditchford and Surrendell and were familiar, relaxed figures sipping their coffees in cafés close to Mirren's West London home. That was then. Surrendell had come and gone. The Parsenn Sally dream was over and it was now time to move on.

But she was loath to hurt Galitzine's feelings, trusting him as you might a big brother figure. 'He was a very good shoulder to lean on away from the showbusiness fraternity and that kind of trivia,' said a chum. 'But passion? No. They had been on a long, slow burn out. She was bored. Yup, that was it. Bored. She'd got such a buzz when she'd been with blokes like Malcolm McDowell. There had been real electricity. She needed that kind of energy in her life when she wasn't working.' What was to follow caused much amusement among Mirren's friends and relations.

Earlier that year, in the autumn, she had agreed to do a photo shoot for *Cosmopolitan* magazine and she had been impressed by the laid-back style of the photographer James Wedge who had built a highly complimentary reputation for himself among the society sets from Mayfair to Belgravia. He was 'in' with the right people and organisations, alongside the likes of fellow high-grade snappers Terry O'Neill, Terence Donovan and Brian Aris.

Mirren usually gave photographers and journalists a wide berth. She had been wary of media attention from early in her career when she made *Age of Consent* with James Mason in Australia. She had no idea then that she could be 'linked' romantically with just about anybody. And she was not street-wise enough to realise that once you had thrown off your clothes for nude scenes, you were bound to have a certain notoriety. She was not keen on the image the press had given her.

But distinguished Wedge, a well-read art lover with ambitions to become a full-time painter, was a very different, aloof creature from the photographic hordes who crowded around her at festivals or photocalls. Friends described him as 'quietly dark, funny and hugely talented'.

She was thrilled by the set of pictures he produced for the magazine and told him so in a handwritten note. He, in turn, ensured that she was sent a set. Eventually, after a month's silence, he nervously plucked up the courage to invite her out to dinner. Much to his surprise, she happily accepted. And they embarked on a romance which was to stumble on until Liam Neeson came roaring into her life four years later. Not that her old friend and escort Galitzine was impressed. He wasn't especially fond of Wedge from the moment they had met briefly at Mirren's home and misunderstood each other during a conversation. Galitzine, not a man to shy away from a confrontation, returned the very next day to see the well-built, bearded Wedge, whereupon a brawl broke out on Mirren's doorstep.

As always in love triangle punch-ups, there are three sides to every story. But one thing was certain – Wedge had come off worst and was nursing a black eye and sore ribs. Mirren fled the scene when they tore into each other.

Mirren watchers were amused, but she was not. 'It was vile, because they weren't strangers,' she said. 'They were two men I liked and I felt mortified and embarrassed. I didn't want either of them to get hurt but they were both traumatised. I wasn't flattered by it. It wasn't about me at that point. It was about them, their egos, their hurt feelings, the pain of the situation.'

The press soon heard about the disagreement between the jealous, often explosive Galitzine and the fashion photographer, and he promised her that he would 'play it cool'.

Wedge was hugely embarrassed by the whole business and retreated to his country cottage with Mirren where they pottered around in his vegetable patch. He rarely spoke of his feelings for Mirren, but did open up on one occasion. He described her as 'delightful' and claimed they had even discussed marriage and having a family together. But their work kept them apart and 'the whole subject would be put on the shelf'. Their relationship was calmer. He didn't have Galitzine's experience of tantrums around the house due to a complex part she was playing. He said, 'Helen was always very easy to be with and was a very creative person. She played different characters. Sometimes she was playing a less domineering role, but that did not change her. That didn't change her character. I was very fond of her.'

Wedge spent many years and a lot of hard-earned cash renovating an old Baptist chapel called Church Gate Hall near

Putney Bridge in south-west London. The chapel, with its fabulous vast windows and vaulted ceilings, served as his home- cum-studio before he put it on the market for £700,000 and retired with his wife Amanda and their two daughters to the countryside to paint for a living.

They now live in a superb farmhouse fitted with all the mod cons just outside Sherborne in Dorset. He had only good memories of his years by Mirren's side, saying he found the experience 'educational'. But he insisted there was nothing 'dramatic' in their final parting of ways. He said, 'I can't really say why we split up eventually. Helen was spending more and more time in America because she wanted to do more film work.'

What remained clear was that the talented Wedge still occupies the warmest of places in her heart. She regarded him as a 'great photographer' and later confided that he released on film a new uninhibited spirit exclaiming, 'He experimented with sexuality. He used images of sexuality, or sexuality itself, whatever it is. We worked together, did photographic work together. The thing that was imposed on me from the outside was crude and vulgar and distressing to you, and disturbing. That big tits, blonde hair, that Diana Dors blowsy kind of thing, wasn't pleasant. I was interested in sexuality and fetishism and all kinds of stuff. I think Madonna got it right. I loved the sex book she did. I thought it was fantastic.'

Mirren was a paradox. Everyone wanted to know her, especially the boys. She had this extraordinary effect on the male of the species. But nobody realised just how shy she could be. One night she was out clubbing with Wedge when she went to pieces. 'Maybe I am too serious and I suffer from a lack of confidence,' she said. 'The other night James and I went to a party, one of those glittery film affairs with directors wandering around. I walked in and just froze inside and out and ran into a corner. I couldn't cope with it at all. Pathetic, isn't it? But I just can't survive in those kind of surroundings, even though I should have got it out of my system by now.

A 20-year-old Mirren makes her mark at the National Youth Theatre, with her raw performance as Cleopatra in *Anthony and Cleopatra*.

Clutching her Variety Club award for *The Duchess of Malfi* and, *inset*, the performance that won her the award.

A highly respected Shakespearian actress, Helen Mirren has won acclaim for playing a variety of the playwright's characters. *Above*: Practising the lute for a role with the RSC, on the banks of the Avon.

Above: With Eric Porter before setting off on a US tour with the RSC.

Below: Playing Cleopatra opposite Alan Rickman's Anthony.

Above: With artist Nicholas Egon in a restaurant in Swiss Cottage.

Below: At the 89th birthday of Ben Travers, pictured here with Joan Plowright.

The versatility of Helen Mirren means that she never fails to make an impact on screen as well as stage.

Above: With John Shea in a scene from *Hussy*.

Below: With Ben Kingsley in the 1988 film, *Pascali's Island*.

Some of the film roles that Helen Mirren will always be remembered and admired for. *Above*: As Caligula's voluptuous mistress, Caesonia in *Caligula*.

Above: With Bob Hoskins in *The Long Good Friday*.

Below: *Gosford Park*, the film that won her an Oscar nomination. She is pictured here with Ryan Philippe.

'It seems such nonsense people wandering around saying "super" and "fantastic" to each other. Perhaps that's what comes over in interviews for jobs, that I'm being snooty or superior. But I am not.'

Galitzine remained in contact with Mirren. She prides herself, even today, on her lasting friendships with her ex-boyfriends. In 1986, Galitzine found happiness marrying the Marquis of Queensbury's niece Emma de Bendern, with whom he has had two children. Emma, a qualified aromatherapist and reflexologist, had met him 17 months earlier at a London party and was taken, she told friends, by his 'dry sense of humour and straightforward approach to life'. Ironically, Galitzine had been bitten by the movie bug himself and had moved into film production. He'd been assistant art director on the Stephen Frears film *The Hit* starring Terence Stamp, and was working in the Seychelles as Art Director on the real-life desert island story *Castaway* with Oliver Reed and Amanda Donohoe shortly before he tied the knot with Emma.

Sadly, their marriage failed. Galitzine fell in love again and now lives with his second wife off the Kings Road in Chelsea, West London. But he has always maintained his friendship with Mirren and is fiercely protective of her. A friend commented, 'He was besotted with Helen for such a long time and she was this unobtainable fantasy for him. She has a special place in his heart.'

And what of Mirren? With *Excalibur* behind them, Mirren and her new love Neeson – 'her lovely Irishman' – returned to her London home in Fulham to start a new life together, having introduced her briefly to his parents in Ballymena. They took to her instantly, though his slightly awe-struck mother was so subdued over tea, he laughed, 'Look, she may be Russian aristocracy, but she's not royalty! Be normal!'

Liam was so different. He was everything, she told friends. She imagined that, if she were to marry, this could well be the groom. Those who knew her best thought she had never been so happy and relaxed. One said, 'They were just absolutely right for each other but, funnily, she thought she was too old for him just because of the six-year difference. She always thought, wrongly, that he would go off with a younger woman. We thought it played on her mind.

'He, on the other hand, loved her wisdom and sense of humour. He thought she was perfect, and that kind of stuff about him being with a young dolly bird, or something similar, was demeaning. But she'd allow work to create too many chasms between them ... some of us thought quite deliberately, as though she was scared of making that final commitment.'

Hilariously, or so they thought, their 'passionate' love scene was actually axed from *Excalibur* when the night arrived for the royal première of the movie before Prince and Princess Michael of Kent in July 1981. Director Boorman said, 'It wasn't because they were getting overexcited, nothing so colourful. I'm afraid we needed to make cuts. It was too long. Certain scenes had to go.'

But their celebrations were also cut short by the tragic death of Mirren's father Basil at the age of 66 after a short illness. The family was devastated. He had been a fit, athletic man, always keen to take a yacht around the Thames Estuary on a Sunday afternoon. He had barely had time to enjoy his well-earned retirement.

A friend said, 'Helen, as you'd expect, took it very badly. It was all so unexpected and, though her sister Katie was obviously there for their mother, Helen felt she should also be around as much as possible. It was her first real experience of death. Liam was like a rock for her. He was very good. She will never forget him for that.'

In the background, however, she was urging Neeson to get on with his career. He may have often joked about having some 'catching up' to do, but he was only half jesting. Having just made his first major movie with the likes of Boorman, Nicol Williamson and Mirren herself, he wanted more and as soon as possible. He said in his soft Irish brogue, 'I just got the bug. Suddenly, there was this lovely euphoria, not because I thought I was great or anything, but because there was a smell to it. Maybe it was the subject of that particular film, the telling of Arthurian legends. I have always loved myths and mythology. But that's what films basically are – story-telling.'

It wasn't long before he was on his travels to Italy to make the special-effects sci-fi dragon adventure *Krull* for director Peter Yates with Lysette Anthony and Francesca Annis. Mirren loved telling her family and friends that her 'old man' was off 'fighting dragons'.

He was packing his bags again soon and heading into deepest Buckinghamshire to make the mushy TV mini-series of Barbara Taylor Bradford's *A Woman of Substance* with Jenny Seagrove playing the heroine of the piece in a cast which included Deborah Kerr as the mature Jenny, Megs Jenkins and Barry Bostwick.

After two largely deliriously contented years in each other's company, Mirren was pleased but concerned. They were spending very little time together and now he was off to the other side of the world. She'd been on stage at the Royal Court and done some TV work. Her biological clock was also ticking away, as she was constantly reminded by friends. But that was of no concern, because she had not changed her mind about babies.

But now there was most definitely a problem. She knew Neeson wanted both marriage and a family, something she was not able to provide. Was it better to part now or stay together for the inevitable later parting of ways?

The solution, in the end, was self-inflicted via their careers. Director Roger Donaldson wanted Neeson to play seaman Charles Churchill in the sweeping nautical saga *Bounty*, a big-budget remake of *Mutiny on the Bounty* with Anthony Hopkins playing Captain Bligh and Mel Gibson as the noble Fletcher Christian. They would be away for months filming in New Zealand and Moorea in French Polynesia. And Mirren, in what she sensed might be a breakthrough for her, was wanted in Los Angeles to play a Russian cosmonaut in *2010*, the sequel to Stanley Kubrick's epic *2001*. They temporaraily went their separate ways.

Neeson knew they were drifting apart in 1983 while he encouraged and partly inspired her to make the award-winning Irish drama *Cal* with John Lynch.

Fate, in any case, was about to take another hand. Shortly before she was due to leave for Russia to make *White Nights* with director Taylor Hackford, they sat down to discuss their future. She had to spend more time in America if she was to make more of an impact with the Hollywood studios. He was still keen to have a baby with her. His mother badly wanted him to have a baby with Mirren. It was not to be.

They smiled, they kissed and they finally went their separate ways in the spring of 1985. And they were still more than just very fond of each other. She sold her home in Fulham, London, soon after, now as fully prepared as she could possibly be for her new life in California. Her mind was made up, she said, as she wept buckets of tears. Never had Mirren been in such distress over a man.

Her sister Katie and close friends offered words of comfort. She was convinced before Hackford appeared on the scene that she'd never find another soulmate like Neeson. But her circle agreed that she had done the right thing by letting him pursue his career and his private dream of a devoted wife and family. And he never forgot her. There were always the warmest of handshakes when they met at awards ceremonies and charity dinners.

The tall Irishman melted at the mere mention of her name while he was in London promoting *Under Suspicion* with Laura San Giacomo. He thought long and hard before saying, 'Ah, Helen ... what a bright lady and beautiful. She is and will always be one of my dearest friends. She was very special to me. But I can say nothing more. Gorgeous, yes, gorgeous.'

Diplomatic Neeson hasn't apparently changed at all since their parting. He always had quite a track record with the ladies and set his standards high, say friends in the business. There was a veritable bevy of outstanding screen beauties waiting to take Mirren's place by his side, and there is a long list of women he has dated and lived with. The roll call includes Julia Roberts, Barbra Streisand, Sinead O'Connor, Jessica Lange, Cher, Diane Keaton and Brooke Shields. It was Shields who later said when asked about his appeal, 'Let's just say he is the most physically awesome man I have ever seen.'

And Neeson's star soared higher still into the heavens after Mirren allowed him to slip away quietly from her life. He shone in the absorbing *Suspect* with Cher playing a mute on a murder charge; he made Micky Rourke look second-rate in the second-rate IRA caper *A Prayer for the Dying*; and he was excellent trading emotional blows with Diane Keaton in the morality drama *The Good Mother*. Many believe he made his breakthrough playing a lunatic film-maker giving Clint Eastwood a hard time in *The Dead Pool*.

And that private dream was realised. He was to fall hopelessly in love with Vanessa Redgrave's gorgeous daughter actress Natasha Richardson who co-starred with him in a scintillating run of Eugene O'Neill's *Anna Christie* on Broadway in early 1992. Her marriage to theatrical impresario Robert Fox ended and Neeson was in clover, landing a Tony award and getting the girl. And what a bonus was waiting! A certain Steven Spielberg was in the stalls watching him sparkle. Days later, Spielberg offered him the lead role in *Schindler's List*. The part of the real-life war hero who saved the lives of countless Jews who worked in his factory won him an Oscar nomination.

Today, Neeson must believe he's been blessed, having survived a body-shattering crash on his motorbike near their home in Upstate New York. Doctors thought he might not walk again. Instead, he fought back, got himself superfit and makes £5 million a movie. He starred in the nuclear-sub blockbuster *K-19: The Widowmaker* and Martin Scorsese's *The Gangs of New York*. And he remains happily married to Natasha, the mother of his two children.

And what of Mirren? Before Hackford entered her life, she reckons she had had over 100 marriage proposals. She smiled, 'Actually, it is 140 all together, and I take each one absolutely seriously. But I am too cowardly to get married. Marriage means so much ... it means I will find it difficult to ever do so, I believe. The best I expect most of all from a man – good sex and a good laugh, but not, of course, together. I require a great deal of protection because I always get into trouble of one sort or another.

'But I've been incredibly lucky that each of the people I have been involved with has been better than me in some area and has taught me something. I still love the people who have loved me and I hope they still love me.'

Close observers of Mirren's lengthy love-in with Neeson believe that they were doomed from the moment the Irishman 'broke out' career-wise, in *Excalibur*. They saw him become more confident in his ability, less in need of almost daily re-assurance from the live-in lady he treated like royalty. In the twelve months before they finally parted, there was a string of fierce rows.

An actor friend, who had joined their circle of chums at various bistros around the World's End in Chelsea, recalled how Mirren would hold court on the subject of acting, making detailed references to the lives of her stage heroines Dame Peggy Ashcroft and Dame Sybil Thorndike. She'd casually recount her tales of 'Larry in Manchester' – her role alongside Laurence Olivier – and 'Johnny in Rome' – her nightmare on Caligula. Her lover would meanwhile be quietly seething on the other side of the table.

'Liam had just about the longest fuse you could ever imagine,' said the friend. 'But there were occasions when Mirren was on one of her acting rolls, so to speak and you could almost see the smoke coming out of his ears. Sometimes he'd go to the loo, light a cigarette and stay there to cool down. Sometimes he'd jut quietly leave the restaurant and walk up and down the street. Then there were the moments when he went. And when Liam went ... trust me, he went. On one occasion, he held a glass so tightly in rage that the stem snapped off and a cut opened across his thumb, with blood dripping down. When Mirren asked if there was a problem, he just about managed a fake grin, wrapped his handkerchief around the wound and head for the door.

'When he blew, she was just petrified. He once screamed at her, "Who the bloody hell do you think you are, Vivien Merchant or maybe just plain Lily Langtree." Mirren's head would go down and she'd go extremely pale. They had more and more of those rows.'

From their early passionate days together on *Excalibur*, they had partied hard and fast. The wine flowed and, as it flowed, tempers became frayed. Often, her maudlin bursts of melodrama would set him off in a rage. 'As I often do when drinking wine, I became very dramatic,' she confided. 'That's definitely the Russian in me. I remember saying, "Don't you understand, Liam? It's all very well for you. You are a … man!! I am doomed." I was convinced I was going to come to the end of my useful life as an actress.

What was clear was that their two substantial egos were not going to settle under one roof. As Neeson's career picked up, he didn't want to be tied down. He didn't mind making commercial movies and collecting fat pay cheques, so long as there were opportunities to lip away to the quality independent film sector. Mirren was of much the same persuasion. But whose ambition was on a higher level? Who was willing to pack a bag and not return? The answer was abundantly clear to those who knew them best. As one confidante and former neighbour put it, 'Helen could have had Liam forever, for keeps, if that's what she truly wanted. The sad thing, or that's the way we saw it, was that she actually *did* want that, but she was too scared to admit it to herself. Instead, she let it be known that she was holding Liam back, that she could never give him what he wanted, that kind of devotion. On the other hand, she was determined. She was through with Britain, fed up with Margaret Thatcher, even though she admired her, and was completely fed up with the way she was being treated by what was left of the British movie industry. She believed he could make it internationally if she left there and then, but that if she left it for another year or two, the chance would be gone. She once hinted that she thought that Liam would find a younger "filly" to replace her, so she was doing both of them a favour. We all knew she was fooling nobody. She loved him to death … she was just frightened of not living up to his expectations. And she wanted that success. She needed that success, even if it meant being alone for good.

But she was not alone for long. The big question her friends were asking was this: when she jetted off to America to join Taylor

Hackford, was she madly in love, was she riding an upwardly mobile career curve or was she running away from a man who had finally got under her skin?

Could it be possible that she had truly found her White Knight as she gazed across the gently ebbing waterways of St Petersburg, the romantic Venice of the North, as she made *White Nights*?

And there again, did Mirren even need a man permanently in her life?

'I have made sure I am never dependent on a man,' she said. 'It doesn't matter how much they love you. If anyone has economic power over you, you are in a hole and you can be bullied.'

8

GONE WEST

The euphoria of *The Long Good Friday* was over almost before it had begun, though in America the film was seriously rated whenever it was played. In Britain, the gangster yarn which heralded the irresistible rise of Bob Hoskins was unceremoniously placed on top of an ever-growing pile marked 'cult movies'.

Where did Mirren go from here? On stage, there was a scramble to see her. Her portrayal of Webster's Duchess of Malfi was widely acclaimed, many pointing to the tragic scene after she has lost her husband and children as a definitive moment in gifted stage craft. Her anguished cry 'I am the Duchess of Malfi' still sent shockwaves through the auditorium at Manchester's Royal Exchange Theatre.

Her stage career was rock solid. Mirren joined Patrick Magee and Stephen Lewis for Irish playwright Brian Friel's three-hander *The Faith Healer* at the Royal Court in March 1981, playing a middle-aged Irish woman looking down an endless dark pathway towards the future. She was also taking the *Duchess of Malfi* to the Roundhouse and preparing for her début as a producer with a lunchtime play she was presenting at the King's Head in Islington, North London.

The following year she was to play Cleopatra – her second interpretation of the part – in a studio production of *Cleopatra* at The Other Place in Stratford with Michael Gambon as Antony.

She rated her performance as probably the best thing she had ever done, but she failed to pick up the Best Actress award for her work. The rejection further convinced her that it was the right time to bail out of Britain.

'I did feel that I was great,' she said, eschewing her usual modesty. 'I thought that was the best I could be on every level.' She slipped out of the Laurence Olivier Awards feeling bitterly hurt at her failure. 'I thought, Fuck it, that's it, they obviously don't want me,'she said. 'They don't like me. They hate what I do. I'll go somewhere else. I didn't have much acclaim. I wasn't being asked to do any work in England. Nobody was actually asking me to do anything. Suddenly, Hollywood seemed a way of saying, "Fuck you, England." '

There was more classical stage work begging before she boarded a plane. She tackled Thomas Middleton and Thomas Dekker's Jacobean comedy *The Roaring Girl* at the main RSC theatre perched beside the River Avon. The period feminist treatise was set in the poorest streets of London in the seventeenth century and was based on the exploits of a woman called Moll Cutpurse who insisted on living her life as an equal in the disease-riddled underworld of the capital. Mirren enthused, 'The ideas expressed were amazing for their time. They show that feminism is no recent thing and there are some lines there which I certainly enjoy saying. The only difficulty is the Jacobean slang. Moll was quite a woman. She fought and drank with the men. She may even have dressed as a man, which is something I am not doing. Not on this occasion anyway.'

Cleopatra and *The Roaring Girl* were both well received, with Mirren quick to contradict certain critics who felt that the Queen of the Nile should always feature an Elizabeth Taylor lookalike.

'Cleopatra was not a great looker,' she confided, as if demeaning her own physical attributes. 'Her power came through emotion, through her wit, speed of thought and verbal adroitness.

'Everyone has a strongly formed idea of what she looks like. I'm not going to look like that. I'm trying to make the appearance of her as unimportant as possible.'

Movie-wise, however, she was in a vacuum. *Excalibur*, the big-budget, knights-of-olde romp with Columbia Pictures, was about to happen. But she needed more work and all that seemed to be on offer silver screen-wise was the low-budget art-house story *Priest of Love*, starring Ian McKellen as the author DH Lawrence. It was shooting that summer in England and Italy where he wrote *Lady Chatterley's Lover* two years before his death in 1930. She had virtually no decent film work on offer so she took a small, insignificant and anonymous part in the story of Lawrence's flight from Britain following the suppression and burning of his novel *The Rainbow*. By his side was Frieda von Richthofen, the ex-wife of his university professor, whom he had married in 1914, and who was the model for Ursula Brangwen in *The Rainbow*. Janet Suzman played Frieda, with the fabulous Ava Gardner as American camp follower Mabel Dodge Luhan, with James Faulkner portraying Aldous Huxley. The tepid drama was released in Britain in January 1982 with little confidence by Enterprise Pictures. It was greeted with disinterest.

By the weirdest twist of fate, Mirren was to play Frieda herself four years later in a new account of Frieda's life while she was still married to academic Ernest Weekley in Nottingham. Central Television made the TV film *Coming Through* with Kenneth Branagh in the star flashback role of Lawrence. Alison Steadman played a central figure, a visitor to the modern city, who learns through the eyes of a young man why there's such a universal obsession with the writer. Alan Plater, who co-wrote *Priest of Love*, penned the new small-screen drama.

For the first time in her career, Mirren found herself out of work. It was for only a few months, but she was bereft. She watched daytime television for the first time. She read. And she was mostly bored. But at least she could catch up with some socialising. She said, 'Being out of work is one of my worst failings. I'm not good at it. I just watch the damn thing all day ... *Crown Court*, *Afternoon Plus*, anything that's on.'

But Helen Mirren was never one to stay out of the headlines for long. The BBC had signed her up to perform in what the *Sun* billed as 'telly's most explicit sex scene yet' in writer Edna O'Brien's play *Mrs Reinhardt*. Little was left to the imagination, they drooled, while American actor Brad Davis, the late, diminutive star of Alan Parker's award-winning movie *Midnight Express*, seduced her in a shower.

BBC Head of Plays, Keith Williams, made no apologies for the scene which was 'central to the story', though their American co-producers had to make a two-minute cut to ensure that the drama was suitable for the PBS network.

Mirren played a devastated wife who flees to Brittany in France when she finds her husband is having an affair with a younger woman. She meets a young American who outwardly appears charming. The play was broadcast on BBC2 in October 1981.

But Mirren didn't have to wait long for another high-profile role. She returned to familiar territory in a new BBC production of Shakespeare's *A Midsummer's Night's Dream* with a viewer-friendly cast of Robert Lindsay, Nigel Davenport, Brian Glover, Phil Daniels and Nicky Henson. Elijah Moshinsky directed with some difficulty, according to Henson, later to star on the box himself as the successor to Kenneth Cranham in the Laurence Marks and Maurice Gran series *Shine on Harvey Moon*.

Peter McEnery played Oberon to Mirren's Titania. They rehearsed for four weeks and filmed the play in days on multi-videocameras. Director Moshinsky had been ambitious with his set at the BBC's West London centre, going for 'total realism' using freshly planted trees and huge earth mounds pelted by gallons of water to keep it 'alive'. Henson, who played Demetrius, said, 'We turned up for work and it absolutely stank, and I mean *really* stank. All of us, including Helen, were holding handkerchiefs to our noses. The nurse had to be sent for with smelling salts at one point because it was just so awful. As we went on, so it got worse. Much worse. You could almost touch the stench outside the studio in Wood Lane it was so disgusting. This was supposed to be a prestige production, but it was rapidly turned into farce. The earth became mud and the mud became slime. You really had to watch your step when you weren't trying to hold your breath. The crew would have been amused were it not for the fact they were in the same position. We all grinned and bore it, including Helen.'

Henson had, in fact, met Mirren when she was a student teacher en route to the National Youth Theatre back in the mid-Sixties He was appearing in the musical *Camelot* and he became a fan as they had a drink together with friends in the saloon bar of the Opera Tavern in Drury Lane. 'She was so striking,' he said. 'People noticed her. Then Harold Hobson, the critic, raved about her and he sort of lit the blue touch paper. She was two different people, either up and down ... and has that appeal ... to the fellas. She's all about sex and domination. There is something foreign about her, probably to do with her Russian background, which was exciting.

'She was no English rose. She was this free spirit and it was Swinging London and nobody thought about class. You thought about cracking it and she was definitely going to crack it. But she hadn't changed when we met again, she was still terrific fun to be with.'

They got to know each other well, later going to the annual Equity Ball in London's West End. 'When actors talk about Mirren ... it's about SEX,' he laughs. 'Sex with perhaps a touch of lust. Men fancy her like mad and women admire her. They would love her sex appeal.

'But she was never a flighty character. She was quite serious at another level. It's that Russian thing again. She would cross the line and be dangerous. Nothing threatened her artistically. She still has this animal magnetism, even though she's moving into a different area now. She is now this Grande Dame.'

After she made *Excalibur* in Ireland for John Boorman, finding romance with Liam Neeson, her agent Maggie Parker had lined up more television work.

She starred with Nigel Havers and Ian Holm in *Soft Targets,* the BBC's *Play for Today* which was broadcast in October 1982. Holm played a homesick Russian diplomat who smells a plot at a high-society wedding. Then she returned to the Shakespearian classics playing Imogen in a BBC/Time-Life production of *Cymbeline*, again with director Moshinsky as the driving force. But he wisely kept a dry set this time around for Richard Johnson, in the lead role, and the ageless Claire Bloom.

The influence of Liam Neeson and all things Irish was strong at this time in Mirren's life. She wanted to be involved in a project which said something about the problems the Irish faced, encapsulating real human dilemmas. She wasn't interested in the rights and wrongs of the the Troubles. That wasn't her territory. But she did care about the effect the long, gruesome conflict was having on ordinary, decent people. Hence her dedication some 13 years later to making *Some Mother's Son*.

Neeson had briefly earlier met director Pat O'Connor in Dublin. The director, who's now married to the American actress Elizabeth Mastrantonio, studied at UCLA and had just turned 40 but was still a relative novice in the film industry. Over a drink, O'Connor told him he was casting *Cal* and explained how pivotal the female lead actress was to the entire story. 'If she didn't click with whom I have in mind, then I'm in real trouble. *We're* in real trouble.'

Neeson suggested that O'Connor take himself off to the Royal Court to see a certain lady called Helen Mirren in action in *The Faith Healer*. O'Connor thought of Mirren more as a screen sex symbol and a serious stage actress than necessarily the kind of subtle personality he required to pull off the role of Marcella in his drama. But once he'd seen her in *The Faith Healer*, later meeting her, he was convinced. The £2 million film would mark the debut of the 22-year-old brooding, Ulster-born actor John Lynch with his gaunt, pallid complexion and coal-black eyes. He was still at drama school in London.

And the film turned out to be Mirren's finest cinematic hour to date.

Cal, based on Bernard MacLaverty's novel, was a bleak love story set against the backdrop of sectarian violence in Ulster. He was a 19-year-old hunted IRA activist and she was the Italian widow of an RUC officer who worked in the local library. Cal also happened to be heavily involved in his murder. But she would be his salvation, his redemption.

Mirren's hair was now shorter and dark. Her accent was Irish. Though wanting to make a 'serious, well-intentioned Irish film', she nevertheless had grave doubts about *Cal* before and during the making of the movie in the dusty town of Drogheda and Newbridge, which doubled for Belfast. She queried the violent nature of the story. She wasn't happy about shedding her clothes once more for another love story. People had warned her not to take the part, though Neeson believed her pairing with the moody, James Dean-like Lynch would be sensational. He was right.

Mirren, on location in late summer 1982, was a mass of uncertainty and indecision, rewriting her lines as she went along while calming the nervous young Lynch. Why was she in Ireland? Did she have 100 per cent faith in the story? 'I'm one of the school that likes to get up and go to work in the morning,' she said. 'You've just got to take everything that is offered to you, within reason. There's an awful lot of good actresses around.

'You start off with intuition, then you get bogged down in technique, then a wonderful fusion starts happening. It's a great moment in any actor or actress's life, but, in the case of the actress, it's the very moment nobody wants you to work any more because you're not young and pretty enough. That's the point I am at now.'

Director O'Connor was convinced he had the right formula. He said, 'I felt that Helen would be right because she is strong and interesting and has this marvellous intelligence. From being a vamp a few years ago, she has turned into a very beautiful woman.'

John Lynch echoed his feelings. 'I was very frightened working with Helen,' he confided. 'But she was lovely, just great.'

She need not have had any fears. The movie in which she shed her image of hooker-cum-sex bomb was an award-winning critical success.

Her insecurity, however, followed her into the Eighties. There were times she'd wake up in a cold sweat and Neeson would calm her. She'd be convinced that her career was in freefall, that she'd never work again. The demons wouldn't go away.

'You would think acting would get easier as you get older, but it doesn't,' she said. 'You are always on the edge of the abyss, the fear that you can no longer do it. It's no wonder some actors are such astronomical drunks. With films, it is so easy to lose a sense of identity. You know, in your heart, you're a puppet in a very technical medium, another "thing", perhaps no more important than the sunset or any beautiful piece of lighting. Yet, conversely, everyone rushes around treating you like a goddess. No wonder so many movie stars become monsters. The key thing is to try and feel in control of your own destiny.

'When I was making *Cal*, I suddenly thought I had lost my craft. I hadn't. But I thought I had and that made me feel terribly insecure. Basically, it was to do with not being in control, that what you were doing would be for all time on film and that you'd watch it on the bloody television in, say, five years time and be confronted with it over and over again. Those thoughts can be very nerve-racking.'

In January 1984, a new chapter in Mirren's life was about to begin. Hollywood was finally beckoning. They had heard about the former convent schoolgirl from the Thames Estuary. And what they'd heard was good.

Director Peter Hyams had seen enough of her in *Excalibur* and *Hussy* to suggest that she was absolutely right for the £14 million thriller *2010*, the sequel to Stanley Kubrick's mind-numbing, celluloid inter-gallactic epic *2001: A Space Odyssey* which was released in 1968.

The urbane Hyams was on something of a roll so far as 'life up there' was concerned, having having just written and directed *Outland*, a clever Big Brother-style science-fiction drama which was a box-office success for Sean Connery.

The plot of *2010* was basically simple and light years away from the moralising of issue-driven Kubrick. Earth was on the brink of war and scientists, dominated by the self-motivated military, wanted to return to Jupiter to learn the fate of the craft taken into another dimension by the astronaut played by Keir Dullea. And what was that floating black monolith about, anyway? Science-fiction aficionados were keen to hear the voice of Hal, the crazed, deluded master-computer back in action. What they got was more of a Wild West tale. Hollywood prefers answers and a spot of gunfire.

But for Mirren, this was – or at least could be – the turning point. Her romance with Neeson was in danger of becoming stagnant. Much as she adored him, she saw no long-term future for them together. But, for the moment at least, she would concentrate on her career.

She would be playing tough Russian cosmonaut leader Colonel Tanya Kirbuk, a role which again took her back to her roots. Her Russian was, in fact, more or less non-existent and she needed a voice coach to make her sound like the genuine article.

She rented an apartment in Hollywood on the same block where Bette Davis once 'reigned' and soon actually got to take tea and mull over the great days of Tinseltown with the legendary star who lived nearby. Every morning, she drove proudly through the studio gates in her red Mustang convertible, usually wearing her trademark knee-length, red leather boots.

'I feel I have sold out slightly by taking an American movie, especially as I took the job without reading the script,' she grinned. 'But it seemed such a treat to go to America. I had only been once before with the RSC, so I was prepared to waive my naturally artistic thing.

'But the day I arrived, I just felt this great pressure lift off my head. I felt free. I realised I hadn't been happy professionally for two or three years. There is this predjudice in Europe about American actors, that they're not serious. It's all glamour with them and the rest. But they were wonderful.

'To be honest, I'd got to the point where I was in despair

professionally in England. I felt I was carrying a lot of excess baggage which I couldn't shake off. Producers, casting people, had this version of me, this sexual independent image. I came to America and suddenly nobody treated or cast me like that. It was such an enormous relief.'

And while she waited for other roles, she did the tour of agents who told her how much they had enjoyed *The Long Goodbye*, showing their confusion with *The Long Good Friday*. The agents were largely fun, lived on another planet, and barely spoke her language. Some of the roles they had on offer were palpably ludicrous. A friend remarked, 'Helen had to pluck up all her courage to get to their offices and occasionally needed a very large glass of wine to get her going. This was definitely not her scene. Most of them had seen nothing of her work because she had been on stage or in largely art-house-type stuff. They were talking about a sequel to *Killer Tomatoes* or maybe working with John Travolta and she was hoping they'd say, "How do you feel about Michael Douglas or Paul Newman?" It was hilarious, but it was not a meeting of minds!'

It wasn't long before she was on the move to share another apartment on Orange Drive just off La Brea Boulevard, taking the small 'maid's room' overlooking the back yard. One of her flatmates was a willowy blonde photographer called Rory Flynn, the daughter of swashbuckling matinée idol Errol Flynn.

The situation inspired her and her friend writer Carinthia West to put together the treatment for a new sitcom called *English Muffins* which was about two English girls and an American struggling to survive under the same roof. They likened it to the current UK hit *AbFab*, and were astonished when Universal paid them over £2,000 for the rights. Sadly for them, Tracey Ullman, Dawn French and Co were about to launch the sitcom *Girls on Top* on British television which effectively destroyed her vision.

In May 1984, while she was still filming *2010* on the old MGM lot with co-stars John Lithgow and Roy Scheider, the call came through that the jury headed by Dirk Bogarde voted her Best Actress at the Cannes Film Festival for her portrayal of Marcella in *Cal*. All those doubts she had vanished in the same split-second she was given the news. What's more, it was her first ever award for her work on film. It was celebration time and Mirren and Co grabbed as many bottles of bubbly as they could carry from a liquor store and headed down to the beach at Malibu.

2010 was to do fair to average business at the box office on its release in Spring 1985. The truth was that neither the 'star' names nor the plot were strong or novel enough to take the film into orbit. Words such as 'lacklustre' and 'dull' were bandied around, and Mirren was not particularly surprised. But the Russian she spoke in *2010* was 'flawless' according to the Russian actors on the set, though she never understood her lines. In fact, her accent was so good it was immediately to help win her one of the lead roles in Taylor Hackford's *White Nights*. She was to play a Russian ballerina and the mistress of an exiled ballet-dancing icon played by Mikhail Baryshnikov. The film was made with Gregory Hines in full support as another Cold War dissident in the summer of 1984 in St Petersburg.

Ironically, her real-life Russian family was rapidly disappearing. After her father's death in 1981, her grandmother and her Auntie Olga were also soon to pass away.

But she had also gained family, as the flame of her long love affair with Hackford had been lit.

Once she'd finished work on *White Nights*, she fished around for more work in America before returning to England for a small role in the Channel 4-backed family weepie *Heavenly Pursuits* with Tom Conti. Charles Gormley's story focused on a remedial class at a Scottish school where a couple of miracles are required to make a saint of a local woman. The low-budget adventure, with a fine support cast of Brian Pettifer, David Hayman and Ewen Bremner, wanted to say something about education, the less fortunate and faith. But the messages were jumbled in a morass of sentimentality and it failed to strike any kind of chord. Mirren was in Glasgow for less than three weeks playing the rather saintly Ruth Chancellor who tries to guide sceptical teacher Vic Mathews (Conti) on to the right path. You could almost hear her whispering, 'Yuk!'

What a relief it was to get back on stage in late 1984 to star with Kevin McNally in William Mastrosimone's *Extremeties*. The play was based on the true story of an attempted rape in which the victim gets power over her aggressor and focused on one of the hottest topical issue of our times: were female victims of rape in some way responsible for having led their attackers on through their dress or behaviour? One argument was that men, on seeing scantily clad women in the streets, believed it gave them every right to assault them sexually. It was a well-acted, fine piece of drama.

There was now another matter in hand as Mirren bided her time in London. She had to bid a final farewell to Liam Neeson and go through the tiresome process of putting her Fulham home on the market.

By now, the Hollywood bug had well and truly bitten and she was off to the jungles of Belize in South America and a date with Harrison Ford to make the film version of Paul Theroux's novel *The Mosquito Coast*. On arrival there, she was slightly disappointed by the tiny British protectorate with its army base and clubs for officers. The director was the brilliant Australian Peter Weir, who made the award-winning *Dead Poet's Society* and, more recently, *The Truman Show* with Jim Carrey. He already had a habit of making classy films, such as the black comedy *The Cars That Ate Paris*; the mystical, dreamy *Picnic at Hanging Rock*; Mel Gibson's breakthrough First World War saga *Gallipoli* and the outstanding *The Year of Living Dangerously*, again with Gibson but with the alluring Sigourney Weaver in tow. Linda Hunt was most memorable in his study of corruption and greed in Indonesia for winning an Oscar while dressed as a man, playing Gibson's sidekick photographer. Weir had worked twice before with Ford on the spy yarn *Hanover Street* and the top-drawer thriller *Witness*, which put Kelly McGillis on the map. He knew him well and it was very much the old pals' act, with the late River Phoenix playing one of Ford's screen children.

But Weir wasn't quite sure what to make of Mirren who was keeping a very close eye on make-up and wardrobe. Having just turned 40, she seemed especially sensitive as to how she was going to look next to the glamorous Ford in the family drama. 'I went absolutely to pieces when I met him,' she confided. 'It's so dumb. Me, acting like some little fan. It's not that I don't have confidence in my own ability. I do. But I just get ill at ease around celebrities.'

Amusingly, Ford felt intimidated by her. He told visiting friends that he'd never met anyone like Mirren, comparing her to 'Julie Andrews ... but with lust'. A member of the crew joked, 'Harrison was a tremendous fan and was slightly in awe of her, mainly because of her work with the Royal Shakespeare Company. Though he'd made the *Star Wars* movies and *Raiders of the Lost Ark*, which had made a colossal amount of money, he regarded her as a 'proper' actor, not somebody who raced around doing comic-book stuff for boys.

A senior member of the crew said, 'So, it was kind of fun watching them edge around each other for weeks before they felt comfortable about just getting on with it. They were terribly polite to each other as well. It was like watching Katherine Hepburn and Humphrey Bogart play those wonderful sparring characters in *The African Queen*, but for real. You could tell by the way Harrison would raise his eybrows after a conversation with her and she would kind of lower her head as he walked away that they had some work to do on each other.'

Weir needed her to look washed out and at her wits' end for her role of the docile wife, known simply and rather demandingly as 'Mother'. Ford was the dynamic Allie Fox, a frustrated inventor and visionary who packs up and moves his family to the remote coastal village in pursuit of his Utopian dream which turns out to be building an ice factory.

But it wasn't the happiest of shoots, with Mirren doing her best to compromise with Weir on aspects of the script and herself. The film was an artistic disappointment, one of Ford's few in his golden career and was a total box-office disaster, though Warner Bros were at pains to stress that the budget was kept low at £12 million. It had been a long time since she felt just a little out of her depth and uncomfortable with her surroundings. And perhaps the part of the weak woman called 'Mother' didn't really suit her at all. Throughout her career, she had played to her strengths and her biggest asset was her power, her ability to control. Anyone who called her 'Mother' when she wasn't working was treated to the fully fixed Mirren glare, which was likened to the Gorgon turning her victims to stone.

Being the only woman in the cast, and an Englishwoman at that, didn't lend itself towards the cameraderie she sought in the remote British outpost. She was lonely. She missed her Hackford. And she wished she was back in her newly bought London flat in Battersea, overlooking Battersea Park, quietly sipping a cup of tea.

Belize, one of the poorest countries in the region, reminded her of her African adventure well over a decade earlier. There they were, the men with the fat cigars from Hollywood, the hangers-on around Ford, and there, just a few yards away, were the locals who could live on $5 a week. She'd been used to better hotels and greater comforts while working on movies, but this was different. They were playing a couple battling against the elements, fighting nature. People who'd turned their backs on that kind of 'civilisation'. So, complaints from outsiders with Beverly Hills addresses seemed less than tactful under the circumstances.

The crew were also quick to spot how unsettled Mirren was and went out of their way to keep her 'cool' and amuse her. One senior member of the production team flew in from Los Angeles and noticed how pale and exhausted she had become. One morning, after a lengthy meeting with Weir, he saw a tear trickle down across her cheek. She casually, without any fuss, mopped it aside with a handkerchief and returned to her Winebago. He said, 'It was pretty clear she wasn't enjoying herself. It wasn't that Peter was making things dificult or that she didn't get on particularly well with Harrison. He was a great admirer ... it was just that he had problems talking to her. Actually, he was terrified of her! They were just very different people and she didn't feel "right" being there or being in the role. I think she realised she had made a mistake. But every day it seemed she had to pull herself up to keep going. It was tough for her and she is a tough lady.

'She also had a deep empathy with the country and the locals, as did her partner Taylor Hackford who spent time in the region with the Peace Corps. She thought there should have been a greater sensitivity shown by certain people connected to the production.'

Other members of the cast and senior technical staff mistook her gloom for recurring bust-ups which didn't happen, or friction between her and Ford, which didn't exist. Mirren simply felt sad she wasn't able to play Hollywood's game quite the way they wanted her to. She was not from the grin-and-bear-it school of acting.

'It was terrible torture because I was in terrible conflict with the character. I am notoriously not like that,' she later confessed. 'It's a male-invented fantasy of the nurturing, caring, non-critical, non-argumentative woman, everything which drives you crazy. I stomped around saying, "Bloody men, who do they think they are?" It spilled over into my feelings for Harrison and Peter.' But she insisted that it wasn't the 'age thing' getting her down. 'The really terrible milestone was being 17,' she said. 'It's all downhill from then. I can't understand why 40 is supposed to be so traumatic.'

Mirren, undiplomatically, failed to be impressed with Ford's sexual prowess, even down to his lack of zip in the 'lippo' department. 'He's the nicest, sweetest guy ... but he can't kiss. He finds it impossible on screen. He's probably not very good off-screen either! It's not just me ... other actresses agree with me.'

She was also becoming rapidly disillusioned with the Hollywood star system and the superficial lifestyle. She claimed her superstar neighbours were 'infantilised by the community around them and, at the same time, disdained'.

She said, 'Everybody laughs at their jokes, they get nannies to look after their children and their cars are all paid for. They turn up with two assistants and all this huge kerfuffle. But as soon as they walk on set, they are basically despised. They have no real power.'

Mirren was soon to restore her sanity with the best possible 'elixir': Taylor Hackford and a good stage role. She had made almost a full recovery from her experiences in Belize by the time she got back to England and Battersea in February 1987 to star in Flaubert's *Madame Bovary* which had been adapted by Edna O'Brien at the Watford Palace, just outside London in Hertfordshire.

In the summer, she'd been booked for a prestige TV job, playing a *femme fatale* in a new small-screen version of Terence Rattigan's *Cause Célèbre*, with David Morrissey as her young lover and the veteran acting star Harry Andrews as her elderly husband.

Production executives felt she was still unsettled from her spell in Belize with Harrison Ford and Co. She was tense and unusually touchy. Behind the scenes, bickering and a major row with a national newspaper – which resulted in her later winning £25,000 in an out-of-court settlement – marred what should have been a pleasant excursion to Norfolk where Anglia Television were making the drama.

Mirren's temper snapped over the suggestion that she'd been 'unprofessional'. Whatever she was or might be, Mirren was aghast, especially at being labelled 'Britain's answer to Sean Penn' in an article by a visiting journalist who'd been expecting to interview her.

Briefly, she returned to the gorgeous hillside home she shared with Hackford before considering her next move. Offers of good work weren't exactly pouring in from studio executives she met at parties who always left with a wave and the words 'You'll be hearing from us!' She rarely did.

Though she might not have thought so, Mirren's reputation for playing powerful, smart, attractive women was gently nudging her towards the same much-respected bracket of actresses in Hollywood as Sally Field, Glenn Close, Meryl Streep and Susan Sarandon.

Yet, in a sense, frustrated Mirren was still waiting to be 'discovered'. She could play Russian or French. She could do 'dowdy' and 'dirty sexy', but there remained a barrier between her and the 'A' league, script-controlling casting agents and producers.

Though nobody was spelling it out or able to completely put their finger on the problem, the film-makers who had clout were fascinated by Mirren and at the same time wary. It bothered them. They couldn't tell where she was coming from or where she wanted to go. Her instant body language suggested 'Garboesque', while others decided she was simply 'cerebral'. Was she 'enigmatic'? She'd always claim to be straightforward enough. Down-to-earth. Mmm. Maybe she'd got that one wrong. But all she simply wanted to do was work, quality work, and leave the mind games to the super-agents running Hollywood.

She told a close friend, 'They think I am "intelligent" or trying to be clever and I think some of them are quite stupid. They want to turn non-issues into issues and they want to dumb down at every available opportunity in the cause of a few extra dollars. They talk about movies as though they are hot dogs with the fillings making the difference. I'm afraid we are mostly in two differents worlds.'

And so, while she got good, solid middle-of-the-road scripts to scan, the usual suspects, such as Meryl Streep, could rely on getting first look at almost all the top-drawer material.

Mirren headed back to Europe once more to make the old-fashioned, romantic, turn-of-the-century tale *Pascali's Island*, leaving Hollywood's excesses and prejudices in her wake. James Dearden who created the original story for *Fatal Attraction* had written the piece and was also directing. Mirren played a beautiful, mysterious Austrian artist in self-imposed exile who rises from a swim in the Mediterranean to have a fling with an enigmatic Brit, played by new British acting talent Charles Dance, on a Turkish island outpost in 1908. There's plenty of intrigue boiling away as Ben Kingsley, playing a bored Turkish spy, also has his eye on the divine Lydia Newman, played by Mirren.

At least it was nice to have the guys fighting over her, so long as nobody got hurt. She said, 'After playing a succession of very strong characters, I adored the idea of this soft, romantic woman with two men chasing after her. I particularly love costume dramas, which has probably much to do with my theatrical training. The director had this kind of image of me looking like a Klimt woman with masses of red hair. It was all quite unashamedly romantic. Charles and I were forever swimming naked in rock pools or galloping along the beach on horseback.'

Dance was equally delirious over Mirren who had been 'over committed' when she might have joined him out in India on the award-winning TV serial *The Jewel in the Crown*. They were pencilled as prospective ill-fated lovers Guy Perron and Daphne Manners.

Here he was, two years on, delicately fondling her brow on the dreamily romantic island of Rhodes, which was doubling for a Turkish hideaway. The tall, fair-haired, beautifully spoken Dance proclaimed, 'I don't think there's anybody to match Helen for certain roles. She has talent, sex appeal and she is fiercely intelligent.'

In the summer of 1988, she made the Central Television-backed eco-drama *When the Whales Came*. Written by Michael Morpurgo and directed by Clive Rees, with a backdrop of the Scilly Isles off the coast of Cornwall, she enjoyed the break and the treat of watching the revered Paul Scofield at work. He played a hermit-like character called The Birdman in the period piece about an island community just watching time pass them by until a pod of narwhals are beached. Scofield emerges to warn the locals not to slaughter the creatures or the past will revisit them! John Hallam, Barbara Ewing, Nicholas Jones and David Suchet, whom she'd just left behind on *Cause Célèbre*, were solid in support. Sadly, like a rare species threatened by the elements, the sentimental family drama also vanished without trace.

Mirren came back to London early the following year to vent her finely tuned versatility with the late Bob Peck in the British première of Arthur Miller's double-bill *Two-Way Mirror* at the Young Vic. In the first playlet, she subtly portrayed a woman in an expensive shop assisting an older man to choose a present for his dying lover. In the second, she re-emerged at full blast as a tragic schizophrenic prostitute. The critics gave both her and the formidable Peck, Steven Spielberg's dinosaur expert in *Jurassic Park*, rave reviews.

There was probably nobody better than Mirren when it came to delivering a 'genuine' Russian accent. She'd kept away from television since making *Cause Célèbre*, but was tempted back by the quality of Ron Hutchinson's script to fly into Washington and make the thriller *Red King, White Knight*, a co-production between HBO and the British company Zenith. The not entirely unique storyline revolved around a KGB plot to assassinate the Soviet General Secretary, thereby offering a new threat to America and her allies. Tom Skerritt played the central figure Stoner, an ex-CIA agent brought back into service to ruin their evil plan, while Mirren played Anna, a sophisticted Russian he'd fallen for in Moscow while he was active for the agency. No prizes here for guessing what happens when they stumble into each other again. Will they, won't they? Well, of course, they must. And he still has time to save civilisation as we know it. Max von Sydow looked typically menacing alongside former *Taxi* star Lou Hirsch in a classy cast. And she was introduced to Tom Bell, later to rejoin Mirren in *Prime Suspect*, who'd been drafted in to play a hard-nosed Russian agent.

The Eighties had almost faded away when Mirren resurfaced in a shocker which was to shatter illusions surrounding nouvelle cuisine and the British class structure.

Welsh-born director Peter Greenaway, a former artist, was going through a career purple patch, having just made the period sexual romp *The Draughtsman's Contract*, the modern tragedy *Belly of an Architect*, and the black comedy *Drowning by Numbers*, when he approached Mirren to star with Michael Gambon in his controversial new celluloid 'essay'.

The dapper, urbane Greenaway was the critics' darling who often enraged and outraged his peers with what was described as 'experimental cinema'. More basically, he could put lashings of nudity and graphic sex on screen and dress the whole concoction up to produce 'art'. Ken Russell wasn't impressed. He said, 'What is it about Greenaway's films which makes the flesh crawl? I think it's his apparent loathing of the human race.' The late Derek Jarman, who also stood accused of making pretentious movies, said sarcastically, 'If Gucci handbags were still in fashion, Greenaway would carry his scripts in them.' No doubt the Monty Python mob would have devoted an hour-long special to Greenaway had he been born a few years earlier. He wanted to make films about 'excess'.

Actors literally queued up to 'do a Greenaway' for a small pay cheque in the same way Hollywood stars queued around the block in New York for an audience with Woody Allen. He started making movies when he was 20 and, though he was never box office, his influence on world cinema has been immense. If Harold Pinter had been born a film-maker, he would have been Peter Greenaway.

Mirren was suitably flattered and intrigued when she was offered the script to *The Cook, The Thief, His Wife and Her Lover*, which was to be made at Elstree Studios in Borehamwood, Hertfordshire. 'It's sinful to say, but I had not seen one of his films before the script arrived and my reaction on first reading was just amazement at his talent,' she said. 'Everyone finds all sorts of meanings in it, but my feeling is that it is a modern Jacobean revenge play about the destruction of the world.'

Few others, especially in the British tabloid press, saw the film in the same complex light. Greenaway had assembled a magnificent cast around Mirren, with Michael Gambon as her screen husband and RSC actor Alan Howard as her lover.

The Palace/Miramax co-production placed Gambon in a top London restaurant holding court as coarse, cruel gangster Albert Spica, a man who wore his designer clothes with all the panache of a neon sign flashing across Piccadilly Circus. His language was foul, his worldly knowledge television-fed. He struck fear into his entourage of cronies, including a weak-kneed Tim Roth. By his side was his magnificently coutured, voluptuous wife Georgina, who was both bored and frustrated by her empty life as a 'moll'. She glanced across the restaurant and spotted the academic Howard alone and reading. She was fascinated and physically attracted. Lust took over as they crept quietly away to the toilet and passionately tore off their clothes.

The affair was at first conducted in the trendy restaurant behind Spica's back. His wife and her lover copulated, explicitly, in the kitchen, the poultry larder and meat store with the aid of the cook played by French actor Richard Bohringer.

When they were almost caught by Spica, they made their escape stark naked in a refrigerated van loaded with rotten meat. The professor and his lover are then seen hosed down by the kitchen staff. Howard, who played the character Michael, was then horrifically murdered by Spica's sadistic gang, literally asphyxiated by his own history books.

And with what can only be described as Greenaway's *pièce de résistance*, Georgina took her revenge in a stomach-churning cannibalistic final sequence. The incredible food seen during the movie was served up by the Savoy and the fashions which caused much fuss in the glossies were dreamed up by Jean-Paul Gaultier. The London Voice Choir supplied the eerie accompanying music.

Pornography or art? The old argument flared again. The film stands today, depending on which side of the cinema you are on, as either a classic or trash.

Mirren knew where she stood. 'It was pure, uninvolved sex,' she said. 'I can understand that, it's a fantasy that lies deep in all of us. No names, just get on with it. But the love scenes weren't a problem. Sex is part of human behaviour. The worst bit was having to go naked into the van with all the dead meat and the flies. I did think twice about having to walk around and play scenes at the same time. But because he [Greenaway] has the eyes of a painter, he knows exactly how a scene will look and is able to tell you. That gives you the confidence to do it.'

Others slammed Greenaway's latest escapade as 'annoying and stupid', condemning the hideous violence. Channel 4 at first refused to finance the film because of its 'terrifying script' and ended up buying it. The movie was so popular during the dynamic period of *perestroika* in Russia, that pirated VHS copies were snapped up as soon as they arrived in Red Square. The French turned on the movie and the vile Spica, especially the scene in which he force-fed dog excrement to an unfortunate victim.

The Cook, The Thief ... inspired outcries in the tabloids, and was certainly a landmark movie for Mirren in 1989, during a phase in which she was finding it increasingly difficult finding quality movie work. Her great friend and ally Laurence Olivier had just died and, everywhere she turned, everyone else seemed to be on a roll: Michael Keaton and Kim Basinger were steaming up the screen with Jack Nicholson in overdrive as The Joker in Tim Burton's *Batman*; Meg Ryan was Hollywood's sweetheart from *When Harry Met Sally*; and Sean Connery raked it in playing Indiana Jones's old man in *Indiana Jones and the Last Crusade*. Irish starlet Alison Doody was Indiana's girl, though she may have been 20 years his junior. And Tom Cruise had made far and away his best movie to date, playing Dustin Hoffman's elder brother in Barry Levinson's Oscar-winning *Rain Man*.

There were rumours that all was not well between Mirren and Taylor Hackford. She had certainly become disillusioned with the movie czars of Hollywood and their aggressive, masculine working practices. In the background, her chum Adrian Noble – who was later to become the artistic director of the RSC – insisted that she belonged on this side of the Atlantic. He said, 'Helen is the Queen in exile. It feels like she has disappeared from the theatre here, which is terrible for us. She should come back. She says she will but she has been saying that for the last ten years.'

Mirren was restless and her mind more or less made up. The best work, like *The Cook, The Thief...*, was back in Blighty. She could always leap on a plane to California should a decent part drop through the letterbox. But her opportunity to make an impact on the commercial cinema in America had passed. At least for the moment. But how was she to know that an ex-actress who lived in a mansion on top of a hill 6,000 miles away was about to shape and change her destiny for ever?

9

WHITE
KNIGHT

T all ... urbane ... charismatic ... softly spoken ... the beard is
  Christmas white and neatly trimmed while his hair is dark and
cut well away from his forehead. At first sight, he might well be a
college professor or a razor-sharp Wall Street lawyer in his colourful
selection of designer blazers. Or an explorer about to parachute into
the Amazon

Taylor Hackford is a man who wears his conscience on his sleeve.
And, though he might make a great deal of his Scottish roots, he's
extremely American. If you'd searched high and low from London
to Los Angeles, you probably couldn't have found a less likely
candidate to sweep La Mirren off her feet and one day into a church
for a wedding.

Perhaps. A director who got to know the actress well prior to
her liaison with Hackford commented, 'You always felt with
Helen that she would follow a pattern as far as men are
concerned – sophisticated, most definitely cerebral and usually
British. She certainly hadn't been that impressed by what she'd
seen in Los Angeles as the average American male. But she hadn't

been with anyone on a really serious level for some time. So she was ripe, up for it, so to speak. Also, she'd been getting some verbals about reaching the great "four-oh" and being alone. The timing was perfect.'

He couldn't have been more unlike Liam Neeson, the actor she had just left behind, when they met in early 1984 in London where she auditioned for his film *White Nights*.

It was not a good start, as far as relationships go. Hackford and a script executive turned up 25 minutes late for their meeting with Mirren after taking lunch with Baryshnikov, and she was furious. He recalls, 'I apologised but what I got back was this cold disdain. She was not amused. She had "attitude" and she even smoked. Actresses rarely smoke any more at auditions through fear of giving offence. She was saying "this is me". The small talk didn't work either. That was plain enough. She lost her patience with me finally and said, "Are we going to read?" You don't mess this girl around. Then, she asked me whether there was anything else I needed to know and it was like, when I glanced up, she had gone. Whoosh! She was out of there. It wasn't the best possible start to any relationship, whether it be professional or personal.

'Anyone who knows Helen will tell you she does not like to be messed about. She is a woman who stands up for herself and what she believes. She does not suffer fools gladly and she is immensely professional. I think she wore the expression of a British actress looking at a Californian film-maker thinking, Ah, another Hollywood moron. She would have been brilliant anyway, but she gave an extremely powerful reading ... I think somewhat urged on by wanting to say something to me and my colleagues.'

Hackford may not have realised it but, on reflection, they had more in common than he could have imagined. They had to battle every inch of the way to earn a decent living in often hostile conditions. He was just five months older than her. Though their parents were well-educated, intelligent and resourceful, they struggled to achieve in a manner more suited to their abilities. In

Mirren's case, her somewhat aloof, distant father was of aristocratic Russian stock while Hackford's mother was forced to guard every cent when her husband left her before her baby son could barely walk. Her parents and his mother were of the generations who firmly believed you did the right thing and lived to a decent set of moral values.

He recalled, 'My parents divorced when I was just a few months old. I spent a couple of summers with my father but hardly ever saw him again. My mother had little to no financial support and it was very hard for her. But she was tough, she was a very strong woman. She wasn't a tragic figure, though she had to withstand some terrible things. When I was eight, my brother, who was 15 years older, was electrocuted in an accident at work. Having gone through that, which is something you never truly recover from, she became ill a year later from breast cancer. Still she fought on. She had the will. It was a traumatic experience for me, sure enough, being witness to these things. But you grew up, you became mature. Or you blew it in other ways. You folded.'

Sadly, his mother died shortly before he met Mirren. He says, 'I know they would have got on. She would have adored Helen. They both had this strength in character, this resolve. She wanted to see me happy again. She would have been very excited by Helen. But it's not about how clever she is or I am. There is more to us as a couple than that.'

While he grieved over his mother's death, a new bright light of love was about to ignite his life as he prepared to make *White Nights* on location in Finland, Portugal and Scotland.

The story, by James Goldman and Eric Hughes, basically focused on a rather precious Russian ballet star called Nikolai Rodchenko played by Mikhail Baryshnikov who's on a plane that is forced to crash-land back in the USSR. Past allegiances and loyalties are swapped with new pals Raymond Greenwood, an American dancer played by Gregory Hines, living in St Petersburg and his wife Darya, played by Isabella Rossellini. Will he or won't he dance again with the Kirov Ballet Company? Into the mix came Mirren as the delicious, mysterious Galina Ivanova, his former lover whose career took a nasty tumble when he did a bunk eight years earlier. Bets on who actually made it out of Russia in this romantic Cold War action drama were not taken.

The Columbia-backed movie – with Helsinki and the Finnish towns of Pori and Reposaari doubling for St Petersburg – actually deserved better treatment from the critics though the vulnerable, unworldly character portrayed by Rossellini perhaps caught the eye more than Mirren's slightly icy, manipulative Galina. Beguiling Rossellini, the daughter of the late Swedish screen beauty Ingrid Bergman, was becoming 'hot' Hollywood-wise during this period and *White Nights*, it was hoped by her agents, would help her to shed her 'European art house' label and become a more commercial commodity.

The intention was also to give Baryshnikov a solid, workable vehicle through which to show his talents, and the money men liked the equation. They also had a top-drawer soundtrack featuring Lionel Ritchie and Phil Collins, who crashed into the charts with Marilyn Martin singing the ageless duet *Separate Lives*. Every cent in the budget was carefully monitored by accountants putting extra pressure on Hackford. At one stage, he needed to hire a 747 for extra scenes involving Baryshnikov, but the cost was adjudged as 'impractical' by the studio. Instead, a hump was temporarily moulded on to the fuselage of a much smaller aircraft in a hangar.

For Mirren, forever examining her Russian heritage, it was another opportunity following her cosmonaut in *2010* to explore that Slav dynamic in her personality.

Hackford, it must be said, was and is a film-maker who wouldn't normally allow personal considerations to fog his direction behind the cameras. Yet, here was an extraordinary phase in his life when he had little doubt that a certain flame-haired British actress was indeed occupying his inner thoughts.

A friend said, 'It wasn't exactly as if he was avoiding women or that he had taken a vow of some sort. But he had two boys who were at an impressionable age and he couldn't afford to upset their mothers. He also had his own life.'

But by the time the unit had reached Helsinki, he was smitten by Mirren and flowers were being delivered to her hotel room. She reciprocated with white roses and enchanted the director.

A female member of the crew observed, 'Helen was so taken aback when this enormous bouquet arrived that she couldn't help herself. She burst into tears. Taylor wanted a woman to deliver the flowers because he felt it would make Helen feel more comfortable. He was absolutely right. The lads in the crew thought it was hilarious when Taylor got his bouquet. They thought something might be going on between him and Isabella. They knew she absolutely worshipped directors. So it was left to the ladies to put them right.'

The temperamental Baryshnikov, amusingly, in typical prima donna fashion, heard about the bouquets and demanded to be informed if the director was 'trying to make a point' about the way his artists were handling the script. Hackford, diplomat that he is from his days with the Peace Corps, reassured the Russian ballet icon that this was a 'special' delivery.

A mischievous member of the crew then dispatched a bouquet of flowers to Gregory Hines via a knock on Baryshnikov's dressing-room door to check as to the whereabouts of the American star.

Hines, in fact, never received the flowers, which were gratefully accepted by an attractive hotel receptionist. But an insider recalls, 'Baryshnikov was distraught and wouldn't leave his dressing room for an hour that morning when he heard more bouquets were being sent and this time Gregory was the recipient. He had just been reassured that there was nothing "personal" in it by Taylor. He was now convinced people were hatching plots against him.'

By the time *White Nights* wrapped, Hackford and Mirren were a steady item, though the future for their romance was uncertain. She was considering several projects, including *Mosquito Coast* with

Harrison Ford, an adventure which would take her away from home for several months. He, conversely, wanted to get home to 'nurture' *White Nights* through its release and then spend some time out before making a tribute to rock 'n' roll star Chuck Berry.

Before Mirren arrived in his life, Hackford was one of the best catches on the block in Hollywood. He was free of booze and drugs and had a reputation for being a mild-mannered charmer. He rated high on the dinner-party circuit when there were single women 'on the lookout' and he had friends who were forever trying to manoeuvre him out of his single status. He confided to close allies that he was more than content at being alone and was not in the least interested in marrying for the third time.

While later promoting the psychological mystery *Dolores Claiborne* starring Kathy Bates and Jennifer Jason Leigh, he revealed, 'I guess at some levels Helen and I are quite different people, but we enjoy being together and travelling and reading. I'm not much into sports and neither is she. But we have our places in London, Los Angeles and New Orleans, which I got to discover through a college friend. She just fell for the place and I love England. She likes gardening and we have a pretty big garden back home in Los Angeles. I have worked with her building walls and planting trees. How do I sound? I'm turning us into this funny little grey-haired old couple ... hey, we are nothing like that!

'But I quite like the fact that people in England just know me as "Mr Mirren". That suits me fine. Over in Los Angeles, they tend to want to scramble over her to reach me which I find hugely embarrassing.'

So who was and is Taylor Hackford, the ace film director who made overnight stars of Richard Gere and Debra Winger through his blockbuster *An Officer and A Gentleman*? The same genial Hackford who much later dared to offer words of advice to an acting gladiator, Oscar-winning Russell Crowe, when he became firmly attached to Meg Ryan on the set of his hostage thriller *Proof of Life*.

Hackford was raised by his mother Mary in upmarket, dreamy

Santa Barbara, which is less than an hour's drive along the coast from Los Angeles through Malibu. But he wasn't one of the rich, privileged kids from Hope Ranch or Montecito, the exclusive districts frequented by those who don't have money worries. His home town had firm links to the movie industry, reaching back to the golden silent era of post-World War One America. Charlie Chaplin and Mary Pickford made the town their studio base back in the Twenties. The Montecito Inn was built in 1928 by silent screen legend Chaplin – you'll find his statue in the lobby – while if you stick around out of season today you might bump into Kevin Costner at his new restaurant Epiphany's. Another local, Steve Martin, has been known to drop by, pretending to wait on tables at the Paradise Café.

Michael Jackson's 2,700-acre Neverland Valley Ranch nestles above the city close to the vineyards of the Santa Ynez Mountains. Old money – in the shape of Kirk Douglas and Oprah Winfrey – mingles with a new breed of star such as the emerging Julia Stiles. Fess Parker, perhaps best known as TV's Davy Crockett, owns a large amount of property, including a beach-front hotel and is the city's elder statesman.

Hackford, along with other teens, would watch the crowds of tourists file down State Street while pondering his future. He had little spare cash. His father walked out on the family before he could walk and his mother worked as a waitress in the local Greyhound bus terminal. Though film-makers and artists today enjoy the climate and atmosphere, he made up his mind that he would be on the list of those youngsters leaving town to carve out a career for himself.

After studying at the University of Southern California where he graduated in international relations, he joined the American Peace Corps and spent two emotionally wrought years in Bolivia instead of being drafted to Vietnam. He said, 'It was a very good experience. In the States, you are quite set in your culture, with your TV and just about everything else. When it's all cut off, it's like going cold turkey. You go out with rather naïve ideas of what you can do, but what can a liberal arts student contribute to a Bolivian farmer whose family have been farming that land for generations?'

Though he enjoyed the excitement of his nights in the capital La Paz with other American members of the corps, it was in many ways a frustrating period, leaving him unsure as to where his heart truly lay. The brutal poverty, corruption and depravity he witnessed shocked him and briefly convinced him he should find a career in politics. He rapidly became fluent in Spanish and built up an appreciation and lasting affection for the people of Latin America.

Still lacking in direction, he enrolled at law school where he lasted two weeks. He hoped to get into television, but his stream of job applications and telephone calls got him precisely nowhere. With no experience or contacts, he ended up in the mail room of the highly respected Los Angeles public service broadcasting station KCET, working his way up to becoming an award-winning investigative journalist and part-time pop music presenter.

Incredibly, he picked up enough information about the film-making process to go on and win an Oscar for Best Short Film with his first fictional film *Teenage Father* in 1978, which he intended as a dramatic short subject aimed at school sex education.

While working at the station, he met Lynne Littman who was an original member of the American Film Institute's Women's Directing Program and a fledgling director and producer.

Hackford was impressed by her dedication to her craft and a raft of Liberal causes. Littman was and is a serious-minded woman interested in making issue-driven film projects. They had much in common with his stance against Vietnam and his fascination and enthusiasm for Hispanics. His home office today features vibrant paintings of urban scenes by East Los Angeles artist Adam Hernandez.

His wife-to-be was already something of a legend, having won an Oscar in 1976 for her short documentary *Number Our Days*, which was based on her close friend anthropologist Barbara Myerhoff's field work. Littman's 1986 documentary *In Her Own Time* chronicled Myerhoff's losing battle against cancer.

Hackford was naturally cautious. There had been a brief earlier marriage to his college sweetheart Georgie Lowres, the mother of his eldest boy Rio, which left him wary about serious involvement and suspicious when he analysed his views on romance. But it wasn't long before the Oscar-winning double act were spending most of their nights discussing the future of Planet Earth together before deciding where their future was going to be spent. They fell in love and she agreed to put her career on hold while she raised their baby son Alex. But she was always going to feel frustrated in her 'housewife' role and couldn't wait to make her comeback, which she duly did in 1983 with the acclaimed anti-nuclear drama *Testament*, starring Jane Alexander.

Her relationship with Hackford was already under considerable strain and she was sending clear signals that she needed him to play more of an active part in bringing up their son. He was only too happy to comply. He wanted her to continue her successful career.

But as a loving couple they had already drifted hopelessly apart by the time he cast his eyes on Helen Mirren. More recently, Littman, who lives in the Hollywood Hills, made the TV film *Freak City* for the Showtime Channel in America with River Phoenix's ex-girlfriend Samantha Mathis playing a girl tortured by society for having multiple sclerosis. She also created the teleplay *Having Our Say* for CBS, the tale of real-life African-American sisters Sadie and Bessie Delaney, from the Broadway play and bestseller of the same name.

Hackford left KCET soon after his Oscar success in 1978 and had to spend many a long hour talking himself into playing it Hollywood's way. At first, his experience of studio executives and their underlings left him thoroughly disillusioned with the world's most influential film-making machine. He also had the added responsibility of bringing up his young son Alex with Littman. The compromise paid off.

The huge commercial success of *An Officer and a Gentleman* four years later swept him to glory. Louis Gossett Jr scooped an Oscar for Best Supporting Actor, while the theme song 'Up Where We Belong' also took an Oscar, rapidly becoming the leading anthem selected by couples for future wedding services. Paramount had no idea the old-fashioned love story about raw military recruits and local white trash factory girls would capture the imagination. But the relatively low-budget feature even outpaced *ET* and *Gandhi* at the box office in late February 1983.

Ironically, it was the feisty Winger who gave Hackford his first taste of a public lashing, telling journalists that her on-set experience had been a 'sexist nightmare'.

The beleaguered Hackford, who was straight out of the JFK school of politics and a dedicated Democrat, also stood accused of being pro-military. After Winger's attack, he refused to get involved, saying, 'I don't bad-mouth people I work with.' That philosophy was later to pay dividends when he encountered a certain Russell Crowe in deepest Ecuador. But he felt he should answer criticism about the film's intentions. He pointed out, 'The answer is simple. I make films about working-class people. This guy played by Gere wasn't going anywhere in business and he wasn't the right kind of material for Yale. This was his opportunity to find success. There were also the factory girls with their dreams. Plenty of people can relate to that. Gere and Winger had good material and made it work for them. We did well.'

Indeed he did. But as is often the case in Hollywood, he soon had a giant turkey making a mess on his CV with another romantic tale, *Against All Odds*, starring Jeff Bridges and British newcomer Rachel Ward as lovers, and James Woods, as always, an unhinged villain lurking in the background. The film didn't fare so badly at the box office, climbing above *Terms of Endearment* in May 1984. Pop star Phil Collins became a firm favourite with Hackford, leading to his involvement in *White Nights*. The theme song, 'Take a Look at Me Now', went to number two in the charts in Britain and is still very much a golden oldie classic.

But he showed little or no interest in beating a path to either Sylvester Stallone or Arnold Schwarzenegger's mansions armed with the next Hollywood all-action special-effects blockbuster. He explained, 'I much prefer the idea of having flesh and blood on screen rather than blood or guts. I'm more interested in ordinary people in extraordinary situations. The commercial side of the business has never been that appealing and the people who control it usually don't look to me to make massive $100 million movies. That's not my scene. To be honest, I wouldn't be interested enough to probably make it successful.'

The Eighties, after that initial success, became professionally lean and, at times, personally distressing. His second marriage was over. He confided, 'I have thought about how I am not there for my children physically many times when I would wish to be. But I hope seeing someone fulfilled and creative is a positive image for them to have, perhaps better than having an unhappy parent who is there all the time.'

He made his Chuck Berry tribute and tried his hand at something musical with *Everybody's All-American* which was hammered as 'shallow and superficial' by one of the kinder critics. Based on Frank Deford's novel, the melodrama followed the fortunes of a college football star and his cheerleader girlfriend in the big wide world. Dennis Quaid and Jessica Lange starred. They didn't gel or look comfortable for a single frame. As one wag quipped, 'Everybody's now in need of medication.'

Hackford's directing career floundered and he turned to producing a slate of movies such as *La Bamba* with newcomer Lou Diamond Philips playing the late Richie Valens, and *Mortal Thoughts* with Demi Moore, anxious to send her real-life hubby Bruce Willis off to meet his maker. Moore and Glenn Headley both shone, but nobody paid too much attention.

And so a not terribly happy pattern developed for Hackford. He was the money-raising executive producer on movies such as *Queen's Logic*, an eccentric comedy with John Malkovich and Jamie Lee

Curtis, and the instantly dismissed light comedy *Sweet Talker* with Bryan Brown playing a charming conman chasing Karen Allen around a small coastal resort.

In fact, faith wasn't fully restored in his bankability until he produced the enthralling Muhammed Ali Oscar-winning drama documentary *When We Were Kings* in 1996. Unwisely, perhaps he then turned back towards Hollywood and the commercial film market, going for pay dirt with Al Pacino and Keanu Reeves in the hellish legal saga *The Devil's Advocate*. The original script had been passed around between the super agents before he spotted its potential, recruiting *Delores Claiborne* writer Tony Gilroy to make radical changes. Pacino had turned it down on five earlier opportunities but he liked Hackford's new vision. The character representing the devil was now a half-crazed successful lawyer as played by Pacino. The moral of the story leaned heavily towards free will and taking responsibility for our lives. He saw the movie as a 'cautionary tale for the Millennium'.

Hackford saw the tale as a warning, setting it against the background of the legal world. 'Evil can be funny and seductive,' he said. 'The devil inside you presents you with the thing you want most. The film company had tried it their way with the script and now it was my turn. Hollywood is full of exploitation movies with a lot of sex and monsters and no ideas.' He was also a huge fan of Pacino, describing him as 'the best American actor ... Too often, film stars become famous because they have a certain talent and they are rewarded with high salaries, pampering and adulation. They won't risk changing. Al is this little guy from the street, an incredibly smart, self-made man. He thinks this is one of his best performances, no matter what Hollywood has to say about it.'

The Devil's Advocate, based on Andrew Neiderman's novel, with Pacino in the central role of John Milton and Reeves as his protégé Kevin Lomax, was not a great critical success, though South African-born newcomer Charlize Theron dazzled as Reeves's screen wife. Roger Ebert of the *Chicago Sun-Times* commented, 'But the movie never fully engaged me; my mind raced ahead of the plot, and the John Grisham stuff clashed with the *Exorcist* stuff.' But Hollywood liked what it heard coming from the box office. The film more than made its money back in the USA following its release in Autumn 1997, and made a handsome £60 million on the international circuit. It was also to become a massive video smash.

Yet Hackford came to be somewhat preoccupied with the devil again three years later when he headed south to Ecuador to film *Proof of Life* with Russell Crowe and Meg Ryan. At first sight, he couldn't believe his luck. He'd got the dream cast – the new Hollywood golden boy coming off the back of the blockbuster *Gladiator* and an Oscar nomination for *The Insider,* with America's own saccharine sweetheart Ryan in tow.

It was a whopping-budget hostage movie set against the backdrop of the fictional lawless South American country of Tecala, which was so obviously doubling for Colombia. But Hackford was the 'victim' finally held hostage by the unscheduled love affair between the New Zealand-born rough-diamond Crowe and Ryan who was on the verge of parting permanently from her actor husband Dennis Quaid.

Their affair and Hackford's reaction came after a string of mortifying incidents, the like of which seem only to have struck down Terry Gilliam in the film business. The story centred on the abduction of an American engineer, played by David Morse, by a mob of thugs brandishing a naïve list of ideals alongside their weapons.

He loosely based his drama on the real-life kidnapping of businessman Tom Hargrove and an article in *Vanity Fair* magazine. He was originally hoping to get Harrison Ford assigned to the lead role. But when Ford dropped out, he took the advice of his director chums Michael Mann and Ridley Scott who had just worked with Crowe. 'All I needed was to see him in action in *Gladiator* and *The Insider*. In one movie, he's this hulking Roman soldier and, in the other, a brilliantly intelligent boffin. He was perfect. But he wasn't easy. I knew he wasn't going to be easy. He can be very difficult. But then so can I. While we were out there, he went from being more or less unknown to this superstar, but he didn't change. He just challenges you. He doesn't hold back. If something is bothering him, he lets you know.'

Even before filming got under way, tensions were running high. The peace and calm of the rainforests outside the capital Quito were shattered by a series of volcanic eruptions. The Army was then called into action after an incursion of Colombian guerrillas from across the border. Within days, the police were mounting road-blocks into the major cities after two local civil dignitaries were kidnapped. Hackford, formulating his plans in Los Angeles with Warner Bros executives, was getting especially bad vibrations. Next, news was flashed via CNN that a bunch of politically frustrated South American Indians had occupied the Congress. The point of no return had been reached and, before any further discussions could take place, he was on a plane clutching his master script.

Days were soon lost to the appalling weather during one of the wettest seasons on record. His vision of dreamy, surreal landscapes became completely obscured by clouds. At one mountain location, 26 members of his crew were evacuated because of altitude sickness. Reality was now firmly imitating art. One of the film's local actors, Pietro Sibille, was stabbed outside a restaurant after a brawl with other diners. And then absolute tragedy struck when Will Gaffney, David Morse's affable stand-in, was killed in a car crash.

Morse, after several clashes with Hackford, almost pulled out. He later told me, 'The trouble is that Taylor sometimes doesn't know when to cool it, when to back off. He'll shout and he'll demand and actually forget why he's doing this stuff. He made his apologies, which showed what a professional and gentleman he is. I think he wanted to put us through hell to give the true experience of being in hell. Whatever, it worked.'

Hackford was under such strain he spent a small fortune on

'soothing' telephone calls to Mirren who was filming back in Europe. During their long romance and marriage, she had never heard him in such a state of professional distress. A friend said, 'Taylor was this tower-of-strength figure and always had been. He never seemed to have doubts about what he was doing and the direction he was heading in. Suddenly, he sounded so vulnerable. She was very touched and sympathetic. Whatever was happening, she told him that he must not let it get to him because his concentration will go. It was like being the captain of a ship who leaves the bridge with the icebergs dead ahead. He knew everyone was looking to him for guidance.'

Everyone, that is, except for Russell Crowe, who had some fixed ideas about how hostage negotiator Terry Thorne was going to secure the release of Peter Bowman.

Troubled Hackford was equally confounded by Crowe's relationship with Ryan, who was being paid a reported £10 million for the discomfort of 'roughing it with the lads in the jungle'. The crew's loyalties were divided on the issue of 'jungle love'. While some were in Crowe's camp, acting as message-carriers and gofers, others sided with Hackford, who was subtly attempting to sabotage any on-set canoodling.

The timing of individual meal breaks were hastily rearranged by Hackford's senior aides, making it difficult for Ryan to join Crowe. 'Spies' on the set would regularly report on Crowe's movements. He'd suddenly get calls to 'script-revision meetings' or 'additional make-up sessions', which would eat into his spare time. He'd vent his anger on the furniture in his Winnebago while confused Ryan anxiously waited to grab his attention.

A member of the crew, who hailed from Seattle, revealed, 'The funny thing was that, in many ways, the thing going on between Russell and Meg actually assisted the emotional impact between them. But there also had to be this danger. They could never feel truly comfortable together because her husband's life was at stake in the story and she was a woman in turmoil. It was very difficult to play and Hackford had never been in that position before and, to an extent, resented having to deal with the extra baggage.

'These weren't kids but mature powerful actors worth a great deal of money. But there was something quite funny about them putting their "Do Not Disturb" sign up, only to hear a familiar knock-knocking on the door only minutes later asking one or both to deal with something quite trivial. We knew what was going on. It was an impossible situation. It didn't affect their portrayals of the roles at all, but Crowe got terribly irritable at times. Much as he respected the director, he was a bachelor and felt his private life was totally his own.'

Hackford today recognises *The Proof of Life* as a grey landmark in his career. It was a film he had hoped he'd be proud of and, in many ways, he is. But the reality was that it was a missed opportunity. 'You get out there in the jungle or the high altitude and everyone is saying, "Why are we here and why are we going through this?" You want to be Mr Nice Guy during this process, but it's not possible. But there you are, up in the mountains, with the studio calling, saying, "Why aren't you back here? When are you coming back?" There were people nervous and frightened. There was plenty of stuff going on and, all through this, you are trying to put a movie together.'

Hackford somehow kept the £50 million movie on schedule for its release just before Christmas 2000. But the critics were fairly unanimous.

Kenneth Turan of the *Los Angeles Times* suggested that audiences were influenced in a negative sense by the gossip surrounding Crowe and Ryan. He wrote, '*Proof of Life* is an ambitious film that aims to examine the human equations behind the abductions. But for all its good intentions, it's not as subtle as it might be, and it's finally pitched too broadly to achieve the level of emotional truth it aims for.'

The off-set romance between Crowe and Ryan had, indeed, overshadowed the drama. They virtually balked at taking part in any publicity campaign connected to the film on the basis that they would be quizzed over their activities in Ecuador.

Ryan was rightly concerned. Her marriage to Quaid was over and she had a young son to consider. Crowe was his usual indignant self, cursing journalists as he went about fixing them with hostile glares.

Hackford tried to be sympathetic, even though the loss of the double act to market the movie would prove to be cataclysmic. 'It's a very thorny, difficult, sensitive area,' he conceded. 'The only thing I can do is get the word out and hope. People say there's no such thing as bad publicity, but I'm not so sure. A lot of people read material about the film and think they know everything, which isn't the case. The point of the movie gets lost.'

His prayers weren't good enough. The movie took less than £40 million following its release in the USA and did average to poor business in Europe. It was clear by this time that he was laying part of the blame at Crowe's door, to which the rugged Kiwi responded by calling Hackford an 'idiot' at a press conference in London.

Hackford responded by saying there was nothing 'personal' between him and Crowe, but added, 'I can see why Russell would take my comments personally, because he was involved. You can have the most lovey-dovey of relationships with somebody but, if that doesn't translate into results on the screen, then I don't care.'

Hackford has trouble believing a 'superior' being played a part in bringing him and Mirren together. He was raised as a Protestant but is now a 'confirmed agnostic', somewhat cynical about organised religion. He smiled somewhat wryly, 'I think if you're in the movie business and you want to make working-class films within that system, you have to possess a basic optimism about the human spirit.'

He declared a year after the movie had been made that he was still talking to Crowe who, by that time, had parted with Ryan. But members of his entourage did not expect him to work with Crowe again, no matter how much he respects his talent.

One commented, 'Taylor thinks Crowe is quite brilliant. But he also thinks he is quite capable of self-indulgent, juvenile behaviour which he should be above having already achieved so much. He believes Crowe would be a better person if people stood up to him and put him in his place. Instead, he takes advantage of people's weaknesses. He has to learn the meaning of the word "humility".'

After the fiasco in Ecuador, Hackford could hardly wait to see Mirren and his sons again. Throughout their relationship, he was acutely aware that she had little to no experience of dealing with children, although she was extremely close to her nephew Simon. American teenage boys were another ball game.

In fact, she had never even lived with a man who had previously been married with a family. His son Rio, now 34 – who once held high hopes of making it as an actor – was fumbling his way through adolescence and had natural concerns about which way he'd be heading after high school. His younger son, Alex, was only five and living with his mother. Hackford smoothed the way for Mirren to get to know Rio and, perhaps surprisingly, they became firm friends.

He says, 'I raised him with Helen's help and support. These things are always going to be difficult. I held joint custody of my youngest who spent part of the week with me. To them she was "Helen" and, after we married, she remained "Helen". In situations like that, you can't expect affection but can expect and get respect. Helen is a very astute woman. It wasn't long before the boys took to her in a big way. It's an old story – they wanted to see their old man happy.

'Helen would have made a great mother, the best. But it wasn't to be. I would have loved to have seen her as a mother. We would have had children if she had wanted to. That decision had to be hers and we had many discussions in that area. But my children have had the experience of knowing and loving her.'

With their clean-cut images and lack of skeletons in the cupboard, gossip columnists have made feverish but as yet unsuccessful bids to find a flaw in their romance, especially when Mirren returned to spend more time in Europe in the early Nineties.

With dancer Mikhail Barishnykov in *White Nights*.

Above: Prince Charles greets Helen Mirren at the premiere of *2010* in Leicester Square.

Below: Presenting an Emmy to *X-Files* star Gillian Anderson.

Holding the Bafta she won for her portrayal of tough policewoman DCI Jane Tennison in TV's *Prime Suspect*. She is pictured here with fellow Bafta winner Holly Hunter.

Looking stunning on the red carpet, Helen Mirren arrives at a Bafta awards ceremony.

With husband, film director
Taylor Hackford.

Top left: Arriving at the 2007 Golden Globe Awards.

Top right: Helen Mirren became Dame Helen Mirren at Buckingham Palace in December 2003, and three years later starred as Her Majesty in *The Queen* (*bottom*).

Top: Helen Mirren in the hugely popular *Calendar Girls*, pictured here with (*left to right*) Linda Bassett, Julie Walters, Celia Imrie, Annette Crosby and Penelope Wilton.

Bottom: With Jeremy Irons in the highly acclaimed *Elizabeth I*.

Helen Mirren has amassed an impressive array of awards. (*Clockwise from top left*) Winner of the Outstanding Lead Actress in a mini-series or movie for *Elizabeth I* at the 2006 Emmys; Best Actress for *The Queen* at the 2006 Venice Film Festival; Best actress for *The Queen* at the 2007 Oscars and picking up the award for Best Actress in a movie/mini-series at the Golden Globes, 2006.

The *Daily Mail* suggested at one stage that she'd had a fling with a member of a film crew – and posed questions about their 'open marriage' without being able to track down any other parties. It was true that they'd often spend up to six months of the year apart, living and coping with all the regular temptations and distractions which go with movie-making. But old-fashioned Hackford made it clear to close friends that he considered they had a 'real commitment' to each other. He admired her intelligence and fierce independence, but could be irritated by her 'secrecy'.

He said, 'In terms of the woman behind the actress, there's no question that she is a very exciting person and she has a sensuality which is palpable. It's easy to talk about somebody from the exterior, but you reach other depths when you have been together this long.

'I do love her candour. I have the utmost love and trust for her. If she spoke in a destructive way, I wouldn't hesitate to speak up. But she is always very true to herself.'

She once said, with a wide smile, 'The problem with Taylor is that he's very American and loves to share things. They like to have things out in the open. Whereas, I am this curious blend of Eastern Europe and Scotland through my mother. The Scots keep everything to themselves and the Russians go from mystery to mystery. But my secretiveness drives him potty.'

A backstager who worked with Hackford in the Eighties said, 'Taylor would do his thing, which, in Californian terms, was fairly academic, while she would do the same. But a lot of folk got it into their minds that they had an "open" relationship. They were both mature people. He had two marriages behind him and she'd lived with a couple of guys. So nobody was probably going to get hurt.

'Taylor is one of the easiest-going guys you could wish to meet, unless roused. He knows what he wants work-wise and intends getting it. That's what he has in common with Helen. He could be seen to be abrasive.

'But he was beside himself with anger one Monday morning when he came in. Somebody had suggested at a dinner party over the previous weekend that he must be a "swinger" and so must Helen. They thought it was so "modern" and "free-thinking" that they could have different partners and still remain so close. Taylor wanted to empty his dessert over this lady's head. Helen wouldn't stand for him sleeping with another woman and vice versa. He wasn't interested, in any case. He wanted her. He was fairly consumed by her in a very short space of time.'

Hackford made it plain to anybody who cared to listen that they had a 'healthy, adult and loving' relationship. Many were surprised when they finally married in a church with all the trimmings. After all, he wasn't a religious man.

Nobody was more thrilled than Mirren when they sashayed down the red carpet together in Hollywood in March 2005 shortly before his biopic of the legendary Ray Charles was hailed on Oscars night. Ray, which had been budgeted at $40 million, scooped $75 million in the US and another £50 million worldwide. Jamie Foxx, who made his breakthrough as hitman Tom Cruise's chauffeur in Collateral, won the Best Actor Oscar having already won a Golden Globe for his portrayal of the late rags-to-riches blind jazz pianist and singer from Albany, Georgia, who beat drugs and racism to become an international musical icon. Hackford went on to pick up a Grammy in 2006 for his work on the soundtrack of the movie.

Mr and Mrs Hackford, despite their flourishing careers, are making new efforts to change their working schedules. They own a spectacular Spanish-style property and have six acres to grow their own fruit and veg in their huge garden high above Hollywood in the hills, a short drive away from Hackford's ex-wife, Lynne Littman.

They take breaks in America and escape to their apartment in the French quarter of beleaguered New Orleans. In Europe, there is a house in Provence they rarely see. His hobbies include collecting photography and South Western turquoise-and-silver belt buckles and watchbands. They fondly call each other 'Hel', and 'Tay', and she once spent five minutes hiding, giggling and wiping the mascara from her eyes in the washroom at a première when a radio reporter, on overhearing her abbreviation for his name, introduced her husband mistakenly on air as 'Decay' Hackford.

Hackford said, 'We both wanted to live our lives to the full and have a good career and that is something we both achieved. But we also discovered how important it was when you found the right person. When you do, you have to grab that time and grab that person and hold on tight. I spend every second I can with Helen when I am not working and our relationship has got better and better.'

Talk to him about epitaphs and perhaps the best film he ever made, *An Officer and a Gentleman*, and he says, 'I have no idea how I would feel about *An Officer and a Gentleman* now. I hope it would stand up as a study of the working classes, specifically of a man whose only route to self-esteem was through the armed forces. That's what I intended. If it comes across as Reagan-era jingoism, that's not at all what I intended.

'When critics want to take a slap at me, they say things like, "Taylor Hackman directs each film as if it's his last." That's exactly how I feel about each film, I do, so I end up admiring their perception!'

Mirren, not surprisingly, knows him better than anyone and she says with pride, 'There is something very special about him. He can change the atmosphere of a room when he walks in. He couldn't be more different from me and I love him for that. He can be difficult and forceful and I love him for that, too.

Mirren used to glibly respond to media enquiries about her own love life with the stock response of how she would set her alarm an hour early: 'Not just to make love but to talk and fondle, to have an hour for us together.' She'd qualify this by describing how they would enter their 'own little world'.

That situation, it now seems clear, has changed to eliminate any carnal physicality. More of that, much later. In recent months, however, she has been candid enough to admit that Hackford was certainly no romantic but what she got from him was 'so much better'.

With a true aura of affection, she said, 'Loyalty and truthfulness and, you know, manliness in the proper sense. I'd take those qualities over a romantic evening with a bullshitter any time.'

10

IN HER
PRIME

The Thatcher era was almost over in Britain and the ITV network was just about to undergo the most radical change in its history. The 'nice guys' at popular Thames Television were among others soon to lose their franchise, having upset the Grande Dame in Number 10, leaving the path clear for the wealthy new boy on the block, Michel Green at Carlton Television, eventually to end up running the entire TV shooting match with Gerry Robinson at Granada Television.

Thames, through its TV film and series production arm Euston Films, had been a veritable fountain of ingenuity. It had given birth to that racy Flying Squad yarn *The Sweeney* and the rock musical odyssey *Rock Follies* in the Seventies, and stunning thrillers such as *The Fear* and *Widows* in the Eighties. Who would be taking over their mantle?

The other ITV companies seemed largely obsessed with period crime pieces and old-fashioned sleuths who always held a door open for a lady. You could take your pick between London Weekend Television's Hercule Poirot and the velvet glove-like David Suchet.

Ruth Rendell's *Inspector Wexford*, starring George Baker, had just yawned into action for TVS, while Roy Marsden as the noble Scotland Yard detective, DCS Adam Dalgleish, had hit the bullseye without causing too much fuss for Anglia Television.

Women? They were still hanging on to their male colleagues' coat-tails in the 'all-action' *Dempsey and Makepeace*, starring Michael Brandon and pouting Glynis Barber, or playing 'headstrong' Northern girls such as Jan Francis in YTV's *Stay Lucky*, which featured Dennis Waterman as a Cockney wide-boy on the run from the London mob. It was pretty dire material. For feminism on the box, read 'zero'. Vivacious, likeable Jill Gascoine turned up as DI Maggie Forbes in LWT's *The Gentle Touch*, playing a woman whose life was split between her roles as a wife, mother and cop. And *CATS Eyes* from TVS was simply a critic's answer to a prayer as Gascoine returned to head up a 'special intelligence squad' with nubile Leslie Ash and Rosalyn Landor in tow. The multi-talented Don Warrington was their boss and appeared, not surprisingly, totally perplexed, running what was laughingly known as 'Covert Activities, Thames Section'. If you were on the lookout for craggy cops, you had to travel north of the border to catch up with ex-amateur boxer Mark McManus in STV's *Taggart*. He was definitely grim and gritty. Ah yes, and an opera-loving mastermind by the name of Inspector Morse had arrived on the scene for Central Television with the rejuvenated and now much-missed John Thaw.

Nobody was sure of the future in 1990 but a large number of ITV executive-sized heads were on the block unless that old fruit of 'instant success' could somehow be attained. Granada Television drama chief Sally Head, fresh from a spell at the BBC, had a hard act to follow sitting behind her desk at the company's London headquarters in Soho's Golden Square. Granada's track record was fairly littered with rich veins of gold from Evelyn Waugh's magnificent *Brideshead Revisited* to the monumental, mysterious *The Jewel in the Crown*, based on Paul Scott's *The Raj Quartet*.

She had inherited *The Adventures of Sherlock Holmes* with Jeremy

Brett poised to make a comeback as Baker Street's exemplary crimestopper and the extremely average cop series *El CID*, which starred Alfred Molina as the Costa del Sol-destined DS Blake.

It was a cold, damp winter's morning in early 1990 when script executive Jenny Sheridan approached the much-respected Head with the words, 'How would you feel about a series based on a high-flying policewoman?' After a further brief conversation to ascertain the origin of the idea, Sheridan was enthusing to the now very excited Lynda La Plante. The commission was hers. Here was an opportunity which might have come straight from heaven; women in television making a hard-edged, controversial TV drama about a 'real' lady cop.

Within four months, Head and Sheridan were sitting around the table with their colleague, script executive Gwenda Bagshaw, glued to La Plante's rough draft script.

Helen Mirren's name was already in the frame to play DCI Jane Tennison. Executive Producer Head said, 'We were on the lookout for a new direction. We had such high standards at Granada following on from shows such as *Jewel in the Crown*. But when I saw the script I thought, "Wow, this is amazing." It needed work doing on it, but it had almost everything going for it. I then thought about casting and the only person I ever took it to was Helen because I admired her work so much. Within a couple of days, she came back with a resounding "yes". She also loved it. The funny thing is that when I told my family who was going to play the part, they had not got a clue who she was. I'd seen her theatre work but missed most of her movies. But to the punters, she was still an unknown quantity.'

At the network centre, they were then operating what was known as the 'flexipool' system, a kind of comedy and drama quota expected on the production line from each major ITV company. *Prime Suspect* was given the green light without any hesitation.

Enter real-life cop DCI Jackie Malton, who'd been advising programme-makers on police methods and plotlines for the best part of a decade. Ultra-professional Malton, a perfectionist and workaholic, bore a striking resemblence to Tennison in many ways and La Plante and Mirren were not slow in picking up on this handsome bonus. As hard-drinking, chain-smoking Malton was soon to reveal, she'd also had what could only be described as an extremley fractious relationship with certain male officers in the force.

Over a period of six months, they scrapped and argued their corners until the final draft of the script dropped on to Head's desk. She cast her eyes over the way La Plante had skilfully drawn Tennison and knew she had something unique. They had all agreed on the avoidance of explicit sexual content which cheered Mirren, an actress accustomed to seeking out the pages in the script where she disrobes and climbs between the sheets. In fact, she'd often joke with her former agent, saying, 'Come on, never mind the rest of the script ... where are the dirty bits?'

Tennison has been passed over time and again to lead a murder investigation, so, when one of her fellow DCIs has a heart-attack just before he's ready to charge their prime suspect, she sees her chance to lead a major inquiry. But the murder squad she takes over is hostile to her; the men upstairs are eager to pull the plug on her investigation; her personal relationships suffer from her obsession with work; and the prime suspect remains elusive. Tennison has her work cut out for her as she and her team work their way through computer data trails, leg-work, intuitive leaps, chases, arrests and confessions to find the killer.

The gripping cycle of cop thrillers was born with an opening story about a serial killer who preyed on hookers. John Bowe, later to be a regular in the TV soap *Coronation Street*, was mesmeric as the unhinged, twisted George Marlow, with the wonderfully versatile Zoe Wanamaker playing his foul-mouthed common-law wife Moyra Henson. They were a dream duo.

One of the main themes was how Tennison would deal with sexual hostility from within. Tom Bell, as the menacing, crude and stubborn DS Bill Otley, was her office 'shadow', doing his utmost to sabotage and usurp her authority at every opportunity. John Benfield would be playing her sympathetic, level-headed boss DCS Michael Kernan, with Tom Wilkinson, later to win an Oscar nomination for his portrayal of a grieving father in *In the Bedroom*, cast as her frustrated lover Peter Rawlins. There was even a small part with a couple of lines for actor Ralph Fiennes in his pre-*Schindler's List* days as Michael, the boyfriend of one of the murdered women.

Head gasped as she read Tennison's brutal and bruised address to her rebellious team – 'Look, I know what you have heard about me, that bloody Jane Tennison. That bloody Jane Tennison. She'll come storming into your nick, the balls of your best officers trailing from her jaws, spraying people with claret, calling people Masons, threatening resignation. Well, I just wanted to tell you that I am not a complete maniac.'

And Mirren had a confession of hers to make about suddenly being in a top-dog position in a man's domain. Just how much fun was it telling the lads what they were going to be doing? She confided, 'Yes, I did quite enjoy taking charge, being in control in a situation where everyone else was a man. It was a first.'

Mirren, ironically, had partially left Britain because she couldn't stand the harsh regime of Maggie Thatcher and Downing Street's relentless alleged persecution of those less fortunate. Yet, here she was, ostensibly playing a Thatcherite character, from the Eighties 'me' academy. A woman in a man's world who must win. A woman who can cut a man in half with a smile. And a woman who can appear sympthetic enough to drag a confession from a devious killer and, in the next split-second, be seen drawing on a cigarette with the trace of a satisfied smile creeping across her jawline. There was indeed nothing 'gentle' about Tennison and this was to show itself in her dismal private life. Men didn't use her. They never got the chance. Her 'family' was down the cop shop along with her life. Nobody was going to get in the way of that. Mirren had got the role under her skin as though she was a blood relative. There were very few cracks in her portrayal of Tennison.

Mirren had her mapped out like a navigator charting the Atlantic and sounded almost Thatcheresque discussing her alter ego. 'Tennison is someone who absolutely and uncompromisingly doesn't do anything that you could call feminine,' she disclosed at the time. 'She is a character who has rejected manipulation, which, historically, is the way that women have gained power. You hate it but you know that it's the only way to achieve your ends. Women are taught to smile, to be pleasant, to be charming, to be attractive. To say things like, "You're a darling, thank you so much." They get their way like that. Tennison doesn't do that. She doesn't say "please".

'I thought it was the right time to do a role like that. It's the kind of part you'll find only on television because cop movies are very male. This is the role I have been waiting for. Certain roles are exactly right. I was the right age and the right mentality. I don't have to pretend to be anything other than what I am. Actresses complain about there not being enough strong roles for women. This is the kind of role they are seeking. She is driven, obsessive, vulnerable, unpleasantly egotistical and confused. But she is damn good at what she does and is totally dedicated. She is very much alive.'

Jackie Malton was also convinced they were creating landmark television. She remarked, 'You're never going to please everyone. We thought we had done great work. But one of the actors spoke to a copper who said the script was crap. I said to our producer Don Leaver, "Ask 12 cops about the story and you'll get 12 different answers." It's boring. That's why writers like to work with me. I am positive and I know what I'm talking about. They are stuck with me at the end of the day and I tell anyone who cares to listen, "Look, this is a police drama, not a documentary." '

She ensured that any obvious blips were sorted before Mirren stood in front of a camera. 'I caught her one day standing with her arms folded against the upper half of her body. I had to tell her that cops never take that position physically, they'd look on the defensive. That kind of body language does not inspire confidence or belief.'

What's more, Mirren badly needed 'public exposure' in the UK. She had spent years on and off in Hollywood but had very little to show for it, apart from a much-improved bank account. She was beginning to convince herself that her future belonged in Britain where she felt 'artistically rooted'. The independent film business may not pay as much as the Yanks, but the work was quality with a big Q.

She had never wanted a TV career and had turned away great bundles of scripts from producers who had used the likes of Felicity Kendal, Penelope Keith and Alison Steadman. But here she was at another career crossroads. It was time for her to put aside her prejudices and play the fame game.

Mirren jetted into London from Tuscany where she had been making the romantic drama *Where Angels Fear to Tread*, directed by Charles Sturridge from EM Forster's novel, with Helena Bonham-Carter and Judy Davis. Mirren said, 'I flew in, had my hair chopped off and started the next morning.'

In fact, there was little call for make-up before she arrived on the North London set to greet director Christopher Menaul, whom Head had met while he directed *Casualty* at the BBC. She could almost touch the euphoria enveloping *Prime Suspect* as the crew and cast assembled to shoot the opening story in the King's Cross district of London, before economics dictated that they all board a train a couple of days later to Manchester to shoot the rest of the story. Interior scenes, representing Tennison's London HQ, were filmed at 'Maxwell Towers', an office block previously owned by the discredited media mogul Robert Maxwell in the heart of the city.

And it was a very different Helen Mirren who appeared on television on the evening of 7 April 1991. Her fair hair, once a delightful, lively, tumbling red mass, had been transformed into a harsh, severe new look which the nuns at her convent school would have warmly approved of for any middle-aged mum. She wore a minimum of make-up, turned up at the office in dark, dowdy suits and puffed like Stephenson's Rocket. Her portrayal of Tennison was ice-hard but not ice-cold as she showed her boys who was boss. There were no signs of weakness or indecision.

The critics, from the tabloids to the broadsheets, idolised TV's latest cop. 'A belter of a suspense thriller,' cried *Time Out*. 'Riveting viewing' gasped the the *Mail on Sunday*, while the *Sunday Times* purred, 'Moves at a cracking pace'. The *Sun* agreed, adding, 'Pulls no punches.'

The critics on both sides of the Atlantic – the show was a huge smash on the PBS network – may have been ecstatic, but Lynda La Plante's glee was muted by her own lack of business acumen and her sense of injustice. The rights to the television series were held by Granada Television, though she would always stand to benefit financially as the ultimate creative force. The movie rights were then sold on to Paramount in Hollywood, who threw names like Meryl Streep and Glenn Close into the hat as the silver screen's American-style Jane Tennison. The last word was that they were getting 'significantly closer' to putting a deal together with Michelle Pfeiffer, to take Tennison on to the streets of New York, though Susan Sarandon has also entered the running as a late outsider.

Though La Plante has been quietly preparing for a return of the small-screen chracter, she also secretly drew an outline for a big-budget American movie and had that tucked away in her office safe. But Paramount sources suggest that the company is more likely to use their own tried and tested screenwriters on the project once Pfeiffer has committed to the role in which Ed Harris would play her partner with James Woods as a serial killer.

The anxious La Plante was aware of the mistake she had made when Granada attempted quietly to change facets of Tennison's character for *Prime Suspect 2*. Senior executives in the company were disturbed over just how tough Mirren's portrayal had been. They wanted to see the character 'lighten up'. 'The warts 'n' all was too full of warts,' said one. 'Where was the romance?'

La Plante was far from convinced and Sally Head was also involved in deciding which way the character should go. Amid much angst, writer Allan Cubitt was brought in to develop La Plante's storyline and create the sequel with a central theme focusing on racial conflict in and out of the force.

Incandescent La Plante said, 'I created that character, fought tooth and nail for that character, but when I disagreed with what they wanted to do with her, they said "Fine, we'll bring in another writer." That was a hard slap in the face, so I went through the slow process of learning how to form my own production company.'

La Plante is a much wiser and richer woman today, through her company's new slate of TV dramas, and is proud of having revolutionised the way crime was depicted in TV dramas, such as the BBC's *Silent Witness*, starring Amanda Burton.

She says, 'Before *Prime Suspect*, nobody ever went into the incident room, the forensics labs or the mortuary. I have to do a tremendous amount of research, because whatever I do will be copied within months. As soon as a script is finished, it goes off to the police, to the pathology labs and to the barristers. I defer to them on all things.'

In America, the critics eagerly awaited a follow-up to the opening drama. Amy Taubin of the New York-based the *Village Voice* said, '*Prime Suspect* reinvents both the psychological thriller and the police procedural, not merely by making the detective a woman but by allowing her to triumph over the misogyny that's both outside and within the law.'

Incredibly, there was so much behind-the-scenes bickering and political wrangling at Granada Television that there was a strong possibility of another *Prime Suspect* story never seeing the light of day. Jane Tennison's successful first adventure had been brought in reportedly for just over £1 million and was voted a hit by viewers.

But the price of making the sequel had spiralled to double the previous budget. Executive producer Head was determined however, as was Mirren, not to let their favourite copper just fade away without a fight.

Inside ITV, sceptics predicted that Granada wouldn't risk the outlay on *Prime Suspect 2*. Enough strings were finally pulled by the progressive, tenacious Head to get the show back on the road within 12 months. Head, who was something of a Fay Weldon *aficionado*, having turned her controversial tomes *The Lives and Loves of a She-Devil* and *The Cloning of Joanna May* into small-screen gems, needed to make changes. She had listened carefully to in-house criticism over Tennison's lack of warmth and dubious sex appeal. The subject matter was deemed in some quarters to be 'too dark and relentless'. Writer Allan Cubitt, who made the award-winning *The Land of Dreams* with Anthony Sher and Rudi Davies, had seen most of his work produced on stage. With the guidance of consultant DCI Mike Fuller, then at the age of 33 one of the highest-ranking black police officers in Britain, he penned the new script which sent Tennison in two new stressful directions.

The second murder investigation focused on the body of a young girl lying in a shallow grave in the back garden of a terraced house in a largely Afro-Caribbean neighbourhood in London. Her job is made tougher as the local community is bubbling over with hatred for the long arm of the law. And her love life becomes the subject of office gossip when she falls for younger black cop Robert Oswalde, played by the promising Colin Salmon, who was making his TV début.

Many of Tennison's 'boys' were back in the line-up, except DS Otley, alias Tom Bell, who was being 'rested'.

Salmon, now 42, was born of mixed British and Ghanaian parentage and spent his childhood in the East End before moving with his family to Luton in Bedfordshire. He'd had it tough. His mother killed herself when he was 24 during a bout of depression. He busked patiently as a musician before getting his acting break at the Tricycle Theatre in Kilburn, North London.

He'd never seen *Prime Suspect*, although he'd been an admirer of Mirren's since seeing her in *The Long Good Friday* over a decade earlier. He became a regular in Pierce Brosnan's James Bond set-up as CIA operative Charles Robinson and appeared in the saga *Die Another Day*. By a bizarre set of circumstances, he had to audition with writer Cubitt, acting out his passionate love scene with Mirren. 'He's cute,' quipped Salmon, 'but I had to dig deep for that one. Once we got chatting, though, I went for it. The whole thing was so intense.'

It was a seven-week shoot with the bulk of filming again in Manchester at Maxwell Towers, where a genuinely spooky discovery was made by one of the squad. Flicking through the files left by journalists in the building, one in particular stood out – The Moors Dossier, a background report on the infamous killers Myra Hindley and Ian Brady. The entire cast shuddered over the discovery, which director John Strickland found disconcerting. Strickland, who had worked on *The Bill* and was once nominated for a BAFTA award due to his excellent technical work on *Smiley's People*, replaced Chris Menaul behind the cameras for the mini-series which was screened in late 1992.

The tall, striking Salmon admitted to being jittery when the moment arrived for his love scene with Mirren. The affair between Tennison and Oswalde was a slow burn followed by a megaton blast. He said, 'We'd had this earlier scene together in which there was stuff going on from her to me which was like an incendiary bomb going off. We were only two feet away from each other. I could feel her breath.

'When it came to the love scene, we went for it as much as you can when there are 13 strangers in the background crowding into the room. What became clear to me was that she was a great snogger. She has gorgeous lips. We giggled a lot. I think you could say that she set me up for other roles since then. The great thing about Helen in *Prime Suspect* is that she is The Hunter in almost every respect. She turns the tables. If you are a man and she is hunting you, there is no escape.

'There is something dangerous sexually about her. She reminded me of women I knew when I first came to London, feisty women, black women ... strong women.'

Father-of-four Salmon, who starred in the recent action video-game movie *Resident Evil*, was an instant hit as Oswalde with Granada Television earmarking him for a spin-off show of his own. That didn't happen, but the BBC saw his potential and signed him up to play another detective called Charlie Nolan in *Deep Secrets*. But the pilot episode never made it into a series.

Mirren's deft but deadly touch left a lasting impression on Salmon. In one scene, tenderly, she had to take hold of the hand of a dying man, played by Tom Watson, and extract the vital confession. Salmon said, 'The guy he played was a nasty piece of work, a real shit. But she needs to elicit the truth so she holds his hand and uses her sexuality. Then, she calmly goes into the bathroom and washes her hands to rid herself of that evil. It was wonderful ... it left me gasping.'

Prime Suspect was by now very much Mirren's 'property' and she guarded her territory fiercely when she had to. Outsiders invaded at their peril. Salmon was given another kind of insight into Mirren the actress when a young unknown actress breezed on to the set for her only scene in the drama. He noticed that the girl 'fancied herself' and was obviously not adverse to letting others know about her talents and ambitions.

He grinned, 'I noticed Helen "clock" her. When she did her scene with Helen, she just wasn't in it. Helen made a point of blowing her away, of acting her out of the scene. The director was left with no choice but to keep the camera on Helen because of the intensity of her performance. But it was also her way of telling the girl, "Watch ... learn ... say nothing."

'The girl was being put in her place. She did nothing combative at all. It was so subtle and so clever without ever being nasty. She can't stand fools. The men around her tend to get like girls ... she has this amazing ability to knock people off-centre.'

There was drama off-set as well when Mirren realised she was being 'stalked' at her Manchester hotel, The Victoria and Albert, by someone security men later described as an 'over zealous fan' from the Salford district of the city. At first, she was convinced the young prowler who roamed the corridors of the hotel in the early hours was a national newspaper journalist hungry for a scoop. But one night she spotted the mystery man 'spying' on her from a fire escape and she raised the alarm, sending security men scampering across rooftops.

The hotel then spent a week monitoring her calls and mounted a 24-hour watch on her suite. Finally, the intruder was again seen climbing the fire escape and apprehended.

A member of staff said, 'Helen was absolutely terrified. At one point, her mother was also staying at the hotel and she buzzed her room and got her to join her. We doubt whether she'd done that since she was a child. We played the whole thing down saying it was probably press, but whoever it was had also delivered some very cranky notes which we vetted and held on to. This lad was definitely very scary. Once we had got our hands on him and got all of his details, we gave him a final warning. He was just a fan, fixated on her, so we left her out of it. That was then. Times have changed. Today, we'd hand him over to the law.'

What was instantly noticeable about *Prime Suspect 2* was the metamorphosis of Tennison from a dowdy, frumpish schoolma'am into a chic, smartly dressed, well-coiffed glamorous forty-something.

Unit publicist Anya Noakes, who first met Mirren on *Pascali's Island* while she was working as Ben Kingsley's PR girl, said it was a welcome change from the Tennison of old. 'She looked washed out on the first *Prime Suspect*. They softened her up. Previously, she looked so grey and strained,' she said. 'By number two, it was a different woman. She looked relaxed and comfortable, they dressed her less severely, gave her feminine pink blouses and colourful clothes. She was also more comfortable with own abilities.'

Prime Suspect 3, which was transmitted in December 1993,

delved into the seedy world of London's rent-boy community, highlighting the plight of young male prostitutes usually hired briefly for sexual gratification by middle-aged men. The mini-series, through some of La Plante's best and darkest writing, sent shockwaves through the executive boardroom at PBS in America, where the feeling was that the material was not suitable for family consumption. But, after careful rather than wholesale cutting, they were able to air the feature.

The story turned away from Tennison's conflicts with male chauvanism to her personal conflicts with her staff.

Tom Bell also returned to the fray as a tamer, more compromising DS Otley, but the drama was almost but not quite stolen by David Thewlis as a particularly vicious pimp called Jimmy Jackson and Scotsman Peter Capaldi, who, months later in March 1994, was proclaimed the toast of Edinburgh as an Oscar-winner for his short film, *Franz Kafka's It's a Wonderful Life*.

Capaldi sets the mood for the third instalment as the perpetually frightened Vera Reynolds singing *Falling in Love Again* in the mould of a campish Marlene Dietrich in a modern upmarket gay bar. Tennison is getting over the break-up of a long-running affair.

Variety said, 'Tom Bell's hard-assed cop is a miniature of underplaying, especially in his gradual rapprochment with his female boss. As the pimp (and prime suspect), David Thewlis is a magnetic study in sleaze. Peter Capaldi makes a sad, touching transsexual. But it's still Mirren's show.'

Thewlis, one of Mike Leigh's favourite actors, scooped awards for his portrayal of a trashy misogynist in *Naked* and was again picking up the plaudits for his repellent portrayal of the worst kind of human parasite. Christopher Hitchen in *Vanity Fair* proclaimed, 'The second most memorable face in the series belongs to David Thewlis, who plays a snarling, whining, crafty pervert. As with his stellar performance in *Naked*, Thewlis gives us the wised-up, gone-wrong tones of junk Britain.'

And the episode closed with a real shocker for *Prime Suspect* fans.

Troubled Tennison took herself off to the GP to learn that she was pregnant. The suspect in this particular case was her old flame American psychologist Jake Hunter played by Michael Shannon. Was Tennison really about to become a mum? Was she going to throw off the chains of her mind-torturing occupation and get herself down to Mothercare?

The answer was soon revealed when Mirren returned in *Prime Suspect 4* with a new expensive format of three one-off TV films which were shown over April and May in 1995. Sally Head and her production team knew they would be under severe pressure to produce guaranteed ratings. They were also determined to maintain what had been a high-quality structure. Like Mirren, they were looking for the best in every department ... and they got it.

The Lost Child had the emerging, popular John Madden as director. Three years later, he was being fêted as the Golden Boy of Hollywood while his modern classic *Shakespeare in Love* picked up the Best Film award, plus Oscars for Gwyneth Paltrow and Judi Dench. The distraught Tennison has had an abortion, deciding not to sacrifice her career for a baby. She has also moved up the promotional ladder to Detective Superintendent. Writer Paul Billing appropriately took her anguish and used it as part of the plot about the search for an abducted baby, a single mother and a cruel convicted child sex-offender, played with gusto by Robert Glenister. He was the prime suspect, but his arrest was badly bungled. Tennison, her private life still in disarray, is faced with a siege situation in which Glenister's screen girlfriend Anne Sutherland, played by Lesley Sharp, and her two children are held hostage.

Writer Billing, who went on to create *The Murder Rooms* for Ian Richardson, said, 'We had her pregnancy terminated in the opening scenes to put her through additional stress and then bring her into the dilemma of the mother who had lost a child in another way. Hence, all the angst.

'It was interesting to see Mirren's reaction to the script,' he added. 'She had seen the horrors befalling children in *Prime Suspect 3* and knows having a child herself will ruin her career. Helen understood perfectly where the characters were coming from and whether it was due to her own personal situation or not, she was genuinely moved.'

Changes were in the air in the drama department at Granada Television and producer Sally Head was replaced by producer Gub Neal for what looked like being the final instalment in Tennison's adventures. She later resigned to go 'independent' and has since been responsible for dramas such as the BBC's Victorian sex saga *Tipping the Velvet* starring Keeley Hawes and Rachel Stirling.

Billing said, 'There's no doubt in my mind that there was room for another episode, especially one which puts Tennison in extremis, but it's a question of finding the right storyline. Has La Plante still got the magic?'

Next on the *Prime Suspect* production line was *Inner Circles*, in which a seemingly straightforward murder of a country club manager led Tennison into the depths of a hidden political scandal and the cruelty of the British class system. The story, penned by Eric Deacon and Meredith Oakes, gave ex-*EastEnders* soap actress Sophie Stanton the opportunity to shine as Tennison's sidekick DS Chris Cromwell. The case put her at odds with both the DCI she supplanted and upper-crust powers in the local community.

The final tale in the trio, *Scent of Darkness*, saw Paul Marcus return as director with Guy Hibbert writing the story about a series of brutal sex murders disturbingly similar to the pattern of Tennison's first major case. She has to deal with the possibility that either she arrested the wrong man or a copycat killer who has murdered two women was out there on the loose. Tennison was herself suspended, but that didn't stop her going on the trail of the killer, especially when a third woman was abducted and the police had just three days to find her. For once, Tennison isn't alone in her suffering.

Stuart Wilson – Mel Gibson fans will recall him playing the villain of the piece in *Lethal Weapon 3* – played a criminal psychologist who took a fancy to our heroine. But anyone expecting sizzling sex scenes was disappointed. And the in-demand Mr Wilson, who starred with Sigourney Weaver and Ben Kingsley in *Death and the Maiden*, was soon given his marching orders out of her bedroom.

Mirren, having leaped into bed with Colin Salmon and Stuart Wilson, was naturally disappointed when writer Guy Andrews decided not to have her falling wildly in love when he created the fifth *Prime Suspect* instalment *Errors of Judgement*, which was shown in October 1996. Instead, she had a cold one-night stand with a high-ranking copper who later betrayed her. She half-heartedly complained with a grin, 'I certainly wouldn't have minded a hot to very hot love scene, but they wouldn't write one in.'

Andrews's story, directed by Philip Davis, took the out-of-favour Tennison from the Met to Manchester for a stint as community relations officer in large schools. She saw this move, quite rightly, as a form of demotion and wanted to get back where the action is. But Tennison is given the chance to redeem herself when a drugs dealer, played by another former *Coronation Street* stalwart Chris Bisson, was shot. And in between leaping into bed with her boss DCS Ballinger, portrayed by ex-*Brookside* favourite John McArdle, she marks down the psychotic local drugs lord known as The Street, played by Steven Mackintosh, as Public Enemy No 1.

Producer Gub Neal, who went on to make the drama *Painted Lady* with Mirren for ITV, wasn't alone in fearing failure as they went back into production with a new drama for Tennison and Co. He said, 'Somehow, we had to match the others, be that good and get 14 million viewers. It was a tall order. Had the viewers tired of Tennison? We were going to find out. We needed a good script, which we got, and we had Helen. John Thaw may have been brilliant as Morse, but I think she took *Prime Suspect* into a different zone. With her, you could explore a different type of policing, something painful, something going down different avenues. Tennison was very different from what had gone before. John Thaw was brilliant as Inspector Morse, but was essentially the old-style

British cop from the old school carrying the weight of the world on his shoulders. Helen wasn't especially fond of the police and wasn't trying to do a public relations job for them.

'She was playing a character in conflict, which is Helen's strength. Tennison isn't a nice person, but then the best characters are not nice. They tend to be self-obsessed, like Robbie Coltrane in *Cracker*, or John Thaw as Morse. She may be a woman in a man's world, but in her heart she is a woman and she never surrenders her vulnerability.

'The thing about Helen is that she is just as sexy now as she was 20 years ago. She has this power. She is switched on. She can be intimidating. But she is almost always very good fun.

'You know, we tried to make her look less attractive because that worked with the story being in Manchester and the tone of the story. We tried to crucify her every morning in make-up and it didn't work.

'We put her through the mincer, even trying to dress her drably. But no matter what we did, she came out looking fantastic.'

Neal would have liked to have made *Prime Suspect 6* in South Africa with the backdrop of violent crime in the streets of Jo'berg and Mirren turning Tennison into a 'Kate Adie-like figure'.

'Was Tennnison past her sell-by date? We thought she might be, but she certainly wasn't. I'd bet on her to draw a massive audience.'

When Sally Head, Lynda La Plante and Helen Mirren combined on the original *Prime Suspect*, they could have had little idea of the international impact of the drama which has now been sold to over 50 countries.

La Plante wanted to make her creation as authentic as possible. She based the original drama on a real-life case, but cuts needed to be made to scenes where Tennison 'roughed' up a suspect. For *Prime Suspect 3*, she interviewed vice squad officers and abused children, spending long, grim periods with teenage prostitutes in 'Cardboard City', a rotting, makeshift shanty town under London's Waterloo Bridge, a short walk from the House of Commons. The tale was also rooted in reality, and a paedophile who made threatening noises in La Plante's direction was eventually arrested.

La Plante says, 'I think I broke a mould but I was very lucky to have a mould-breaker so willing to work alongside me. I just wish they had more respect for the women who really hold these jobs. They are not 25 years old. They are women who have come to that position after many, many years of hard work moving from squad to squad, working on the streets dealing with tremendous discrimination along the way.

'There is prejudice against women, jostling to keep on top. If two detetctives are on a case, the man will open the car door for the woman, very polite, but it will be the rear door so he can sit in the front where the power is. A squad of young detetctives will be especially hostile to a woman if she replaces a much-loved guv'nor, as I had happen in my script.'

The series has to date won a total of 25 awards from around the world, including three British BAFTA 'Oscars' for Mirren and two American Emmy Awards for Best Mini-Series. And there may be more to come when DS Tennison makes her return to the small screen.

Mirren was always keen to play it again and believed the audience would welcome the return of the lady cop whose private life was a battlefield. She remains convinced that Tennison is more than just a symbolic character dreamed up to entertain the masses. She sees her as a powerful, dynamic feminine force making a statement to women in their everyday lives.

'She isn't always a nice person,' she admits. 'She can be selfish and driven. Those aspects are actually quite attractive in that they are forceful and dramatic. I hope this is a turning point in the way people view female characters.

'I try not to make a big deal out of this whole thing about women's roles because life is tough for actors and actresses in general. What I always say is that you have got to change women's roles in life before you get better roles in films, television and theatre.

'What Lynda La Plante showed clearly was that you could write a great role for a woman who is not a victim or that slightly

American idea of a tough businesswoman. She showed that women can be very ambitious and very vulnerable.'

Throughout the Summer of 2002, boyish, Andy Harries, the new Controller of Drama for Granada Television, held secret meetings with Lynda La Plante and Helen Mirren to discuss the possibility of a new *Prime Suspect*. The possible shape for a new adventure was already in Lynda La Plante's mind but they agreed that, due to her extreme workload on several other TV dramas, writer Peter Berry should be brought in to mould the teleplay. Berry was a proven and much respected wordsmith with credits such as *A Life For A Life – The Stefan Liszko Story* and the compelling movie drama *The Luzhin Defence*, starring John Turturro and Emily Watson, to his name. David Boulter would produce and a new TV wunderkind was deftly inserted into the brew. Director Tom Hooper – Harries quipped, "God ... he looks about 18 ... hate him" – was fresh from his success directing the award-winning TV drama *Daniel Deronda*. Hooper was well known to Granada stalwarts from directing episodes of their hugely successful long running thirtysomething comedy drama series *Cold Feet*.

The behind-the-scenes blend was firmly set while Berry forged and, with La Plante's support, a completely new career perspective for Jane Tennison, seven years after her near-death experience in Manchester. Now she was back in her natural habitat in Central London, heading up a new murder squad. Politics would be coming into play as crime figures showed over 30 unsolved murders on the books and 70 ongoing murder investigations. And there was another political hot potato, the immigrant issue. Tennison rattled her sabre and caused a flap at the Home Office when she investigated the killing of a young Bosnian girl who was brutally tortured to death. When the prime suspect turns out to be a 'minor' war criminal given a new life in the UK after identifying higher profile war criminals in Serbia, her quest for justice became increasingly complicated. The case threatens to bring an end to her career. But just as she sensed she had little left in her life apart from her job, along comes a good-looking and much younger journalist Robert West, played by Liam Cunningham.

Forty-two-year-old Dublin-born Cunningham was working as an electrician in the mid-Eighties before deciding to try his luck as an actor. More recently, he has appeared in the movies *Dog Soldiers* and *The Abduction Club*. He also worked for Granada on an episode of the Robbie Coltrane series *Cracker*.

Observers felt that for *Prime Suspect* to truly work again Tennison needed a passionate love interest. La Plante and Mirren herself believed viewers would be more gripped by a tale in which their heroine had a solid shoulder to lean on. Though there were concerns of 'taste' in upper executive echelons at Granada Television, the younger man element also met with Mirren's enthusiastic approval.

A senior source at Granada said, 'We could go nowhere without Helen and after such a long abscence it was clear to her that Tennison just couldn't be forever this "woman alone" thing. There had to be a man and she preferred the idea of a younger man rather than an obligatory kind of father figure. But, it was a fascinating relationship because Robert West, the character he plays, scares the hell out of Tennison with his passion for her. She hasn't given of herself for so long. There was tremendous electricity between them. There had to be' to make it work. We wondered whether Liam reminded her of her old flame Liam Neeson, intelligent and charismatic. When she first met him she turned to a somebody she knows well from the production team, curled her lip as only Helen can do and grinned "Ooo yes, he'll do very nicely!" The love scenes were dealt with discreetly, though. Helen wouldn't have it any other way.

Writer Berry has crafted Tennison a completely new team at 'the office' including Ben Miles – a former regular in the rural medical saga *Peak Practice* – as her right hand man Det. In. Finch. Mark Strong, who might just be recognised by *Prime Suspect* addicts as Det. In. Larry Hall from *Prime Suspect 3* played Det. Con. Hall.

Tennison's prime suspect, Milan Lukic, was played by Eastern

European idol, Moscow-born Oleg Menshikov who starred in the Cannes Film Festival award-winner *Burnt By The Sun*.

The £3 million two-parter *Prime Suspect 6: The Last Witness*, a co-production between Granada and WGBH (Boston), was aired in the UK on ITV on 19 November 2003 and in the US by the Exxon Mobil Masterpiece Theatre on PBS on 18 April 2004. Generally, reactions to the drama were excellent with more BAFTA, Emmy and Royal Television Society award nominations raining down on Mirren and the production. And, though nobody had to step up on this occasion to collect a prize, the critics were full of praise.

Robert Bianco wrote in *USA Today*, 'At the center, of course, is the marvel that is Mirren's Tennison - a woman who demands respect and an actress who commands attention. As long as there are still actors and characters of this caliber, all is still well with the TV world.'

While the *Sun*'s (UK) Ally Ross enthused, 'It was quite simply one of the TV drama events of the year … The real triumph of *Prime Suspect* is Saint Helen Mirren. The woman's still got it.' And he begged Mirren not to send Tennison into retirement.

There was no intention on her part or that of Granada to do so.

Executive producer Harries had pulled off one of the biggest TV coups of the year by re-launching *Prime Suspect* and Mirren on the beleaguered ITV network. It would not be long before he'd be taking a seat around a table with Mirren, director Philip Martin and writer Frank Deasy to discuss Tennison's poignant farewell in Prime Suspect 7.

He says, 'The show has been a cultural zeitgeist, always looking at modern issues, always wanting to be controversial. Helen Mirren? She is unique.'

11

WILL THE REAL
JANE TENNISON
STAND UP?

So who was and is Jane Tennison, the vulnerable but dedicated cop immortalised on television by Helen Mirren through the pen of writer Lynda La Plante? Was she total fiction? If not, how much like the genuine article was her fictional creation? Today, there are still only a handful of senior female detectives working in the Metropolitan Police region.

There can be little doubt that sexism and racism is still rife among the rank and file who proudly collect their pass-out diplomas from police training colleges up and down the country every summer. Jackie Malton felt nothing but pride as she stood in line, the polished buttons on her new uniform gleaming in the afternoon sunshine. Here she was, a raw recruit in a man's world. The Midlands newspaper executive's daughter was about to enter the lion's den, but she was ready for a scrap. She knew how to use her claws if need be. She may not have been the brightest school kid in Leicester, but there was no question about how tenacious she could be. She was the one who took on the bullies in school, the gutsy little redhead who had a thing about justice and equality. She may not have had many boys trailing her to the local picture house, but girls always felt safe in her company. They could confide in her as she was a good listener, genuinely interested in their problems.

While her chums were racing home to catch Cliff Richard and the Dallas Boys on the pop show *Oh Boy!*, she'd avidly be tuning into the ground-breaking cop series of the day, the BBC's *Dixon of Dock Green*, created by Ted Willis, and its ITV rival *No Hiding Place*, with a certain acting newcomer Johnny Briggs playing DS Russell. And then she'd hide behind the sofa, keeping her eyes firmly closed as aliens threatened Earth via an underground station in the science-fiction chiller *Quatermass and the Pit*. Malton was fascinated by the law, and if she had had academic leanings, she would have almost certainly been a solicitor tied to the criminal courts. She was ambitious. But she knew that that wasn't going to be possible. Instead, it was going to be a long hard slog, making her way through the police ranks to a senior position. And she wasn't going to be deterred. She wanted to prove to doubters that it was possible for a woman to find career contentment and satisfaction from a job in the Force. The sceptics, naturally enough, included her parents, who hoped she would find a more conventional career for a young woman. But the excitement of the idea and the challenges were enough to convince Malton that she had made the right decision.

What she had not quite bargained for was the reaction of the boys in blue to her sexuality. Jackie Malton was gay and had spent a good deal of her teenage years coming to terms with that reality. But she could never have forecast how the sexual element of her lifestyle would come into play as she boarded a train bound for London in 1979. Like a plotline from *Prime Suspect* itself, blackmail, fear, corruption and hate would become all-too-familiar ingredients in her day-to-day existence.

She recalled, 'There was nothing theatrical about me, but I was an 11-plus failure. I dreaded the whole exam thing. That would seem to define you for ever. When I was a kid in the Midlands, I wanted to work in TV but I didn't know in what capacity. My best subjects were English Literature and English Language, but I just loved the idea of being a TV star.

'I don't know why, but most of the stuff I watched on television was connected with darkness of one sort or another. In cities or in prisons. I did a project on prisons at school. I had this area of my mind which manifested itself in an obscure way. It wasn't channelled in a particular area. But I knew I had to join the police in order to get where I am today.'

Malton skilfully, diplomatically, climbed the ladder of promotion, permanently aware that she was having to deal with rampant sexism along the way. By the time she'd made it into the Flying Squad at Rotherhithe at the southern end of the Blackwall Tunnel in the early Eighties, she was a highly commended plain-clothes detective. On her first day in the office, she was given a partner who made Jack Regan from *The Sweeney* look like the Sugar Plum Fairy. He was rough, jaded and a fully fledged, paid-up bigot. She said, 'When we were introduced, he looked me straight in the eye and said, "Why don't you fuck off, you cunt?" I think it was fair to say I was taken aback. He was making it pretty clear where he was coming from. It was nothing new to me, but it was so nastily blatant.'

For weeks afterwards, she would leave the office to go on jobs only to find herself regularly stranded in the dark, dingy backstreets of docklands, whereupon her driver would mysteriously disappear. 'There would be no warning,' she said. 'It was like a little game they were playing, to test your patience, to see how far they could push you. I'm only human, I'd be furious, going absolutely potty. But I didn't let them see it. I'd somehow get back to the station. The better I dealt with it, the less it happened. They were basically saying to me that they didn't want to work with a woman. They didn't have any choice.'

What gave the cruellest, typically macho officers the most pleasure was to see women openly break down in front of them. The higher the rank, the better the 'result'.

Malton was a star cop who progressed steadily to Flying Squad status and became an obvious role model for Jane Tennison, deploying her every waking hour to progressing her career at West End Central in the heart of London.

She said, 'You had to be strong. If anything, you had to be stronger than the guys. In a sense, they did you a favour. They made you stronger. I was a leader. If I crack, their confidence in me waivers.'

She kept her emotions firmly under wraps. When an 18-month-old child was raped and murdered, a young male officer sobbed in her arms. He begged her not to discuss his moment of weakness and she promised never to repeat the episode. When she returned to the sanctuary of her own office, she allowed the tears to flow.

Few doubted that she was ten years ahead of her time working on rehabilitation projects at Holloway Prison and other schemes aimed at improving parenting skills of criminals and police officers, which is now a pet hobbyhorse for Tony Blair's New Labour Party in the war against crime. She set up a special unit to study and deal with domestic violence while serving in Hammersmith, London, and later in the Nineties ran a safe-sex campaign among the rent boys on the dimly lit backstreets around King's Cross.

She said, 'It was a period of innovative change and you had to keep up if you wanted promotion. You couldn't stand still or just go with the flow.'

There was resistance to her methods in the Eighties while she was serving as a DI at West End Central in Savile Row. She had just been approached by ITV's *The Bill* to advise on a rape story with the possibility of her becoming a more permanent consultant. She was ecstatic. But within days, she was bitterly despondent when a deputy assistant commander merely accused her of 'wasting' her time.

There were also areas of police life she found more difficult to deal with because of her sexuality. There were few serving, high-ranking women officers in the Met at that time and the men in her office were keen to know what made her tick ... in every sense. The vicious smell of blackmail also lingered in the air, so long as she kept her secret to herself. But she broke any possibility of another officer having that kind of hold over her by revealing her sexual identity to her superiors.

'My sexuality wasn't clear to me as teenager,' she said. 'You don't decide at 14. Everyone wants to be the norm, whatever that is. But you work for institutions which bring you into conflict. Nobody wants to be different from their best mates. I accepted that people are homophobic, they don't understand. I don't know why I was given my sexuality. It wasn't choice. Whether I like it or don't like it, that's what I am stuck with. I didn't particularly want to have it. I didn't choose. In the '60s, '70s and '80s, you wouldn't choose. The attitude towards homosexuals then was appalling.

'I knew, but I didn't do anything about it. I am sure I have always been gay. But it's not a black-and-white thing, you have a struggle with it until you come to accept it. In your conscious or unconscious, you might feel your natural pull is towards somebody of the same sex. You want to be normal, to lead a normal life. Get married and have two kids. But it's not going to happen. It's a very sexual world and you have to fit into the rules and the hurt that goes with it.'

The pressure to conform was enormous in the Force, but she wasn't going to walk away. Or be driven out. And she often paid a high price by way of being tormented as a figure of fun.

'You were either a dyke or a bike ... and I was a dyke,' she confessed. 'They attacked my sexuality. They said I wasn't a real woman because I was a gay. They couldn't accuse me of sleeping my way to the top, there was nothing there for them and that made some of them more angry. And there were the others who wanted to sleep with you as if they were going to straighten you out. You'd got it all wrong and they were going to prove it to you. The guys always tried to take sexual advantage. They wanted to give me a good "rodgering" and told me I hadn't been treated right, that was why I preferred women. I was this trophy waiting to be taken ... but it never happened. They reacted the same to women, whether gay or not. If I had a pound for every time I turned a guy down, I'd be very rich. The guys really fancied their chances. Men would persist. There was even one who said, "Well then ... can I watch?"

'Please don't make me sound like a victim, because I wasn't. You just had to be insensitive. At Christmas, you'd have dildos dropped through your door. It was just one of those things. That was their idea of humour. Or they thought they were doing you a favour, like you needed this stuff! But I was one of the "lads" in the main and that was fine. When I was 40, they threw this surprise birthday party for me and that was smashing, when I least expected it.

'But the truth was that, if you were up-front with your sexuality, it was no real problem. If you weren't going to tell, they would guess in any case. If you made it plain where you were coming from, they would walk away. The joke was over. I, for the most part, worked with a great bunch of blokes who were terrifically supportive. I was very fond of the blokes and they were fond of me.

'The thing was that – I have never said this before – but I don't have to hide this any more. The whole issue about sexuality was one about protecting family, but it is my journey. You had to fight the system.

'I didn't get involved with women in the Force. I kept that side of my life out of the police. The whole thing was a nightmare because *I* was a nightmare. I drank a lot, smoked a lot and worked all hours for ten years in order to maintain myself in the police and keep up with everyone else. But *I* did these things. It wasn't anyone else's fault.'

The year was 1990 when 'Feisty Jack', as she was known, was put in contact with Lynda La Plante by a former officer pal called Peter. The writer had already had a degree of success with the feminist thriller *Widows* which had first been broadcast in 1983 while *Civvies*, her violent tale about a mob of former SAS hard-nuts, was about to be transmitted. They had dinner at La Plante's mansion on top of Kingston Hill in Surrey. Malton, in jeans and bomber jacket, was slightly taken aback by the size and grandeur of the property tucked away off the main road. She was even more surprised by the reaction of La Plante's ex-husband Richard who, she claims, was brusque to the point of outright rudeness. She said, 'I don't know what was on his mind, but he sort of looked me up and down when he opened the door, and said he thought I must have the wrong place. I don't know whether he misheard me or was just being stroppy. He was definitely being off-hand, so I told him to stop messing about as though he was doing me a favour. They wanted me, it wasn't a case of me chasing them. Then Lynda appeared and everything was fine.'

La Plante explained that she had got the idea for the fiercely independent female DCI from an episode of *Crimewatch*. Malton flicked through the rough draft of *Prime Suspect* and was full of enthusiasm for the storyline and the possibilities of turning Tennison into a permanent TV fixture. And she was quick to spot the similiarities between the facets of the fictional character and her own. Here was a woman who put her career first, a woman with a vulnerable streak, a loner who hated losing. Her closest fictional relative was probably Clarice Starling, the FBI agent who was a memorable match for Hannibal Lecter in Thomas Harris's *The Silence of the Lambs*.

Malton was shadowed by La Plante for months while she interviewed hardened criminals and observed autopsies. She was impressed by her businesslike manner at the station where her uniform was almost always a smart, tailored suit and lower ranks always addressed her as 'Ma'am'. She never touched a male officer. Any kind of contact could be regarded as a sexual statement. And she never, ever allowed her emotions to spill out in the workplace.

'I believe in fate, that your journey is mapped out for you,' said Malton, who very quickly became La Plante's 'sounding board' while she developed Tennison's plotline in the opening story. It was

215

a meeting of minds. Both agreed on the direction in which Tennison should go, that here was an opportunity to develop something unique. 'Lynda sucked me up like a sponge,' she said. 'She was very clever, she couldn't get enough of me and my stories. I could have been boring with a husband and two children and just had traffic stories to tell, but mine were about violent criminals, the worst, those who enjoyed causing pain.'

Sadly, back at the 'office', things hadn't been quite so cordial. There were still the dark, depressing periods when she'd hit the bottle and chain-smoked. When the pressure was too great. The crunch came when she decided to take a walk through a career minefield as a witness against an officer who was suspected of corruption and of planting drugs on suspects. Ironically, she was never called to court to give evidence before the officer concerned was jailed for 12 months.

But her stance and determination sent shockwaves through the ranks at West End Central. One morning, she entered the canteen and witnessed a silent walk-out by officers who'd heard about her 'grassing' on a mate. The stunned Malton became a target for abuse and loathing which would, in time, lead to her making her exit from the Force to find a new life.

Suddenly, the worst kind of pornographic literature was being stuffed through her letterbox in bundles. Extreme images were accompanied by phallic symbols of almost every description. Every morning for months, she feared what she might find lying on her mat. She dreaded the sound of the postman's knock. The effect of the long and vicious campaign against her was that she suffered from post-traumatic stress disorder and panic attacks.

She said, 'The campaign just petered out. I don't know why. I never found out who was behind it, although I had my suspicions. I was just glad it was over.'

Malton was in her mid-forties and perhaps felt she had, in any case, gone as far as she could. Above all, she wanted her sanity restored. She wanted to quit boozing. And, more importantly, she could actually see a fulfilling, exciting future for herself in the world of television. That teenage dream was now a distinct possibility.

'I was a brilliant cop because I was good with people,' she says. 'I gave of myself. I didn't make judgements about people's lives. I related to people who had problems. I gave people back their dignity. I empowered them, gave them an opportunity, whether they were victims or villains. I gave a lot and they gave to me. I had relationships with hookers ... 101 different types of people and I was compassionate.'

Soon after meeting La Plante, she was introduced to Mirren over dinner. There was an instant rapport, respect and admiration. She said, 'Helen was very striking, she had and has a sense of presence ... with or without make-up. The first time I met her, she was very natural and lovely.' It was the start of a three-way partnership which was to inspire one of the classic TV police dramas of the Nineties.

Then she heard, much to her surprise, that Granada Television, who were making the show, were considering putting Tennison on screen as a gay senior detective. La Plante, who was not initially averse to the concept, went away to consider the switch but told executives that they would be risking a hostile audience. The idea was dropped and never brought up again.

Malton also felt that the show would not have been a massive ratings hit if the writer and producers had gone in that direction. Looking back at her work on *Prime Suspect*, she said, 'I think I am more vulnerable than the character you saw on screen, but you don't see that. Helen doesn't necessarily show that same vulnerability. She doesn't put herself through the hoop the way I did.

'But nobody could have played Tennison the way Helen did. I could see why men took to her so much. She exudes sexuality. I also respect her because she can be aloof when she wants to be. She can hold people at a distance and I respect her for that. I'd like to be more like her. She gives so much, and then the shutters come down. There are "spikes" around her which make her the actress she is.

'You can feel as if you are in deep sisterhood with her over women's issues. When she wants to be, she can be quite frightening, intimidating, in as much as she is powerful with her presence. I have got enormous respect for her. I have to say, *Prime Suspect* couldn't have been successful without her. She didn't need anyone to tell her how to play the part.

'One day, though, she took me by surprise. She said she didn't like DCI Tennison, which kind of hurt me; I took it as a personal insult. She didn't like the character because she was so hard, self-centred, self-obsessed and driven. Then, later, just as I was about to leave the Force, she said she was learning to love Tennison and that meant a lot to me. One of my best friends was dying at the time and that was such a boost to me.'

On set in Manchester and London, she was also able to 'bond' with the boys in Tennison's squad, feeling relaxed in the company of Tom Bell and John Benfield. Only Craig Fairbrass kept his distance.

She said, 'They had a tremendous respect for Helen. She was the star but they revered her. One thing I learned that stayed with me was that there is no magic in television. It is hard work. Damn hard work.'

Prime Suspect was, in effect, to save her life. Her involvement with La Plante and Mirren and her advice as a leading consultant took her away from her usual police work and gave her a new impetus. She was major influence on *Prime Suspect 3*, which was shown in 1993, in developing the transsexual and homosexual characterisations. When the series was brought to a conclusion by ITV network chiefs in 1996, by which time Malton was a DCI, she was convinced that it was also time for her to make her move. She had also worked on *She's Out*, the steel-edged sequel to La Plante's Eighties tale *Widows*, which again starred Anne Mitchell. By this time, the TV bug had well and truly bitten.

She said, 'I might have been a troubled soul trying to find inner peace, but I had stopped drinking by 1992. I just got fed up with being sick, waking up with hangovers and feeling like shit. I haven't had a drink since. Without question, *Prime Suspect* had a profound effect on me. More than anything, the show tapped into my creativity, which I didn't know I had. And it was cathartic after all the crap I had gone thorough. I had a new direction, a new reason to wake up.'

Fate was to take another hand while she plotted her future at Fulham in West London. She was sickened by the endless hounding she had had to endure over having 'put the finger' on another corrupt police officer. The cutting remarks hurt and there was no further promotion in the air.

Then, she was struck down by a painful knee injury and, after securing specialist advice, she resigned in 1997 to collect a well-earned pension.

Within 12 months, she had created her own company, Prime Crime, developing police-based television and film storylines and character ideas. She has had input into series such as *The Bill* and its spin-offs *Beech is Back* and *Burnside*, while retaining her association with La Plante through *Trial and Retribution*.

She said, 'I actually had 11 women in my team before I left. They were so loyal to me. I was one of the best in terms of "guv'nors" and I was a good cop. If you were good, you were OK, no matter what the other baggage was.

'Lynda said I was cut out for television work, but you had to believe in yourself. Writers don't have, in the main, that experience of the darkness of life. At Christmas, I worked with the Crisis organisation and the homeless. You think, there but for the grace of God go all of us.'

When I met her she lived alone in a cosy cottage in the surrey countryside. The atmosphere is more *Miss Marple* than *Sweeney*, as she pours coffee. Patterned drapes and cushions with Laura Ashley-type designs colour the walk-through lounge with a smart iron spiral staircase leading to the upper floor. The garden is a maze of hanging green plants and pots in a rustic setting.

She has a slight red tint to her hair, and she speaks without a trace of the Midlands accent she left behind as a teenager. Her manner and approach appears straightforward and businesslike. She's is not one for small-talk and has learned, through experience, to be guarded.

On the surface, it's hard to believe this slightly built woman in jeans and a loose check shirt had to deal with hardened villains, rapists and drug-dealers on a regular basis. That's exactly what she did while earning the admiration and respect of almost every officer who came across her, except the corrupt or most sexist.

Writer La Plante also got to know her well during her 'consultancy' period. Remembering an initial meeting at her home, La Plante observes, 'She might have been someone in the fashion world, immaculately dressed, vivacious. She went through my draft script with a big red pencil saying, "Nonsense ..." or "She'd never do that ..." or "She'd have to go through the Super ..." But she also said at the end, "I don't know how you're doing it, but you are getting inside my head."

'Jackie won through because a woman is bound to be up against all sorts of handicaps in this job. One of the reasons there aren't more senior women detectives is that it is a very steep promotion ladder. You have to go up it quickly or not at all. You need to have been out on the streets very early, learning the basics. DCIs are young these days. In real life, Morse would have been pensioned off years ago. If a woman misses a few years having children, she's off the escalator. Jackie has foregone all that. She eats, sleeps and breathes the job. And she's against any short cuts for women.'

Malton, who has just turned 50, believes the Force is changing, but slowly. 'There are far more opportunities for women now in the police,' she says, pointing to the prejudicial unofficial 'ceiling' of 10 per cent of women in the Force. 'But it's not true that there are certain jobs women don't want to do anyway. It is a tough, difficult job, but why should you put yourself on the line? That seems to be the problem now.'

No matter. She played her part in TV history. *Prime Suspect* made its mark with the public, as well as the Force itself, who now use

Tennison's dark, edgy adventures as part of their courses for cadets at the Hendon Police Training College.

The series was already a ratings success when Merseyside senior cop Alison Holford decided to 'go public' when her rise to the top abruptly came to an unexpected halt.

'I know we had a huge effect,' said Malton. 'We came along at the time Holford was having her problems and its timing in that sense couldn't have been more perfect. The public were able to see for themselves how senior policewomen could be treated unless they stood up for themselves.'

Malton, as we talked, had just finished work as story consultant on the new two-part ITV thriller *Sirens*, starring Daniela Nardini, Greg Wise and *Prime Suspect* 'old boy' Robert Glenister. Glamorous Scottish actress Nardini, who made her TV breakthrough in *This Life*, played a detective hot on the heels of a serial rapist operating around London's canal system.

Ironically, Malton never handled a murder inquiry or chased a serial killer. Her speciality, if there was such a thing, was arson. And now she has entered a new war zone in the cut and thrust world of television, though as a creative consultant she doesn't have to deal with the politics at the ITV network headquarters or Greg Dykes's latest policy plan at the BBC. She believes the public will welcome the return of *Prime Suspect*, no matter where it is set, just so long as Helen Mirren is back in her trenchcoat.

'It wouldn't work without her. Trust me,' says Malton. 'I'd like to think she'll end up a happy lady. Perhaps she'll go off with somebody from outside of the Force and say, "Up yours." Yes, that would be something I'd enjoying seeing.'

And she should know. She's been there.

The L-shaped white-walled mansion, complete with a baronial hall and glass-panelled swimming pool overlooking the landscaped garden, stands just off Kingston Hill in Surrey and is a monument to the outstanding success of Lynda La Plante.

When she turns into the drive of her £4 million mini-estate, she glows with pride. At one time, La Plante hardly ever left her office. The woman behind *Prime Suspect* had to keep writing just to preserve the prestigious roof over her head. But La Plante doesn't have to worry about the mortgage any longer. And the office has moved to give her some breathing space.

These days, she grafts away with her small team at La Plante Productions in Wardour Street, once the centre of the movie and TV production industry. Colleagues can see with their own eyes just how well the lady has done, whether she's dining at Mezzo or slipping into Groucho's for a natter with old mates.

Make no mistake, La Plante is a tough cookie. She's worked hard to get this far and she has no intention of losing her lifestyle. Too much sweat and too many tears went into creating what she has today.

You half suspect she'll let loose a gaggle of heavies she met during research should you step out of line with her. Certainly, you'd cross her at your peril. If you should hear the expression 'Now, you won't let me down, will you?' be prepared for repercussions. One writer who fell foul of La Plante chose his words carefully. 'She's not the most forgiving of souls. You get a chance with her and, if you let her down, you're out and you stay out, no matter what you say or do. People were tough with her once. They let her down, they gave her a hard time. Somewhere along the way, she said to herself that she wasn't going to get far in this business being weak. She'd been in that position herself and it wasn't much like fun. Now she has clout. Real clout.'

Typical of the woman, she bought her fabulous home in 1987 for £400,000 and had it renovated at huge expense. She was then married to American thriller writer and judo black belt Richard La Plante, whom she met in 1975. Finally, she ended up almost having to write just to keep the expensive roof over her head. Her talent shone through. La Plante in the Nineties became an 'industry', the TV crime writer with the golden keyboard.

Looking back at her step up in the property market, she said, 'We moved on the promise of me getting a couple of fantastic advances from America for my work, so we spent and spent. But the agreements never materialised. I adore the place, but it's just as well I'm a workaholic. In the business, they call me Morecambe and Wise. I say, "Hold on, I've got to write a play. I'll be back in a minute", just like Ernie.'

She confessed that her house ate up every penny she earned, turning her life into a 'nightmare'. The telephone call from California she was waiting for never happened. She'd hoped she'd hit the jackpot and there was going to be a big-budget adventure movie starring Mel Gibson and a deal on the screen rights to her first novel *The Legacy*. It didn't happen. But she is no stranger to disappointment.

La Plante was born Lynda Titchmarsh in Crosby on the outskirts of Liverpool. She was regarded as bossy and exhibitionist, not averse to scalping her sister's dolls and dunking them down the toilet. She was aware she had a problem with words by the age of 12 but was not diagnosed as dyslexic until much later. She went to RADA at 15 to train for an acting career, gaining the new name Lynda Marchal in the process. The peer rivalry and bitchiness got to her within days. 'I hated the place,' says La Plante, who is now in her mid-fifties. 'They can be very cruel there. I once complained to the principal about being cast as an 89-year-old woman all the time, and he said, "My dear, that's all you'll probably ever play. You're a very plain-looking person, small and rather squat." I thought, Thanks very much, but it had a profound effect on me. I don't think I reacted very well at that time to criticism. Maybe I was too sensitive for my own good.

'It's only now or latterly that if somebody said to me, "No, you can't," I'll think, Oh yes I can, or they will give me the drive to carry on, to prove them wrong.'

For 20 years, as Lynda Marchal, she tried to make her name as an actress by appearing in series such as *Bergerac*, *The Sweeney*, *Fox* and

Minder. 'I enjoyed it, but I never had a lucky break,' she said. 'I was loud and I had red hair and I played a lot of hookers. But it was all leading to a dead end.'

She was spurred on to write some 20 years ago when she appeared in *The Gentle Touch*, the TV series about tough woman cop Maggie Forbes played by Jill Gascoine. She was again cast as a prostitute and she told Gascoine she thought the script was a load of rubbish. When she was told it was one of the better scripts, she wrote the outlines to four new plots herself.

They weren't used but one, marked 'brilliant', eventually blossomed with reworking into the smash-hit series *Widows* about four women who commit a robbery their late mobster husbands had planned. Ann Mitchell starred as the gang's acid-spitting leader Dolly Rawlins and she made a welcome return in the sequel, *Widows 2*, in 1985. La Plante had taken the original script to leading feminist TV drama chiefs Verity Lambert and Linda Agran, who were both to become firm friends. Now she was being taken seriously.

Hollywood suddenly sat up and took notice and she was ecstatic when her agent rang with a lucrative offer from the Walt Disney organisation. They flew her first-class out to Los Angeles. Statutory bouquets of flowers fell into her arms on arrival. Krug champagne on tap was waiting in her hotel suite. If she made a move, there was a stretch limo waiting. 'They gave me the kind of treatment I'd always dreamed about when I was an actress,' she recalls.

Then she spent an hour trying to sell them the plot of *Widows*. After she had mimed every gunshot and grisly murder, ex-Walt Disney chief Jeffery Katzenberg turned to her and said, 'Yes, that's fine, Lynda, but where are the laughs, where's the humour?' Susan Sarandon and Geena Davis had yet to co-star in *Thelma and Louise* and the concept of women making men look silly as they rode off into the sunset was a largely unchartered area for the average Hollywood movie executive, even the super-smart Katzenberg, who later masterminded the success of *Shrek* at DreamWorks.

Patiently but forcefully, she explained that her gangster yarn was no slapstick farce. He paced around his desk before punching the air dramatically and shouting, 'OK, we'll do it!'

But, within a month, her dream was in ruins. La Plante was in 'turnaround' land. Fuelled by one glass of red wine too many, she made a series of abusive telephone calls to her so-called 'backers' 6,000 miles away. 'Those bastards,' she told me. 'I was so naïve. I thought I had cracked it. Had I hell! The trouble was that, at the end of the meeting, one of the executives sneakily asked me for a note on *Widows* explaining the rough plot. He then sent a copy to everyone, killing off the film! I was very naughty ringing them up while I was drunk. God knows what I said. I still feel ashamed. I was in such a fury, but I wasn't going to let those people destroy me. The whole business was insane. They told me they bought *Widows* as a vehicle for Bette Midler. Bette Midler? Then they were comparing it to *Butch Cassidy and the Sundance Kid.* Total madness. Those same people were then telling me how wonderful I was. What a bunch of creeps!'

The brief flirtation with Hollywood inspired the former actress to write her second novel *Bella Mafia*, which went hurtling into the bestseller list.

After *Prime Suspect* won her a much-coveted BAFTA, she supplied the plot outline to the sequel which was written by Alan Cubitt. But she made her comeback on *Prime Suspect 3.*

Between scripts, she'd pen novels such as *Entwined*, which was her fourth, about twin sisters separated in the concentration camp at Auschwitz.

But she's at her best writing for television, and followed up her success in *Prime Suspect* with *Civvies*, which was actually created years earlier, and the boxing yarn *Seconds Out*, switching channels to work for the BBC.

The night she collected a British 'Oscar' from BAFTA for the first *Prime Suspect* was the highlight of her career so far. Unfortunately, within hours of clutching her prize, she was close to tears over allegations of a judging mix-up which would have seen Alan Bleasdale get the accolade for *GBH*.

Scouser Bleasdale's brilliant black comedy, starring Robert Lindsay, focused on political life on Merseyside. The storyline interwove corruption and hypocrisy with a healthy supply of farce from Julie Walters as Lindsay's screen mother. Lindsay Duncan played a temptress with a mission to destroy a fictional local party leader called Michael Murray.

To this day, La Plante privately believes there was a conspiracy to undermine her, to make her peers and the public believe there was something 'dodgy' about her victory. Rumours circulated that a circle of high-ranking ITV and Channel 4 executives had been lobbying hard for Bleasdale, already a firm favourite with BAFTA for his *Boys from the Blackstuff*. When *Prime Suspect* came out of the envelope, a row developed, which took little time to reach the national press. BAFTA officials had never heard or seen anything like it before. One senior BAFTA figure who was involved in the affair said, 'We were never really aware of any major row or bitterness between Mr Bleasdale and Ms La Plante. There's always jealousy in the showbusiness fraternity between actors and writers, but it's always kept under control. There isn't a law which says we have to like each other. The knives seem to be out, from both quarters. As far as we're concerned, everything was absolutely above board so far as the voting was concerned. People have their favourites work-wise. They always will. They were both tremendous pieces. There were a lot of people who just assumed *GBH* would win because it was topical politically and dealt with issues and personalities who were around at the time, whereas *Prime Suspect* was much more of a straightforward story with quality writing and acting. For once, we weren't politically correct.'

'It was deeply upsetting,' La Plante says. 'I have the award but it will never mean as much to me now. I can't even look at it. That highpoint was tarnished.'

But La Plante, with her ring of steel in place, hurled herself back into her work through the BBC series *Civvies*, a gangland saga based on paratroopers adjusting to dull, poorly paid urban life. There was also *Framed*, a new caper set against the backdrop of the Costa del Sol, and *Seconds Out*, which took a close look at the unsavoury aspects of the boxing game ... not forgetting her new novel *Entwined*.

La Plante is proud that her work is commercially attractive, but she would never want to emulate Barbara Cartland or Mills & Boon. 'I find it difficult writing these romantic women's books where "her breasts fell from the lace and her lips were trembling" and the underwear is by Janet Reger. I can't get into that.'

On the *Prime Suspect* series, she knew there was a certain pressure, mostly from the 'suits', to get Helen Mirren to disrobe and expose those ample curves. Ratings were everything. They didn't believe La Plante could sustain her success unless the public were given lashings of nudity. Mirren in the buff would be a massive publicity bonus. La Plante was unmoved. Throughout, from the opening *Prime Suspect* to the last, six years later, nobody saw much more than a flash of Mirren's upper arm, even during her 'torrid' one-night stand with another detective in *Prime Suspect 5: Errors of Judgement*.

'People say, "Sex scenes, please," and I say "Sod off." Humping scenes are a turn-off.'

La Plante was not impressed by the BBC's support when they launched her new series *Lifeboat* – a kind of kiss 'n' tell drama set in stormy waters off the Welsh coast – in 1994. An insider said, 'The series needed more time to develop and a bigger budget. It was made on a shoestring. They could probably have used a couple of "names" as well, but the general feeling was that the BBC went off the idea at an early stage.'

But she was on song with the third part of the *Widows* trilogy *She's Out*, which again brought Dolly Rawlins, alias Anne Mitchell, back into confrontation after serving an eight-year stretch. It wasn't long before she introduced an entirely new principally court-based drama *Trial & Retribution*, which, twelve stories later, is still going strong. There was another new crime drama, *Mind Games*, which starred Royal National Theatre actress Fiona Shaw as a former nun who turns effective criminal profiler. And she created a new crime series *The Commander* for the ITV network starring the popular Ulster-born actress Amanda Burton.

Perhaps most daring and challenging of all has been her revamping of her British hits to break into the American television market. She took *The Governor*, which she co-produced, and co-wrote with Natalie Chaidez, and which co-starred Janet McTeer, and conjured up a new sophisticated version called *The Warden*. Ally Sheedy took the lead role of Helen Hewitt, who was ably supported by Sam Robards and Lindsay Crouse in running the toughest jail in America. TNT put their dollars into the drama which was shown in January 2001. She also co-wrote a new version of *Framed* starring Rob Lowe and Sam Neill, a tale which first appeared on British screens a decade earlier. And she was thrilled when her Americanisation of *Widows* was broadcast in August 2002 with Rosie Perez, Mercedes Ruehl and Brooke Shields, proving that the fair sex can break the law just as well when given an opportunity. Michelle Pfeiffer has optioned the film rights to her novel *Cold Shoulder*, which is centred on a lady cop.

She has many admirers in the upper echelons of American television. In fact, California-based Steven Bochco, the brilliant creator of the superb *LA Law* and *NYPD Blue*, reckons that La Plante has been one of his major influences in the Nineties through *Prime Suspect*.

La Plante, who has now also written eight novels, has paid a high price on a personal level for being a one-woman industry. In 1975, she met and married Richard La Plante. They hoped for a family but, following fertility treatment, she went through a premature menopause, so children of their own were ruled out.

They were an odd couple when you saw them together. He was

tall, fair-haired and boyish, with the muscles of a body-builder. She was a tiny 5ft 2in, with a mane of curly flame-coloured hair. She strode confidently, especially at parties and awards ceremonies. He shuffled uncomfortably in her wake. They got into their own routine with 'his' and 'hers' offices at their Surrey home, usually keeping a distance until lunchtime. Richard ensured they worked out three mornings a week and they doted on their two Irish wolfhounds. He may have been able to knock her into shape physically, but emotionally they were out of step with each other, though refusing to admit it, by the turn of the Nineties. Sadly, by the time they were divorced in 1996, he seemed generally to have only unkind things to say about her, suggesting that she could never have won her glittering prizes without his support. He was the one who put his career on hold.

'I was obsessive about my work,' she said. 'Lunchtime would come around and he'd say, "Are you having lunch?" and four hours later I would appear. Or I'd say I'd be ten minutes doing something else, and I'd be six hours.' She viewed their parting of the ways as 'amicable', but agreed that 'the writing did it'.

Nobody has yet managed to take away her fabulous house on the hill, not that she's ever complacent about gremlins lying in wait on the horizon. Though she may often write about 'low-life', when she wants to get away from it all, she jets across to her new chic retreat by the shoreline in The Hamptons, an extremely well-to-do sailing spot a short drive upstate from New York. And at the age of 62 she now shares her life with her three-year-old adopted son Lorcan. An adoption agency located the boy for her in Florida when he was six months old.

It's easy to imagine that the first lady of TV crime climbs into bed with a huge grin on her face. After all, what about all those in the business who said she'd go nowhere? The producers who held out little hope for her. And the rest of the sceptics who sighed when she said she was now writing for a living.

'It's good having the last laugh,' she said. 'It's no good looking back. But I did get a certain amount of pleasure about proving them wrong. Now? I just do what I'm best at. I do what I enjoy. That's my pleasure. And I'm free to do it. Freedom is the best.'

12

Oscar, Where Art Thou?

When Helen Mirren was 25 she went to see a palmist. 'I was really depressed and fucked up,' she confided. 'I went to a hand-reader, this Indian guy in a funky neighbourhood. He said, "The height of your success won't happen until you are in your late forties." From that moment on, I felt much better because I realised I didn't want to know what was going to happen. I just wanted to get on with it.'

Mirren couldn't have made a better prediction if she'd written it herself. There was no real reason for her to be that miserable at the time. She was a rising star with the RSC but was unsure about how badly she wanted success. What price was she willing to pay?

Now here she was gazing across the Lido in Venice 20 years later and the demons had not gone away. But she had always heeded the palmist's words. She knew that there was something waiting for her. After an extraordinary career spanning 25 years, the public still didn't know her. It didn't seem possible, but in Chelsea and Hampstead she was an artistic darling. Media people worshipped her. If you read the *Guardian* or the *Observer*, you could rattle off most of her movies. And there was even a band of red-blooded red-top readers who'd fantasise about her as they dozed off at night. Remarkable, then, that she was still largely undiscovered. That was about to change.

When she was filming *The Comfort of Strangers* with Christopher Walken, Rupert Everett and Natasha Richardson, she took the call about making a new TV crime story called *Prime Suspect*. The script followed. She'd never wanted to make a television series but this was a 'pilot', a one-off show which had the makings of widening out into so much more.

She would be rushing back to London as soon as she'd finished filming director Paul Schrader's vision of Ian McEwan's dark novel, which he himself had co-written into a screenplay with Harold Pinter. Walken, a master of the macabre, and Mirren played a wealthy married duo who lure a younger, unsettled English couple into their dangerous sexual web. Schrader's bid to turn one of McEwan's novels into a compelling movie, however, fell well short of that other Italian spine-chiller, Daphne du Maurier's *Don't Look Now*. The subject matter may have been in part the loss of innocence. But the movie also lost its audience after its release in March 1991.

Just over a month later, *Prime Suspect* was launched on the ITV network in Britain and a new heroine was born. Mirren had suddenly matured. The Sex Queen was no more. She wore little make-up to reveal the lines of age. Her clothes were dull. But she was real. The public – an amazing 14 million of them – were spellbound. Jane Tennison showed the guys how to do it and didn't mind putting them in their place.

The *Sun* joined the chorus of approval, saying, '*Prime Suspect* pulls no punches ... it rams them down your throat.'

Mirren saw Tennison as a heroine, a role model. She had three female icons herself – wild rock star Janis Joplin, Margaret Thatcher and pop queen Madonna. She said, 'Janis was very strong and passionate, a fantastic and uncompromising performer. She may have been out of control so far as drink and drugs were concerned, but she did not control her own destiny. Margaret Thatcher was a great image to young girls. They know nothing about politics but they could look at pictures of world leaders and see a woman there. Now it looks as though it is back to grey suits. Madonna combines great business acumen, incredible self-discipline and a wonderful talent, and yet she remains a rebel.'

By July 1991, she was starring at the Young Vic in Tom Kempinski's farce *Sex Please, We're Italian!*, playing a Neapolitan mamma who's had a secret affair with a priest. But she confided that she could see something of herself in her new TV character Jane Tennison.

'Early on in my career, for sure,' she said, 'I was more like her in terms of being uncompromisingly committed to personal ambition, but I don't think I am now. I wanted to do it because it was such a good part. It had great subtlety and social comment. But the first I knew of how well it had gone was through my mother who told me everyone at the bridge club was talking about it.'

She was also feeling homesick for Hackford. Their separations had grown longer over the last 12 months since her return to Europe. 'That's when I really hate it,' she said. 'Because it's so much more dangerous. We write and then we forget. He's not a great letter-writer. We should call more but we don't. I get frightened for us.'

She said, 'Moving away from your country gives you a different aspect and it gave me a great education in finding what I call the genius of England and that is the British people, the English character full of wit and strength. I had to go away to fall in love with it all over again. I couldn't bear England any more. It really depressed me. Maybe it was a kind of vanity but I didn't feel that my kind of acting was accepted. I felt what I was trying to do was not understood. So I went to America to see if I fitted in better there, or if I had anything to learn.

'I also moved to America to be with Taylor because I felt it was my destiny. When a change of life decision hits you, it's like a wave breaking on the shore. You can't hold it back and you can't avoid it. That's what happened to me.

'But America could never be home to me. I love England, seeing the trees without their leaves and, most of all, I love the theatre. I'd forgotten just how brilliant it is and I am desperate to do some more.

'What I wanted to do originally was make films in France in French. My own personal taste has been more towards European than American film. I don't basically like American films. I think they're fairly stupid. But it was totally impractical. I couldn't speak French and they had all these great, lovely French actresses around.'

Mirren was soon on her travels again back in Italy making *Where Angels Fear to Tread* in San Gimignano and Siena in Tuscany. This was Merchant-Ivory land on a smaller scale. The £4 million London Weekend Television-backed remake of EM Forster's novel saw her portraying Lilia Herriton, a well-to-do widow who falls in love with a much younger man played by Rupert Graves. But she dies giving birth to his son, leaving relatives to travel to Italy to take care of the infant. The prim and exceptionally proper Helena Bonham-Carter and Australian star Judy Davis picked holes in each other superbly. The Edwardian period piece, set against the backdrop of life in Europe in 1906, was beautifully directed by Charles Sturridge but lacked any real passion. But it made excellent television fodder when shown on ITV in November 1992.

It was the summer of 1991 and Mirren was still missing Hackford. She'd just been to see the movie *Parenthood* starring Steve Martin and had left in a flood of tears. Her maternal instincts got the better of her, she explained, while she dwelt on motherhood. 'It is incomprehensible to me,' she said. 'I have always loved children but I decided that the biggest contribution I could make to the ecology of the world is simply not producing a child. In the end, I was crying over this film because I would never experience that unconditional love you have for a child.

'Not having a baby is not necessarily some huge tragedy in a woman's life. I genuinely and absolutely do not regard it as a tragedy in my own. I know of people who can drive themselves crazy with these imagined "tragedies" in their lives. They have been told this is how they will feel, should feel. Then, they comply with that. I refused to be that kind of victim.'

Prime Suspect 2 was shown just before Christmas 1992 and swept straight into the British television Top Twenty with 14 million viewers. It involved a 'new look' Tennison with a brighter wardrobe, smart hair-do and full make-up. Mirren said, 'What was interesting about returning was that, like her, I had changed also. Not in a major sense, but you are different 18 months down the track. I had more confidence and that's part of the story, confidence leading to errors.'

The makeover was a winner, even if the non-smoker almost got herself hooked on cigarettes by inhaling too much nicotine during filming. The two-part thriller was set in Brixton but was filmed in the Moss Side district of Manchester as a cost-saving device.

She was thrilled that the second story also left a lasting impression. She said, 'It's the kind of part you'll only find on television because cop movies are very male. I went down on my knees and said, "Thank you, God," because it was the perfect role that rarely happens in one's life. Lynda La Plante showed clearly that you could write a great role for a woman who isn't a victim or a tough businesswoman.'

Her bi-continental career with its lengthy separations from Hackford still troubled her. 'It can lead to wonderful reunions,' she said. 'It's a lot to do with immense trust. For the last seven years it has worked well, but not without difficulty. Most men over 50 can't deal with a woman having a career.

'I'm still as ambitious as I ever was. I know it is something I should get rid of but I don't seem able to. I always want more. I always want what I haven't got and ignore what I have got. It has led me into trouble. It ultimately gives me pain because I am in a permanently dissatisfied condition.

'But Taylor is an extremely developed man, thoughtful and understanding. But he's difficult and forceful at times, the most difficult man I have ever lived with! I hate being pushed around, but we are both committed to each other.

'I've always believed that sex with men is fine, just don't clean their houses. I don't even mind if my men are domineering, providing they like women. But there are a lot of men who are frightened of and fundamentally loathe women.'

Little attention was given to her low-budget politically charged saga *Bethune: The Making of a Hero*, which was released in Autumn 1993. Ted Allan wrote the film from his own novel while Phillip Borsos directed. She had a small role as the plucky wife of heroic Dr Norman Bethune, played by Canadian veteran Donald Sutherland. The Canadian, Chinese and French co-production, which was largely made in Montreal, also starred Anouk Aimee and Helen Shaver.

Mirren was thrown into a very different arena in the BBC psychological drama *The Hawk*, which was released in December 1993. The £1.8 million thriller mirrored the real-life bloody tale of the Yorkshire Ripper who preyed on prostitutes in Yorkshire and Lancashire. Written by Peter Ransley, who created *Underbelly*, it was loosely based on the experiences of the Ripper's wife Sonia Sutcliffe. She had to get inside the mind of Annie Marsh, a mother-of-two who believes the father of her children might be the kind of man who butchers young women. The film was made on an industrial estate in Bristol, close to where the BBC still make their long-running hospital drama *Casualty*.

Since *The Cook, The Thief, His Wife and Her Lover*, she had not stripped for action on screen. And she has not taken her clothes off for a love scene since *avant-garde* director Peter Greenaway used her to eye-shattering effect in his brave nude world. Her agents were turning away work in which producers wanted her to peel away the outer layers and trade off her old image.

The Hawk was a welcome change. She confessed, 'I loved doing it and it was a relief that I didn't have to take my clothes off.'

Prime Suspect 2 won an Emmy in Pasadena, California, in September 1993 for Outstanding Mini-Series, the award being accepted by producer Paul Marcus. So, a wave of euphoria greeted *Prime Suspect 3* which was shown on 19 December 1993. The mini-series was a gritty, often despairing study of the rent-boy trade in London with Tennison zig-zagging her way through sexual perversity like a soldier in a minefield. One teenage lad was about to die from AIDS, others were abused in children's homes. To add authenticity to the drama, real transsexuals and transvestites also figured in the plot which was deemed too provocative for American television and was cut by PBS. At one stage during filming, Mirren burst into tears over the anguish of a lad who had been sexually abused in a children's home. 'I cried and found it difficult to go to the next scene,' she said. 'We had to break and just soldier on. But it was very distressing. We just hope it had that effect on viewers. Seeing children on the streets making a living out of prostitution, taking drugs and being streetwise and vulnerable is shocking.'

And there was no doubt that the series, after only two instalments, had totally changed her career for ever. Mirren said, 'It has been a turning point for me. It has helped me find the grown-up within me and it's the first time I have actually stuck with a role. I have changed. I don't lose my keys all the time and I own a computer and washing machine which I never had before.'

The new La Plante offering also made it a record British BAFTA win for the third year running for Mirren. 'The show has given me a tremendous amount of confidence. I don't have to pretend to be anything I am not. I don't have to be glamorous any more. It's a wonderful feeling. To be honest, I wasn't very confident before. I know we all say we would like to be young again but, funnily enough, I wouldn't go back to being 22 now with all those insecurities and fears. Those dreams and anxieties. At my age, you don't have to worry any more.'

In spring 1994, she returned to the stage at the Albery Theatre in London in a Bill Bryden production of Turgenev's moving period masterpiece *A Month in the Country*, to play Natalya Petrovna, a helpless victim of her own passion, the wife of a wealthy landowner who's obsessed by her son's tutor. The immaculate John Hurt was put in the shade by Joseph Fiennes's bashful tutor.

Her views on the young male of the species, as always, were fascinating. And she was, as always, a mass of contradictions. 'I much prefer younger men,' she said, forgetting a certain gentleman she had left behind in California. 'It's nothing to do with looks or physique, it's to do with social attitudes. Men over 40 are dinosaurs in their attitudes or, if they are not, they are self-conscious, trying to react to modern feminism. Younger guys take it for granted. That's why I have never gone for older men.'

She was being offered virtually no work in America but the effect of *Prime Suspect* being shown on the Public Broadcast network was sending out some very good vibrations. She was painfully honest over her record in the Nineties. She said, 'I follow in Taylor's wake over there. I am shoved aside. My status in Hollywood is basically zero.

'I have been mainly in second-class films, but what can you do? There is no British film industry. So you take what you can get. The box office calls for nudity and the public like to see people taking their clothes off. When I was young, I never thought I was pretty. It was the age of Twiggy and I was unfortunate because I had big breasts. They were out of fashion and I felt awful. I feel so good they are back in.

'I'm not kidding, I want to be incredibly rich and famous. Think of the unlimited money. You do hardly any work and you are only required to be mediocre and you have an endless supply of sycophants!

'I read about these million-dollar salaries for a few weeks' work and I am so jealous. The only thing missing is fun. The big stars I have met seem to be gloomy and neurotic. But I still want that work in Hollywood. Do you hear me?!'

But Mirren was an acquired taste for too many leading super-agents and producers. She was 'too classy', 'too strong' and 'too old'.

Another of her movie oddities, *Prince of Jutland*, was also about to be released and disappear just as quickly. Gabriel Axel directed this retelling of *Hamlet* in early 1994, reverting to the original Danish source material but retaining the opening scenario. Mirren starred as Queen Geruth to Irish star Gabriel Byrne's role as Fenge. Christian Bale and Brian Cox joined a gold-plated supporting cast including her ex-*Prime Suspect* buddie Tom Wilkinson, Kate Beckinsale, Freddie Jones, Saskia Wickham and Steven Waddington.

But Mirren had good cause to cheer in February 1995 when Hollywood went crazy over another period piece, *The Madness of King George*, which swept four Oscar nominations. She earned her first ever nomination for her portrayal of the sympathetic yet disciplined Queen Charlotte in the historic epic, which started life as the Alan Bennett stage play *The Madness of King George III* at the Royal National Theatre. Nicholas Hytner directed the stage production and also made his movie début on locations around England at Arundel Castle in Sussex, Broughton Castle in Oxfordshire and the Royal Naval College at Greenwich.

The story focused on how George, played by Nigel Hawthorne, became hopelessly unbalanced in 1811, apparently suffering from the blood disorder porphyria. His behaviour became wholly eccentric to the point where he attacked his son the Prince of Wales, played by Rupert Everett, in full view of the Court and swore violently at those who irritated him. He was 'tortured' back to health by his physicians, led by Ian Holm. They bound and gagged him to a chair, forced him into freezing cold baths and piled leeches on his body to bring him to his senses. The versatile Hawthorne, known to the public in Britain through the TV sitcom *Yes, Minister!*, also won a nomination. He was magnificent, while Mirren showed new levels of compassion as his queen.

There was much hilarity in England over Hollywood's initial attitude to Hytner's film which had been funded by Channel 4 and the Samuel Goldwyn Company. The American distributor insisted on changing the original title by dropping the 'III'. They believed this would remove any confusion over what had happened to the original film about King George and the sequel! In London, they laughed all the way from Wardour Street to Soho Square.

Mirren did not endear herself to members of the Academy, however, with her blasts at the British monarchy and the movie industry on both sides of the Atlantic. In one interview, she described Princess Diana as 'nauseating and half crazy, poor thing'.

Mirren, though highly regarded by her peers, was not in favour by those in a position of power in Hollywood. They regarded her as 'haughty' and 'arrogant'.

One hardened senior studio executive said, 'The trouble with Mirren was that, though she might not say so, she came across as somebody who thought they were above it all. Slightly superior. It's that British thing about stage acting and coming from the Royal Shakespeare Company. That "You may have the money but we have the talent". That's fine. But in Hollywood, it's about the size of box office and making sure you have the right friends. She was never box office, and Taylor Hackford may have had a few successes but he never possessed that much clout.

'It's admirable that she has always been her own person, that she has largely stuck by her principles. But where exactly has that got her in terms of universal acceptability or bankability. Sorry. She isn't in most wish lists when we're talking about the big-budget movies.'

Jane Tennison returned to the small screen on 26 February 1995 in *Prime Suspect 4*, with a batch of three new integral stories. Mirren, armed with a new £350,000 contract from Granada Television, allegedly complained that she wanted a 'hot' affair with a new character, criminal psychologist Patrick Schofield, played by Stuart Wilson. The British actor was making a name for himself in Los Angeles in roles such as the vicious villain in *Lethal Weapon 3* opposite Mel Gibson.

Oscar nomination or not, Mirren was not about to play the Hollywood movie games in order to scoop awards. Much as she craved the recognition, as one friend put it, 'She's just not the kind of girl to parade herself and wear a fake smile. It's simply not her style ... end of story.'

Mirren, meanwhile, was playing it cool. She said, 'Success makes me much more nervous than failure because it usually means you get identified with just one role. The two most dangerous things in an actor's life are success and failure. I'm also nervous of trusting what a fickle industry like the acting community really thinks. I don't need the accolades of others to make me feel good.'

The Oscar was not to be. The prize for Best Supporting Actress went to Susan Sarandon who starred in another real-life drama, *Dead Man Walking*, with Sean Penn.

Instead, Mirren headed for the bar with Taylor Hackford. She said later, 'You don't want to get too excited about awards. When I lost out at the Oscars, I immediately left my seat and headed for the bar to drown my sorrows. It was great fun, actually, because all the other losers were at the bar.'

But Mirren had much, in fact, to cheer. She at last made her Broadway début in *A Month in the Country*, securing a Tony nomination for herself, and pulled off one of the big ones, winning the Best Actress award at the Cannes Film Festival for *The Madness of King George*.

For once, she wasn't the bridesmaid and the surging crowd by the Palais du Festival roared as she stood proudly next to Jonathan Pryce, who had just won Best Actor for his portrayal of Lytton Strachey in *Carrington*. The actress who feared being 'corrupted' by success seemed quite at ease.

Actress Janine Duvitski, who'd starred with Mirren in Dennis Potter's *Blue Remembered Hills* some 20 years earlier, had a small part in *The Madness of King George*, and has never forgotten her friend's act of kindness when she 'dried' one morning while filming at Eton College. She said, 'I had a terrible day. I had stepped in for another actress who had to deliver five lines but I kept on getting it wrong. Every time I got it wrong, they had to reset the carriages with the horses and the royal procession. I couldn't believe what I was doing.

I was in a terrible state. But once I panicked, it got worse and worse. Helen was facing me and everyone on the set knew the words but me by that time. She was mouthing the words to me ... she was very sweet, trying to cue me. She could see the desperate look in my eye.

'Helen hadn't changed at all. She still had this sexuality. She had matured, she'd got *Prime Suspect* in the bag and suddenly she was a public face. But she was still alluring, still interesting. *Prime Suspect* was brilliant for her. There are so few good female parts around, instead of having to be this young, pretty thing for ever.'

Mirren put herself back in the firing line with her next project, *Some Mother's Son*, a semi-fictionalised account of the death of IRA hunger-striker Bobby Sands at the Maze Prison in Belfast as part of the 'Dirty Protest' in 1981. He had fasted for 66 days. He was 27, MP for Fermanagh and a martyr for the Republican cause. Mirren was immersed in the issues and morality of the piece, co-written by Jim Sheridan, the director of the Oscar-winning *My Left Foot*, and Terry George, a convicted IRA terrorist. He was jailed for six years in 1975 for possessing arms. He co-wrote the Oscar-nominated *In the Name of the Father*, starring Daniel Day-Lewis, a film noted for its sympathetic stance towards Sinn Fein.

Mirren, apart from playing Sands's mother, became a 'film-maker' for the first time in her career, taking the title of Associate Producer and lining herself up with George and Sheridan to take the flak. And take the flak she did, from Ulster through to London, where so-called representatives of the 'silent majority' were outraged by the tone of *Some Mother's Son*, which was being backed by Columbia Studios.

Mirren was possibly influenced by her past relationship with Liam Neeson when deciding to get so involved with Irish politics through the film, which was made in the quiet Irish coastal resort of Skerries. Some felt her film hindered the peace process, while fiery Protestants such as Ian Paisley wanted her hung, drawn and quartered.

Brad Pitt, who earlier played an IRA assassin in *The Devil's Own*, considered flying over for the role of Bobby Sands but Mirren and Co plumped instead for John Lynch, who had played alongside her in *Cal*.

Co-producer Arthur Lappin jumped to the film's defence, denying they were cashing in on the Troubles. He said, 'We are not seeking to condone or forgive IRA violence at all, but to understand the nationalist position, as we feel the Tories and Unionists at the time had an astonishing amount of air time.'

Mirren, herself a committed anti-monarchist and Republican, was more specific. She said, 'That's the predjudice of the people looking at it. It deals with a moment in history 16 years ago. To me, its about the creative force in women and the destructive force in young men, how women are the carriers of life and young men can be the carriers of death. You see it time and time again all over the world. The film is controversial but it is a controversy which must be addressed.

'I had spent time there but, like everyone else, I knew fuck all about the situation, really. I wanted the film to reflect all the confusions and contradictions of a civil war. I put a lot of personal effort into it.

'The trouble is that only anti-IRA propaganda is acceptable to some political commentators. They consider it taboo to portray the enemy as human.' And then, she snapped, 'I wasn't an apologist for the IRA. There is no way I would make a film which makes heroes out of IRA bombers. They are cowardly assholes, the people who plant these bombs. This is about the love of mothers for their sons.'

Distribution of the £10 million movie was held up until early 1997 because of political in-fighting and criticism. Even Sands's real-life sister Marcella refused to join forces with Mirren. She said, 'Our family are not involved in an advisory capacity, nor do we support any films in production. This is just a way of exploiting for financial gain a very painful time for us.'

Mirren was stung by a volley of fierce rebukes. Right-winger Peter Hitchens, then of the UK *Daily Express*, cried, 'Why does she despise and trample on the opinions and loyalties of the viewers who have made her a star?' He called the film 'politically dishonest, despicable'. The film did well critically and financially in America but the well-orchestrated campaign of hostility damaged its performance in Britain.

At least she could fly back into the arms of Hackford free of charge. Virgin chief Sir Richard Branson signed her up for a series of airline commercials which netted her £200,000 worth of tickets instead of a fee. Mirren was seen curled up in Upper Class, like a cat which had run off with the cream. But a bright press spark spotted that the legs on screen perhaps looked just too good to be true and model Cindy Ward, aged 28, stepped forward to confess to being the very cute body-double.

It was just as well that they didn't use realistic footage of Mirren in the Upper Class cabin. She confided, 'I do like to make an effort when I fly out to meet Taylor. I always put my hair in curlers for the flight. I don't want him standing at the airport, hiding behind a pillar, thinking, Dear God ... I can't be seen with ... *that*.'

Mirren's long association with the Showtime cable channel and the start of her American TV career was launched soon after through the TV drama *Losing Chase*, which also marked actor Kevin Bacon's directorial début. The feature was made in the small town of Bronte, Oakville, and Cabourg, Ontario, and the visually beguiling Martha's Vineyard. Mirren played Chase Phillips, a wealthy businessman's wife on the verge of a nervous breakdown. Hubby Richard, played by Beau Bridges, hires a comforting aide Elizabeth, played by Bacon's real-life wife actress Kyra Sedgwick, to move in and care for their two children. But Elizabeth has problems of her own, not least taking a fancy to troubled Chase. The film focused on their relationship. Mirren preferred to keep her clothes firmly on during a bedroom scene involving Sedgwick, claiming she was not going to give voyeurs a treat. She said, 'From watching the porno channel in New York, one of the biggest turn-ons for men is watching two women have sex together.'

She was right. Her performance won her a Golden Globe award, though comedienne Joan Rivers ruined the evening for her with some spiteful commentary over her fashion sense. She'd recorded the awards on her video and, when she sat down to watch, Rivers was in overdrive. Mirren recalled, 'I'm sitting there watching it and she looks straight at me and says, "Helen, if you're out there ... let me tell you, honey ... you've got to get your act together!" I spent the night in tears.' She said she was now 'dreading' turning up at any awards ceremony in America in case Rivers had the microphone.

The Mirren family came together in August 1996 to share their grief. Kit Mirren died peacefully in a Southend nursing home at the age of 89 after a series of strokes. For three months her daughter had been flying back and forth across the Atlantic to join her elder sister Katie by their mother's side.

She had decorated the room at the home with pictures and items from the family house in nearby Leigh-on-Sea. 'I am so grateful she didn't die in her sleep,' said her youngest daughter. 'It happened over nine months, a stroke and old age. She was stepping further and further back from life. It was hard but absolutely wonderful and I mean wonderful in the sense of her being at peace.'

Mrs Mirren, like her husband Basil, had stayed very much in the background during their daughter's rise to fame. They were not première or first-night people, explained their actress daughter. Once, she recalled, she wanted to give Kit a taste of luxury, whisking her away to the fabulous five-star Crillon Hotel in the heart of Paris, overlooking Place de la Concorde for a break. Mirren said, 'She took to that like a duck to water. But she was a hopeless housewife. She was born to be a diva.

'My mother was a night person. She would be hoovering at two in the morning but she could never wake up to make breakfast.'

Mirren couldn't help wishing her mother could have tuned in to see her winning an Emmy Award for Best Actress for *Prime Suspect 4: Scent of Darkness* only a month later, but it was not to be. The Americans were by now addicted to her antics as Tennison.

Viewers were stunned to witness their favourite TV law enforcer having an abortion in the opening sequences of *Prime Suspect 5: Errors of Judgement* in October 1996. And the feminists in her fan club were mortified when she had a one-night stand with her CID boss. But the critics and the viewers were generally agreed that the episode dealing with drugs trafficking in Manchester was yet another triumph. And with that, the lonely cop went off into the night.

With Tennison close to handing in her warrant card, she made a rare appearance on British television in the ITV drama *Painted Lady* which was written by Allan Cubitt who penned *Prime Suspect 2*. She played a wayward character called Maggie Sheridan who ended up in the gutter after dabbling in drugs and booze. But Sheridan pulled herself together in rehab when her benefactor was murdered. She went on the trail of the killer with screen buddie Michael Maloney having reinvented herself as an arts dealer. Iain Glen and Lesley Manville co-starred, along with Italian idol Franco Nero..

With her mother's death very much on her mind, she'd also flown to Toronto to film *Critical Care* for the veteran director Sidney Lumet, who made the classic post-Holocaust study *The Pawnbroker*. The hospital-based 'comedy drama', derived from Richard Dooling's novel, teamed her up again with Kyra Sedgwick and a cast including Anne Bancroft, James Spader and Albert Brooks. Spader played a medic who gets emboiled in a legal battle between two half-sisters fighting over the care of their comatose father and his $10 million estate. The hospital needed to keep all their patients alive for their insurance cash. The subject matter, despite raising valid points about medical insurance, was largely in dubious taste. And bearing in mind Mirren's recent loss, it was a film she could have done without in every sense.

A couple of odd jobs were on the horizon while Mirren pondered her next move and her December 1997 wedding to Taylor Hackford in Scotland. This was a period of her life, quite rightly, when there were other priorities. And, for the first time, her career went on the back burner.

There were some jobs she could do which would not interfere with her new life as Mrs Taylor Hackford. She put her voice to the part of the Queen of Egypt in the DreamWorks epic animated musical saga *Prince of Egypt*. But sing, she could not. So she made way for chanteuse Linda Dee Shayne at the appropriate moment.

And she had the most curious of 'appearances' in the Latin comedy docu-drama *Sidoglio Smithee* which was filmed by Jorge Molina during a film festival in Cuba.

And then, it was back to work. *Prime Suspect* director Christopher Menaul crossed the Atlantic to Toronto to take the helm of her next TV project Showtime's *The Passion of Ayn Rand*. Eric Stoltz, Julie Delpy and Peter Fonda as her screen husband also figured in the real-life tale about the right-wing philosopher and novelist who founded an American political movement which extolled individualism to the point of selfishness and even cruelty. Her fair hair was tucked out of sight under a dark, severe, mannish wig as she recruited and indoctrinated youngsters into her cult. Rynd, born Alisa Rosenbaum, was a Russian immigrant to America, which gave Mirren, with her Slav heritage, an angle to use for the woman she was portraying. Her ideological manifesto was based on the 1943 novel *Fountainhead*.

When Ronald Reagan was elected President in 1981, he said she had inspired his policies of dismantling the social safety net to force the lazy to work, coupled with tax cuts to the needy. The £5 million drama also focused on her promiscuity. At the age of 50, she fell in love with one of her protégés, 25-year-old Nathaniel Brandon, played by Stoltz.

The TV film was premièred in America at the Sundance Film Festival in January 1999 and was another Emmy award-winner for Mirren. She was by now no stranger to controversy, having survived a barrage of contempt over *Some Mother's Son*. And she violently disagreed with almost everything Rynd had to say. But she empathised with her as a woman. She said, 'My perception of her was that she was a woman of extreme intellectual power and extreme emotion and passion. She struggled with those conflicts.'

In October 1998, Mirren made her long-awaited début at the Royal National Theatre playing Cleopatra for the third time in her career under the direction of Trevor Nunn. Her Antony was former RSC legend Alan Rickman, whom the public had got to know through films such as *Truly, Madly, Deeply*, *Die Hard* and *Robin, Prince of Thieves*, depending on which side of the Atlantic you ate your popcorn. The production did not fare well with the critics. Benedict Nightingale of the London *Times* claimed they lacked 'momentum, intensity, excitement, texture and depth'. He largely blamed Rickman's performance – 'lacking vocal clarity' – for the production's deficiencies. But he praised Mirren's 'irony and mockery', saying she would have done far better with 'another director and another leading man'. Others, like the *Mail on Sunday*, cared to focus more on the aspect that, at the age of 52, she was naked in the scene leading to the deathbed climax of the play. While heaping praise on Mirren for 'looking as good as she does', they wanted to know why she was naked. 'The nudity is certainly not necessary to drive or illuminate the action.' Sheridan Morley disagreed, proclaiming, 'Helen is just at the right age to play the part.' Mirren may have shrugged off the criticism, but Cedric, the asp used in the play, escaped from its backstage box and disappeared for ever.

Rejection and recognition seemed to come in equal helpings. In the summer of 1999, students and fans crowded around while Mirren, wearing a gold-and-white hood and black cape, was made an honorary graduate and given the title Doctor of Letters of St Andrew's University in Scotland.

By November, she was back in the West End at the Theatre Royal in the Haymarket in *Collected Stories* by American playwright Donald Marguilies. Mirren played teacher and short-story writer Ruth Steiner to Anne-Marie Duff's pupil-cum-stalker Lisa

Morrison, as they discussed the ins and outs of civilisation as we know it. Reviews were mixed, but Mirren was thrilled to be back in the West End. Benedict Nightingale of the *Times*, believed she was at her 'most incisive'.

Mirren returned to London in 2000 to star in Tennesse Williams's *Orpheus Descending* at the Donmar Warehouse. Nicholas Hytner, who brought her success directing *The Madness of King George*, directed the Mississippi-set story about the lonely shopkeeper's wife condemned to a loveless marriage until a mysterious stranger, played by Stuart Townsend, arrives in town to snatch her from her self-made hell.

In 2001, she had another hit on Broadway, starring with Ian McKellen in August Strindberg's *Dance of Death*. The play, set in Sweden, focuses on a feuding married couple played by Mirren and McKellen, who are preparing to celebrate their twenty-fifth wedding anniversary.

They were rehearsing the drama in a room near the theatre on 11 September when the World Trade Center was destroyed by terrorists. She was badly shaken but said, 'We saw the cloud of smoke go up and we heard what had happened, but then we carried on,' she said. 'We thought there was no point in standing and gawping, it was better to carry on with what we were doing.'

But Mirren's movie career at the turn of the century was looking decidedly 'quirky', without much meaningful development. She'd been back in Los Angeles making the dark comedy *Teaching Mrs Tingle*, in which she played a battle-axe of a high school teacher who got her kicks out of torturing pupils showing enthusiasm or confidence. Mrs Tingle was a wrecker of teen dreams and adolescent self-esteem. She made Roald Dahl's Miss Trunchbull look positively cuddly. Katie Holmes and Barry Watson played the teen duo who teach Tingle a lesson by holding her hostage in her own home until she agrees not to have them expelled. In America, the title of the Miramax movie was *Killing Mrs Tingle*, an unfortunate choice in light of the increasing number of attacks by lunatic gunmen on teachers and pupils alike. The film was withdrawn from German cinemas after a wave of school violence. In one incident, three 14-year-old boys upset by poor marks obtained a gun and planned to kill three teachers. Distributors re-released the film, after changing the title to *Saving Mrs Tingle*. But, in Britain, distributors were so unimpressed by the theme, the film only made it to video in January 2001.

The British weren't exactly backing her other new little movie *Greenfingers*, an old-fashioned comedy drama with a huge worthy heart, in a similar mould to two other recent comedies – *Waking Ned* and *Saving Grace*. It was based on a true story and Clive Owen starred as a repentant killer called Colin who's sent to an experimental 'open' prison where he realises he's got a gift for all things horticultural. Enter Mirren as the celebrity gardening guru Georgina Woodhouse, who wants to take Colin and his eco-friendly band of lags under her wing and all the way to that silver cup at the Hampton Court Palace Flower Show. Without restraint from newcomer director Joel Hershman, who also wrote the story, Mirren played Woodhouse as a cross between matronly Margaret Rutherford and *Ab Fab*'s frenetic Joanna Lumley. Natasha Little was cute as her daughter. The Americans liked the yarn, which would have suited Dirk Bogarde down to the ground in 1961. Irish star David Kelly and Mirren's long-time pal Warren Clarke were excellent, and Owen's star is still rising.

Mirren, herself a keen gardener when she's back in California, didn't expect *Greenfingers* to cause a rush of blood at the cinema and simply said, 'When I read it, I thought it was absolutely charming. It was a sort of throwback to the Ealing comedies. It had a sort of spirit about it.'

Her uncertain movie future was now in the hands of a studious Australian, a reformed wild American and a veteran film-maker who'd never worked in England before. And her star was to soar like never before.

Fred Schepisi would be the first to admit he had nothing in

common with the blue-collar community in Graham Swift's novel *Last Orders*. But the rugged, charismatic Aussie director, who gave us the sophisticated *Plenty*, the subtly romantic *Roxanne* and the hopeless (in every sense) farce *Fierce Creatures*, was touched to the point of tears by the camaraderie of the central characters.

The story revolved around three old friends – Ray, Vic and Lennie – played by Bob Hoskins, Tom Courtenay and David Hemmings. They met in their favourite watering hole to prepare to fulfil the last order of their lifelong friend Jack, played in flashback by Michael Caine. Mirren played the seemingly loyal Amy, butcher Jack's unglamorous widow, while Ray Winstone, everyone's favourite 'heavy' in the British movie and TV business, was brought in to play Caine's screen son Vince, a second-hand-car salesman.

As the story unfolded through flashbacks and on a drunken road journey to the seaside resort of Margate, they open a can – or barrel-load – of worms, aided by the angry Vince who never saw eye to eye with his dear old Cockney Jack-the-Lad dad. Ray still dwelt on his past affair with Amy and what might have been, while she feels deep anguish and guilt over the handicapped daughter Jack refused to acknowledge. The central event of the film was the magic scattering of Jack's ashes in the English Channel and the build-up to the final sequence on the end of a jetty was electric.

Producer Elizabeth Robinson watched Mirren walk into the Soho Theatre in Dean Street to rehearse with 'the lads' before the cast moved on to locations in North London, Canterbury and Margate in Kent.

'They clearly all adored her the minute she walked in,' said Robinson, an American who worked on *The Man Who Knew Too Much* with Bill Murray. 'She has this incredible charisma, especially with men. I don't think I have seen anything quite like it.

'I have seen plenty of other actresses who are attractive turn it on, but there was a quality about her which, wow, is hard to find, especially when you're looking for a double. It's not just a question of finding a lookalike.'

They found newcomers Kelly Reilly to play young Amy and JJ Feild to play young Jack, two real discoveries for the future. Robinson said, 'We searched high and low for somebody who had that quality and, in the end, Kelly looked less like Helen but had that sexual charisma.'

The film was shot during the windswept, rainy autumn of 2000, a bonus as it happened, as producers didn't have their work cut out making the atmosphere and the terrain look as miserable as possible. Amusingly, when they needed rain and wind for the climax, the sun emerged from behind the clouds. 'There were floods everywhere and people were getting sun tan lotion out,' laughed Robinson.

Last Orders, which was premièred at the British Film Festival in Dinard, Brittany, in October 2001, was budgeted at around £7 million and will take some time getting its money back. The major-league cast agreed to work for old-fashioned peanuts – unofficially, none were paid more than £50,000.

Robinson said, 'I read the manuscript while I was making another film. I knew it was going to be so hard to get this made, though I love a challenge. The subject matter is unpopular – old age and loss. But I think it's more about friendship. It's very difficult to explain without people greeting you with silence. Fred and I fell in love with it. For the British, it felt like an episode of *EastEnders*. For us, it was about our fathers and friends and about my dad and his friends in Michigan, Detriot.'

But *Last Orders* was a critical success story. The London critics handed Mirren their Best Supporting Actress award, and the cast won the Best Ensemble Performance from the American National Board of Review.

And so Mirren took off to small-town Keremeos in British Columbia, Canada, for a date with Jack Nicholson and Sean Penn, who was directing a new low-budget drama called *The Pledge*. 'The Feminist' was about to meet 'The Womaniser' and 'The Wild Man'. As she told a friend, 'If you believed half of what was written about either of them, you wouldn't get on a plane. They are tremendous professionals, very unusual men, each with their own tremendous appeal.'

Actor/director Penn, who was once married to Madonna, had seen Mirren on stage and believed she was perfect to play the role of a psychiatrist assisting police in the raw, tense thriller, based on a 1950s crime drama by the Swiss author Friedrich Durrenmatt.

The story followed jaded Nevada lawman Jerry Black, played by Nicholson, who was preparing to take well-earned retirement. But in his last few hours in the job, Black was drawn into a murder case, promising the heartbroken mother of a murdered young girl that he will find the killer.

A mentally unbalanced Native American played by Oscar-winning Benicio Del Toro is accused, but Jerry can't believe that the police have arrested the right man, even though they had a confession and a corpse after he killed himself. But something doesn't seem quite right to the veteran cop who discovers a link between the murder and past attacks on young blonde girls.

Dark and moody, *The Pledge* gave Nicholson an opportunity to enhance his reputation as a 'serious' actor in small independent films, such as his other recent drama, *About Schmidt*.

The Pledge, with other cameos from Robin Wright Penn, Mickey Rourke and Sam Shepard, was beautifully photographed and directed by Sean Penn, who also co-wrote the script. Penn's film was greeted warmly by critics and the public alike at the Cannes Film Festival in 2001. He'd already got a reputation there with his two previous movies, *The Indian Runner* and *The Crossing Guard*, which also starred Nicholson. Nobody could put their finger on why the critics in America had been so hostile to the drama or why so many of Jack Nicholson's fans wouldn't buy a ticket. But by the time *The Pledge* arrived on the Cote D'Azur for its European première in May 2002, industry pundits were already saying it was dead and buried.

Mirren was pure dynamite during her one big scene with Nicholson who was, it must be said, wary of Mirren before Sean Penn introduced them. 'What should I call her?' he enquired of

Penn. 'I mean, is it Miss Mirren, Ms Mirren or Helen? Or Toots?' 'Toots' was his affectionate nickname for his long-time live-in partner Anjelica Huston.

Penn thought for a second or two, before suggesting either 'Helen' or 'Miss Mirren'. He said to Nicholson, 'But I'd definitely give the "Toots" a miss. I don't think that will work.'

When Penn introduced them, Nicholson grinned, 'Well, hello there, Toooo ... Helen,' measuring the reaction carefully. 'Now you don't mind me calling you "Helen" do you?' She was smitten. Mirren later remarked to a friend, 'Nicholson is quite extraordinary. He could say a totally meaningless word like "milk" and make it sexual. He is so funny. No wonder women adore him.'

Director Robert Altman had never made a film in England. The revered veteran, white-bearded film-maker notched up a huge commercial success with *MASH* in the Seventies and later sculpted a string of superb ensemble pieces, including the Hollywood exposé *The Player* and the dark, comedic *Short Cuts*. The critics and film aficionados universally worship him. But nobody expected Altman, at 75 in the twilight of his career, to conjur up *Gosford Park*. The country house mystery thriller worked to an ingenious formula in which the period television series *Upstairs, Downstairs* met Agatha Christie and came back via Raymond Chandler. The blend was clever, but he needed a well-crafted script.

Altman approached the original *Upstairs, Downstairs* creators Dame Eileen Atkins and Jean Marsh to provide the goods. But Atkins wasn't keen. 'I was sick to death of *Upstairs, Downstairs*, but Jean wanted to have a go, so we had a go,' she said. 'I didn't want to give up years of acting to write, either. But I was a bit bolshie and made it a mystery and not a thriller. He didn't like the treatment, so that was that. I was thrilled that I didn't have to write it.'

Instead of Atkins and Marsh, he turned to actor Julian Fellowes, giving him a full brief but explaining that they would also be improvising much of the dialogue. The plot was played out in Gosford Park, a magnificent country estate to which Sir William

McCordle and his wife Lady Sylvia gather relations and friends for a weekend shooting party. The group included a countess, a Great War hero and British matinée idol Ivor Novello. As the guests were assembled Upstairs, their maids and valets swelled the ranks of the house servants in the kitchens and corridors Downstairs. The cast was stellar, with Michael Gambon leading as Sir William and Kristin Scott-Thomas playing Lady Sylvia. The Upstairs guests included Maggie Smith, Charles Dance, Tom Hollander and Jeremy Northam as Novello. Downstairs people included Mirren as Mrs Wilson, the housekeeper, who spars endlessly with Mrs Croft, the cook. They were joined by Emily Watson, Richard E Grant, Derek Jacobi, Alan Bates, Clive Owen and American teen idol Ryan Phillippe, who played a visiting film producer's fake Scottish valet. The rich comedy then took a successfully melodramatic turn, lurching into whodunnit territory after Sir William was bumped off.

For Mirren, it was reunion time with Gambon, her co-star in the RSC's *Antony and Cleopatra* in 1983, and Clive Owen, who she had just sprayed with insecticide in *Greenfingers*. And she fired on every cylinder.

Eileen Atkins wanted Maggie Smith's aristocratic role in the film, but was originally offered the part of the stoic, cold housekeeper which was tailor-made for Mirren at her most dowdy. Dame Judi Dench was set to play the cook in the early days of pre-production. Atkins said, 'They said there might be some "shifting" part-wise and they were very apologetic. They told me I'd make a better cook.'

Co-producer Bob Ballaban had the unenviable task of smoothing over ruffled feathers in the casting department until everyone was 'satisfied'.

Atkins knew Mirren from their days in New York in the mid-Nineties when they were both nominated for Tony awards. They'd meet regularly just off Broadway in the restaurant Une, Deux, Trois next to the Broadhurst Theater to gossip and whinge over who'd grabbed roles they wanted. Atkins said, 'Helen would often do the arranging. She was good at that. Peter Hall would often join us as an old friend. He called Helen the "The Mother of All Russia" because of the way she went about organising us, which infuriated her.'

They sat together during rehearsals at stately Wrotham Park in Hertfordshire and were stunned when, one morning, Altman approached and warned them of a new twist in the plot. Atkins said, 'He said, "I am going to make you sisters. You will come away with me now and we will improvise." I am terrible at improvisation, whereas Helen is brilliant. She is so good I hate it.'

Atkins also noted during filming how careful Mirren was in make-up to get it absolutely right.

'She was terribly exact with her hair pieces, which to some may not be important,' she said. 'But she is so clever because she knows that you are the way you look, if you are an actor. I behaved stupidly and badly at the time. I wasn't paying attention. I wanted a gingery-grey curly wig and she just wanted one piece of hair to be different from the rest. She knew exactly how she was trying to look to get the soul and body of her character. She wanted to show this imperfection.

'She is amazingly good-natured and fun. Most of all, she is very, very good at what she does. The difference between her and most of us is that she has always had glamour and she is not afraid of sexuality, which is why she was superb as Cleopatra.

'She has this wonderful sense of humour. When she worked with Joan Plowright on this Chekhov play, there was this terrible fuss one day when one of the actors disappeared, just got up and left. They had to pull one of the stage staff in for the part. There was no time to rehearse. Plowright told everyone this and there was a silence before Helen looked slowly up from a book she was reading and simply said, "How exciting!" We fell about laughing.

'I think it's the norm for actors to be wild and then settle down in some kind of way. She was wilder than most. She wants danger and excitement, but you have to be dangerous or you are not interesting.'

Gosford Park earned Mirren her second Oscar nomination as Best

Supporting Actress in March 2002. Again, she lost out, this time to Jennifer Connolly for *A Beautiful Mind*. The real-life story of the disturbed mathematician John Forbes Nash was directed by Ron Howard and starred New Zealand-born Russell Crowe, who won an Oscar for the second year running.

She said of Gosford Park, 'On that film, I was very proud of my fellow British actors, I have to say, because they gave themselves up to it absolutely wholeheartedly, and generously, without any egos at all. Of course, we all have egos ... all actors have egos, there's no question about that ... but they gave of themselves very selflessly, and with a lot of dedication.'

Mirren was philosophical, going off for a cool glass of wine and an early night with Taylor Hackford. She told a friend with a grin, 'At least when they say, "We wondered where she got to," at least they will know.' Her role as melancholy housekeeper Jane Wilson in *Gosford Park* won her awards from critics in America and an ensemble award from the Screen Actors Guild. Altman's film was a definite turning point. Hollywood had noticed and applauded. They thought she had vanished off the face of the earth, and here they were recognising her again. And there wasn't a special effect in sight.

If it could happen late in the day for Jessica Tandy in *Driving Miss Daisy*, and for Dame Judi Dench in *Shakespeare in Love*, who's to say where Mirren will be in ten years' time? Film critic Barry Norman has followed Mirren's career for 30 years and believes she could be on the verge of even greater things.

He said, 'I rate *The Long Good Friday*, *The Madness of King George* and *The Cook, The Thief, His Wife and Her Lover* as the best things she has done on screen and, the truth is, that she'd be a much bigger star if she'd been attached to an industry which believed in the power of women. We don't like actresses very much here or in America. Mirren never slotted into Hollywood, but there's no doubt she could suddenly be huge. She still looks terrific. The first sin in Hollywood is to be old and the second is to look old.'

For Mirren, a new chapter was about to begin.

13

FROM THE DALES
TO REDFORD

Tragedy, death, disaster ... extremes of emotion. They can inspire great pieces of literature or movies which linger in the memory. Take a band of redundant steel-workers stripping down to their thongs in order to pay the rent. Or what about an ogre who lives in a swamp with a singing donkey?

When Tricia Stewart suggested to her fellow Women's Institute chums that they pose nude for a fund-raising calendar in aid of the Leukaemia Research Fund, she had little idea of the consequences. Within weeks of the calendar being published, the tasteful pictures of the middle-aged women baking madeira cake and stirring lemon curd while wearing little more than a string of pearls were being wired across the globe from Los Angeles to Sydney.

Not only did 53-year-old yoga teacher Tricia and her friends become overnight celebrities, their lives in the Yorkshire backwater of Rylstone would never be quite the same. The downside of the human interest story was that the real inspiration for the high-profile strip came through heartbreak. Tricia's close friend Angela Baker, 56, was devastated when, in 1999, her husband John, the father of her two grown-up children Rachel and Matthew, died from non-Hodgkins lymphona within months of being diagnosed. The dedicated, charming Baker, the assistant National Parks officer for the Yorkshire Dales, lived up to his nickname of 'Mr Sustainability' for his devotion to protecting the environment for future generations.

Once the calendar became hot property, the 11 women from Rylstone and the nearby villages of Grassington and Cracoe found themselves subject to further exposure. They did radio and television. They took a bow on the Royal Variety Show. They rode in limos and stayed in palatial hotels. They called at Buckingham Palace to leave calendars for the Queen and her mother. Terry Wogan 'plugged' them on his radio show while the playwright and author Alan Bennett, himself a Northern lad, wrote to them saying, 'Don't be seduced by showbusiness. Victoria sponges are much more worthwhile.'

Incredibly, it wasn't over. They took themselves off on a city-to-city promotional tour of America. Their last port of call was Los Angeles and the hugely popular *Jay Leno Show*. When they had done their sums, 200,000 calendars were sold in America alone and they had raised in excess of £500,000 for leukaemia research. They were jubilant. There were, however, arguments breaking out between the old friends over their future direction. Some didn't want to tread the celebrity path any longer. They wanted normality.

And Tricia, a tall, striking blonde, had a crisis of her own. Her businessman husband Ian was having an affair with somebody else's wife while she was busy getting 'airtime' for fundraising.

And their story is still rolling. Most of the women from the WI, which was based near Skipton, could hardly wait to see themselves being portrayed on screen in the new £3 million film *Calendar Girls*, with Mirren and Julie Walters co-starring as the best pals who stripped off to raise cash for charity.

They were instantly recognisable, even though their names were changed to Chris and Annie. Ciaran Hinds, recently seen in *The Road to Perdition* with Tom Hanks, played Chris's devoted husband

Rod, while TV sitcom star John Alderton played Annie's husband John who is seen dying from cancer.

The story was strongly fictionalised to take the 'heat' out of any lasting real-life angst in the village of Cracoe where many of the women, including Tricia, still live.

Screenwriters Juliette Towhidi and Tim Firth invented a totally new character called Ruth, whose husband Eddie, played by George Costigan, does a bunk with another local woman. But the betrayed wife, played by Royal National Theatre actress Penelope Wilton, manages to survive the blow and surface with the proud smile of a woman who has retained her dignity.

Producers Suzanne Mackie and Nick Barton of Harbour Pictures had a battle on their hands getting *Calendar Girls* made. Before they got backing from Walt Disney's wealthy film division Buena Vista, they were stunned when comedy star Victoria Wood came in to take over the film as a vehicle for herself. They would have lost a crippling small fortune, having already commissioned writer Towhidi to write the first draft. They had not been expecting any hiccups. Their company had the right pedigree. Among their productions, they could list the BBC comedy drama *The Wimbledon Poisoner* starring Robert Lindsay and Alison Steadman, *The Vanishing Man* starring Neil Morrissey for ITV, and *Boswell and Johnson's Tour of the Western Isles* starring Robbie Coltrane and John Sessions. They had a history of quality TV product for a relatively small outfit.

But they had to sweat it out for a month before being told that the WI wanted them to take control of the film instead of the popular Wood. Mirren and Walters, whose daughter Maisie once suffered from leukaemia, had been pencilled in by the film-makers to play the main characters from the day they commissioned the rough draft.

Producer Barton said, 'We felt that the combination of Helen and Julie would be very powerful. Both would bring humour and drama to their respective roles. They had never worked together before. But they are both fine actresses. Julie can really move you. She had a strong rapport with Angela Baker. She understands what loss means and how devastating it can be, especially when she had to deal with her own daughter's illness.' His partner Mackie added, 'With Helen, it is instinct. She is strong, powerful. Tricia is probably one of the most compassionate people I have met, which is why she did what she did for Angela. That struck a huge chord for Helen.'

The double-act were delighted by the script and the real-life WI women from Rhylstone, bonding over dinner before the film went into production in the Yorkshire villages of Kettlewell, Skipton and Burnsall in summer 2001. In the film, Rylstone will be known as Knapley. The WI agreed to a deal, in which part of the proceeds from the movie will also be going to leukaemia research.

There was, however, a clear division of feeling in the village once the film company got the green light from their backers. Only six of the eleven real-life women involved wanted to collaborate with the producers. The remainder decided it was time to slip back into the shadows and the welcome anonymity of the past.

The story of the women and their extraordinary calendar will concentrate on the effect fame has on Tricia and Angela and the fictional Ruth. But the producers make no excuse for dumping the sub-plot of the affair between Tricia's husband Ian and his mistress Lesley Barrett who left her husband.

Other members of the WI band from the Yorkshire Dales were played by Linda Bassett, who starred in *East is East*; Annette Crosbie, perhaps better known as Victor Meldrew's wife from *One Foot in the Grave*; Celia Imrie, one of the stars of *Bridget Jones's Diary*; and Geraldine James from *Jewel in the Crown* and *Band of Gold*.

Mackie said, 'Tricia and Ian are happily together and we became good friends with them. By the time we became involved in the story, there wasn't a question of us going off in that direction in any case. Whatever he had been involved in, it was over. There was this perception that it was a bit of a potboiler but very quickly that was dispelled. It has a lot more depth and substance. Finally, it is about how being in the media spotlight can destroy friendships.

'Ruth's story was much more complicated in that her husband

goes off with somebody else and she has to pull herself up and find her own self and is liberated.'

She believed the dynamic combination of Mirren and Walters had the kind of appeal to make the film attractive and entertaining to Northern factory girls and City high-flyers. 'Helen and Julie are women whom other women respond to, who can tell a story honestly without it being exploited,' she said. 'They set the tone. The comedy was inherent in the story. The comedy is at its most funny when they are there being natural. Having "comedy actresses" instead of them would have cheapened it.'

For Mirren, it's another fascinating change of career direction. Mackie said, 'I think Helen and Tricia share an energy. They are dynamic and charismatic people. They are very intuitive, very strong. Tricia was the dominant one in the group. She had the original idea. Julie very much mirrors Annie in many ways. Angela was the heart of the calendar because of her husband's death. There is a vulnerability about them both. Helen will surprise people, as she isn't known for her comedic roles. She is one of the most instinctive and passionate actresses of our time.'

'We had such a giggle doing the calendar,' said Angela Baker, who will be forced to relive her husband John's death during the film. 'We decided we wouldn't show any nipples or furry bits.'

The makers of *Calendar Girls* – the movie was dubbed 'The Full Brontë' by media wags – have respected their wishes. 'No, definitely no furry bits,' said Mackie.

The film was still certain to inflame old rows and jealousies in the once quiet, remote Yorkshire villages. Locals were asking why the film's makers backed away from the real-life scandal involving Tricia's husband, and have made accusations that she 'hogged the limelight', turning their efforts, as one put it, into a 'showbusiness fiasco'. One villager, who asked not to be named, said, 'Some people like to be the centre of attention, others do not. Tricia falls into the first category. That is fine for her. But the whole point of why we were doing what we were doing was getting lost along the way. Some of us feel used.

But if the film does anything for the charity involved, we can't complain. We just hope it ends there. We want to reclaim our lives. We're not showbusiness personalities.'

The warm, touching movie - 'cute' some Americans called it - was directed by Nigel Cole on location in Yorkshire and at Shepperton Studios and was given a rousing reception following its world premiere at the Cannes Film Festival in May 2003. Tricia Stewart and Angela Baker flew down to the Cote D'Azur glamour spot to walk the red carpet with Mirren and other members of the cast and pose for photographers splashing in the Med on the Carlton Hotel beach before taking afternoon tea with the world's media. And the double-act from Up North were even given walk-on parts in the film.

Mirren herself was in fine form alongside the mercurial Julie Walters telling tea-partygoers, which included myself, 'I have to say that, when I was a youngster, when I first took my clothes off for a film, if someone told me I'd be doing it again over 30 years later, I'd have died laughing. But it's all in such a good cause and such good taste, I didn't have any problem with the idea. I don't think anyone else did either. These roles keep coming my way.' She pauses and grins: 'It must be because I have a certain reputation.

'I was like the cheerleader when it came to the nude scenes because I have done it so often. I kept on telling them it would be great and there wouldn't be a problem. But some of the other girls had never stripped before so all power to them. It's tough, you know, if you are in your fifties, let alone your sixties. But I think it was liberating. I have always found it to be ultimately liberating. It's just the thought of it that puts you off. It's actually much worse when you are younger because you are a kind of sexual object. The reality is that I am not.

'But let's be honest, though, you don't get to see too much in the film, do you? I mean, this isn't *Last Tango in Paris*. These are genteel ladies from Yorkshire! I really admired their courage and their commercial flair. We had such fun as well, and I think I've made one of the best films of my career!'

Later, far from the madding crowds of the Croisette, she confided, 'I did have my concerns about the film. I was in two minds about doing it. I felt in the wrong hands it could go all wrong and be just titillating, or trivial or silly. Or worse, gratuitous. I'd stand accused, yet again, of just wanting to get my boobs out.

'It was a quirky, difficult subject and could be seen as being bland, middle-aged, Middle England, middle-class, middle everything. I was worried about that. It could have been so mundane. It is often so hard to get a story out of real situations. But the writer Tim Firth did a fantastic job. So I said, 'Yes' and crossed my fingers. After the first read-through with all those fabulous actresses, I thought, Wow, this is going to be good!

'It was the first time in my life that I have actually been with a whole group of women. Often it's a group of guys having a laugh and you're the one on the outside wistfully looking in. We just laughed and we got drunk. We laughed all the time about stupid things, like regressing to school, would be the best way to describe the feeling. We'd be laughing hysterically about something completely stupid.'

The film was released in the UK on 29 August and the critics were unanimously in praise. Peter Bradshaw of the *Guardian* (UK) wrote, 'This genial comedy, directed by Nigel Cole, with an excellent, tightly constructed script by Tim Firth and Juliette Towhidi, accentuates the positive. There's lots of wit and pluck.'

Mark Kermode in the *Observer* (UK) commented, 'Despite the unnecessary schmaltz, *Calendar Girls* is a jolly romp with its heart in the right place.'

And in America, from Los Angeles to New York, the critics were largely charmed. Roger Ebert of the Chicago Sun-Times wrote, 'That the movie works, and it does, is mostly because of the charm of Mirren and Walters, who show their characters having so much fun that it becomes infectious.'

At the box office, *Calendar Girls* proved to be one of the small big hits of the year taking £20 million in the UK and $30 million in the

US, apart from later DVD sales. The lady herself greeted the news with the kind of chagrin which has become her trademark: 'Goodness, a Helen Mirren film which makes money ... whatever next!'

In fact the triple effect of *Last Orders*, *The Pledge* and *Gosford Park* had already paid off in a big way for Mirren in Hollywood where she was back in favour. Robert Redford needed a 'strong personality, somebody who could blow me off screen', to play his wife in the new thriller *The Clearing*, which was being made in Asheville, North Carolina, and Pittsburgh, Pennsylvania. Oscar-winning Redford played a wealthy business executive who was kidnapped by a bitter disgruntled ex-employee played by Willem Dafoe, who starred in *Platoon* and more recently played the villain in *Spiderman*.

The Fox Searchlight drama was being directed by Dutchman Pieter Jan Brugge who produced the award-winning *The Insider*, *Bulworth* and *The Pelican Brief*, which starred Julia Roberts.

Redford, wearing his director's hat, had plucked British actresses such as Brenda Blethyn out of the pot before, but Mirren was no stranger to him through her long-standing American connections. In the drama she conducts negotiations for Redford's release and a source closely connected to the production said, 'It was vital to have somebody very assured and strong, somebody who could take control in any stress situation. Bob said there were only a handful of women of a certain age who could do that ... she was up the top of the list. It was made pretty clear to us that she wouldn't have gone for it if it just meant hanging decoratively on to his jacket for the duration. She wanted a real part with balls. That's what she's got. Bob really admires her.'

The Clearing, which was premiered in Los Angeles in June 2004, left her with mixed emotions. At one stage, during an emotionally charged scene with Redford, tears gently rolled down her face. Even when director Brugge called, 'Cut it,' she was still visibly upset. But she refused to discuss her obvious distress. However, Mirren did later confide that her younger brother Peter's death at the age of 53 had triggered her genuine outpouring of grief. The teacher had grown more distant from Helen and her sister Kate in his final years, according to family friends. He had no interest in showbusiness and certainly none in the age of celebrity. If anyone queried the connection between his name and his illustrious sister, he'd merely smile and mutter, 'Yes, I'm very proud of her. She's a very talented girl. Now, we really must move on!'

He was something of a rolling stone, never feeling settled or content. Past neighbours recalled him as a 'broody teenager'. One said, 'His problem seemed to be that he wasn't sure who or what he was. He felt very British but he was very aware of his aristo Russian blood. There seemed to be something of a battle going on there between the different facets of his personality. He was much more like Kate, studious and serious.'

Mirren rarely mentioned Peter in her many interviews. Soon after finishing work on *The Clearing*, she said, 'I had been bottling it all up for too long. I had to repress my emotions when it happened and then I moved straight on to film with Redford. I didn't have time to absorb the pain.'

Helen and her sister agreed that his death was private family business and would remain as such. There had been no rows, no bitterness. Just sadness. In essence, both girls and in particular Helen wish they had spent more time with him. They hoped over the years he would become less insular. It was not to be. He wanted a quiet, almost isolated life. Tragically, it was also to be cut short. And his funeral was shrouded in secrecy.

Mirren's latest American movie adventure received mixed reviews. In essence, the critics weren't sure what to make of it. The essentially downbeat climax also confused audiences. Much of the action was slow and drawn out and there was little chemistry between Redford and Mirren in the short time they actually appeared on screen together. Ruthe Stein of the *San Francisco Chronicle* liked what she saw, however, commenting, 'The brilliance of *The Clearing* lies in its ability to tell parallel stories and make both equally riveting. The movie is as much about cracks in the Hayes' seemingly rock-solid marriage - the biggest being Eileen's [Mirren] concern that her love for Wayne [Redford] is not reciprocated - as it is about his kidnapping.'

Glenn Kenny from *Premiere* magazine gave the drama, set against a cosy Pittsburgh suburb, the thumbs-down. He wrote, 'Moviegoers of a particular aesthetic bent are apt to bemoan the dearth of character-driven films coming out of Hollywood at any given moment, complaining of a cinema that values sensation over narrative nuance. And I can kind of get with that. So this particular pill is an even more bitter one to swallow when first-rate talents set out to create a subtle, considered, mainstream narrative film and wind up falling flat on their faces.'

After making *Gosford Park*, Mirren was able to fly back briefly to New York to make a cameo appearance in the Hal Hartley-directed black comedy *No Such Thing* – a modern-day take on the classic *Beauty and the Beast* fable – which was filmed principally in Iceland with a largely Icelandic cast, though Julie Christie also has a cameo as a doctor. The often poignant film, which only made it to video in the UK, starred Sarah Polley as Beatrice, a timid, lowly aide to a dynamic TV network boss played by Mirren. When her cameraman fiancé disappears on an assignment to locate a monster in a remote part of Iceland, she begs Mirren for the opportunity to find the lost crew. En route to Scandinavia, she miraculously survives an aeroplane crash and becomes a minor celebrity herself.

Good scripts were pouring in but Hackford has never put pressure on her to spend more time at their Californian retreat. She says, 'I've quite often been separated from Taylor for long periods because of my work. I don't mean in a slavering, apologetic sort of way. I mean, I am completely independent from Taylor and make my own career decisions. In fact, I am very secretive, almost embarrassed to discuss things. I rarely tell him about a project until I have done a deal. It drives him crazy. But I have worked at our relationship in the sense that I have sometimes given up work for Taylor. I have never done that before. Maybe it's a big mistake. I mean, basically, it's best to look after yourself first.

'He's difficult and forceful and I love that. We're totally committed to each other. The great thing about him is that, when push comes to shove, when something big happens, he always does the right thing either by himself or with other people.

'He can be terrible, awful. Sometimes I don't like him very much at all. But when there's a problem, he always does the right thing. I really love him and always will. I was very happy before but we have walked through this new door together and it feels in many ways as though we are entering something new. Before I met Taylor, I had this romantic dream of starting again, from scratch, living in a seedy hotel on Sunset Boulevard. Instead, I live in a big house with a swimming pool ... and I love it.'

Everything in the Mirren camp appears to be in order. Her sister Katie was understood to be back teaching in the Southend area, while her nephew Simon, her 'adopted' son, had thrown himself into screenwriting and was putting an episode of a well-known TV series together. 'He's not afraid of women and he's never an arsehole like these neurotic men who are all messed up,' says Mirren. 'It's not in his nature because he is so open. He's mercurial in temperament, emotional and he will cry, but he's also very manly and that's a wonderful mix. That was why he got on so well with Liam Neeson when we were together. Liam grew up around women.'

Taylor Hackford doesn't wear his heart on his sleeve. He's a supercool Californian. But he confesses that he can hardly wait to see his wife coming through the door of their Californian home. He said, 'What turns me on most about her is her talent. I was definitely smitten from the start. She was fabulous to work with, very smart and intuitive. You can feel the pain and ambition of the women she plays through her eyes. I can read her in our private life as well. There can be complications when you get to read somebody that well. What is special about her is that she is not a narcissistic actress. She has a professional ego but she is totally real.

'I don't find it difficult that she is in sexy scenes either. They are not the easiest things to do, but it's crucial to get performances that are real on the screen. I ask actors to step up to these kind of situations, so it would be unrealistic not to expect others to ask this of Helen.'

Hackford said he's 'desperately sad' they haven't worked together since their introductory film *White Nights*, and gets angry about the 'sexual tyranny' in the film industry which eliminated her from many prestigious projects making the rounds. He said, 'It's sickening and tragic for women in a profession like ours. Their star rises at 18 and sets at 35 and that's usually about it in terms of big money and big parts. For the guys, they go on from their mid-thirties through to their late-fifties and beyond.

'The trouble is that Helen is a woman of a certain age and they are not going to build films around her. But she has a great sense of her own worth and she is responsible for her own fate. If, when she was in her early twenties in the UK she wanted to go and be a sexy bombshell in Hollywood, she could have done so but she chose to go off to Africa and work in the theatre with people like Peter Brook.'

American television viewers are also about to get several different 'tastes' of Mirren. Before making *Calendar Girls*, she jetted off to Rome to star in a Showtime TV remake of *The Roman Spring of Mrs Stone* with Brian Dennehy and newcomer Oliver Martinez, who starred in the recent drama *Unfaithful*. It was based on Tennessee Williams's novella, and she plays an actress who wants to get away from it all after the critics tore her apart for being too old for her latest part. But her husband, played by Dennehy, dies from a heart-attack during the journey. After deciding to stay on in Rome to mourn, she falls for a much younger man played by Martinez. The novella was originally filmed in 1961 starring Vivien Leigh and Warren Beatty as her Italian paramour.

Eyebrows were once again raised, though not by Mirren, as the media fussed over how a woman nudging 60 could get it together with a young lad like Martinez. There was much talk of 'steamy scenes' and 'hot clinches' in a romantic drama palpably being made for a family television audience in America.

Mirren joked, as she lounged in the Roman sunshine, 'I felt like a very lucky girl. Olivier is incredibly good fun. He is very self-deprecating and enjoys making fun of himself. He is absolutely adorable. He's French but he comes from a big working-class family so he's got that street thing, which is very sexy and he's really smart. But the best thing about him is his sense of humour. As for the so-called sex scenes, I think he was more embarrassed than I was. I was the one saying, "Don't worry, Olivier, the best thing sweetie is just to do it and not make a big deal out of it." He didn't.'

The handsome dark-haired Latin has been a permanent fixture in the life of Australian singing star Kylie Minogue while she battled cancer. But, while they filmed in the Lazio district of the city, he was still involved with American actress Mira Sorvino. Mirren said, 'He wasn't going out with Kylie then. He was going out with Mira Sorvino and she came to the set. So I don't know what happened with Mira. I would imagine a bit of heartbreak went on, actually.'

The Roman Spring of Mrs Stone, which was directed by Robert Allan Ackerman and adapted by Martin Sherman, was shown on the Showtime channel in the US in May 2003.

Showtime then handed Mirren the opportunity to direct on screen for the first time in her career, making her début on the science-fiction short film *Happy Birthday*. The piece was an adaptation of a Keith Laumer short story called *Placement Test*, about a hierarchical world where citizens take tests to determine their place in society.

Hardly pausing for breath, she also joined the cast of the new *Dynasty*-like CBS network drama series *Georgetown*, playing a Washington hostess and newspaper mogul who has ongoing battles with her family after her husband leaves her a controlling interest in his newspaper empire. And in the Turner network TV movie, the real-life story *Door to Door*, which had been co-written by *Boogie Nights* actor William H Macy, she played the fiesty mother of a man suffering from cerebral palsy. The inspirational weepie followed brave Bill Porter (Macy) battling the illness across four decades while he become a successful door-to-door salesman.

The touching biopic won a total of six Emmy awards. Macy, who also wrote the screenplay, collected Outstanding Lead Actor and Kathy Baker, playing a genteel, lonely alcoholic who sees more in Porter than his selling ability, took the award as Outstanding Supporting Actress. Kyra Sedgwick also co-starred as a romantic interest in the quirky, dark but warm-hearted teleplay, set against the backdrop of Portland, Oregon, in the 1950s but actually filmed in 28 days on location in Vancouver. Mirren was nominated for her work as Porter's mother, who suffered from Alzheimer's disease.

Porter was 69 and still selling via the internet when *Door to Door* was shown and Macy struck a chord when he said, 'We watch the Ozzy Osbournes and the Spidermen because we want the thrill of seeing the oddball or the fantasy superhero. But I think stories about the ordinary Joe who triumphs are a lot more interesting.'

Ironically, Mirren often felt that, *Prime Suspect* aside, much of her TV work in the US went totally unrecognised in Europe where it was usually shown on cable or satellite. Certainly that was the case with another biopic, The Passion of Ayn Rand, which won her an Emmy in 1999 for her portrayal of the philosopher and novelist. The director of that piece happened to be Christopher Menaul who had previously worked with her on Prime Suspect.

Mirren dib-dabbed around American television like a child passing the time of day in a fairground amusement arcade. She later took a small but memorable role as a junkie in the long running NBC drama *Third Watch*, confiding, 'It is rather sad that some of my best work just gets completely unnoticed because it stays in the US and doesn't travel. But, contrary to a lot of opinion in the UK, there is a lot of good work on American television if you hunt it down or, better still, if it comes to you directly. Sometimes, I like to do a friend a favour and sometimes something amuses me enough. And sometimes I think, Wow, this is really very, very good!'

After finishing work on *Calendar Girls* at Shepperton Studios Mirren took a well-earned break with Hackford at their Los Angeles home. She also thumbed through the script of another impressive Walt Disney-backed movie project *Raising Helen*. Jack Amiel and Michael Begler had penned the screenplay and veteran Garry Marshall was directing. The affable, almost cuddly uncle figure Marshall cut his teeth on Robin William's *Mork and Mindy* television series in America in the Seventies and had marched on to make the box office mega hits *Pretty Woman*, *The Princess Diaries* and *The Runaway Bride* with Richard Gere and Julia Roberts. Marshall wasn't just about laughs. He'd also won critical approval for *Beaches* with Barbara Hershey and Bette Midler and the Al Pacino, Michelle Pfeiffer fast-food romantic drama *Frankie and Johnny*.

What also massively impressed Mirren was the name of Joan Cusack on the probable cast list allied, with Oscar nominated starlet Kate Hudson, the daughter of Goldie Hawn. The often underrated Cusack has been one of America's foremost character actresses for well over a decade having appeared with her actor brother John Cusack in the critically approved *Grosse Pointe Blank* and Nick Hornby's *High Fidelity*. Mirren was revealed to be one of her most ardent fans. Marshall had actually met Hudson as a child while making the class conscious farce Overboard with Hawn and her actor step-father Kurt Russell. The 'Helen' in the comedy which was set against the backdrop of the modelling business in New York and Los Angeles was in fact played by Hudson as Helen Bradley, a personal assistant to Mirren's character, the boss of a top modelling agency.

By late February 2003, Mirren was on set with Hudson, Cusack and John Corbett who'd enjoyed his first real blast of publicity playing the hunky teacher in *My Big Fat Greek Wedding*. One story already making the movie rounds is that Marshall kept referring to Hudson as 'Goldie' and was 'amazed by their similarities in style and movement.' Hudson took his confusion in good spirit but jokers in the crew decided the director should pay $5 into a 'foul-up' box every time he made the error. By the end of the shoot there was enough cash in the box to fund a 'wrap' party, actually thrown by Goldie Hawn for the crew.

Raising Helen, which was made in New York, New Jersey and Universal Studios, wasn't released until May the following year, following a long session of heated behind-the-scenes arguments and sessions in the editing process. Walt Disney executives at Buena Vista were demanding rewrites and the return of Hudson to reshoot long after the film had wrapped. As one Disney source said, 'Somebody got it badly wrong in the casting process and it just isn't funny. You are supposed to laugh and then cry. Not fall asleep.'

The film died a slow death at the box office, taking over $40 million, and not being the complete disaster many had predicted. Mirren, however, escaped any criticism.

Critics suggested that the concept might work as a TV sitcom or, as the *Chicago Sun-Times*' critic Roger Ebert put it, 'a pilot for a TV sitcom', before adding, 'But it was hardly worth the price of a movie ticket.'

Ty Burr in the *Boston Globe* wrote that the movie 'works so hard to be inoffensive that you may well be offended'.

Stephen Hunter in the *Washington Post* conceded his fondness for Hudson saying, 'It's hard to frown upon her, even when the material seems thin and spun out for too long. She immediately took my heart hostage with that crinkly smile and the utter decency she conveys, and so I want to please her somehow. Too bad the movie won't let me.'

Eleanor Ringel Gillespie of the *Atlanta Journal-Constitution* was more harsh: 'It's one of those bogus "sincere" pictures, a schmaltz-ridden mediocrity without an honest moment in it.'

Mirren and comedy is not a cocktail to everyone's taste. But nobody should underestimate her ability to get laughs either. She positively dazzled when she took over from Glenda Jackson as the serious actress everyone wanted as their 'stooge' following Eric Morecambe's untimely death. And she has made countless hilarious, deadpan appearances on Dawn French and Jennifer Saunders's TV comedy specials.

What with the latest surge of interest from Hollywood and American television companies, Mirren is in danger once again of neglecting the British stage. But as Dame Judi Dench and Dame Maggie Smith still 'reign' supreme, at least in London's West End, perhaps her strategy is right. She remains at a distance. She wants to spend time at home with Taylor Hackford and their pets. She wants to potter around their garden.

Having reinvented herself once as a TV detective, she's convinced she can repeat the trick. Many believe she will one day, in the not too distant future, be 'crowned' as the genuine successor to those in the elite group of theatrical royalty.

John MacKenzie, who directed her in *The Long Good Friday*, says, 'She was always a great actress and, in particular, a great stage actress, but she wanted to be more of a film star, which I always found curious. When she is on stage, she is absolutely incandescent. She has tremendous presence and feel for a character.'

The UK *Daily Mail*'s former theatre critic Michael Coveney told me, shortly before the transmission of *Prime Suspect 6: The Last Witness*, 'She has been the darling of the critics in Britain since the doyen of their circle Sir Harold Hobson salivated watching her star in the sixties in *Antony and Cleopatra*. She has always been a bit of a sex bomb and has always had a unique quality on stage, that special indefinable X factor. I have always marvelled at the range and variety of her career. She was doing very serious stuff early on but she kept disappearing. But I think we will have Dame Helen very soon and she will take over from Judi Dench and Maggie Smith.

'She can be very funny but she is best at erotically charged emotional stuff. There is no trickery either, she comes straight at you, very intense. Most of all she has this naughtiness. But she is more likely to take a risk than any of her peers. This is a key chapter of her life.'

Few would disagree.

14

NOTHING LIKE A DAME

There is no doubt that Helen Mirren will look back on 2003 as one of the great landmark years in her life. Within two years, her name was on everyone's lips from the world of television to cinema.

Calendar Girls had given her the career notoriety she had been missing, especially in the UK. And the rebirth of *Prime Suspect* – to be shown weeks after the release of the movie – was a masterpiece of timing. Even if the movie only brought in the punters from Yorkshire by way of the Harrods Food Hall crowd from upmarket Chelsea and Hampstead in London, she was assured of her fish-and-chips following tuning into her return as Jane Tennison, complete with shock horror sex scenes hyperbole. Timing, as she'd often remark, is everything.

But there were other more surprising developments unfolding at Buckingham Palace where the Queen was approving the recommendation of Mirren becoming a Dame in her Birthday Honours list. Her lefty image and rebellious past mattered not one iota to the reigning monarch. It was time she was recognised by the great British Establishment as being one of their kind. Under the heading if you can't beat them, join them at their private members clubs and feel the privilege, she was being given the opportunity to plant one foot very firmly in the upper-crust camp and enjoy those little luxuries which come with a noble title.

Mirren, if anything, was hideously embarrassed at the thought she was selling out in any form. 'I feel very ambivalent about it actually,' was her immediate response. 'I don't like seeing letters addressed to Dame Helen Mirren. It makes me feel peculiar. It doesn't feel like me. I know this sounds like famous last words, but I will never use the title. I don't think I shall ever call up a posh restaurant and say, "Oh, Dame Helen here, my usual table if you please…".'

So, what finally convinced her, following her rejection of an award in the mid-1990s, that there was in fact nothing like a Dame? Mirren freely admits she would not have accepted the honour 20 years earlier because it would have been seen to be 'too Establishment'.

Friends confided that she turned down an OBE in 1996, still feeling uncomfortable with the idea of the monarch bestowing an 'imperialist' title upon her. But the lady was indeed for turning, claiming her views on the 'absurd, ridiculous, little monarchy' had mellowed over the years, and she actually liked some of the royals. She had met Princess Margaret through her gardening pal Roddy Llewelyn many years earlier in her 'hippie period' at their rural Berkshire commune and at dinner parties in London.

Her own Russian aristo background had swayed her against privilege and the class system from her earliest days in Leigh-on-Sea, though her life with Taylor Hackford in California had thrust her into the upper echelons of Beverly Hills Krug-swigging society. No, you didn't find La Mirren munching toast with a cuppa at a transport café any longer.

At premieres and on film sets, she was already royalty. Doors swung open, stretch limos arrived on time and travel was always first class. Mirren had a pretty thorough understanding of how the Royals lived and was convinced that nobody thought less of Diana Rigg, Maggie Smith or Judi Dench because they had risked 'Dame-nation'.

She was able to justify her change of stance thus: 'The whole concept of aristocracy I loathe but it dawned on me that by having a monarchy perhaps it has saved us from becoming like Argentina or having a fascist dictator state.

'I gave myself a week to think about whether or not to accept the honour. I talked to people in my industry and they were unanimous. They said, "You have got to do it." It was surprising to them slightly, and embarrassing because I thought of myself as the naughty one.'

Her anti-royal feelings still lurk but now remain mostly buried way beneath the surface. She said, 'I still hate the British class system. I hate those drunken toffs at Annabel's [a well-established and 'in' London nightspot]. I have never been there but I imagine them all and I'd like to line them up against a wall. They are nauseating in their sense of entitlement.'

Her entire family were thrilled, especially her sister and nephew Simon.

As for Taylor Hackford, he quipped, 'Does that mean I have to leave the room facing you? How shall I address you in the morning?'

To which, she quite regally responded, 'You, sir, are dismissed!'

One of her closest friends said, 'Taylor, who's a pretty straight, studious kind of guy, loved ribbing her about the title. He wondered whether he should be trailing her in the street or announcing her arrival whenever they entered a room. She loves him not taking the whole thing seriously because so many Americans do. They would do anything to get to Buck House and be made a peer of the realm which is out of the question in any case. Let's just say Taylor was impressed without being overawed. He liked the idea of Helen being 'elevated' in stature. He believed she had never truly had the recognition she deserved from the great British public. Women had always admired her and felt intimidated by her while the guys still fancied her like crazy, especially media executives.'

She was constantly being propositioned by 'the suits' running British television and some very important men in Hollywood. Flattered though she was, she'd always give them the same brush off line which they could never deal with: 'How very sweet of you.' One well-known senior executive at the BBC just stared in amazement when she whispered her stock 'no way' response to him on the Carlton Beach in Cannes, after he'd just offered her 'one hell of a weekend' in Monte Carlo.

A close friend of Mirren told me, 'You would not believe just who has propositioned her over the years from Whitehall to Hollywood. One director even threw in a five-picture deal in the 1980s for one night with her. There was also a junior government minister under John Major's administration who had inherited a stately home and suggested they share it every weekend when she was available. When she explained that she was a married woman, the politician said she could bring him along as well. She just stared and gave him the "How sweet of you".

'At one point in the Seventies, it was almost offensive *not* to make a pass at Helen. So many men made the assumption she was the kinkiest thing around because of many of the roles she played. In fact, sexually she has always been fairly straight, apart from what you'd call an "experimental" period when she puffed on the odd joint in the early 1970s which she just thought was "hilarious". But her earlier experiences, when certain guys gave her such a hard time and seriously molested her, made her extremely wary of guys who came on strong.'

Mirren duly collected her award from Prince Charles at Buckingham Palace on 5 December 2003, soberly dressed in a dark two-piece suit and pearl earrings with her fair hair brushed back. Very Dame-like indeed. Taylor Hackford was by her side but the tattoo on her left hand from a drunken night on an Native American reservation in Minnesota created more of a stir. The two interlocked crosses, she explained, denoted 'love thy neighbour'.

To this day, she prefers people not to use her new title. She says, 'The only time I am called "Dame Helen" is when I am on British Airways. Actually, there I quite like it. Coming home from America, you step on the plane and it's "Dame Helen, it's lovely to have you on board". I feel as if I have already left the US and am back in Britain. When people do call me "Dame Helen", it's like "Who? Oh yeah, right." That's not to say I am not incredibly proud. I am. But I find it surprising. I never felt I've done enough to warrant the title. I still don't. Only my best friends call me "Hell", though.' Now she is grinning: 'Just think, "Dame Hell". What a head turner!'

No matter that she was a reluctant Dame. In the eyes of the British nation, she was still very much a scintillating object of desire which made her natural casting as the sensuous Christine Mannon in the National Theatre's production of Eugene O'Neill's epic *Mourning Becomes Electra*. The play opened just a few weeks earlier in November, within days of the TV critics raving about her comeback in *Prime Suspect*. It was the kind of dream role – the adulterous lover of a much younger man (Paul McGann) who plotted to poison her suffocating older husband – tailor made for her.

Remarkably, she had only appeared at the National once before, with Alan Rickman in Antony and Cleopatra. About which she commented, 'One performance here is not enough for me. I should definitely have done more in my life.' The play, some four and half hours in length, was chosen specially for her by Nicholas Hytner, the director of the National Theatre and the mastermind behind the superb stage and film productions of Alan Bennett's northern school saga *The History Boys*.

And she was thrilled, saying, 'The great thing about the play is that it's absolutely driven by women. The men have very good complex roles but the drama is driven by Christine and her daughter Lavinia [Eve Best].' Her grin grows wider into a girlish giggle: 'It's all about revenge, sex, incest, lust and hatred. It's like five brilliantly written episodes of *Dallas* rolled into one.'

The play was set in New England just after the American Civil

War as Ezra Mannon's return from the field of battle swept an entire family into a violent spiral of revenge. O'Neill's variation on the Greek tragedy *Electra* relocated the action and focused on the repercussions as well as the bloodshed. A passionate tornado of a play which also starred Tim Pigott-Smith explored the wildly destructive forces of jealousy and desire unleashed when Lavinia discovered that her mother, the intoxicating Christine, had dared to take a younger lover. Designer Bob Crowley's massive set will be remembered both for its aesthetic and mechanical qualities. It changed smoothly from the outside of the Mannon mansion to its interior. With a crumbling, tattered Stars and Stripes canopy, the house symbolised the end of the American Civil War and the start of the new family era in the New World. The set then breathtakingly metamorphosed into a ship's deck and lower quarters.

In the *British Theatre Guide*, Philip Fisher wrote, 'The real highlight is in the acting, first of Helen Mirren, who combines passion with calculating hatred, and then of Eve Best. In short, a long night's journey into brilliance.'

With electrifying reviews of *Electra* still luring fans to the Royal National Theatre, there were gathering whispers in the corridors of theatrical dreams of a new, mammoth small-screen version of *Elizabeth I* being developed by BAFTA- and Emmy-award-winning author Nigel Williams in league with the UK-based Company Pictures, the independents behind Channel 4's hit series *Shameless*, *Anna Karenina* and the critically acclaimed Peter Cook biopic *Not Only But Always*. Would the epic two-part biopic become Helen Mirren's crowning glory? The challenge of playing one of the most powerful, intelligent and successful rulers of England could be just too good to pass on for the Essex girl with the dazzling classical streak. Was the world now ready for 'Tudor Tennison'? Writer Williams and producers George Faber, Charlie Pattinson and Suzan Harrison from Company Pictures were masterminding the production in collaboration with Francis Hopkinson, the newly appointed Senior Commissioning Editor in Channel 4's drama department.

From their point of view, it was all systems go. Oscar-winning Jeremy Irons was 'very interested' if they could come up with the right lead lady, as was Dennis Potter favourite Patrick Malahide and newcomer Hugh Dancy. All they had to do was get Mirren on board. Few others were in the running to play Good Queen Bess or the so-called 'Virgin Queen' in the later stages of her reign.

There was talk of the Dames Dench and Rigg but the age factor would rule them out. As the production was likely to be international in flavour with Home Box Office as the chief US financial backer, they required impact on that side of the Pond. So, out of the running went Sarah Lancashire and Amanda Burton. There were even discussions, albeit brief, on comedy actresses Caroline Quentin and Jennifer Saunders.

The casting was quirky but novel with both capable of carrying the role. But as an insider at Company said, 'It was Mirren or Mirren basically. The feeling was that nobody was as sexy in middle age, nobody was more desirable and nobody could "feel" the part better than her. Sarah Lancashire maybe lacked power, but the danger of going with somebody like Jennifer would be the risk of not being taken seriously because of her Dawn French double-act connections. In any case, she'd be lacking in American appeal. Helen had it all because of *Prime Suspect* on PBS and her recent movies. She was a known quantity.'

Writer Williams, who created *The Wimbledon Poisoner*, *Uncle Adolf* and *Dirty Tricks* for television as well as *Fortysomething* (a six-part series adapted from his book), had no doubts. Perhaps the problem was that, ever since Flora Robson embodied Elizabeth in *Fire Over England* in 1937 (reprised in *The Sea Hawk* three years later), renowned actresses virtually queued up to deliver their version of Elizabeth. Bette Davis was memorable enough in Henry Koster's *The Virgin Queen* in 1955 which also briefly featured a little-known Joan Collins playing the wench Bess Throckmartin. There was Glenda Jackson in the BBC's *Elizabeth R* and a hilarious, slapstick, irreverent Miranda Richardson in Richard Curtis's Rowan

Atkinson comedy vehicle *Blackadder*. And, even as they sat around a table off Dean Street in London's Soho, the BBC were preparing the hugely talented actress Anne-Marie Duff for their very own bio-series *The Virgin Queen*. And would young moviegoers start comparing their 'Liz' to Judi Dench's Oscar-winning portrayal in *Shakespeare in Love* or Cate Blanchett's magnificent tender Oscar-nominated powerhouse in *Elizabeth*?

Williams's polished, well-researched script focused on the second half of her reign when her fertility and therefore the diplomatic trump card of her procreative powers were on the wane. Here was an opportunity, though not in a million years would she say it, for Mirren to 'out-Dench' Dame Judi and put certain 'heiresses' to her acting kingdom such as charismatic Cate firmly in their place. Apart from *Prime Suspect*, rarely was she tempted to enter the telly arena.

But Mirren took little persuading once her nerves had settled down over lunch with Williams, the affable ex-BBC denizen Faber and her old buddy Tom Hooper who directed *Prime Suspect 6: The Last Witness* and the rapturously received docu-drama *Longford* starring Jim Broadbent. And she was thrilled to discover that the nature of the piece would cover the two great loves of the Tudor queen's life, the Earl of Leicester (Irons) and her later tragic infatuation with the charming, courageous and doomed Earl of Essex (Dancy). As Williams put it, 'The evidence we have of her table talk, poems and speeches showed her also to have been a persuasive and eloquent speaker who, in spite of occasional lapses into Tudor brutality, was also gifted with that rare virtue of supreme rulers, compassion for her fellow creatures. The political machinations of this period played an important part in the story, taking us into the corridors of power and presenting the Elizabethan governmental machine in all its complexity.

'But the real focus was on Elizabeth herself. Essentially, *Elizabeth I* was the story of private faces in public places and my fascination in writing the script was the way in which the violent passions of the time informed, created and distorted the great events which every schoolboy thinks he knows but doesn't. Authenticity in both history and drama is very often an illusion.

'I wanted the audience to feel they had a ringside seat at the great events of the late 16th century, events that set the pattern for so much of our history and whose bitter religious conflicts have uncomfortable resonances in a world that seems increasingly to be divided, not united, by faith. This was the story of the woman behind the mask in a violent and turbulent age. A fiercely intelligent, outstandingly courageous and passionate woman, her tragedy was that her head and her heart could never be reconciled.'

Tessa Ross, Channel 4's Head of Film and Drama, made Mirren feel even more at home with the subject matter, saying, 'This felt like a killer combination of acting, writing and producing talent, tackling the extraordinary and resonant story of a middle-aged Elizabeth fighting to retain her power in a hostile, male-dominated environment.'

Mirren immersed herself in books on the Tudors before boarding a jet clutching biographies by Anne Somerset and Alison Weir. The former Soviet republic of Lithuania was used as 16th-century London and Home Counties principally for cost-cutting purposes and because many old buildings and backstreets lent themselves to that era. She relished her trip back in time to 'discover' Elizabeth the woman and the monarch, saying, 'I read some of Elizabeth's own writings, as well as books on contemporary Elizabethan life. All you can do is look at history through the eyes of all the different historians, and then make up your own mind based on the evidence. What we do know are certain things commented on at the time. You look at those truths and make up your mind about how and why they happened. Why did she shut herself away for four days when she discovered that Leicester was secretly married? Why did this discovery lead her to banish him from court for seven years? Why did she refuse Essex something, only to give in to him after he, in turn, locked himself away for four days? We know these things happened, but we don't know why. So, as actors and creative people, we fill in with our own imaginations what we think may have happened. I also studied paintings, portraits and contemporary pictures of the period, as well as buildings – particularly the Tower of London, which is not far away from where I live. Portraits are valuable to a certain extent, but they're a very false image of someone – especially in those days, as they were painted for political reasons.'

In taking on the multi-layered role, she was also aware that she too was taking yet another step in the direction of TV history. What was it about Elizabeth which fascinated film makers and writers? She said, 'I think there are many explanations for this. One is that she was so brilliant at branding herself. The image of Elizabeth is so iconic. If you put the gear on, you look like her. So she'd branded herself very, very well. She was highly conscious of marketing herself. There's also the reality that, sort of accidentally, her reign covered rather an extraordinary time in British history and, indeed, in the history of the world: the discovery of the New World, the stealing of the wealth of Central and South America, which suddenly made Europe exceedingly rich, which in turn opened up art and science and all kinds of things. It was an extraordinary period in European history.

'Then there's the fact that she was a woman, which was obviously hugely important, and that she reigned for such a long time. That was very rare; even for someone to live that long was unusual. And there's the mystery of her sexuality, the so-called Virgin Queen. Did she or didn't she screw? Supposedly she didn't, and yet her life is full of relationships with men that are quite excessive and incredibly intense.'

Could Mirren see some parallels here between herself and the character? Here she was yet again playing a strong, wilful, determined and single-minded woman. She says, 'Elizabeth was alien to the concept of becoming a feminist icon as she was also to the concept of a democracy. She did very well in a man's world. She was intelligent, ambitious, egotistical and probably quite vain. However, it was all of these attributes combined which made Elizabeth the very powerful person she was.'

The £5.5 million production spent three months in Lithuania on the Baltic coast where the interiors of her Whitehall Palace were recreated in a giant sports hall in Vilnius before cast and crew returned to London. Critics later agreed Williams's *Elizabeth I* went beyond the myths to the woman subjected to a humiliating gynaecological examination when contemplating marrying a French prince, to ensure she was still able to have children. To the woman who ran a country and yet who wasn't allowed to marry the man she loved. And, poignantly, to the woman who, in her mid-fifties, conducted a passionate affair with a man half her age, a man whose arrogance eventually led him to mount a desperate challenge for Elizabeth's throne. Williams set his two-part story in England in 1579, some 20 years into her Protestant reign, and facing two enormous challenges, the question of the succession to the throne and the threat of the Catholic powers as represented by Spain. Illuminating the grimy, lustful underbelly behind the opulence and formality of the English court, he also focused strongly on her relationship with her scheming but trusted adviser and lover Leicester, who ruthlessly dealt with all political and emotional threats. Their relationship also formed the prism for two other major events – the execution of Mary Queen of Scots (Barbara Flynn) and the War with Spain. Part One culminated with the death of Leicester and the British victory over Spain, juxtaposing her public celebration and private grief.

Part Two followed the latter period of her 45 years on the throne, dealing with her tumultuous relationship with the Earl of Essex and how, with the aid of her adviser, Robert Cecil (Toby Jones) she maintained power. The story culminated in the execution of Essex for treason, and in her glorious but lonely ascendancy into the pantheon of great British rulers.

The mini-series was transmitted over two weeks in September and October 2005 and resulted in universally glowing reviews. Brian Lowry of *Variety* sung her praises thus: 'Nor does the word "sumptuous" quite do justice to this Lithuanian-shot production, which features a theatrical array and sprawling sets as well as wildly baroque costumes, highlighted by Mike O'Neill's spectacularly regal frocks. Still, peel back the outward finery and this is ultimately Mirren's show.'

Another Emmy was to be Mirren's reward for her outstanding performance, to add to the previous award for *The Passion of Ayn Rand*. Two months later, she went to New York to collect her prize looking ravishing in a sweeping full-length cream Morgane Le Fay Victorian-style gown with an emerald and diamond necklace and laughed that she was considering auctioning off the high-heeled designer shoes she wore on the night. Mirren stumbled when she walked to the stage and then raised eyebrows across America by joking that she almost fell 'a**e over tit'.

For director Hooper, it was a pleasure to see Mirren acknowledged yet again for capturing extremes of emotion so superbly. He commented, 'With lesser actors, you risk going over the top incredibly quickly. But she has the ability to take extreme positions and root them, make them feel incredibly real. One of her great gifts is that she carries a tremendously strong sense of reality with her as an actress.'

Elizabeth I was shown by Channel 4 on 29 September 2005 and in America the following spring. The critics were unanimous. Kathryn Flett in the UK *Observer* gushed, 'You couldn't take your eyes off Helen Mirren's charismatic, hot-blooded, flirtatious, and intermittently tantrum-throwing Bess.'

John Preston in the UK *Sunday Telegraph* commented, 'There was a lot to applaud here. It looked terrific. The dialogue sounded rich and authentic – never lapsing into authentic prithee-speak – while the chokingly tight atmosphere of court had been well captured.'

Rupert Smith in the UK *Guardian* was equally enthusiastic: 'The acting, sets and costumes were gorgeous,' while the UK *Express* boomed: 'Mirren reigns supreme.'

By an extraordinary twist of fate – but again featuring Jane Tennison – Mirren was to play both *Elizabeth I* and *Elizabeth II* within an 18-month-long period.

The name of the complex but ingenious game was to reproduce the many facets of the Queen in her entirety in the chaotic, unsteady and often tearful week immediately after the death of Princess Diana in September 1997. Few could have predicted the impact of the car crash in Paris on the British government and the royal family. The glamorous princess had caused huge waves to gather and crash against the Establishment, rather than sitting quietly and disappearing from public life.

The inspiration for the film which moved co-producers Christine Langan and Granada's Controller of Drama and Comedy Andy Harries was a modern story rooted in ancient history which could involve every soul in the nation. Here was the tale of the princess who had everything and saw her fairytale shatter into a million pieces. Here was a modern princess learning to love again, cruelly killed in her prime following a terrifying car chase away from ruthless paparazzi photographers. And a controversial love affair cut short before it could blossom. The public was instantly devastated by her death and the tabloid press, in almost pantomime-like fashion, were cast as the devils in the face of universal anguish.

But, tabloid headlines apart, it was another aspect of her death which caused Langan and Harries to become engrossed in a film idea. They had just made the award-winning TV docu-drama *The Deal*, about the almost perverse relationship between Tony Blair and Gordon Brown and the birth of the New Labour Party in the UK before and after they seized power through the 1997 General Election. Michael Sheen starred as Blair with David Morrissey as the PM in waiting. It had been written by Peter Morgan and directed by Stephen Frears, the film maker who made his explosive Hollywood debut with the Oscar-winning period piece *Dangerous Liaisons* and won over the pseudo-intellectual movie crowd with *The Grifters*. The colourful Frears, who cut his teeth on the Albert Finney thriller *Gumshoe*, the essentially art-house *My Beautiful Launderette* and the Joe Orton biopic *Prick Up Your Ears*, had just engineered a magnificent return to form with the Second World

War vaudeville saga *Mrs Henderson Presents* starring Judi Dench and Bob Hoskins.

Harries and Langan saw *The Queen* as a mini-personality-driven epic but with a grander, more ambitious sweep of a movie than *The Deal*. This was a story which would pit the old-fashioned formality of the world of the British royal family, both in the rugged countryside surrounding their Scottish retreat of Balmoral and in the elegant drawing rooms and private quarters of Buckingham Palace, against the casual modernity of the newly elected Blair and his entourage of slick, image-conscious and hyper-cynical aides.

For Harries, it was the recollection of how the royal family and the Queen reacted to the news of Diana's death that proved the deciding factor, the concept of a family so preserved by tradition that it couldn't and wouldn't break with protocol to deal with the tragedy.

'Diana had been a great cause of tension while she was alive,' said Harries. 'It was inevitable that her death would present the monarchy with perhaps the biggest challenge it had faced in 50 years. What fascinated me most about the story of Diana and the Queen was an ageing monarch whose reign was rooted in Victoriana being challenged by a young princess, who, thanks to a catalogue of bad judgements, had been absorbed into her family. Diana had an extraordinary aura about her.'

Harries was confident Peter Morgan had the skill to write a screenplay that was authentic and dramatic. Nobody was 'hotter' in the art of screenwriting with a historic flavour in the UK. His joint adaptation with Jeremy Brock of the bloody Idi Amin biopic *The Last King of Scotland*, directed by Kevin Macdonald and starring Forest Whittaker, won them a Bafta screenplay award, while his screenplay of the period story *The Other Boleyn Girl* – based on Philippa Gregory's novel – is proving to be another gold-star addition to the CVs of Eric Bana, Scarlett Johansson and Natalie Portman. His *Henry VIII* won an Emmy as Best International Drama in 2004 and more recently he wrote the controversial and harrowing real-life murder story *Longford* which starred Jim

Broadbent and Samantha Morton. He'd also written the well-received stage production *Frost/Nixon* which starred the multi-talented Sheen as the TV icon and Frank Langella as the disgraced American president.

Morgan, just 43 at the time of writing, was intrigued by the prospect of dramatising events around Diana's death for the big screen. He said, 'It soon became clear that the interesting aspect was how the royals reacted in the week between her death and the funeral. It was a family in crisis, locked up in the closed world of Balmoral. The Queen decided that to protect the boys all televisions and radios were to be removed so they were living in total denial. They were bunkered up in an institution, propped up by sycophancy, and they weren't told what was going on in the outside world. A very strong anti-monarchist feeling was in the air, stoked by the media which realised that the spotlight of guilt was being beamed in its direction.'

Morgan says he went to see 'everyone and anyone who would talk' and adds perceptively, 'There are a lot of biographers of both the royal family and the Blairs and they all have their sources from equerries to secretaries to butlers to maids and civil servants. There's a lot of material but it's a question of sifting the real from the embellished.'

He was also quietly amazed when Mirren the Monarch appeared on set, padded but with virtually no make-up. He said, 'She had completely metamorphosed without any prosthetic assistance.

'When she arrived on set, she was very much Helen in a wig. I remember at one point she mischievously moved my hand so it came to rest on the breast of a naked statue and she was very appreciative of one handsome crew member in particular whispering to me, "Cor, he's a bit of all right." A week later, in costume, she was a totally different person. People were simpering like total idiots and almost curtseying.'

The £5 million production, a collaboration between the French Pathe International group and Granada, had actually gathered in momentum much earlier while Harries was overseeing *Prime*

Suspect 6. At a read-through, he watched with interest as other members of the cast and production team arrived. He said, reliving the moment as though it were a religious experience, 'As they filed in and saw her sitting there, they all gave her this little deferential nod and I remember thinking, Blimey, she's just like Queen. Which, of course, she was. She is the reigning queen of British drama. A little light went on in my head. We'd just filmed *The Deal* and I had found it incredibly exciting to do a drama about real people, a real event. I was wondering what we could do next … and there it was, in front of me in that room. I thought, She even looks more than a bit like the Queen. This is her!'

The gargantuan project meant Mirren delving through piles of videos and books and working with a dialogue coach to be able to conquer the Queen's world-weary voice. From early days, she felt she had one unique advantage. 'I look terribly like the Queen actually,' she smiles. 'If I had to wear a dark wig for a role, I looked like Princess Margaret, but I knew I was going to look very much like her. I thought *The Deal* was a fantastic piece of work, so I knew I would be in very good hands. It's delicate material, dangerous material in a way, so you have to be confident that the people you are working with have the intelligence and the ability to put a story like this on screen without a cheap betrayal of the subject.

'But I did a lot of research. I'm not very good at mimicry and, even if you are the most brilliant mimic in the world, you'll only capture 50 per cent of what the real person is. Given the iconic status of the Queen, I was terrified. I was more nervous about this than almost any other role.'

Despite her years of experience in period work, she was not afraid to ask for advice from her co-star Michael Sheen who also played Blair in *The Deal*. He advised her to work closely with voice coach Penny Dyer to feel comfortable with the voice and mannerisms when they began shooting. Mirren also invited the actors playing her family in the film to her home. It was more of an afternoon tea-party atmosphere when veterans James Cromwell from *L.A.*

Confidential and *Babe*, who was to play the Duke of Edinburgh, Sylvia Sims, alias the Queen Mother, and Alex Jennings, who portrayed Prince Charles, filed in for the 'Royal seminar.' And she forged a special bond with actress Helen McCrory who was to play Blair's hyper-critical wife Cherie.

Mirren, relaxing in a hotel lounge just off the Strand, said, 'The challenge was negotiating the fine line between giving an accurate portrayal of the person and tipping into caricature. You don't want the audience caught up in your brilliant impression or impersonation. You want them to believe who you are and go on your journey with you in an imaginative way. If the impersonation is too brilliant it can mean the truth is too intrusive. Sometimes you have to step back from the truth because in theatrical drama it can jar the audience out of their imaginative engagement with what you are doing.

'You have to get the hair, the hands, the stance, the walk and the voice. I had photographs of the Queen all over my trailer and watched tapes all the time. It was a bit intimidating because each time I watched them I would feel as if I was failing her. Failing the inner person. There was one piece of early film, a simple little thing of about one minute of Elizabeth as a young girl, aged about 12, getting out of a car and walking forward to shake somebody's hand. I found it very touching. I watched it over and over. The more I studied her, the more extraordinary she became, as a person, as a psychology because she is so incredibly iconic and well known, and yet we don't really know her at all. She's back within herself almost on a continuous basis.

'But it's not a neurotic place or a confused place. It's a very steady place, quite a confident place. It's a place of incredible self-discipline and then she steadily comes out from that point. That was the person I was constantly trying to fight my way towards. The most valuable research for me was looking at the Queen as a young girl, and reading the rather nauseatingly grovelling book that Crawfie [Marion Crawford] wrote, *The Little Princesses*, which was invaluable because she saw Elizabeth as a little girl and you really saw clues into the character, I thought, through that book.

'I haven't actually often played living people. I've avoided it because I think you're in a no-win situation. You'll never be half as good as the real person. All you can do really is fail. In fact, this is the first time I've ever played a living person. I've played people who were alive but are now dead, except for *Calendar Girls*. You can't imagine how intimidating and scary it is to contemplate playing a real person. It's terrifying. Especially knowing that down the pipeline I'm going to sitting here talking about it, and that's the most scary thing of all, because it's a bloody hot potato. You know you're going to be under scrutiny, people will ask you what do you think about the monarchy, about Diana.'

She pauses and says, 'But it was an interesting thing to do, as an actor, because there you are, inhabiting a real person's soul and I've long realised that you can never be half as good as a real-life person if you happen to play someone like that. You realise that all you can do is try and that the worst thing that you can do is fail! The trick about life, I always think, is learning how to deal with it!'

But even Mirren couldn't imagine how she would have felt if she had been made a Dame of the British Empire after the release of *The Queen*. Would she have been able to face the monarch? Would she have received the award at all? 'I have had no contact with the Palace [Buckingham Palace] over the film, so I really don't know whether they have seen the film or they approve. My instinct tells me they have seen the film and that the Queen would have approved. I hope she sees my performance as heartfelt and honest. Whatever she thinks, I hope she can see that I did my best for her. I would hate to think that I stripped her of her dignity in any way or shape. I don't know, I have no idea. It's not my place, how can I say. I suspect the royal writer Robert Lacey was asked the same question. He said, "Well, I think the Queen will say, "Well, that could have been worse – could I have a gin and tonic please?"

'With Elizabeth II, she's alive, she's with us. She's incredibly important to us. It's really a different thing. I think all I can do really is be me as her. I cannot be her. I've never lived that life. I don't know what it is like to be woken by bagpipes every morning, to wear the most beautiful underwear all my life, to never have a run in my stocking, though I suspect she does actually because she's not into clothes. One of the most fascinating things about her is her lack of vanity, her utter lack of interest in what she wears, which is alien to me because I love clothes.'

Mirren never took sides on the great Diana v the royals debate following her death. While in the past she was a critic of the institution of the monarchy, she was clearly a fan of Elizabeth II, describing her as 'utterly without vanity'. And, ploughing into the debate shortly before filming started, she commented, 'I'm not a monarchist but I am kind of with the Queen on this one. I think the film was sympathetic to the Queen in an objective way. The hysterical reaction to Diana's death certainly polarised opinion. I'm not sure I really got it. I wasn't in England at the time so I was blissfully separated from it. I was quite grateful I wasn't in England.' There is a pause and she agrees that she has mellowed. The Mirren of old, the Seventies hippie, the high-school rebel, would surely have been sickened by the media infatuation with a Queen facing an almost impossible dilemma and the public outpourings of grief for a naive but vivacious princess.

She confessed that her family was and had been fervently anti-monarchy. She said, 'They thought it was all a load of old rubbish. I remember the days when we all stood up for "God Save The Queen" after the last film of the night in the cinema. My family hated all of that and the class system. That's how I was brought up. But I have somewhat mellowed on that issue and I am not quite so hysterical as I used to be. In fact, I am not certain where I stand on it and what does it matter anyway!

'It becomes banal and silly to rally against the monarchy. Just being rude, as you get older, you think, Oh, it's infantile. But people have woken up to the truth that she was always there. She was constant. She's gone through fashions and politics and maybe ten Prime Ministers. I think the Windsors have served us well, fantastically, she particularly. The Queen has served us so well. It's a fascinating thing about her, she won't perform or act something she doesn't feel. I don't think she feels that is part of her job. Her job is to be dignified, gracious, but, above all, serious. She has two kinds of smile. And sometimes it is a genuine smile and you can tell she is enjoying herself.'

Principal photography began on *The Queen* in London on 13 September 2005. Production designer Alan Macdonald had the task of finding suitable alternatives to Buckingham Palace and Balmoral, where most of the film was set. He whittled down an initial list of between 25 and 30 suitable castles and mansions in Scotland to the three chosen for Balmoral interiors and exteriors. They were Cluny Castle in Aberdeenshire, the Glenfeshie Estate in Invernesshire and Blairquhan Castle in Ayrshire. Other locations included Goldsmith's Hall in London for the Chinese Room in Buckingham Palace, Brocket Hall in Hertfordshire for the Queen's bedroom and drawing room, and RAF Halton in Bucks for various Buckingham Palace state rooms; and Southend Airport in Essex was used for Northolt. Costume design was in the capable and experienced hands of Consolata Boyle who used archive footage to get the 'country' feel of their fashions as they relaxed on their Scottish estate.

Mirren said, 'I was really, really nervous about it. But, once I started, I just loved being in that character. I loved being in her personality. It was like getting into a car. You loved being in the interior. You loved driving. It wasn't a particularly luxurious car. It wasn't a particularly fast car. It was a car you could depend on.'

But coming to terms with the less than flattering costumes was a struggle for Mirren after glowing in the magnificent array of bodices and gowns provided by costume chief Mike O'Neill on *Elizabeth I*. Her nerve broke one morning on set when she caught her reflection in a full-length mirror and ended up sobbing quietly into a handkerchief. She said, 'At my first fitting, the costume designer brought all these horrible-looking clothes, all these walking shoes and tweed skirts. After playing Elizabeth with the brocades and jewellery and fabulous other stuff, well, I cried. I just burst into tears. Then I thought, You know what, Helen, you *have* to wear them. Let go of the vanity and the sense of prettiness. You know, the moment I put those clothes on, I suddenly found the Queen's walk. It came quite naturally in those shoes.'

She even tried the look out on her neighbours who she says 'fell about laughing' because of the uncanny likeness. Mirren soon came to admire the monarch she once simply viewed as a privileged anachronism. She said, 'What drew me to her was her lack of vanity. If you look at pictures of her as a young girl, she was like Elizabeth Taylor. I mean, she was gorgeous. She had the most beautiful figure, tiny waist, wonderful legs, that gorgeous white skin. She was honestly, unbelievably beautiful but I suspect that even as a girl she was completely without vanity yet with a huge sense of duty and order, and that's very interesting in her psychology as a girl. It's a lack of ego. It's where you go through vanity and ego into another place and that is one without choice. Once she understood she was likely to become Queen, she had no choice. It would have been a slow realisation perhaps, but once she understood it she could not say "No".

'Her uncle [Edward VIII who became the Duke of Windsor after his abdication] had said no and to her this was an unbelievable betrayal of everything the monarchy stood for. In the wake of that, she couldn't say no, so this destiny was going to envelop her and I suspect that's the point at which she travelled through vanity and ego into that place where there are no choices. My perception is that, once she had done that, like Elizabeth I, she accepted it totally. She didn't waver.'

Director Frears confessed that he feared a media backlash which would at least divert much of the attention away from Mirren and the rest of his cast. Extra security was hired to patrol the set and nobody was to disturb the main members of cast without both the producers and the director being aware of the intrusions. But, at the end of the day, Frears was candid about the film's intentions. There was no hidden agenda. He said, 'The gap between what people are expecting it to be and what it is will be very great. I'm expecting journalists to look for trouble and the film itself doesn't supply trouble. The act of impertinence is in the making of the film. But it has nothing shocking or scandalous to say that isn't in the public domain. But the very act of treating the Queen like a woman rather than like a cut-out of the sovereign is in itself shocking.'

The Queen was released on 15 September 2006, almost a year to the day after Frears gave the order for 'Action!' There was barely a poor review. The UK *Daily Mail* verdict was 'Magnificent' while *The Times* pronounced it 'Brilliant'. *Time Out* magazine also liked what they saw, trumpeting, 'Helen Mirren is superb.'

USA Today was equally ecstatic, summing up her performance: 'It is Mirren who must pull all of this together and she does it beautifully. Her Elizabeth is an intriguing combination, an intensely private person, yet mistress of all she surveys. This immovable object has met the unstoppable force that is actress Helen Mirren, one of the great masters of modern screen acting.'

And of course, the awards began tumbling in her direction. At the 2006 Venice Film Festival, in a shimmering Neil Cunningham chiffon gown and £2.2 million necklace in white gold, with 60 carats of Bulgari diamonds, she took the Volpi Cup for Best Actress for *The Queen*.

The film also won Best Screenplay for the modest low-key Morgan. Everyone agreed that justice had been done.

As that doyen of critics Pauline Kael once observed, 'No other actress can let you know as fast and economically as she can that she's playing a distinguished and important woman.'

Her co-star Michael Sheen was also quick to heap praise on Mirren: 'She has real courage and complete control. Some actors have this recklessness, this risk-taking, but they don't have discipline … That's why she's able to give you these glints of the Queen's humour, mischief and ability to read people. It's Helen having all these things together, intuition, courage, risk-taking, and discipline.'

After the hoo-hah had died down at the Lido, she claimed, jokingly, that she and Taylor Hackford were waiting for a dinner invite from Buckingham Palace. 'Oh, yes,' she grinned mischievously. 'Playing the Queen was tough all right. I'd like to see her playing Jane Tennison!'

15

PRIMED TO SURVIVE

Every much respected established actor has that moment in time or space, often enough on screen, when they wish they could shrivel up into a tiny ball and be kicked into oblivion. Helen Mirren may have had her reservations about certain sequences in Ken Russell's *Savage Messiah* and privately expressed dissatisfaction and dismay at the exploitative nature of Don Boyd's *Hussy*. And she was on the verge of taking *Penthouse* guru Bob Guccioni to court with the revered senior members of the cast of *Caligula* following the discovery of certain 'insertions' in the post-production process. But she could say with her hands clasped firmly together as a measure of her sincerity that, on stage, from *Teeth n' Smiles* at the Royal Court to *Mourning Becomes Electra* at the National, she had no regrets about lending her name to the billing.

Which brings us to the virtually forgotten low-budget American gangster movie *Shadowboxer*, which was shown to much indifference at the Toronto Film Festival in September 2005, and released in a handful of cinemas in July 2006 before duly vaporising through lack of interest in a matter of weeks.

Mirren was talked into taking the co-starring role in the £3 million movie by New York fringe producer Lee Daniels, who was making his directorial debut on the feature, which was to be made in spring 2004 in Philadelphia and small-town Pennsylvania. Indie maverick Daniels, 47, had been associated with two class productions, the Oscar-winning *Monster's Ball* with Halle Berry and Billy Bob Thornton, and the intense child-abuse drama *The Woodsman*, in which Kevin Bacon gave one of his finest performances, with his real-life partner actress Kyra Sedgwick by his side. Harlem-based Daniels was co-producer on both movies and had fallen in love with William Lipz's tale about a female assassin diagnosed with terminal cancer who carries out one last job aided by her lover, who also happens to be her much younger stepson. Off-beat, dark and dangerous were three words which immediately applied to the project. Anjelica Huston and Wes Bentley were pencilled in to star with Macy Gray and newcomer Vanessa Ferlito, but the two leads soon became unavailable. Instead, after finding a gap in her diary, Mirren agreed to participate, with Cuba Gooding Jr and Stephen Dorff joining her on location. Graphic violence and bad language laced with nudity ensured the film was given an 18 rating in the UK and an R in America. Though both Mirren and Gooding won praise for their work, the film took barely $400,000 following its premiere at the Arclight in Los Angeles.

Daniels, who garnered a reputation for delving into subject matter others wouldn't touch, later said in defence of *Shadowboxer*, 'People don't understand my movies or they love my movies. There is no grey area. That's OK. Because, if everyone did get it, I think I'd be doing something wrong.' He candidly added that he was able to secure big names because they wanted to work in movies which were 'adventurous' and a 'little Euro, a little homo and a little ghetto'.

Of Mirren, he declared, 'I wanted somebody who would be as daring as the material required and she gave me her soul. She threw down the gauntlet in the most positive sense.'

He had been reluctant to cast Cuba Gooding in the role because of his comedic background but was swayed when Gooding told him, 'You know nothing of my struggles,' and by the manner in which Halle Berry had sounded off over *Monster's Ball*. She raised the heat in his Harlem office to a new scorching level, telling him, 'Who exactly are you to say a beautiful young black woman can't have her problems?' Berry, of course, got her role and the Oscar.

But *Shadowboxer*, without major promotional backing and mainstream distribution, was a financial semi-disaster waiting to happen, though through DVD and cable it may make a small long-term profit. Mirren was disappointed with the outcome; though, as her agents reminded her, she had *Elizabeth I* in the pipeline for television and *The Queen* also waiting to happen. There was also the climax of *Prime Suspect* due to go in front of the cameras in spring 2006.

The extremely garrulous Daniels, the son of a police officer who was shot dead in the line of duty when he was 13, was thrilled that Mirren and Gooding would forgo their usual Hollywood-sized salaries to work for him for close to a month in less than five-star conditions in the backstreets of Pennsylvania. He said, 'These people came into my world for some Tootsie Rolls and some barbecue potato chips. You all made my dream come true and I had nothing to pay you but love. I want to tell the kids that want to make a film, you can do it, you will do it and don't take no for an answer.'

Ferlito, who starred with Jude Law and Juliet Binoche in 2006 in *Breaking and Entering*, echoed those thoughts, saying, 'The experience was amazing and your job is easy when you love the people.'

Mirren, recognising that *Shadowboxer* was unlikely to ever see the light of day, put the whole project down to experience. And simply forgot about it, unless challenged. Daniels, from the US indie cinema, was a wacky but fun character, way out of her normal professional experiences and she was full of admiration for the 'super-cool' Gooding and Dorff.

Her agents and her instincts were proved right. *Elizabeth I* and *The Queen* would, within the space of 12 months, grant her international recognition. And, of course, her public in the UK and America were demanding a climax to *Prime Suspect* and a farewell to Jane Tennison. They did not have to wait for long.

Prime Suspect 7: The Final Act had in fact been talked about for over ten years. How were they going to end it with Tennison? Could she be put out to grass and then returned to active duty to hunt down a serial killer she knew only too well? The possibilities were endless and nobody, naturally enough, was talking. Whatever form the drama would take, one aspect of the show was guaranteed – a huge audience. *Prime Suspect 6* drew in 11 million viewers. They were hoping to sail past 13 million. Mirren couldn't have planned it any better than if she had Lynda La Plante as her chief adviser. Here she was basking in the glory of *The Queen* and positive fallout from *Elizabeth I*. Her street cred was at an all-time high. And Granada, with just a little bit of help from the lady herself, could hype the adventure up to transmission day and beyond. So long as Tennison could breathe a breath, or in her case lift a whisky glass, there was something to chat about. And, unlike her jaded screen alter ego, Mirren was positively peaking.

It had taken years to talk Mirren back into action in *Prime Suspect 6* on the proviso that she would make one final journey as the detective, cutting a sad, lonely figure. She said, 'I was in a very privileged position of being able to do theatre and film projects in between each *Prime Suspect*. Television is very powerful and can stick to you like glue. I did feel by the mid-1990s that I was becoming too identified with Jane and I wanted to put an end to that. Over the seven-year gap after series five, I was approached on a number of occasions but I just didn't feel I was ready. Then the producers came back to me at a time when I felt I had put enough distance between myself and the character. Not only had I got my own identity back as an actress but the script was just so strong that I felt able to move forward.'

The terrier-like Andy Harries was back in the helm as executive producer while Andrew Benson produced. Philip Martin would be directing Frank Deasy's pacy, riveting script which centred on the murder of a teenaged schoolgirl and the perilous issues facing children and adults alike in urban Britain. Martin's credits included the BBC's *Hawking* which starred Benedict Cumberpatch while Deasy created the brilliant *Looking For Jo Jo* with Robert Carlisle and the gaunt coming-of-age movie drama *Prozac Nation*, which starred Christina Ricci, Anne Heche, Michelle Williams and Jonathan Rhys Meyers.

Deasy had cleverly chiselled a completely new landscape for Tennison. Here she was on the last leg of her journey as a cop, burned out, reaching for the bottle. A sad, lonely middle-aged woman, almost a sociopath. Her ailing father Arnold, again forcefully played by veteran character actor Frank Finlay, was dying from cancer while her estranged sister and niece buzzed around like mosquitoes, tormenting Tennison over her self-inflicted solitude. From her past team came Robert Pugh as the solid DS Simms.

Casting director Doreen Jones pulled off a battery of masterstrokes, reining in the Irish star Brendan Coyle to play her boss DCS Mitchell and the ever popular Stephen Tompkinson, lately seen as vet Danny Trevanion in ITV's *Wild At Heart*, to play the central figure of flawed headteacher Sean Phillips. Tompkinson, who emerged through the mining drama movie *Brassed Off* and the BBC series *Ballykissangel*, was keen to be involved. He said, 'When I took the call from my agent, I had said "Yes" before she could finish the sentence. Here was a chance to work with one of the greatest actresses there is. Taking a part in the final *Prime Suspect* was the quickest decision I have ever made.'

Jones also signed up actor Gary Lewis, seen playing Jamie Bell's father in the film version of *Billy Elliott*, as the murdered girl's heartbroken father. But perhaps her greatest 'trick' was to employ Tennison's past nemesis, actor Tom Bell, to return as the once hardened, acidic detective Bill Otley to remind her of her own alcoholism and inner demons. But, by one of the cruellest pieces of fate, life came to reflect art as the mesmeric Bell collapsed and died days before transmission of *Prime Suspect 7* on 5 October. He was 73 and had led a difficult life, both professionally and privately. In the 1960s, through films such as *The L-Shaped Room*, the Liverpool-born Bell was destined to join the ranks of Albert Finney, Tom Courtenay and Alan Bates as yet another northern working-class lad not giving a toss for the old boys network acting Establishment. Sadly, the often aggressive, argumentative Bell put one too many a powerful nose out of joint and lost his way before he had the opportunity to fully shine.

That said, he made forceful, dynamic appearances in the Emily Lloyd breakthrough movie drama *Wish You Were Here* and as real-life gangster Jack 'The Hat' McVitie in *The Krays*. Bell, one of Britain's finest character actors, was indeed his own worst enemy. As he once said, prophetically, 'If you act, you need to have threat. Without threat, nobody notices you.'

Helen Mirren and Granada dedicated *The Final Act* to Bell as a touching, poignant gesture as the last line of the rolling credits.

There were months of extraordinary behind-the-scenes wrangling before the final draft of *Prime Suspect 7* came to rest on Andy Harries's desk. Neither Lynda La Plante nor Helen Mirren wanted to see the character killed off, even though the concept was a ratings buster. La Plante, who parted company with the show as a writer after the third series, had doubts as to the direction it was taking. She held back from launching a full-frontal attack on Granada but commented, 'I just find it very sad for the end of a great female character somebody has to say "Make her a drunk." Why?' She added that she was 'glad' she had nothing more to do with the drama.

Fierce arguments as to the climactic scenes of *The Final Act* raged from Manchester to London as Harries, Deasy, Mirren and producer Benson struggled to compromise. The scenario which resonated most obviously was for Tennison to meet her death by the blade of a knife before the killer was seen being led away. But Mirren plumped for an alternative course, suggesting the character would simply 'walk proudly off into the night', failing even to celebrate her retirement or a successful last case.

So, the door was left wide open for a future 'special' in which she could return for a final bout of glory. And Mirren had the final say, giving writer Deasy a huge hug for his work. Harries made it clear to associates that he would have been happier if TV's top cop had departed with a heroic, but dignified gasp of triumph. A senior source who worked on the production told me, 'The bottom line is that, whatever Helen Mirren wants, Helen Mirren gets. But she's always more subtle than that. If she wants something, it can be with the look of an eye, the turn of her head, a quick stare, or a walk away, and look up to the ceiling. Then, maybe a smile. But, when it comes to television in the UK, she definitely feels she can be, say, more aggressive in determining script and plot. In fact, all aspects of the production, if she feels she has to make a point. But, give her her due, she will never ever throw a tantrum unless there is a very good reason. Usually it is because somebody isn't being professional enough. She does not suffer fools gladly. If somebody is getting up to no good, she will fix an eye on them and then on the director and then a few quiet words will be spoken and the matter will be resolved. In the case of *Prime Suspect*, she felt as though she had a duty to ensure the final scenes had the ring of truth and reality about them.'

Mirren, however, claimed she did not dictate the ending. Those close to her suggested she much preferred the idea of Tennison being killed rather than committing suicide. But she admits there was a 'collaboration'. She said, 'A four-hour drama is a difficult thing to bring to the point that you see on screen. That involves many drafts and editing. But what we started with was an incredible first part, a wonderful piece of work. The second part came later. But I never read a whole four-hour script.'

But she was sure she was doing the right thing by calling for what might be an indefinite break in Tennison's career. She said, 'You can't go on doing something forever. I think it's long enough. I came back to it extremely reluctantly the last time [in 2003 after seven years away], and only on the proviso that it was a really good script, and they came up with a really good script. I thought then, It's a fantastic role, and I'm allowed to make a big contribution, so do it. I was worried that maybe the world had moved on and *Prime Suspect* might look a bit of a dinosaur. There has been so much police drama since the first series, some slightly cloning it, some very different. So I said I would do one more and see whether it worked. If it did, I would do another one. That was always the deal. We did the last one and it was successful. So I thought, Great, we will do that last one. And I like the way it ends, it's not a *Dynasty* wedding!'

The last mini-series was filmed over 11 weeks in late spring 2006 and early summer on locations around London including Elliott School, in Pullman Gardens, Putney; Northwick Park Hospital in Harrow; King's Cross; Hampstead Heath and a drab office block in Holborn, which served as base camp for the police operation.

The plot of *The Final Act* never veered from being simplistic – the identity of the real killer being somewhat telegraphed long before Tennison realised how serious an error of judgement she had earlier made. Many of her best scenes were either with her father (Finlay) or the sexually frustrated headteacher and prime suspect Phillips (Tompkinson) or his screen daughter Penny Phillips, admirably played by Laura Greenwood.

The final scenes seemed to fizzle out faster than necessary, as though director Martin was himself dissatisfied with the material at hand. Tennison silently vanished into the night, the viewer unsure as to the fate of the killer and the other suspects in the case. Unsatisfactory? Nobody was saying on the record but one source close to executive producer Andy Harries commented, 'People at the top would have liked a more solid conclusion. It didn't have to be all blood and bullets, or a long drawn-out speech by Tennison. Just something more memorable, to get a fix on. But the creative powers that be and Helen won the day on that one. They knew what she wanted, what she was looking for by way of an acceptable script she could deal with. Something with a touch of intellectual appeal, nothing obvious. So that's what they gave her. Even Mirren herself got dragged into the hype at times pretending she had been killed off. If that had really been the case, the storyline would have been leaked to add a million or three on to the ratings. But nobody could seriously say when asked about the climax, "We end in a whimper rather than a bang." That doesn't interest anybody.'

As she sipped nothing headier than water, she reflected on her 15 on-off years as Tennison. 'I can't say I will miss her terribly,' she says. 'But I hope she has made an impact. I hope she has opened the door for other strong-minded women in TV drama. It wasn't actually completely groundbreaking in the sense of having a female cop on television but I think, in terms of the issues we dealt with, with us going for realism, and very hard-hitting dark stories, now that was the groundbreaking part. The sexism within the police force struck a nerve and the show really caught the zeitgeist. Not just in terms of women in the police force but of women in all professions that were traditionally perceived as the domain of men – women in the legal profession, in the medical profession and in many business environments. The setbacks they had all experienced were in some ways uniform, and suddenly being held up for everyone to see.'

From her very first outing as Tennison, she confides that she was dominated by the character and writer Lynda La Plante. It was essential the blonde long-haired, impeccable Mirren looked like a hard-nosed female detective, and at six in the morning on her first day on set her hairdresser Trevor Sorbie arrived and 'chopped all my hair off'.

She says, 'Lynda had written a sort of selfish, self-obsessed, egotistical and untidy sort of person and that's what made her great. But, of course, she changed. There are really profoundly disturbed people out there and she has seen it all. No matter how strong a person is, facing those horrors is going to have an effect. Consequently, she was in a very precarious position psychologically by the time we reached the conclusion. I think the sheen had gone off her. Her sense of drive and ambition has lessened and there was a greater sense of reality and cynicism.'

Executive producer Rebecca Eaton was convinced *Prime Suspect* had gone in the right direction with Mirren's drive and work rate being a central part of their success. She said, 'With each *Prime Suspect*, she grew into the part and became interchangeable with

Jane Tennison. The viewers got to know Helen and the authenticity of her acting, and loved her. It is the thing you look for in any ongoing series: the audience falls in love with the character. Jane Tennison is not a particularly lovable character. It's a tribute to what Helen is doing with the role.' She described the final *Prime Suspect* as an extreme close-up of Tennison's life. She said, 'It's the perfect way to finish. Tennison must deal with her alcoholism and her career's end.'

Mirren was determined not to allow the last adventure to become sensational or gratuitous, purely for the sake of ratings. She said, 'That would have been the obvious and wrong way to go. The thing that I find happens a lot on television is "What can we do that's more than we did before?" Things get more and more sensationalist, more and more horrific, until it becomes absurd. I always wanted *Prime Suspect* really to have its feet firmly on the ground in the recognisable world.'

Prime Suspect: The Final Act was shown over two weeks in October 2006 in the UK and a month later in America where her fans were waiting to see her back in action as that telly cop as soon as possible. The American magazine *Esquire* said *Prime Suspect* was 'the most sustained example of great acting in the history of television'. Critic Tom Shales wrote, 'Her portrayal of Tennison is ice hard but not ice cold, a brilliant parlay of backbone and heart.'

Director Ken Russell rates her work on *The Madness of King George*, *The Comfort of Strangers*, *Gosford Park*, *The Cook, The Thief, His Wife and Her Lover* and *Last Orders* as her finest work. But he says she 'broke the mould' with her portrayal of Jane Tennison in *Prime Suspect* 'inventing a truly complex and sexy detective'.

He said, 'That she can apply that precision of hers to a portrait of self-willed lack of inhibition as she did in *Savage Messiah*, so early in her career, gives you a clue to her talent. One feels her mystery, even when she's showing all. You never quite get at the all of her. And you get the idea any of her characters would be sure to save something just for themselves. Helen can't play anything less than a powerful woman.'

Neil Midgley of the UK *Telegraph* summed up his experience: 'Mirren put in a bravura final performance as Tennison, fighting her twin demons of loneliness and alcoholism as well as London's criminals.'

Caitlin Moran in *The Times* wrote, 'The old girl went out in style' and 'the tension throughout left you mildly ill.'

Helen Mirren remains the Golden Girl of British stage and screen. From early September 2006, when she reigned supreme in Venice, there seemed to be no stopping her. Giving new nuance to the acclamation 'The Queen is dead. Long live The Queen', her performance as the British monarch was hailed by critics and audiences alike in Venice. The Rome newspaper *La Republica* headlined 'Queen Wins Venice's Heart'. The British trade publication *Screen Daily* predicted that Mirren's performance in The Queen was likely to be ' crowned with a host of awards nominations'. The online film commentator David Poland wrote that the actress lived 'at the centre of the work, underplaying the role to within an inch of not connecting with us, but keeps us firmly at the end of the leash until it is time to show us this very reserved character's heart. 'The French news agency Agence France Presse reported that Mirren, director Stephen Fears, and cast members received a 15-minute standing ovation at the film's screening. It made no odds that she almost fell flat on her face a few days later in New York when she collected her Emmy for *Elizabeth I*.

She arrived at the microphone as demure as ever wearing her very best schoolgirl grin and then calmly announced that she almost fell 'arse over tit'. She later threatened to auction off the high heels. A week later she was 'crowned' Best Actress by the New York Film Critics Circle before America's National Society of Film Critics also gave her their Best Actress prize. The Hollywood Foreign Press followed suit in January 2007 in Los Angeles, awarding her a Golden Globe. Her acceptance speech was almost regal in stature.

Wearing a fabulous Chopard pear-shaped golden pendant on a white gold and diamond chain, she said, 'Thank you so much to the Hollywood Foreign Press. In 1952, a woman called Elizabeth

Windsor, at the age of 24, walked into literally the role of a lifetime and I honestly feel that this award belongs to her because I think you fell in love with her, not with me, and I just try to make her as truthful to herself as possible. However, she already has an orb that protects her, so I will gratefully receive this one.

'I want to thank the writer Peter Morgan, incredible, extraordinary. I want to recognize him, and also our director Stephen Frears. And obviously, our producers Andy Harris and Christine Langan, who really conceived the whole thing and also without them and without Scott Rudin, I obviously wouldn't be standing here. So thank you very, very much. It is a great honour.' The Screen Actors Guild also voted her as Best Lead for *The Queen* and leading actress for her portrayal of Elizabeth I in the HBO/Channel 4 (UK) mini series *Elizabeth I*.

A tearful Dame Helen, looking magnificent in a cream silk Jacques Azagury gown and a fabulous £200,000 Chopard necklace, dedicated her Best Leading Actress BAFTA on February 11 to her 'mentor', actor Ian Richardson who died earlier that week. The pair starred together in 1968 movie *A Midsumer Night's Dream* – the actress's second ever film role – and she insists the veteran star who found fame late in his career through David Nobbs's TV satire House of Cards , played a huge part in her success story. After lifting the award she fought back tears to tell the audience at London's Royal Opera House, 'Many years ago when I started off as an actress I had the immense good fortune to work with an actor who was so generous in sharing his craft. He became a mentor to me, he helped me believe in myself. Ian Richardson, I'm not too sure I would be here today if it wasn't for you.'

Writer Morgan said it came as no surprise to him that Queen Elizabeth would never watch his award winning movie because she doesn't want to watch someone else depict her on screen. The 80-year-old Royal wasn't keen to relive what was arguably the most painful week of her 55-year reign, the period after Princess Diana's tragic death in August 1997. A source close to Buckingham Palace had revealed, 'It's hard enough for her to have to look at a video of herself after an event. But to try to watch somebody else being you is almost impossible. The Queen is not a great film person. There are small cinema rooms at (her homes) Buckingham Palace, Sandringham and Balmoral, but the Queen rarely takes advantage of them.' Morgan commented, 'If the Queen hasn't seen it, that's very, very sensible. It speaks hugely in her favor.'

His screenplay continued to cause some controversy, even in the skies. All references to God in the airline version of the film were bleeped out by an overly zealous employee of Jaguar Distribution, the company that provided it to the airlines.

According to the news agency AP, the unnamed employee was instructed to remove all profanities, including blasphemies. 'God ' was bleeped seven times, including the moment when a character remarked 'God bless you, ma'am'. A.P. later said that Jaguar would be replacing the edited version with the original.

Mirren's stunning portrayal made her the hottest Oscar favorite ever with Ladbroke's in the UK quoting an extraordinary 1-66 on for her to lift the golden trophy. In America they were calling her nomination a shoo-in award despite the fact that Judi Dench for *Notes On a Scandal,* Kate Winslet for *Little Children,* Penelope Cruz for *Volver* and Meryl Streep for *The Devil Wears Prada* were all more than worthy contenders in the running. A spokesman for the UK bookmakers William Hill said, 'Mirren is the shortest price we have ever had for the nominations'.

There was even a battle raging behind the scenes to dress the actress. Designers were queueing up to bask in the reflected glory while international jewelers vied to drape her in diamonds. Hardy Amies, once Her Majesty's favourite fashion house, dressed Mirren for the London premiere of *The Queen.* She then wore Jacques Azagury creation for her BAFTA. Jasper Conran dressed her in a coat dress for e New York gala a few weeks later. Every fashion house from Chanel to Armani queued up to dress her for her date with Oscar in Hollywood, putting aside as much as £400,000 to tempt her into their 'corner'. She thought it was hilarious that an actress in her Sixties had suddenly become the 'It' girl. But the fashion houses made it clear that they would dress her for free for an entire year. Prada even offered to dress her husband Taylor Hackford. She actually hated travelling so much she'd occasionally kit herself out at charity shops soon after touch-down. At the 2006 Emmy Awards she confessed to buying her 6-inch plastic platforms on Hollywood Boulevard for $49 99.

The Queen was also causing something of a trend setting fashion stir. A month before the Oscars, a shopper stalked into the Barbour section of the Peter Elliot store on Madison Avenue, New York, demanding of Maggie Archambault, the manager, 'Have you seen *The Queen*?' 'Actually, yes.' responded Ms.Archambault, recalling a 1970's garden party. 'No, *The Queen* the movie,' the customer shot back. 'I'd like the coat that the Queen is wearing in it.' On the weekend immediately following the movie's release on September 30 2006, no fewer than 20 customers requested the coat worn by Mirren in the film sequence at her country retreat at Balmoral. Ms. Archambault said the coat, the Beauford, had been emblematic of the sort of breeding money can't buy. It is also the key component in a rusticated wardrobe exerting a strange new pull on the popular imagination.

The glamourous vision that was to appear at the Oscar ceremony at the end of February 2007 was in stark contract to the elderly image of the monarch she created for *The Queen*. Her hair grey, her eyes lined, and wearing a specially designed padded body suit to expand her physique, Mirren couldn't have appeared much more unattractive on screen. But the illusion, as millions have now seen, was without question the most exciting and convincing transformation she had ever made.

And so the stage was being set. Friends of the star said she was definitely beginning to feel 'shaky' over the worldwide attention. But she was refusing to take any form of substance for her nerves, and that included alcohol. She freely admits she gets tipsy easily, and would never want to appear intoxicated onstage.

She explained, 'It's a bit of a roller coaster ride ... and you can't drink. I can't anyway. I'm too scared to drink and then make a t*t of myself. It's much too scary to do that. Some of the award shows you do there is alcohol on the table, there's wine and things. You have one afterwards and drown your sorrows usually. I've lost a lot of awards in my life. I'm brilliant at going, 'Oh, I'm so glad she won! She's fantastic! I'm a worm by comparison! I don't deserve it at all! I don't know why I'm here! 'Mirren also refuses to eat at glitzy awards shows, adding, 'You're too nervous and excited and insecure; you don't want beans in your teeth when they start taking photographs.' Mirren pauses for a moment, 'I would take a $1,000 bet that you could go to any newsstand in the world and find one magazine cover devoted to Diana. It was so extreme. The public had been fed imagery of Diana for so long – and then to have it suddenly taken away. It was just incomprehensible to all of us that we'd never see another picture of Diana in the newspaper. What we had was a heroine addiction.' Mirren laughs at her little pun (after taking the trouble to point out it is heroine 'with an e').

The media world focused on Los Angeles and the star jammed Kodak Theatre for the 79th Academy Awards on Sunday night, 25 February 2007. Mirren arrived on the red carpet in a stunning full length Christian Lacroix white gown and a £1 million worth of Chopard diamonds, waving a Union Jack. For once she admitted she had prepared herself to a deliver an acceptance speech, commenting, 'If I get to say it tonight, it will be the last one ever.' She was followed down the red carpet by glamour queens Jennifer Lopez, Penelope Cruz, Cameron Diaz and past Oscar winner Rachel Weisz. Kate Winslet, another Oscar hope, conducted her own regal theme by carrying an 18 carat gold bag with three coins from the days of Alexander the Great embedded into it. Other true Brits in line to pick up an award included Peter O'Toole for *Venus*, director Paul Greengrass for *United 93* and Stephen Frears, director of *The Queen*. As it was, there had never been a hotter favourite in the history of the Oscars than Mirren to scoop Best Actress. Bookmakers stopped taking bets the Friday before the ceremony and some even agreed to pay out early. But you could still cut the atmosphere with a very sharp knife as her name was read out as the victor on the night. Amazingly, she was the only Brit on the night from 20 nominations to take the short walk to the rostrum with Martin Scorsese's *The Departed* making the greatest impact as Best Film and Best Director. It was also no surprise when Forest Whitaker was named Best Actor for his quite stupendous portrayal of Ugandan dictator Idi Amin in the British made biopic *The Last King of Scotland*.

But Mirren, taking a deep breath after giving Hackford a peck on the cheek, was going to step up to live her dream, even though she had temporarily lost an earring in the madness.

Clutching the prize the late James Mason had predicted she would one day make her own on the set of her very first movie, she said, 'I've got my purse in one hand, my earring in the other. Thank you, Academy. Thank you so much. This is a huge honour. You know, my sister told me that all kids love to get gold stars, and this is the biggest and the best gold star that I have ever had in my life. I want to share my gold star with my fellow nominees, those brilliant, brilliant actresses who gave such amazing performances this year. I also share my gold star with the filmmakers, with Stephen Frears, with Peter Morgan, with Andy Harries and all the producers and all the filmmakers and the cast. Thank you. Now you know for 50 years and more, Elizabeth Windsor has maintained her dignity, her sense of duty, and her hairstyle. She's had her feet planted firmly on the ground, her hat on her head, her handbag on her arm and she's weathered many, many storms, and I salute her courage and her consistency. And I thank her because if it wasn't for her, I most, most certainly would not be here. Ladies and gentlemen, I give you The Queen. Thank you. Thank you very much.'

Backstage, moments later, looking far more relaxed and being decidedly cheeky, she sipped a Vodka and lime juice while taking on the world's Press. She confided that she would be going off with hubby Hackford, sister Kate and other members of the Mirren clan for a celebration dinner and party. In her regulation hand on hip, sky-high confidence stance, she confessed about her role in *The Queen*, 'I was very, very nervous before I started filming. Once I started I was fine but the idea of it was very intimidating. There are other real-life people I have played that people know but don't quite know. But Elizabeth is such a familiar person to the world, so identifying, that it was doubly intimidating. Tonight, I felt quite calm. I honestly felt so deeply honoured to be nominated in a year when there were so many great performances by women. To be nominated was a huge honour. Just to be here was everything to me. To win, which is a silly word because we're not athletes, is just great.

'I don't think of myself as our only big winner. I think we won big time because we were clearly identified for our ability.' She took a sip of her drink and added, 'I think it's wonderful that I live in a country that allows us to make a film like this. There are many countries that would not allow it. It was generous of the Royal family and the Queen to sit back and not interfere. It was very gracious and noble of her. And no, I am not expecting a phone call invited me to lunch or dinner. Putting politics aside, I do believe she is a noble person in the best possible sense of the word. That is nothing to do with class but everything to do with spirit.' And then it was off for a burger, a sashay at the Vanity Fair party with family and close friends and … home to bed. The night of her life was over.

Where does Mirren go from here? In the 1970s, she was bobbing up and down like a cork on the ocean, unsure which direction to move in. By the 1980s, she was an established force who intimidated Hollywood and yet didn't quite fit with the British Establishment. By the 1990s, she had been resurrected through *Prime Suspect*.
With media attention approaching fever pitch, there might have been reason to believe that she would at long last be in line for the role which gave her the much needed springboard to commercial celebrity. *The Queen*, which cost $10 million to make, had already earned over $60 million by the time Mirren had arrived to join the throng of 3000 at the Kodak Theatre on Oscar night. When *Prime*

Suspect was created and pitched to Hollywood, studio chiefs at Universal who bought the rights had sound reasons for rejecting her in the glamorous lead role. But one senior executive candidly told me, over a drink following the Golden Globe Awards, 'Though we think she is a great actress, a lot of kids from the Mid West have not got a clue as to who she is and they won't be going to see *The Queen* either. We'd sooner do this *Prime Suspect* movie our way, with our script and our legs, so to speak.' Their rejection will no doubt leave both *Prime* writer, Lynda La Plante, and Mirren disappointed. They were both keen to keep a firm British slant on the action should the film have American backers. Instead, the studio wants to see an 'American broad' in the frame. They are still talking about Michelle Pfeiffer and Glenn Close while Kim Basinger could well be in pole position, trying to kick-start her career yet again, with Melanie Griffith and Demi Moore also being considered to play the hard nosed cop. As one film colony insider suggested 'Universal still want a nitty gritty script which will equal *Jackie Brown*. They see the movie version of *Prime* as maybe something Quentin Tarantino would want to look it. Lethal, bloody but with a lot of humour.'

Mirren may have had a premonition that much of her work could well still be on the British side of the Atlantic. Shortly before the Oscars ceremony she put the Hollywood house she shared with Hackford up for rent at £20,000 a month. Their six bedroom, nine bathroom property which once belonged to silent movie star Dustin Farnum, a protégé of Cecil B De Mille, included a large guest cottage.

And now *The Queen* may prove to be – apologies for the pun – her crowning glory. Those who have studied her career believe she moves in cycles of achievement. Roughly every year she selects the kind of projects which seem sure to give her a certain notoriety. Just when you think she'll never strip again, she'll be hosed down in the nude by director Peter Greenaway for *The Cook, The Thief, His Wife and Her Lover* or gets the Women's Institute all shook up in *Calendar Girls* or get herself seduced by a young, dark-eyed handsome man in *The Roman Spring of Mrs Stone*. She enjoys causing a stir, takes pleasure from the sound of men in pinstriped suits shuffling nervously in the stalls. Certainly, she has reached the pinnacle of her trade as an actress. The 'new' inspired Mirren isn't afraid to play her age without make-up or go nose to nose with Robert Redford on a movie set if need be. And she will still deny her own sexuality rather than allow the tabloids to use her as a tacky figurehead. She says, 'I have never understood the sex-siren thing. I appreciate beauty and I know I am not beautiful so I know it is not to do with that. I appreciate overt gorgeousness, sexiness, Marilyn Monroe. That kind of thing. I know I am not that. So I don't see it and I don't get it. People see me as strong but I have always felt more the person being destroyed than the destroyer. Sexuality can be a weapon of enormous power that you have for a fairly brief period in your life. You are more aware of that when you are young.'

Acting, she says, 'is all illusion, anyway. All an actor can and must do, is make whatever you are playing as believable as you can. Actors should be ready to take a chance. We are all rogues and vagabonds, or at least we should be. I loathe it when I see my colleagues acting like mild-mannered solicitors from the suburbs! Get out there and put it on the line, for Pete's sake!' She pauses and grins mischievously. You know she means it when she says, 'I'm afraid, playing safe is not an option for me.'

And she cites an example. 'John Boorman once cast me as Morgana in Excalibur, in 1981 and Nicol Williamson as Merlin, because he knew that Mr. Williamson and I could not stand each other. He [Boorman] thought that it would be great to see that hostility on screen. I think he was right. Now that, that is inspired. Although it took quite a bit for me to agree to do it, I am sure that was in equal measures of loathing on Nicol's part as well!'

Her career prospects were on an upward curve. But what of her solid, secure marriage to Taylor Hackford? Since his Ray Charles biopic *Ray* starring Jamie Foxx caused a stampede at the box office in 2004, he had been working on television projects and playing 'Mr Mirren' while she promoted *The Queen* across America. A man quietly confident of his standing as a film maker and a gentle soul given respect and warmth by all those who know him well. But their romance and their relationship has also, not surprisingly, changed radically over the last 20 years. Mirren used to quip, by way of an escape from media intrusion, that she had a habit of setting her alarm clock to buzz an hour early in the morning so she could wake up to enjoy a sunrise session of passion with her husband.

But, having evaded probing of her own fascinating love life, she reportedly let it slip to a senior member of cast on *The Queen* while members of the crew were within earshot that their nocturnal passions had finally evaporated into mere friendly hugs and pecks on the cheek. She innocently revealed, as one senior member of the production was later able to relate, that changes in her marital life had apparently taken place soon after her 60th birthday. Mirren was discussing the chemistry between her *Roman Spring* co-star, the French actor Olivier Martinez, and his pop-singer girlfriend Kylie Minogue when the regal Mirren, normally reticent over such intimate matters, blurted out, 'Days gone by, I'm afraid for me. I was 60 and out in the sexual sweepstakes. Mind you, I like to think I did it well for longer than most.'

Further discussions between the two women implied that, while she still 'fooled around' with Hackford, especially after a few glasses of wine, their bedroom had now become a shrine to sleep.

The production member confessed, 'We were quite taken aback because Helen is still so sexy, what man could resist her? But her attitude seemed to be: "Been there, done that, won't do it any better", while it seemed his was to watch and admire her, almost voyeur-like when she was disrobing her finest French lingerie.'

'We thought she was joking at first but then she said she was being serious. She said, quite loudly, to the actress sitting next to her, "Darling, when I'm in the right mood, I could still turn a dead ferret on! But no sex please, I'm a pensioner!" She was howling with laughter. But she seemed very contented with her private life, no matter what the sexual content may have been. But then, after they had been chatting away for about an hour, not giving a toss about anyone within earshot, Mirren suddenly lost her nerve or realised others had been listening in. She stood up and said, "Please forget I said any of that stuff, just got a bit carried away, didn't we." Then, she took off.'

The intrigue certainly adds to her chic mystic.

One of Hackford's friends on the West Coast said, 'They'd meet up now and again when work allowed it and be the best of buddies. She certainly made it clear that she had no ambitions to meet anybody else or fall hopelessly in love again. He felt the same way. They had both matured in the nicest possible way to avoid the grief which afflicted so many showbusiness couples. Hackford treasured and respected her like no other. They were the greatest of friends.

Another source who once worked at the offices of her agent Ken McReddie summed up her romance with the astute and charming American film director. She said, 'They complement each other very well. He has a fascination with artistic pursuits and the people of Latin and South America and the Third World and she is also very socially conscious. He is close to his sons and so is she, but in no way is she a stepmother figure. She is their friend and preferred to be called Helen from the start. As Hackford accepted that Helen wasn't interested in having any children of her own, he encouraged her to spend as much time as possible with them. He knew she was never going to be a mumsy character. That just wasn't in her make-up, though Helen would never admit she was probably too selfish and jealous by nature to have children of her own. Throughout her life, there has been a line which she will never go beyond in the context of showing her emotions privately. She'd call it her stoic Russian side. But, outside of her sister Kate and nephew Simon and her husband, there were very few people she felt she could confide her deepest thoughts in. She was always very clinical about any sex scenes she had been involved in. She not once thought any of them had been a turn-on. She thought the whole process was mechanical, going from A to B to C. She wasn't particularly aware of her sexuality. She was never truly a flirt. If a man did ever get the wrong idea at a reception or party, she would be quick to correct any impression he might have got.'

Two very well known members of the House of Lords also clearly adored the actress in the 1970's, albeit innocently. In the days she lived in Fulham, West London she was close to both Melvyn Bragg and Jeffrey Archer. They showed more than a passing interest in her taking major parts in their projects. She had just swopped her temperamental live-in partner Prince George Galitzine for photographer James Wedge while Bragg and Archer remained in the background. Both men, say friends, were clearly enchanted by the girl who had been dubbed the sex queen of the Royal Shakespeare Company. Bragg, who had been introduced to her by director Ken Russell, was keen for her to play poet's wife Dorothy Wordsworth in a prestige TV project, a role later taken by Felicity Kendall, the ex wife of playwright Tom Stoppard. Jeffrey Archer would wine and dine her on the basis that he had some books up his sleeve which would make perfect mini-series. He felt she would be dynamite in one particular tale he had in mind.

Bragg and Mirren remain great friends. Today, the much respected Bragg is still riding high as an ITV arts chief while Archer – once Chairman of the Tory party – fell from grace after being jailed for four years for perjury and conspiracy to pervert the course of justice.

Mirren still looks absolutely fabulous, especially when she's floating down the red carpet in Eavis & Brown or another Amies creation. The eyes are eagle-like, predatory and perceptive. The slightly crooked nose has attained a nobility while her facial lines denote the experience of pleasure and excitement. While she refrains from launching attacks on the Beverly Hills set who regularly undergo cosmetic surgery, she says she's not in line for a face-lift. She said, 'I would say to parents they should put their children through school to become plastic surgeons, there's so much money in it. But the reality is that we are all going to get old and you'd better relax about that fact and deal with it. My mother always said, "Don't worry about getting older, darling, nature has a wonderful way of maturing your mental facilities so that you don't mind the physical side." Ideally, I'd have long and beautiful legs. Instead, I have short, fat legs. I would have liked that Left Bank Bohemian look, flat-chested with long dark hair. Instead I have footballer's legs.

Two very well known members of the House of Lords also clearly adored the actress in the 1970's, albeit innocently. In the days she lived in Fulham, West London she was close to both Melvyn Bragg and Jeffrey Archer. They showed an interest in her taking major parts in their projects. She had just swapped her live-in partner Prince George Galitzine for photographer James Wedge while Bragg and Archer remained in the background. Both men, say friends, were clearly enchanted by the girl who had been dubbed the sex queen of the Royal Shakespeare Company. Bragg, who had been introduced to her by director Ken Russell, was keen for her to play poet's wife Dorothy Wordsworth in a prestige TV project, a role later taken by Felicity Kendall, the ex wife of playwright Tom Stoppard. Jeffrey Archer would wine and dine her on the basis that he had some books up his sleeve which would make perfect mini-series. He felt she would be dynamite in one particular tale he had in mind.

Bragg and Mirren remain great friends. Today, the much respected Bragg is still riding high as an ITV arts chief while Archer – once Chairman of the Tory party – fell from grace after being jailed for four years for perjury and conspiracy to pervert the course of justice.

'Me, sexy? I don't know why men think I am sexy. I suppose it's because I look as though I have always just got out of bed. I used to get upset at being described as sexy. I wanted to be taken seriously. Now I accept it. It was never easy being true to yourself when others were so keen to pigeon-hole you. I was enraged by the sexism I encountered, exacerbated by the way I looked. But you have to live with it … and you have to love it.'

Cynics and BBC drama executives bitchily say that she was at her most Machiavellian when she quite deliberately refused to kill off Jane Tennison on the basis that the lady would make a late return to the fray in some form, when the time suited her career most. 'That would be rather stupid of me,' she confesses. 'To categorically say that Jane will never be seen again. But I now wonder if there is anywhere we can take her? To her retirement home in Florida, after her career in the police finishes? Well, actually maybe that is not such a bad idea to let her sort out the Miami police or somewhere on the Keys. Smashing! At the moment, I do not think that she will "come back from the dead". But, in the world of television, who can ever tell?

'But I don't want my obituary to read: "She was the lady who played the policewoman on television." As proud as I am of that role – and I am – I don't want that to be all I was remembered for. I think I'd sooner be remembered as somebody who took risks and went on taking risks. Maybe that's not me but it would be a lovely way to be thought of. Whatever happens, though, I suspect it will be the part I am most remembered for.

'I just know that I never ever want to be past my sell-by date. I think I shall know when it is time for me to go. I do not want to be thought of as "That silly Dame who sits around waiting – and never receiving", and going more than slightly gaga!

'In years gone by, all of my ambitions from way back were based on jealousy. When I was a little girl and went to the theatre, I was always jealous of that girl on the stage. Now I am jealous of people who can do it as well as me. When I was a little girl, I vowed that when I made it I wouldn't just be good, I wouldn't just be brilliant. I would be the greatest thing there ever was. I couldn't see marriage or children or becoming a great theatrical Dame. But I could see me getting a bit notorious.'

Philosophically, Mirren believes she has now come to terms with who and what she is. She understands her roots and that Russian side of her personality. And she equally has much affection for that lost waif who grew up in middle-class anonymous Leigh-on-Sea with the Thames Estuary forever ebbing away in the grey background. She wanted to be 'special'. She yearned to be 'noticed'. Now she has everything she always wanted.

She says, 'Your twenties are simply torture really because you don't know what you are going to be or whether it is all going to work out and you are supposedly an adult but you have not really learned anything. You are always looking for your own place in the world. You think you are wonderful one minute and you are a disaster the next. Your thirties are a wonderful time. Your sixties are brilliant. Life kind of organises itself. You slowly get used to what you are.'

Her return to the Broadway stage or the RSC is long overdue. She has a pile of scripts waiting in her London residence. Hackford, much as he has made London his home, would like to journey back to spend more time with his sons in Los Angeles. Mirren would welcome the opportunity to work Stateside with Steven Spielberg or Martin Scorsese or try something out of left field with Woody Allen in New York.

'What's next? I really do *not* know,' she says. 'There are a few acting offers on the table. Some interesting things. But I am always a person who has found life pretty thrilling. And, when things work out well, I am always overwhelmed with the nice things that people say and write. I am a very, very, very lucky woman. I have had some very nice breaks. I just hope that they keep on coming. That's all!'

Indeed they do. As the awards came raining down, Mirren also keenly eyed a script which had been recommended to her by her teenaged great-niece Natasha. Well established New Line Cinema were about to go into production with a £10 million movie version of Cornelia Funke's best selling fantasy novel *Inkheart*, with Brendan 'The Mummy 'Fraser and Paul Bettany, recently seen in *The Da Vinci Code*, already attached. Mirren was being offered the plum role of Elinor Loredan, the eccentric great-aunt of her heroine of the piece, Meggie Folchart, played by Berkshire born newcomer Eliza Bennett. She beat scores of other girls to the prize role of Meggie with a pedigree ranging from the original cast of *Chitty Chitty Bang Bang* to a co-starring part alongside Emma Thompson and Colin Firth in Nanny McPhee.

The supporting cast is also impressive, with Fraser playing Meggie's wizard-like father Mo, Bettany as Dustfinger, Oscar-winning Jim Broadbent as Fenoglio, Lesley Sharp as Mortola and Sienna Guillory. Locations range from Liguria in Italy to Farnham in Surrey with the base at Shepperton Studios. Iain 'Skeleton Key' Softley, who made an impressive debut with the Beatles biopic Backbeat back in 1994, is directing the fantasy inspired by classic literature about Meggie and her father who live in a house where the characters in books they are reading eerily come to life. The medieval and contemporary fast paced time-travelling tale will most probably be released to co-incide with the Easter break in 2008.

Mirren is thrilled to be back working again while receiving so many accolades. *Inkheart* author, German born Funke, who now lives in Los Angeles and has written over 40 books, was equally ecstatic when she heard that the likely Oscar winner was in the line-up and happily approved David Lindsay-Abaire's (*Robots*) adaption of her novel which has been translated into over 20 languages. Cornelia Funke and Barry Mendel are producing. The behind the scenes team included director of photography Roger Pratt and editor Martin Walsh. Cornelia Funke and Barry Mendel were signed to produce while the behind the scenes team included director of photography Roger Pratt and editor Martin Walsh. Shooting would continue until mid-March by which time there would be virtually no room left on her mantelpiece for any more awards from The Queen.

Amusingly, in her final Prime Suspect tale there was a slice of dialogue between her and another officer who irritates her with his ingratiating manner. ' Don't call me "mum",' she says chiding him at the station house. 'I'm not the bloody queen!.'

Dame Helen, we beg to differ. It's now official.

MAJOR STAGE,
TELEVISION AND FILM ROLES
AND AWARDS

MAJOR STAGE ROLES

1965   *Antony and Cleopatra* (National Youth Theatre) – Cleopatra

1966   *Hamlet* – Ophelia

1967   *All's Well That Ends Well* – Diana

1968   *As You Like It* (RSC) – Phoebe; *Troilius and Cressida* (RSC)
       Cressida; *Much Ado About Nothing* – Hero

1969   *The Revenger's Tragedy* (RSC) – Castiza *ichard III* (RSC) – Lady Anne;
       Hamlet (RSC) – Ophelia; *Two Gentleman of Verona* (RSC) – Julia

1970   *Hamlet* (RSC) – Ophelia; *Enemies* (RSC Aldwych) Tatiana;
       The Man of Mode (RSC Alwych) – Harriet

1972   *Miss Julie* (RSC) – Miss Julie

1974   *Macbeth* (RSC) – Lady Macbeth

1975   *Teeth 'n' Smiles* (Royal Court) – Maggie

1976   *The Bed Before Yesterday* (Lyric) – Ella

1977   *Henry VI Parts 1, 2 and 3* (RSC) – Princess/Queen Margaret

1979   *Measure for Measure* (Riverside) – Isabella

1980   *The Duchess of Malfi* (Royal Exchange Manchester) – The Duchess

1981   *The Faith Healer* (Royal Court) – Gracie

1983   *Antony and Cleopatra* (RSC) – Cleopatra; *The Roaring Girl* (RSC) –
       Moll Cutpurse

1984   *Extremities* (Duchess) – Marjorie

1988   *Two-Way Mirror* (Young Vic) – Angela

1991   *Sex Please, We're Italian!* (Young Vic) – Rosetta
1991   *A Month in the Country* (Albery) – Natalya Petrovna
1994   *A Month in the Country* (Broadway) – Natalya Petrovna
1998   *Antony and Cleopatra* (Royal National Theatre) – Cleopatra
1999   *Collected Stories* (Theatre Royal, Haymarket) – Ruth Steiner
2000   *Orpheus Descending* (Donmar Warehouse) – Lady Torrance
2001   *Dance of Death* (Broadway) – Alice
2003   *Mourning Becomes Electra* (Royal National Theatre)

MAJOR TELEVISION ROLES

Prime Suspect 7 (ITV, two parts, 15/22 October 2006)
As Helen Mirren reprised her iconic role as the formidable Jane Tennison for the last time, she was joined by Stephen Tompkinson, Robert Pugh and Tom Bell who was tragically to die only days before transmission. Retirement loomed large on the horizon for Tennison but, as her exemplary career heads towards its inevitable conclusion, she paid dearly for 35 years of repressed rage and loneliness.

The discovery of the body of missing schoolgirl Sallie Sturdy (Maxine Barton) on North London heathland triggers the hunt for a crazed killer. But, as Tennison and her team worked to identify their prime suspect, the emotional fallout from the brutal murder took its toll on the world-weary and battle-scarred detective. As the investigation got under way, Tennison had to deal with the imminent death of her father (Frank Finlay), but also her addiction to alcohol which she had desperately tried to keep hidden. And, as the pressure mounted to secure a conviction on the high-profile case, the cracks started to show. Her Damascene conversion gripped the nation again as *Prime Suspect* reached a devastating finale. Directed by Philip Martin, written by Frank Deasy.

Helen Mirren	Det. Chief Supt. Jane Tennison
Tom Bell	Bill Otley
Gary Lewis	Tony Sturdy
Frank Finlay	Mr Tennison
Stephen Tompkinson	Sean Philips
Robert Pugh	Det. Sgt. Alun Simms
Laura Greenwood	Penny Philips

Trailer For a Remake of Gore Vidal's *Caligula* (2 March 2006, *Crossroads* for US television). Short film.
Directed by Francesco Vezzoli, written by Gore Vidal.

Helen Mirren	Tiberia
Karen Black	Agrippina
Michelle Phillips	Messalina
Gerard Butler	Prefect Cassius Chaerea

| Milla Jovovich | Druscilla |
| Courtney Love | Caligula |

Elizabeth I (ITV, 29 September 2005. Channel 4 and HBO co-production)
Directed by Tom Hooper, written by Nigel Williams.
With Helen Mirren, Jeremy Irons, Patrick Malahide, Hugh Dancy, Barbara
    Flynn, Ian McDiarmid, John McEnery, Toby Salaman, Diana Kent.

The Hitchhiker's Guide to the Galaxy (BBC, 28 April 2005)
Directed by Garth Jennings, written by Douglas Adams.

| Helen Mirren | Deep Thought (Voice only) |

Pride (BBC, 27 December 2004)
Directed by John Downer, written by Simon Nye.

| Helen Mirren | Macheeba (Voice only) |

Frasier: Coots and Ladders (Episode 256, March 16 2004. Paramount Television
in US and Channel 4 in the UK)
Directed by Kelsey Grammer, written by Heidi Perlman.

| Helen Mirren | Babette the Caller (Voice Only) |

Prime Suspect 6 (ITV, to be screened during the 2003/2004 Autumn/
Winter season)
Seven years have passed and Jane Tennison is back on London's meaner streets
hunting a killer who has tortured a Bosnian girl to death. The two-parter also
focuses on her managing the 'bigger picture', probing 30 unsolved murders and
70 up-and running murder investigations. She rocks some very big boats as she
hunts the man who brutally murdered the attractive young immigrant. The prime
suspect is a minor war criminal who has been given a safe haven in the UK, for
pointing the finger at other Serbian war criminals. Peter Berry's story is set in the
world of asylum seekers and is being directed by Tom 'Daniel Deronda' Hooper.
Directed by Tom Hooper and written by Peter Berry.

Helen Mirren	Supt Jane Tennison
Ben Miles	Det Inspector Finch
Robert Pugh	Det Sgt Simms
Mark Strong	Det Con Hall
Liam Cunningham	Robert West
Oleg Menshikov	Milan Lukic
Clare Holman	Elizabethe Lukic

Prime Suspect 5: Errors of Judgement (ITV, 20 October 1996)

Guy Andrews wrote and Philip Davis directed what many believed was going to be her final adventure. Tennison has been transferred yet again, this time from the Met in London to the Greater Manchester force, where she has to do a stint as a community liaison officer. It's not long before she is once again focusing on serious crime, investigating a seemingly straightforward drugs murder that she believes is linked to a smug, smooth crime boss played by Steven Mackintosh. She has big problems with her hard-nosed boss, played by ex-soap star John McArdle. He may have designs on her but he isn't keen on the direction she chooses to take on the case, for reasons that soon become apparent.

Directed by Philip Davis, written by Guy Andrews.

Helen Mirren	Supt Jane Tennison
John McArdle	DCS Ballinger
Julia Lane	DI Devanny
David O'Hara	DS Jerry Rankine
John Brobbey	DC Henry Adeliyeka
Steven Mackintosh	The Street
Ray Emmet Brown	Michael Johns
Paul Oldham	Toots
Joe Speare	Radio
Paul Simpson	Outboard
Joseph Jacobs	Campbell Lafferty
Marsha Thomason	Janice Lafferty
Vanessa Knox-Mawer	Louise Ballinger
Badi Uzzaman	Mr Ahmed
Anne Hornby	DC Skinner

Prime Suspect 4: – series of three films – *The Lost Child* (ITV, 30 April 1995)
John Madden, later to direct the award-winning *Shakespeare in Love*, helmed theaction from a story by Paul Billing. Tennison's star is rising and she has been promoted to Detective Supt. She leads the search for an abducted child, taken from a single mum played by Lesley Sharp. Robert Glenister scooped rave reviews playing the convicted child sex offender who takes a family hostage after his arrest is bungled.

Directed by John Madden, written by Paul Billing.

Helen Mirren	Supt Jane Tennison
Beatie Edney	Susan Covington
Robert Glenister	Chris Hughes
Lesley Sharp	Anne Sutherland
Tracy Keating	Carolyn Norwood
Richard Hawley	DI Richard Haskons
Jack Ellis	DI Tony Muddyman

David Phelan	DC Pride
Graham Seed	Doctor
John Benfield	Chief Supt Kernan
Tony Rohr	DS McColl
Mark Bazeley	DC Aplin
Chris Brailsford	DC Westbrook
Mossie Smith	WPC Maureen Havers
Caroline Selby	Alison Sutherland

Prime Suspect 4: Inner Circles (ITV, 7 May 1995)
Tennison finds herself locked in upmarket internecine warfare with leading members of a suburban community, when the manager of a country club is found dead in his home. Local police point the finger at two local lads from a run-down housing estate, but Tennison has other ideas and duly causes a political scandal, rocking the social climbing set's boat by putting the wrong questions to the right people.
Directed by Sarah Pia Anderson, written by Eric Deacon and Meredith Oakes.

Helen Mirren	Supt Jane Tennison
Tom Russell	Geoff
James Laurenson	Paul Endicott
Helene Kvale	Lynne Endicott
Jill Baker	Maria Henry
Kelly Reilly	Polly Henry
Gareth Forwood	Denis Carradine
Anthony Bate	James Greenlees
Phillida Sewell	Olive Carradine
Jonathan Copestake	Micky Thomas
Julie Rice	Sheila Bower
Roger Milner	Norman
Tony Spooner	Alan
Hamish McColl	Younger Neighbour

Prime Suspect 4: Scent of Darkness (ITV, 15 May 1995)
A series of brutal sex murders disturbingly similar to the pattern of her first major murder case leads Tennison to the terrible conclusion that she may have sent down the wrong man. Was George Marlow innocent? Stuart Wilson, who made a big impression in Hollywood playing the bad guy in Lethal Weapon 3, stepped into the fray and – and into Tennison's bed – as criminal psychologist Patrick Schofield. But this was to be yet another doomed love affair.
Directed by Paul Marcus, written by Guy Hibbert.

Helen Mirren	Supt Jane Tennison
Penelope Beaumont	Elizabeth Bramwell

Glen Berry	Wayne
Christopher Fulford	DCI Tom Mitchell
Linda Henry	Forensic Scientist
Scott Neal	Geoff
Marc Warren	PC Andy Dyson
Stuart Wilson	Dr Patrick Schofield

Prime Suspect 3 (ITV, 19 December 1993)

La Plante returned to write the grisly tale transferring Tennison to the Vice Squad. It doesn't get much darker than this. Her first assignment is to find the killer of a rent boy with links to a paedophile gang operating from one of London's worst red light districts. Her investigation takes her into the seediest corners of the sexual twilight world. Classy guest stars were drafted in: David Thewlis, from Mike Leigh's *Naked*, portrayed a mealy-mouthed pimp and pornographer, while Oscar-winning Peter Capaldi played Vera Reynolds, a perpetually frightened transsexual. Also high on Tennison's suspect list is Edward Parker-Jones, played by Ciaran Hinds, who runs a youth centre to shelter boys from trouble. Tom Bell makes his comeback as the stony-faced Otley.

Directed by David Drury, written by Lynda La Plante.

Helen Mirren	DCI Jane Tennison
Peter Capaldi	Vera Reynolds
Michael Shannon	Jake Hunter
Greg Saunders	Connie
David Thewlis	James Jackson
Danny Dyer	Martin Fletcher
Tom Bell	Sgt Bill Otley
Richard Rees	Mike Chow
Terrence Hardiman	Commander Chiswick
Mark Strong	Insp Larry Hall
Karen Tomlin	WPC Norma Hastings
Struan Rodger	Supt Halliday
Liza Sadovy	WPC Kathy Bibby
John Benfield	Chief Supt Kernan
Terence Harvey	John Kennington

Prime Suspect 2 (ITV, 15 December 1992)

Jane Tennison has made a full recovery from her earlier exploits and is back on the murder trail, with most of her team intact, after the body of a young black woman is discovered in an Afro-Caribbean neighbourhood. Allan Cubitt penned the storyline in which she causes a stir in the ofice by taking a much younger lover from within the ranks, Sgt Robert Oswald, played by new James Bond regular,

Colin Salmon. She is also sold out by her boss, Chief Supt Michael Kernan, played by John Benfield, who sees her as a threat to his own professional progress. Racism both in and out of the force is the main theme.

Directed by John Strickland, written by Allan Cubitt

Helen Mirren	DCI Jane Tennison
Colin Salmon	Sgt Robert Oswald
John Benfield	DS Michael Kernan
Jack Ellis	DI Tony Muddyman
Craig Fairbrass	DI Frank Burkin
Richard Hawley	DS Richard Haskons
Philip Wright	DC Lillie
Ian Fitzgibbon	DC Jones
Andrew Tiernan	DC Rosper
Stafford Gordon	Commander Trayner
Lloyd McGuire	Sgt Calder
Stephen Boxer	DCI Thorndike
Nirjay Mahindru	Asian PC
Claire Benedict	Esme Allen
George Harris	Vernon Allen

Prime Suspect (ITV, 7 April 1991)

Enter the raw and yet-to-be-tested Detective Chief Inspector Jane Tennison, on the trail of the vicious serial killer, George Marlow, played by John Bow. Tennison's creator, Lynda La Plante, wrote this first episode, that also delved into the sexist world of male coppers. Acid spitting Tom Bell plays Det Sgt Bill Otley, Tennison's arch nemesis.

Directed by Chris Menaul, written by Lynda La Plante, produced by Sally Head and Don Lever.

Helen Mirren	DCI Jane Tennison
Tom Bell	DS Bill Otley
John Benfield	DCS Michael Kernan
John Bowe	George Marlow
Zoë Wanamaker	Moyra Henson
Bryan Pringle	Felix Norman
Tom Wilkinson	Peter Rawlins
John Forgeham	DCI John Shefford
Gary Whelan	DS Terry Amson
Jack Ellis	DI Tony Muddyman
Craig Fairbrass	DI Frank Burkin
Ian Fitzgibbon	DC Jones
Mossie Smith	WPC Maureen Havers

Philip Wright	DC Lillie
Andrew Tiernan	DC Rosper
Ralph Fiennes	Michael

Door to Door (2002, TNT for US television)
Directed by Steven Schachter. Written by Steven Schachter and William H Macy.
With William H Macy, Helen Mirren (Irene Porter), Kyra Sedgewick
   and Kathy Baker.

The Roman Spring of Mrs Stone (2002, Showtime for US television)
Directed by Robert Allan Ackerman. Adapted by Martin Sherman, from
   Tennessee Williams's novella.
With Helen Mirren (Karen Stone), Oliver Martinez, Brian Dennehy, Anne
   Bancroft and Suzanne Bertish.

The Passion of Ayn Rand (1992, Showtime for US television)
Directed by Christopher Menaul. Adapted by Howard Korder from
   Barbara Branden's book.
With Helen Mirren (Ayn Rand), Eric Stoltz, Julie Delpy and Peter Fonda.

Painted Lady (1997, Granada/WGBH Boston for ITV)
Directed by Julian Jarrold. Written by Allan Cubitt.
With Helen Mirren (Maggie Sheridan), Iain Glen, Franco Nero,
   Michael Maloney, Lesley Manville and Iain Cuthbertson.

Losing Chase (1996, Hallmark and Showtime for US television)
Directed by Kevin Bacon. Written by Anne Meredith.
With Helen Mirren (Chase Phillips), Kyra Sedgewick and Beau Bridges.

The Hawk (1993, BBC TV)
Directed and written by Peter Ransley.
With Helen Mirren (Annie Marsh), David Harewood, George Costigan,
   Rosemary Leach, John Duttine and Owen Teale.

French and Saunders Spring Special (2000)

Red King, White Knight (1989, HBO and Zenith, for US television)
Directed by Geoff Murphy. Written by Ron Hutchinson.
With Helen Mirren (Anna) Tom Skerritt, Max von Sydow,
   Tom Bell, Neil Dudgeon, Gavan O'Herlihy and Lou Hirsch.
Cause Célèbre (1987, Anglia Television for ITV)

Directed by John Gorrie. Adapted by Kenneth Taylor from Terence Rattigan's
  play.
With Helen Mirren (Alma Rattenbury), David Suchet,
  David Morrissey, Harry Andrews and Oliver Ford Davies.

Cymbeline (1983, BBC TV)
Directed by Elijah Moshinsky.
With Helen Mirren (Imogen), Richard Johnson, Claire Bloom, Michael
  Pennington and Robert Lindsay.

Soft Targets (1982, BBC TV)
Directed by Charles Sturridge. Written by Stephen Poliakoff.
With Helen Mirren (Celia), Rupert Everett, Nigel Havers, Ian Holm
  and Celia Gregory.

A Midsummer Night's Dream (1981, BBC TV)
Directed by Elijah Moshinsky.
With Helen Mirren (Titania), Nigel Davenport, Pippa Guard, Nicky Henson,
  Robert Lindsay, Brian Glover, Geoffrey Palmer, Don Estelle and
  Phil Daniels.

SOS Titanic (1979, ITV)
Directed by William Hale. Written by James Costigan.
With Helen Mirren (Stewardess Mary Sloan), David Janssen,
  Cloris Leachman, David Warner, Ian Holm, Harry Andrews and Ed Bishop.

Blue Remembered Hills (1979, BBC TV)
Directed by Brian Gibson. Written by Dennis Potter
With Helen mirren (Angela), Janine Duvitski, Michael Elphick, Colin Jeavons,
  Colin Welland, Robin Ellis and John Bird.

As You Like It (1978, BBC TV)
Directed by Basil Coleman.
With Helen Mirren (Rosalind), Richard Pasco, Angharad Rees, James Bolam and
  Clive Francis.

The Collection (1976, Granada for ITV)
Directed by Michael Apted. Written by Harold Pinter.
With Helen Mirren (Stella), Laurence Olivier, Alan Bates and
  Malcolm McDowell.
Caesar and Claretta (1975, BBC TV)

Directed by Claude Whatham.
With Helen Mirren (Claretta Petacci) and Robert Hardy.

Coffin for the Bride (1974, ABC for ITV)
Directed by John Sichel. Written by Brian Clemens.
With Helen Mirren (Stella McKenzie), Michael Jayston, Margaret Courtenay,
  Josephine Tewson, Arthur English, Marcia Fox and Richard Coleman.

The Changeling (1974, BBC TV)
From Thomas Middleton's play.
With Helen Mirren (Beatrice Joanna) and Stanley Baker.

Cousin Bette (1971, BBC TV)
Directed by Gareth Davies. Adapted from Balzac's novel.
With Helen Mirren (Valerie), Bella Emberg, Ursula Howels, Sally James,
  Thorley Walters, Colin Baker and Margaret Boyd.

MAJOR FILM ROLES
The Queen (2006)
Directed by Stephen Frears, written by Peter Morgan.
With Helen Mirren, Michael Sheen, James Cromwell, Sylvia Sims,
  Helen McCrory.

Shadowboxer (2005)
Directed by Lee Daniels, written by William Litz.
With Helen Mirren, Cuba Gooding Jr, Stephen Dorff, Vanessa Ferlito, Macy Gray.

Raising Helen (2004)
Directed by Gary Marshall, written by Patrick J Clifton and Beth Rigazio.
With Helen Mirren, Kate Hudson, John Corbett, Joan Cusack,
  Felicity Huffman.

The Clearing (2003)
Directed by Pieter Jan Brugge, written by Justin Haythe.
With Robert Redford, Helen Mirren, Willem Dafoe, Alessandro Nivola.

Calendar Girls (2003)
Directed by Nigel Cole, written by Juliette Towhindi and Tim Firth.
With Helen Mirren, Julie Walters, John Alderton, Linda Bassett, Annette
  Crosbie, Philip Glenister, Ciaran Hinds, Celia Imrie, Geraldine James,
  Penelope Wilton, George Costigan.

No Such Thing (2001)
Directed and written by Hal Hartley.
With Robert Burke, Julie Christie, Helen Mirren, Julie Anderson,
    Anna Kristin Arngrimsdottir.

Last Orders (2001)
Directed and written by Fred Schepisi.
With Michael Caine, Tom Courtenay, David Hemmings,Bob Hoskins,
    Helen Mirren, Ray Winstone.

Gosford Park (2001)
Directed by Robert Altman, written by Julian Fellowes.
With Maggie Smith, Michael Gambon, Kristin Scott Thomas, Camilla
    Rutherford, Charles Dance, Geraldine Somerville, Helen Mirren.

The Pledge (2001)
Directed by Sean Penn, written by Jerzy Kromolowski.
With Jack Nicholson, Patricia Clarkson, Beau Danile, Helen Mirren.

Greenfingers (2000)
Directed and written by Joen Hershman.
With Clive Owen, Helen Mirren, David Kelly, Warren Clarke.

Happy Birthday (2000)

Teaching Mrs Tingle (1999)
Directed and written by Kevin Williamson.
With Helen Mirren, Katie Holmes, Jeffrey Tambor, Barry Watson.

The Prince of Egypt (1998)
Directed by Brenda Chapman and Steve Hickner, written by Ken Harsha
    and Philip LaZebnik.
With the voices of Val Kilmer, Ralph Fiennes, Michelle Pfeiffer, Sandra Bullock,
    Jeff Goldblum, Danny Glover, Patrick Stewart, Helen Mirren, Steve Martin,
    Martin Short.

Sidoglio Smithee (1998)
Directed and written by Jorge Molina.
With Helen Mirren.

Critical Care (1997)
Directed by Sidney Lumet, written by Richard Dooling and Steven Schwartz.
With James Spader, Kyra Sedgwick, Helen Mirren, Anne Bancroft,
    Albert Brooks.

Some Mother's Son (1996)
Directed by Terry George, written by Terry George and Jim Sheridan.
With Helen Mirren, Fionnula Flanagan, Aidan Gillen, David O'Hare.

Great War and the Shaping of the 20th Century (1996)
Directed by Carl Byker and Lyn Goldfarb, written by Joseph Angier
    and Blaine Baggett.
With the voice of Helen Mirren.

The Madness of King George (1994)
Directed by Nicholas Hytner, written by Alan Bennett.
With Nigel Hawthorne, Helen Mirren, Ian Holm, Rupert Graves, Rupert
    Everett, Amanda Donohoe, Julian Wadham, Jim Carter, Geoffrey Palmer.

Prince of Jutland (1994)
Directed by Gabriel Axel, written by Gabriel Axel and Saxo Grammaticus.
With Gabriel Byrne, Helen Mirren, Christian Bale, Brian Cox,
    Steven Waddington, Kate Beckinsale.

The Hawk (1993)
Directed by David Hayman, written by Peter Ransley.
With Daryl Webster, David Harewood, Helen Mirren, Clive Russell,
    George Costigan.

Where Angels Fear to Tread (1991)
Directed by Charles Sturridge, adapted by Tim Sullivan fromEM Forster's novel.
With Rupert Graves, Helen Mirren, Helena Bonham-Carter, Barbara Jefford,
    Judy Davis.

Bethune: The Making of a Hero (1990)
Directed by Phillip Borsos, written by Ted Allan.
With Inaki Aierra, Anouk Aimee, Helen Mirren.

The Comfort of Strangers (1990)
Directed by Paul Schrader, written by Ian McEwan from his novel
    and Harold Pinter.
With Christopher Walken, Rupert Everett, Natasha Richardson,Helen Mirren.

When the Whales Came (1989)
Directed by Clive Rees, written by Michael Morpurgo.
With Irene Wilson, Paul Scofield, David Suchet, Helen Mirren.

The Cook, the Thief, His Wife and Her Lover (1989)
Directed and written by Peter Greenaway.
With Richard Bohringer, Michael Gambon, Helen Mirren, Alan Howard,
    Tim Roth.

Pascali's Island (1988)
Directed and written by James Dearden.
With Ben Kingsley, Charles Dance, Helen Mirren.

Invocation: Maya Deren (1987)

The Mosquito Coast (1986)
Directed by Peter Weir, written by Paul Schrader and Paul Theroux
    from his novel.
With Harrison Ford, Helen Mirren, River Phoenix.

Heavenly Pursuits (1985)
Directed and written by Charles Gormley.
With Tom Conti, Helen Mirren, David Hayman, Brian Pettifer.

White Nights (1985)
Directed by Taylor Hackford, written by James Goldman and Eric Hughes.
With Mikhail Baryshnikov, Gregory Hines, Helen Mirren.

Coming Through (1985)
The Gospel According to St. Vic (1985)

2010 (1984)
Directed and written by Peter Hyams.
With Roy Scheider, John Lithgow, Helen Mirren, Bob Balaban, Keir Dullea.

Cal (1984)
Directed by Pat O'Connor, written by Bernard MacLaverty.
With Helen Mirren, John Lynch, Donal McCannn, John Kavanagh.

Priest of Love (1981)

Directed by Christopher Miles, written by Harry T Moore from his book and Alan Plater.

With Ian McKellen, Janet Suzman, Ava Gardner, Penelope Keith, Jorge Rivero, John Gielgud, Helen Mirren.

Excalibur (1981)

Directed by John Boorman, written by John Boorman and Thomas Mallory from his book.

With Nigel Terry, Helen Mirren, Nicholas Clay, Cherie Lunghi, Paul Geoffrey, Nicol Williamson.

Hussy (1980)

Directed and written by Matthew Chapman.

With Helen Mirren, John Shea, Daniel Chasin, Murray Salem.

The Long Good Friday (1980)

Directed by John MacKenzie, written by Barrie Keeffe.

Written Bob Hoskins, Helen Mirren, Dave King, Bryan Marshall, Derek Thompson.

The Fiendish Plot of Dr Fu Manchu (1980)

Directed by Piers Haggard and Richard Quine, written by Rudy Dochtermann and Jim Maloney.

With Peter Sellers, Helen Mirren, David Tomlinson, Sid Caesar, Simon Williams, Steve Franken.

Caligula (1979)

Directed by Tinto Brass, written by Gore Vidal.

With Malcolm McDowell, Teresa Ann Savoy, Helen Mirren, Peter O'Toole.

Hamlet (1976)

Directed by Celestino Coronada, written by Celestino Coronada.

With Quentin Crisp, Anthony Meyer, David Meyer, Helen Mirren.

O Lucky Man! (1973)

Directed by Lindsay Anderson, written by David Sherwin.

With Malcolm McDowell, Ralph Richardson, Rachel Roberts, Arthur Lowe, Helen Mirren.

Miss Julie (1972)
Directed by John Glenister and Robin Phillips, from the play by
    August Strindberg.
With Helen Mirren, Donal McCann, Heather Canning.

Savage Messiah (1972)
Directed by Ken Russell, written by HS Ede from his book and
    Christopher Logue.
With Scott B Anthony, Dorothy Tutin, Helen Mirren, Lindsay Kemp.

Age of Consent (1969)
Directed by Michael Powell, written by Norman Lindsay and Peter Yeldham.
With James Mason, Helen Mirren, Jack MacGowran.

A Midsummer Night's Dream (1968)
Directed by Peter Hall.
With Derek Godfrey, Barbara Jefford, Nicholas Selby, Hugh Sullivan, David
    Warner, Diana Rigg, Michael Jayston, Helen Mirren.

AWARDS

2007	Oscars, Best Actress for (The Queen)
2007	Golden Globe, Best Actress (Drama) for *The Queen*
2007	Golden Globe, Best Actress in a Mini-series or TV Movie for *Elizabeth I*
2007	Screen Actors Guild (USA), Outstanding Performance by a Female Actor in a Leading Role for *The Queen*
2007	Screen Actors Guild (USA), Outstanding Performance by a Female Actor in a Television Movie or Miniseries for *Elizabeth I*
2006	Venice Film Festival, Winner of the Volpi Cup as Best Actress, *The Queen*.
2006	Emmy Awards, Outstanding Lead Actress in a mini-series for *Elizabeth I*.
2002	London Critics' Circle Film Award, Best Supporting Actress, *Last Orders*
2002	National Society of Film Critics (USA), Best Supporting Actress, *Gosford Park*
2002	Screen Actors' Guild (USA), Outstanding Performance by a Female Actor in a Supporting Role/Shared Award for Outstanding Performance by a Cast, *Gosford Park*
2001	National Board of Review (USA), Ensemble Performance, *Last Orders*

2001   New York Film Critics' Circle, Best Supporting Actress,
       Gosford Park

1999   Emmy Award, Outstanding Lead Actress, *The Passion of Ayn Rand*

1997   Golden Globe, Best Performance by an Actress in a
       Mini-Series, *Losing Chase*

1997   Golden Satellite Awards, Best Performance by an Actress in
       a Mini-Series, *Prime Suspect 5: Errors of Judgement*

1996   Emmy Award, Outstanding Lead Actress, *Prime Suspect 4: Scent of
       Darkness*

1995   Cannes Film Festival, Best Actress, *Madness of King George*

1994   BAFTA, Best Actress, *Prime Suspect 3*

1993   BAFTA, Best Actress, *Prime Suspect 2*

1992   BAFTA, Best Actress, *Prime Suspect*

1992   Broadcasting Press Guild, Best Actress, *Prime Suspect*

1992   Royal Television Society Award (UK), Best Female Actor, *Prime Suspect*

1985   BAFTA, Best Actress, *Cal*

1984   Cannes Film Festival, Best Actress, *Cal*